TYRANTS

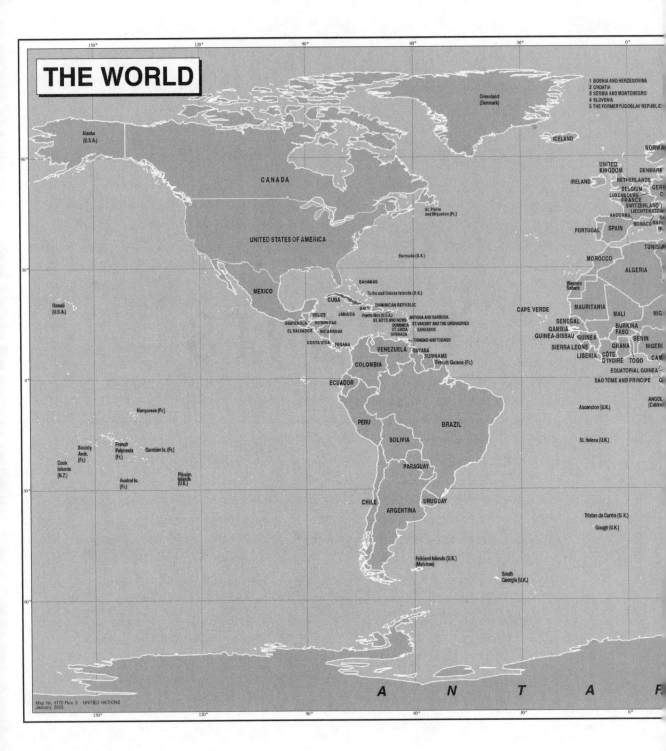

THE WORLD

1 BOSNIA AND HERZEGOVINA
2 CROATIA
3 SERBIA AND MONTENEGRO
4 SLOVENIA
5 THE FORMER YUGOSLAV REPUBLIC

ICELAND

NORWA

Greenland
(Denmark)

UNITED
KINGDOM   DENMARK
IRELAND   NETHERLANDS
BELGIUM   GER
LUXEMBOURG   C
FRANCE
SWITZERLAND
ANDORRA   LIECHTENSTEIN
MONACO   MARI
PORTUGAL   SPAIN

TUNISIA

Alaska
(U.S.A.)

CANADA

St. Pierre
and Miquelon (Fr.)

MOROCCO

ALGERIA

UNITED STATES OF AMERICA

Western
Sahara

Bermuda (U.K.)

BAHAMAS

MEXICO

Turks and Caicos Islands (U.K.)

CUBA

DOMINICAN REPUBLIC

CAPE VERDE   MAURITANIA   MALI   NIG

Hawaii
(U.S.A.)

HAITI

BELIZE   JAMAICA   Puerto Rico (U.S.A.)
ST. KITTS AND NEVIS   ANTIGUA AND BARBUDA
GUATEMALA   HONDURAS   DOMINICA   ST. VINCENT AND THE GRENADINES
EL SALVADOR   NICARAGUA   ST. LUCIA
COSTA RICA   GRENADA   BARBADOS
PANAMA   TRINIDAD AND TOBAGO

SENEGAL   BURKINA
GAMBIA   FASO   BENIN
GUINEA-BISSAU   GUINEA   NIGERI
SIERRA LEONE   GHANA   TOGO
LIBERIA   CÔTE   CAM
D'IVOIRE
EQUATORIAL GUINEA   G
SAO TOME AND PRINCIPE   G

VENEZUELA   GUYANA
SURINAME
French Guiana (Fr.)

COLOMBIA

ECUADOR

Marquesas (Fr.)

Ascencion (U.K.)

ANGOL
(Cabind

PERU

BRAZIL

St. Helena (U.K.)

French
Polynesia
(Fr.)   Gambier Is. (Fr.)

Society
Arch.
(Fr.)

BOLIVIA

Cook
Islands
(N.Z.)

Pitcairn
Islands
(U.K.)

Austral Is.
(Fr.)

PARAGUAY

CHILE   URUGUAY

Tristan da Cunha (U.K.)

ARGENTINA

Gough (U.K.)

Falkland Islands (U.K.)
(Malvinas)

South
Georgia (U.K.)

A   N   T   A   R

Map No. 4170 Rev. 5   UNITED NATIONS
January 2005

150°   120°   90°   60°   30°   0°

CEDONIA

SWEDEN FINLAND
LATVIA ESTONIA
R.F. LITHUANIA
POLAND BELARUS
REP. SLOVAKIA UKRAINE
TRIA HUNGARY REP OF MOLDOVA
ITALY ROMANIA
ALBANIA BULGARIA
E GREECE TURKEY GEORGIA
MALTA CYPRUS ARMENIA AZERBAIJAN
LEBANON SYRIAN
ISRAEL ARAB REP
LIBYAN JORDAN IRAQ
ARAB KUWAIT
JAMAHIRIYA BAHRAIN
EGYPT SAUDI QATAR
ARABIA UNITED ARAB
EMIRATES
OMAN
CHAD YEMEN
ERITREA DJIBOUTI
SUDAN
CENTRAL ETHIOPIA
AFRICAN REP.
SOMALIA
CONGO UGANDA
DEMOCRATIC RWANDA KENYA
REPUBLIC OF BURUNDI
THE CONGO UNITED REP.
OF TANZANIA
SEYCHELLES
ANGOLA COMOROS
ZAMBIA MALAWI Agalega Island
ZIMBABWE MOZAMBIQUE Tromelin Island
NAMIBIA Cargados Carajos Shoals
MADAGASCAR Rodrigues Island
BOTSWANA Réunion MAURITIUS
SWAZILAND (Fr.)
SOUTH
AFRICA LESOTHO

RUSSIAN FEDERATION

KAZAKHSTAN

UZBEKISTAN KYRGYZSTAN
TURKMENISTAN
TAJIKISTAN
ISLAMIC Jammu and
REP OF Kashmir (*)
IRAN AFGHANISTAN
PAKISTAN
NEPAL BHUTAN

INDIA BANGLADESH
MYANMAR
LAO PEOPLE'S
DEM. REP.
THAILAND VIET NAM
CAMBODIA
SRI LANKA
BRUNEI
DARUSSALAM
MALDIVES MALAYSIA
SINGAPORE

Chagos
Archipelago/
Diego Garcia**

I N D O N E S I A

MONGOLIA

DEM. PEOPLE'S
REP OF KOREA
REPUBLIC JAPAN
CHINA OF KOREA

PHILIPPINES

Northern
Mariana
Islands (U.S.A.)

Guam (U.S.A.)

PALAU

FEDERATED STATES OF MICRONESIA

MARSHALL
ISLANDS

KIRIBATI
NAURU Tokelau (N.Z.)
TUVALU

PAPUA Wallis and
NEW GUINEA Future Islands SAMOA
(Fr.)
American
SOLOMON Samoa (U.S.A.)
ISLANDS Niue (N.Z.)
VANUATU FIJI
TONGA

New Caledonia
(Fr.)

AUSTRALIA

Christmas
(Austr.)
Cocos (Keeling)
Islands (Austr.)

TIMOR LESTE

NEW
ZEALAND

C T I C A

The boundaries and names shown and the designations used
on this map do not imply official endorsement or acceptance
by the United Nations.

*Dotted line represents approximately the Line of Control
in Jammu and Kashmir agreed upon by India and Pakistan.
The final status of Jammu and Kashmir has not yet been
agreed upon by the parties.

**Appears without prejudice to the question of sovereignty.

Department of Peacekeeping Operations
Cartographic Section

TYRANTS

THE WORLD'S **20** **WORST** LIVING DICTATORS

DAVID WALLECHINSKY

REGAN
An Imprint of HarperCollinsPublishers

HarperCollins books may be purchased for educational, business, or sales promotional use. For information please write: Special Markets Department, HarperCollins Publishers Inc., 10 East 53rd Street, New York, NY 10022.

For editorial inquiries, please contact Regan, 10100 Santa Monica Blvd., 10th floor, Los Angeles, CA 90067.

FIRST EDITION

Designed by Sarah Gubkin

Library of Congress Cataloging-in-Publication Data

Wallechinsky, David, 1948–
   Tyrants : the world's 20 worst living dictators / David Wallechinsky.—1st ed.
     p. cm.
   Includes bibliographical references and index.
ISBN-13: 978-0-06-059004-8 (cloth: alk. paper)
ISBN-10: 0-06-059004-1 (alk. paper)
   1. Dictators—Biography.   2. Dictatorship—History—20th century.   3. Dictatorship—History—21st century.
I. Title.

D412.7.W36   2006
909.82'50922—dc22   2006043715

ISBN-13: 978-0-06-059004-8
ISBN-10: 0-06-059004-1

06 07 08 09 10 DIX/RRD 10 9 8 7 6 5 4 3 2 1

It is easy to sit in a democratic country and expose the practices of dictators. This book is dedicated to the courageous and creative citizens who live under the rule of dictators and who risk their lives and well-being to bring freedom to their own nations.

CONTENTS

THE WORLD OF DICTATORS

Among the many reasons that President George W. Bush presented to justify his 2003 invasion of Iraq, the one that most resonated with Americans was that Saddam Hussein was an evil dictator who terrorized, tortured, and murdered his own people. Unfortunately, there are still more than two billion people who live in countries controlled by brutal tyrants. We like to think of dictators, such as Saddam Hussein, Kim Jong-il, and Muammar al-Qaddafi, as inhuman personifications of evil. But what is more disturbing is that each of these tyrants is a human being. Each of them had parents and each of them made a series of choices to gain power and to use that power in a cruel manner. What is more disturbing is that none of these dictators can maintain his grip on his victims without the active support of accomplices. And what is most distressing is that many of today's worst tyrants are financed, aided, and abetted by the United States government and by U.S.-based corporations. These unholy alliances have continued whether the president of the United States is a Democrat or a Republican and whether Congress is controlled by liberals or by conservatives.

However, at the same time, Americans have a long and deep tradition of helping tyrannized people around the world and liberating them from the clutches of dictatorship. I hope that, by identifying the worst of today's dictators and by learning what they do to their people, Americans will be moved to pressure their leaders to consistently oppose dictators and to work with the world community to drive them from power.

There was a time when all world leaders were dictators, when all leaders gained power by inheritance or through violence. Even the Athenian democratic period of the seventh to fourth centuries BC would not meet modern standards of universal suffrage. Because three of the major figures during World War II, Adolf Hitler, Benito Mussolini, and Joseph Stalin, were vicious tyrants, they defined our current understanding of what a dictator is. In the second half of the twentieth century, democracy spread rapidly around the world and became so accepted as an almost universal value that now even dictators feel compelled to placate world opinion by staging phony elections.

For the purposes of this study, I have defined "dictator" as a head of state who exercises arbitrary authority over the lives of his citizens and who cannot be removed from power through legal means. To choose the worst dictators currently in power, I have taken into account suppression of those freedoms that Americans and citizens of other democratic nations are able to take for granted: freedom of speech, freedom of religion, the right to a fair trial, freedom to choose elected representatives, and the freedom to disagree with their government. To determine the ranking of the finalists, I have given "extra credit" to those dictators who go beyond normal repressive measures by torturing prisoners and others, by executing political opponents, by causing their citizens to starve or to suffer malnutrition, and by interfering in the politics of countries other than their own. In ranking the worst of the worst, I have also taken into account how much power a dictator actually has. In some cases a dictator lost a few places because, even though his nation's government is harsh and repressive, the dictator himself does not have full control. One such example is Bashar al-Assad of Syria. It is worth noting that most dictators rise to power by replacing other dictators. The fact that a one-party or family dictatorship is so deeply entrenched that its leader can be replaced without its policies changing does not make the current leader any less of a dictator.

Of the dictators included in this book, the first three, Omar al-Bashir of Sudan, Kim Jong-il of North Korea, and Than Shwe of Burma, stand out as being a cut above the others in terms of venality. Bashir is the only dictator currently in power who is responsible for the killing of hundreds of thousands of people. While the media occasionally cover the massacres in Darfur in western Sudan, they usually do so in the context of it being a "humanitarian tragedy," while Bashir himself has remained little known and has generally escaped condemnation. In fact, he has the power to prevent the destruction of villages in Darfur, just as he had the power to prevent the killing and enslavement of innocent people in southern Sudan. In both cases, he has been an enthusiastic supporter of the slaughters.

North Korea's Kim Jong-il is often portrayed as crazy or as a clown. In reality, although he is certainly eccentric, he is a clever politician who carefully follows world affairs and chooses his tactics accordingly. Most of the coverage given Kim Jong-il in the mainstream media deals with his nuclear ambitions and his threats to build weapons of mass destruction. But domestically he runs the most tightly controlled society in the world. While Kim Jong-il himself might watch satellite television news, most North Koreans have absolutely no access to information about the outside world. The normal kinds of political rights and civil liberties that are squashed to one degree or another by other dictators are simply nonexistent in North Korea.

In Burma, Than Shwe heads a military dictatorship that has been in power since 1962. His regime stands out from those of other dictatorships for its use of forced labor in support of both infrastructure projects and for military actions that the Burmese government is taking against a variety of ethnic minorities. Than Shwe is the commander-in-chief of an army that is different from the armies of most nations in that it exists as a nation within a nation. The Burmese military, known as the *Tatmadaw,* runs its own health care system, its own educational system, its own businesses and farms, and its own banks. It is no longer possible to rise in Burmese society without being a senior member of the military.

After leading a successful anticolonial war of liberation, Robert Mugabe was elected the first president of independent Zimbabwe. It was hoped that, like Nelson Mandela in South Africa, Mugabe would guide Africa to a new era of democracy. But with each year that has passed, he has turned increasingly dictatorial, and he has run his country into the ground. Since 1988, life expectancy in Zimbabwe has plunged from sixty-two years to thirty-eight. This destruction of the health of his people is as much an abuse of human rights as arbitrary arrest and torture.

Islam Karimov of Uzbekistan is one of a handful of leaders from the former Soviet Union who have survived the post-Communist transition while retaining the authoritarian methods favored by the Soviets. His name is synonymous with torture, and there is strong evidence that the United States outsourced the interrogation of terror suspects to Uzbekistan to take advantage of Karimov's relaxed moral standards. In 2005, Karimov's excesses came out of the closet when he ordered the massacre of hundreds of his citizens.

The United States and other democratic nations do so much business with China that there is a tendency to turn a blind eye toward the Communist Party's abysmal human rights record. The Chinese Communist Party's strategy of liberalizing its national economy while harshly rejecting democracy has become the model for modern dictatorships. Hu Jintao and his party control all media in China, between 250,000 and 300,000 Chinese citizens, including political dissidents, are incarcerated in "reeducation-through-labor" camps and the conviction rate in normal criminal trials is 99.7 percent. Less than 5 percent of trials include witnesses. China executes more people than all other nations combined and most of those executions are for nonviolent crimes. Amnesty International has reported that school children have been bussed to public executions as field trips.

The case of Saudi Arabia highlights the difficulties that democracies face in trying to support freedom, human rights, and democracy. King Abdullah heads a royal family that completely controls Saudi society. Thanks to the fact that they own the world's largest reserves of oil, they are virtually immune from international criticism and they do not bother to hold even fake national elections. By law, all Saudi citizens must be Muslims. It is illegal for Saudis to follow a different religion. A Saudi woman cannot appear in public with a man who is not a relative. Women are required to completely cover their bodies in public and they must wear veils. Some Saudi women have expressed satisfaction with the restrictions in their country. However, the strict suppression of women is not voluntary, and Saudi women who would like to live a freer life are not allowed to do so. King Abdullah and his relatives follow an intolerant version of Islam known in the West as Wahhabism. Since 1975, the Saudi royal family has spent more than $70 billion financing mosques and Islamic centers worldwide, including more than $300 million in the United States, where most Muslims studying in Arabic use Saudi textbooks, some of which are virulently anti-Christian and anti-Jewish. If Saudi Arabia did not control so much oil, King Abdullah and the Saudi royal family would be treated just as much as pariahs as are Than Shwe and the Burmese generals.

If it were possible to have comic relief in a story as serious as that of the worst dictators in the world, that role would go to Saparmurat Niyazov of Turkmenistan. Niyazov has created the world's most pervasive personality cult, and criticism of any of his policies is considered treason. Among the most bizarre recent examples of his government by whim are his banning of car radios, lip-synching, and the playing of recorded music on TV and at weddings. In 2005, Niyazov also closed all national parks and shut down rural libraries. He launched an attack on his nation's health care system, firing 15,000 health care workers and replacing most of them with untrained military conscripts. He announced the closing of all hospitals outside the capital and he ordered Turkmenistan's physicians to give up the Hippocratic Oath and instead swear allegiance to him. He has also renamed the month of January after himself and April after his mother.

Since his election as president of Iran in June 2005, Mahmoud Ahmadinejad has caused something of a sensation by, among other things, questioning the reality of the Holocaust and suggesting that Israel be moved to Europe or Alaska. His outrageous speeches have been good theater both for his supporters and for foreign opponents who want to demonize him. However, his power is actually quite limited. For example, even with the support of the Iranian legislature, he cannot make law, and he is not the commander-in-chief of the Iranian armed forces. Above the elected government in Iran is an unelected twelve-man Guardian Council of mullahs, headed by Ayatollah Khamenei, who has ruled the nation since the death of Ayatollah Khomeini in 1989. Khamenei is the leader of the military, and the Guardian Council has the right to veto any law passed by the elected government.

Since 2001, Khamenei has undone the reforms that had been gradually changing the face of Iran.

The tiny West African nation of Equatorial Guinea (pop. 500,000) was catapulted onto the international scene when major reserves of oil were discovered in 1995. Since then, U.S. oil companies have poured $5 billion into the country. The majority of Equatoguineans live on less than $1 a day because the bulk of the oil income goes directly to President Teodoro Obiang Nguema, who managed to transfer $700 million into personal accounts in U.S. banks. In May 2004, the U.S. Treasury Department fined Riggs Bank of Washington, D.C., $25 million for its mishandling of Obiang's accounts. In the words of former U.S. ambassador to Equatorial Guinea John Bennett, Obiang's regime "is not really a government," but rather "an ongoing family criminal conspiracy."

Muammar al-Qaddafi, the dictator of Libya, has experienced roller-coaster relations with the West and with the United States in particular. In 1986, U.S. president Ronald Reagan ordered U.S. fighters to drop 2,000-pound laser-guided bombs on Qaddafi's residence. Qaddafi survived the attack, but 100 other Libyans died that night. In a bizarre twist, supporters of Ronald Reagan would hail the attack as a high point of his presidency, a demonstration of how terrorists should be dealt with, and they would claim the West did not have to worry about Qaddafi again after that. Unfortunately, the exact opposite was the truth. Qaddafi increased his support for terrorism, culminating in his involvement in the 1988 destruction of Pan Am flight 103 over Lockerbie, Scotland, which killed 270 people. In recent years, Qaddafi has made his peace with the West in exchange for access to his large oil reserves. However, it should not be forgotten that domestically Qaddafi still runs a brutal dictatorship in which he maintains complete control over all aspects of Libyan life. "Collective guilt" can lead to the punishment of entire families, tribes, and even towns, and freedom of speech, assembly, and religion are harshly restricted. Libyans can even be arrested for "opposition."

Africa's last remaining absolute monarch, King Mswati III of Swaziland, took power at the age of eighteen. Since then he has allowed his country to slide into extreme poverty, with 69 percent of the Swazi people living on less than $1 a day. Swaziland has the highest HIV/AIDS rate in the world: almost 40 percent. The nation operated without a constitution for thirty years. Mswati agreed to implement a new one in 2006; however, it bans political parties, gives Mswati the right to reject any laws passed by the legislature, and grants him immunity from all possible crimes.

General Pervez Musharraf, supposedly an ally in the fight against Islamist terrorism, seized power in Pakistan in a military coup that overthrew an elected government. He appointed himself president in 2001 and then attempted to legitimize his rule by being elected in 2002. However, the election was heavily boycotted and did not come close to meeting international standards. Musharraf agreed to step down as head of the military at the end of 2004, but then changed his mind, claiming that the nation needed to unify its political and military elements and that he could provide this unity. He justified his decision by stating, "I think the country is more important than democracy." Prior to September 11, 2001, Musharraf was an ardent supporter of Afghanistan's Taliban regime. Yet his greatest transgression concerns Pakistan's role in the spread of nuclear technology. In early 2004 it was revealed that Abdul Qadeer Khan, the head of Pakistan's nuclear weapons development program, had been selling nuclear technology to the dictatorships of North Korea, Libya, and Iran. Musharraf claimed, rather unconvincingly, that he knew nothing about this dangerous and illicit trade. He also gave Khan an unconditional pardon.

Aleksandr Lukashenko of Belarus has the dubious distinction of being Europe's last remaining dictator. He was popularly elected in 1994 and immediately began consolidating his power and eliminating any shred of democracy or free speech. As he himself once said, "I look at our old people and the middle-aged generation who are nostalgic for the Soviet Union, and they can see that Lukashenko is a good chap."

No list of dictators would be complete without Cuba's Fidel Castro, who is currently the longest-ruling world leader, having taken charge of Cuba in 1959. His refusal to pass on the mantle of leadership has been his way of saying that two generations of Cubans have come and gone without a single person being worthy of leading the country. Although Castro has mellowed with age, his government continues to control all media and it is still possible to be sent to jail for the charge of being prone to commit a crime in the future.

In 1991, Isaias Afwerki of Eritrea and Meles Zenawi of Ethiopia teamed together to liberate their respective countries from the brutal Ethiopian dictatorship of Mengistu Haile Mariam. Seven years later, Isaias and Meles subjected their own people to a bloody and useless border war that claimed the lives of tens of thousands of people and served no purpose other than to distract the two citizenries from the terrible job the two dictators were doing in running Eritrea and Ethiopia.

Since 1961, Syria has been ruled by the Ba'ath Party, the same party that ruled Iraq until the fall of Saddam Hussein. Bashar al-Assad inherited the leadership of Syria from his father, Hafiz al-Assad, in 2000. Bashar is the balancing point among the various Syrian power forces, including the military, the intelligence service, the nation's ruling party, and the government bureaucracy. Meanwhile, the people of Syria are not free to express their political opinions, much less choose their leaders.

Since achieving independence in 1961, the West African nation of Cameroon has had only two leaders, Ahmadou Ahidjo, who ruled until 1982, and Paul Biya, who has been in power since then. Every few years, Biya stages an election to justify his continuing reign, but these elections have no credibility. In fact, Biya is credited with a creative innovation in the world of phony elections. In 2004, annoyed by the criticisms of international vote-monitoring groups, he paid for his own set of international observers, six ex–U.S. congress-men, who certified his election as free and fair.

The remote Southeast Asian nation of Laos has been ruled since 1975 by the Communist Lao People's Democratic Party, a stultifyingly dull collective dictatorship. The latest number-one elder in Laos is General Choummaly Sayasone, who ascended to the top of the party hierarchy in March 2006.

I am often asked if there is some personality trait that characterizes all dictators. Obvi-ously, they all enjoy the benefits of absolute power. However, I see dictators as falling into three rough categories that are analogous to the different types of rich people. Some dictators inherit their position. This is clearly the case in nations ruled by royal families, such as Saudi Arabia and Swaziland, but it also applies to Kim Jong-il, who took over the leadership of North Korea from his father in what was the first hereditary transfer of power in a Commu-nist country, and to Bashar al-Assad of Syria. The second class of dictators are the company men who slowly and patiently work their way up the hierarchy of a one-party or military regime. Current examples include Hu Jintao of China and Than Shwe of Burma. The last category, and the one that produces the most intriguing personalities, is the entrepreneurs who seize power on their own initiative. Fidel Castro, for example, led a rebel army into Ha-vana and became his nation's leader at the age of thirty-two. Muammar al-Qaddafi was even younger, twenty-seven, when he led an officers' coup in Libya.

All dictators stay in power through violence or the threat of violence, yet most of them try to gain the support of at least some of their citizens, either because they want to believe that they are really loved or because it is simply easier to rule a country if a substantial minority of the population actually does support you. Consequently, dictators use various ploys to gain the support, or at least the acquiescence, of their people. The most common ploy is the ap-peal to patriotism, whereby the dictator tries to equate love of country with devotion to its leader. For example, almost every dictator presents his citizens with a form of this argument: (1) "Our nation is being threatened by an outside force." (2) "Only I can protect our nation from this force and if you oppose me, you are opposing our nation and supporting the enemy." The first half of this equation is often true. The second half never is. Another argu-ment that is used by apologists for dictators is that "conditions are better than they used to be." This is often said in defense of the Saudi royal family and of the Chinese Communist Party, dictators upon whom the West is economically dependent. The implication is that if half as many political prisoners were arrested or executed this year as were arrested or exe-cuted the year before, human rights advocates should shut up and be satisfied that, as bad as things may be, at least they are going in the right direction.

This book has its origins in an annual article that I write for *Parade* magazine. Since

Parade began publishing my lists of worst dictators in 2003, I have been inundated by complaints about my choices. In some cases, I am accused of including world leaders who are not really so bad. Hu Jintao, King Abdullah, and even Equatorial Guinea's Teodoro Obiang have hired public relations firms to promote their governments in the United States, and there are formal networks of Saudi and Chinese apologists who write letters, e-mails, and Internet posts in support of these dictators. In other cases, I am accused of ignoring or downplaying the abuses of certain leaders. More often than not, these complaints deal with Meles Zenawi of Ethiopia and Fidel Castro. It is only natural that people who have been oppressed by a dictator consider him to be the worst in the world. However, without in any way defending these two dictators, I would ask that their opponents take a look at the chapters about some of the other tyrants. I should also note that whatever I write about Castro and wherever I rank him, I am always criticized by both the left and the right. For all the criticism I have received regarding dictators such as Castro, Hu Jintao, King Abdullah, and others, the fact remains that a substantial majority of the complaints I receive have to do with one subject: my refusal to include U.S. President George W. Bush in my lists of worst dictators. For this reason, I have included a chapter about President Bush. George Bush is not a dictator . . . but he does use many of the tactics that dictators use. That's the short answer. For the rest of the details, you'll have to read his chapter to find out.

(George Mulala/Reuters/Corbis)

1.

OMAR AL-BASHIR—SUDAN

THE NATION—Sudan, by size, is the largest nation in Africa and the tenth-largest nation in the world. It shares borders with nine different nations; only China, Russia, and Brazil have more neighbors than Sudan. Since achieving independence from the British in 1956, the nation has experienced only ten years of peace. The rest of the time it has been plagued by a series of overlapping civil wars. Since 1983, an estimated two million Sudanese have died of war-related causes, while five million have been forced from their homes. Since 1993, Sudan has been the world's leading debtor to the World Bank and the International Monetary Fund. Sudan's population of about 38 million is deeply divided ethnically and religiously. Although 52 percent of the population is black, the nation has always been ruled by the minority, who are Arabs. Seventy percent of Sudanese are Sunni Muslims, 25 percent follow traditional religions—referred to as animism or primitive religion by Westerners—and 5 percent are Christians, mostly Catholic. A census taken at the time of independence identified 50 ethnic groups, 570 distinct peoples, and the use of 114 languages, although more than half the population speaks Arabic.

SLAVERY—In recent years, the media have devoted a good deal of attention to the killings in Darfur in western Sudan. One of the most disturbing aspects of this tragedy is that the exploitation of black people by Arabs in the Sudan has been going on for more than 1,400 years. The word "Sudani" in Arabic means "black." This term, along with the words "Nuba" and "Nubia," which relate to one of the areas in southern Sudan populated by black Africans, have all entered colloquial Arabic with the meaning of "slave."

Christian missionaries arrived in the region in the 6th century from Constantinople and Islamic missionaries in the seventh century. As early as 652 a treaty was signed in which Muslim Egypt would provide goods to Christian Nubia in exchange for Nubian slaves. Slave raids in southern Sudan continued almost without a break for the next 1,300 years, no matter who ruled the region—Egyptians, Turks, or local sultans. Muhammad Ali, the Albanian-born ruler of Egypt, invaded Sudan in 1821, leading to sixty years of Turco-Egyptian rule. During this period, which saw the introduction of domestic slavery and the development of slave soldiers, an average of 30,000 southerners a year were seized in slave raids.

Muhammad Ali also founded the city of Khartoum at the confluence of the White Nile and the Blue Nile. In 1885, the forces of Mohammad Ahmed al-Mahdi (Mohammad the Messiah) captured Khartoum and overthrew the Turco-Egyptian regime. Al-Mahdi died the same year and was replaced by Abdullahi ibn Muhammad, known as the Khalifa. The Mahdists expanded the practice of slavery, driving millions from their homes. They also set an unfortunate precedent by demanding that citizens take a personal, religious oath of loyalty to Mahdi and the Khalifa and condemning nonfollowers, even fellow Muslims, as "unbelievers." When British and Egyptian troops invaded Sudan, these rejected Muslims were glad to help overthrow the Mahdists.

The Anglo-Egyptian forces, led by General Horatio Herbert Kitchener, defeated the Mahdist army at the Battle of Omdurman on September 2, 1898, and the Sudan became a possession of the king of England. The British abolished slavery, outraging the Arabs in northern Sudan, who considered the practice not a question of human rights, but a cultural tradition that was being disrupted by foreign invaders. The British also halted the spread of Islam to new areas and assigned separate zones to Catholic and Protestant missionaries, most of whom arrived from Austria, Italy, and the United States. The Americans distinguished themselves by their obsession with clothing the natives.

The Mahdists had never established control over southern Sudan, and it took the British a long time to deal with it themselves. As part of their pacification campaign, the British-led army occasionally burned down villages in the south, just as the Egyptians and Mahdists had done, and they were even known to seize cattle just to prove they had the power to do so. In 1930, the British declared a Southern Policy that stated that the region was African rather than Arab, but because there were few hereditary rulers in the south, it remained difficult for the British to establish consistent authority. In the north, meanwhile, tensions developed between the British and their junior partners, the Egyptians. In the 1920s, the British expelled Egyptian soldiers and administrators and, to counter the growing influence of Egypt in Sudan, they brought back the posthumously born son of the anti-Egyptian Mahdi. The grand *qadi* (judge) of the religious courts was always an Egyptian, but the British ended this monopoly in 1947. After World War II, the British came up with a novel tactic for stemming the threat of Egyptian power in Sudan: they proposed that the Sudan be granted independence, even though few Sudanese themselves had demanded it. When formal negotiations for independence began in 1952, Egypt was included, but the black Sudanese in the south were not.

Sudan's first election, held in 1953, was generally fair, although women were not allowed to vote. (Women's suffrage finally occurred in 1967.) The National Unionist Party, which advocated political union with Egypt, emerged as the largest single party, but it failed to gain a majority of the votes, and a coalition of anti-unionist parties turned union into a dead issue. The new, pre-independence government also showed no interest in sharing power with the black Sudanese and appointed northerners to all leadership positions in the south. This continuation of the Arab view that the southern tribes were not fit to be partners led to a shocking incident in the summer of 1955. When the northern government ordered southern soldiers in the state of Equatoria to transfer north, they refused. In what became known as the Torit Mutiny, the soldiers went on a rampage against the administrators from the north, killing 450 people, including women and children. The northern authorities were outraged, but not enough to ask themselves what could be done to mitigate southern anger.

Great Britain practically forced Sudan to declare independence on January 1, 1956, before a constitution had been written and before the achievement of anything that could be even remotely considered a national consensus. The southern Sudanese were understandably wary of the northerners' intentions toward them. Southern leaders pushed for a federal system that would allow them some regional control, but the northerners took the position that giving the south any power at all would lead eventually to secession or that it would, at the very least, threaten the master–servant relationship that they considered part of their "traditional culture."

Less than two months after independence, an incident took place that would serve as an awful harbinger of the violence that has cursed Sudan ever since. Police in Kosti locked 281 striking tenant farmers in a room. By morning, 192 of them were dead.

The first post-independence election, in 1958, exposed Sudan's deep divisions, as the ruling alliance fractured and the southerners established their own party. A nationwide strike, led by labor unions, the tenant farmers' union, students, and the Communist Party, brought the country to a standstill. On November 17, 1958, the military, led by General Ibrahim Abbud, seized power and declared a state of emergency. This came as a relief to both the Western powers and the USSR, who found a democratic Sudan difficult to deal with. The new government set out to Arabize and Islamicize the south, using Arab traders and Muslim missionaries as a vanguard and then sending in the army to burn villages and to arrest and torture civilians. They also ordered that the day of Sabbath be changed from Sunday to Friday.

THE FIRST CIVIL WAR—In 1962, southern Sudanese living in exile, including students and ex-mutineers, formed the Sudan African Nationalist Union (SANU), which eventually included a guerrilla wing known as Anyanya, which is a type of poison. SANU appealed to the West for support, but the Europeans and Americans were not interested. SANU also received little help from fellow Africans because the Organization of African Unity had pledged to retain all colonial boundaries and SANU'S call for "self-determination" was judged counter to this pledge. Anyanya managed to acquire weapons by hijacking Sudanese government convoys that were transporting arms to pro-Arab rebels in the Congo. Fighting between the southern rebel forces and Sudanese government forces began slowly. The first major rebel attacks started in September 1963. Both sides were ruthless in their tactics. However, along the way, Anyanya discovered the Maoist strategy that guerrillas can survive by befriending the locals and becoming "fish in a sea of people."

Meanwhile, back in Khartoum, things were not going well for General Abboud, who was not the most competent of leaders. Student protests, street demonstrations, and a general strike finally led to a popular uprising that overthrew Abboud in October 1964. A transitional government was formed by Communists and unions of tenants, workers, and farmers, which allowed women to obtain some political rights. Six months later an election was held, but only in the north. The newly elected government made clear its intentions in the south by approving the first large-scale massacres of civilians. When war broke out between Israel and its Arab neighbors, Sudan supported the Arabs, broke relations with the United States, and turned to the Soviet Union, which led to a drastic decline in foreign aid. As the war in the south grew to eat up one-third of the national budget, Sudan's foreign debt doubled between 1964 and 1969, putting great pressure on the northern poor.

Another election was held in 1968, but few in the south were able to vote. By this time the rebel movement had grown large enough to develop bickering factions. They did find it easier to acquire weapons and training because enemies of the Sudanese government, such as Israel, Ethiopia, and Uganda, were happy to supply the rebels.

In March 1972, the government and the rebels signed a settlement, the Addis Ababa Agreement, that ended the civil war. This was the first negotiated settlement in postcolonial Africa, but eventually the southerners would come to regret it and consider it a failure. The agreement provided for the gradual absorption of the Anyanya guerrillas into the national army, but northern troops did not leave the south and many guerrillas chose to go into exile in Ethiopia. Economically and politically, the promises of the Addis Ababa Agreement would turn out to be illusory.

NIMEIRI AND THE INTERLUDE OF PEACE—On May 24, 1969, Colonel
Jaafar Nimeiri overthrew the elected government of Sudan by bringing together the military and the Communist and Socialist parties. Nimeiri would prove to be a completely self-serving politician who would make or break an alliance with any group, so long as it helped him stay in power. For example, by 1970 he had booted out of office all of the Communist ministers who had helped him with his coup d'état. Nimeiri civilianized himself by staging a phony election in September 1971, in which he won 99 percent of the votes. Not surprisingly, the traditional political parties turned against him, so he countered their potential strength by reaching out to the southern rebels and negotiating the Addis Ababa Agreement. Nimeiri then shoved through a new constitution in April 1973 that created a one-party state. That party was Nimeiri's Sudan Socialist Union. He put himself in command of the armed forces and made the judiciary completely answerable to the president (Nimeiri). He also gave the security services broad powers of search and arrest and set up a large network of informers.

Another group of growing influence whom Nimeiri chose to co-opt was the Islamists; religious radicals led by Hassan al-Turabi, a man who would rise to great power after Omar al-Bashir took over as dictator of Sudan. To appease the Islamists, Nimeiri released Turabi from the prison where he had been languishing for seven years. Nimeiri began incorporating the Islamist agenda into his own. He supported Arab Iraq in its war against non-Arab Iran and, in September 1983, he imposed Shari'a, or Islamic, law on Sudan. He also sold out the southern rebels, supporting the 1978 Camp David Accords so that Israel would stop supplying the southern guerrillas. In 1983 he abolished the system of regional councils that had provided the southern Sudanese a modicum of power.

Nimeiri made friends with the U.S. government, which viewed him as a counterweight to pro-Soviet regimes in Ethiopia and Libya. Fully aware that U.S. president Ronald Reagan would support any government that was "anti-Communist," Nimeiri convinced the Reagan administration that the southern rebel forces were Communists. This earned him $1.4 billion in aid, including U.S.-made aircraft that he used to attack southern troops. In exchange, Reagan was able to use the "defense of Sudan" as his excuse for bombing Libya in 1986. Vice President George H.W. Bush visited Nimeiri in Khartoum in 1985 while accompanied, rather bizarrely, by American televangelists Pat Robertson and Jerry Falwell. It was during a return trip to the United States in April 1985 that, after sixteen years in power, Nimeiri's luck finally ran out. After a government-imposed rise in food prices, a popular uprising led to a coup that overthrew him. It was little realized at the time, but the most horrible aspect of Nimeiri's legacy was his creation of the practice of supplying tribal militias to fight as surrogates so that he could deny that the Sudanese army was fighting antigovernment forces. The current Sudanese government is still employing the same tactic in Darfur.

One year after the 1985 coup, Sudan held another election, although only half of the south took part. Sadiq al-Mahdi, the leader of the UMMA party, emerged as the prime minister. Sadiq committed Sudan to becoming an Islamic state. Upon his election in April 1986, he put it bluntly: "Non-Muslims can ask us to protect their rights—and we will do that—but that's all they can ask. We wish to establish Islam as the source of law in Sudan because Sudan has a Muslim majority." This was an unusually bold, or one might say, rash statement, considering that the non-Muslim rebel groups in the south were dramatically gaining strength. In fact, the civil war, which had recommenced, was turning horrifically ugly.

The largest of the rebel groups was the SPLA, led by John Garang, who had earned a doctorate in agricultural economics at Iowa State University and had also attended a U.S. Army infantry officer's course at Fort Benning, Georgia. The SPLA represented the largest of the southern ethnic groups, the Dinka. In 1985 and 1986, the SPLA, desperate for supplies, staged a series of vicious attacks against civilians. But then the SPLA learned a miraculous lesson: if you treat civilians well, they might actually support you. As obvious as this may seem, it is a fact that continues to escape the Sudanese government. In 1987, the SPLA changed tactics. Instead of attacking villages and seizing food and other goods, it imposed a food tax that, once paid, protected villagers from seizures. Since the Sudanese army continued to attack people's homes, the popularity of the SPLA grew and, in 1988, for the first time, it was no longer viewed by other tribes as a purely Dinka army.

The government-supported Murahalin militia, on the other hand, was engaging in grotesque tactics, burning to the ground Dinka villages and killing civilians. It regularly abducted Dinka and sent them north to be kept in slavery or traded, while children, who had been raised non-Muslim, were forced to attend Islamic schools and adopt new names. Captured women were forced to endure genital mutilation.

One particularly infamous atrocity, the Ed-Da'ein Massacre, was carried out on March 28, 1987. Two thousand Dinka villagers, fearing an attack by a Muslim tribe, the Baggara, asked for police protection. The police told them to take shelter in nearby railway freight cars. That night, the police stood by and watched as the Baggara set fire to the railway cars, killing at least a thousand people.

In 1987, the SPLA scored a stunning defeat of the Murahalin and the Sudanese army, which responded to the humiliation by attacking unarmed Dinka refugees in Southern Darfur. Sadiq al-Mahdi had never had the full support of the army, and he further alienated them with his dependency on tribal militias. As the military situation deteriorated and the SPLA took the fighting north to areas previously controlled by the government, the army demanded that Sadiq meet with John Garang and try to negotiate a ceasefire. Sadiq finally agreed. This decision infuriated one of the parties in his ruling coalition, Hassan al-Turabi's National Islamic Front (NIF), which withdrew from the coalition. On June 30, 1989, before Sadiq could meet with Garang, a group of Muslim army officers, led by Brigadier General Omar al-Bashir and supported by the NIF, staged a coup. The coup leaders called themselves the National Movement for Correcting the Situation.

THE MAN—Omar Hassan Ahmad al-Bashir was born in 1944 in Hoshe Bannaga, 100 kilometers northeast of Khartoum. A member of the Ja'aliya tribe, he came from a rural working-class family and attended Ahlia Middle School in the town of Shendi. Bashir's family moved to Khartoum, where he attended secondary school and worked in a garage. Bashir found his niche in the military world. Admitted to a military academy for training as a pilot, he graduated from Sudan Military College at the age of twenty-two and then earned two master's degrees in military science, one from the Sudanese College of Commanders and the second in Malaysia. By 1973, he was serving as a paratrooper in the Arab-Israeli War. Bashir was jovial and well-liked, and his natural affinity with fellow officers would serve him well in the decades to come. He was particularly friendly with those officers who were sympathetic to the National Islamic Front. In late 1985, military intelligence identified Bashir as a potential leader of an NIF coup and he was transferred to remote garrisons, including Muglad, which was used as a base for operations against rebel forces in the south and the Nuba Mountains. As a sign of his solidarity with his own forces, Bashir would choose as his second wife the widow of a fellow officer killed in the fighting.

In 1988, Bashir was promoted to brigadier and put in command of the 8th Infantry Brigade that was fighting the SPLA. He was one of the few senior officers who did not oppose Sadiq al-Mahdi's use of tribal militias and he even proposed formally incorporating them into the regular army. However, he was critical of Sadiq's conduct of the civil war, as well as his decision to negotiate with John Garang. In the middle of June 1989, Bashir returned to Khartoum, supposedly on his way to a training course in Cairo. Two weeks later, he was the leader of Sudan.

TAKING POWER—At first, the 1989 coup in Sudan appeared to be just another power grab by a group of junior officers, the sort of event that happened all the time in Africa. The

Egyptian government, mindful that Egypt had given Bashir a military decoration for his services against Israel in 1973, praised Bashir and offered its support. Likewise, Saddam Hussein, within hours of the coup, rushed off a shipment of weapons as a gesture of thanks for Sudan's support of Iraq during its war against Iran. Libya sent 60,000 barrels of oil, enough to last Sudan the rest of the year, while Saudi Arabia, Egypt, and Iraq threw in some oil for good measure. The United States was required by law to suspend nonhumanitarian aid to Sudan because an unelected government had overthrown an elected one. However, the United States was reassured by Bashir's personal pledge to U.S. assistant secretary of state Herman Cohen that he hoped to emulate secular Turkey.

For his own part, Bashir acted like a typical leader of a successful bloodless coup. He immediately promoted himself to general and appointed himself premier and defense minister. He promised to fight corruption and embezzlement and he offered amnesty to SPLA members if they turned in their weapons. In his first public appearance, Bashir spoke in favor of pan-Arabism and expressed solidarity with Sudan's Arab neighbors, Egypt and Libya. In a surprising gesture of diplomacy, Bashir visited non-Arab Iran and secured aid for a road-building program in exchange for "cooperation with security and intelligence."

Domestically, Bashir pursued policies that were also typical of newly installed military dictators. He suspended the constitution, banned all political parties and trade unions, and closed down the formerly free press. When the presidents of eight labor unions and professional associations submitted a petition for the democratic election of union officials, Bashir had them all arrested. He banned the Sudanese Bar Association, took charge of the appointment of judges (who had previously been chosen by sitting judges), and imposed an Islamic judicial system on the entire country.

To the outside world, the change of government in Sudan was hardly worth noting, and few, if any, observers could have predicted that Omar al-Bashir would still be in power more than fifteen years later. For the people of Sudan, however, particularly those in the south, it soon dawned on them that this was not a typical military coup. Bashir decreed that Arabic should replace all other languages and that although Christians would still be allowed to practice their religion because they were "people of the book," Sudanese who followed traditional religions would be forced to convert to Islam.

Bashir set up a three-part government. The first part, the Revolutionary Command Council, was made up of the fifteen officers who carried out the coup, with Bashir as their chairman. The second part was a more formal national government with twenty ministers, who were either anticorruption technocrats or members of the National Islamic Front. Over the next four years, NIF members would replace each of the technocrats. But the real power was held by the third part of the government, the semisecret Council of Defenders, also known as the Committee of 40, which consisted of NIF members and young military officers. Chaired first by Bashir's old friend from military school, Ali Osman Muhammad Taha, and then by Hassan al-Turabi, the Council members served as "advisors" to Bashir.

This fusion of the Sudanese military with the radical NIF gave Bashir and Turabi the ability to carry out an aggressive Islamist agenda. Students, teachers, and professors of all ages, along with civil servants, were forced to undergo six weeks of military training, during which they were subjected to endless lectures on Islam. In March 1991, Bashir's government issued the Public Order Act of 1991, which set forth an Islamic Penal Code. He restored flogging and amputation and formalized the death penalty for a wide range of offenses, including adultery, embezzlement, dealing on the black market, the vague charge of "corruption" and organizing strikes, not to mention apostasy, the giving up of Islam. Emergency courts were authorized to seize illegal vendors and flog them in public on the spot. Bashir declared that God supervised his judiciary system because He is "all-knowing and all-seeing." The new laws were not kind to women. They prohibited social gatherings in which men and women danced together or mixed freely. In Khartoum State, police broke up wedding parties. Women were excluded from public life and had dress codes imposed upon them. Bashir issued a presidential decree that forbade women to wear perfume or trousers and required them to wear veils and dresses down to the ankles. Some women tried to continue wearing colorful traditional dresses called *thobe,* but the NIF's Guardians of Morality and Advocates of Good began flogging women in the streets. Women who defied other rules were arrested, jailed, and tortured. The government also banned the teaching of art and music, because it spread Western and African culture, and closed down the Institute of Music and Drama at Khartoum University because the NIF objected to classical Arabic music. Needless to say, Bashir's government banned alcohol. But in February 1995, the ministry of health took this restriction even further, forbidding the importation of medicines containing alcohol, including the antimalarial drug chloroquine, which led to a widespread epidemic of malaria. Eighty percent of pharmacies shut their doors and so many doctors left the country that the government banned all travel by medical personnel.

THE MAN BEHIND THE THRONE—To most Sudan watchers, it was difficult to imagine that the thuggish Omar al-Bashir could create on his own the principles of a new rigid Islamic state. Many found it easier to categorize Bashir as a mere front man for the better-educated and more sophisticated leader of the National Islamic Front, Hassan al-Turabi. Although Bashir would prove to be wilier than he at first appeared, Turabi's influence on Sudanese politics is undeniable.

Born in 1932, Turabi was the son of an Islamic judge and grew up in an orthodox family that opposed the more tolerant Sufi branch of Islam that was then popular in Sudan. He graduated with a B.A. in law from Khartoum University, and went on to earn a master's degree in law from the London School of Economics and a doctorate in law from the Sorbonne in Paris. When Turabi returned to Sudan in 1965, he was appointed Dean of the Law School at the University of Khartoum. He was also the secretary-general of the Sudanese branch of the Muslim Brotherhood, an activist orthodox group founded in Egypt in 1928, and to whose ideas he was first exposed in London. At the university, Turabi taught students to give up Sufi mysticism, reject the formalism of Iran's Ayatollah Khamenei, and instead interpret Islam and their own behavior according to Shari'a law. Turabi was particularly popular with foreigners, who enjoyed his lively good humor. In 1970, Jaafar Nimeiri had Turabi thrown into prison, where he remained for the next seven years until Nimeiri decided that he needed the support of the Islamists. Turabi immersed himself in the creation of an Islamic banking system in which depositors are given a partnership rather than interest. Three months after Nimeiri's fall in 1985, Turabi founded the National Islamic Front. He led the party in the 1986 elections, campaigning for Shari'a and universal conscription. This platform did not appeal to the Sudanese majority and the NIF did so poorly that Turabi himself lost in his own constituency in Omdurman. Two years after the election, the victor, Sadiq al-Mahdi, who happened to be Turabi's brother-in-law, appointed Turabi attorney general. In this position, Turabi was able to institute a law that outlawed apostasy, in other words, being a Muslim who gives up Islam. However, the wording of the bill was sufficiently vague to be interpreted to include opposition to the current Islamic government. He also banned public demonstrations by the populist National Alliance, a party that advocated peace negotiations with John Garang and the SPLA. In February 1989, Sadiq promoted Turabi to deputy prime minister and foreign minister.

When Bashir took charge in the 1989 coup, the Revolutionary Command Council had Turabi put under house arrest. However, this was merely an empty gesture of false impartiality, as Turabi's followers continued to operate the bureaucracy for the Revolutionary Command Council. He was released the following year. Turabi tried to promote *Shura,* Islamic democracy, which he described as government by consultation with learned males who come to a consensus, thus eliminating the need for passing written laws. He and his wife, Wisal al-Mahdi, founded the International Organization of Islamic Women. According to their interpretation of Islamic feminism, female subservience has no place in Islam and women can own property, attend public meetings, and take part in political affairs. Non-Muslim women, on the other hand, are nothing more than the spoils of war, property to be owned and disposed of.

The presence of the troops of the United States and other Western nations on the soil (or sand) of Saudi Arabia during the 1991 Gulf War served as a great marketing tool for Islamist leaders, who distributed tapes of their speeches throughout the Arabic-speaking world.

Turabi's tapes did not achieve the widespread popularity of the scion of a wealthy Saudi business family named Osama bin Laden, but Turabi did develop a substantial following. In December 1990, he visited Chicago, where he attended a conference of the Islamic Committee for Palestine and spoke on "Islam: The Road to Victory." One of Turabi's protégés was Dr. Ayman al-Zawahiri, leader of the Egyptian Islamic Jihad and future lieutenant to Osama bin Laden in al-Qaeda.

In April 1991, Turabi, with some financial backing from bin Laden, organized the first general assembly of the Popular Arab and Islamic Congress (PAIC), which brought together delegates from forty-five nations. Although the PAIC would soon gain infamy as a meeting place for terrorists, at the 1991 congress Turabi pulled off a diplomatic coup by bringing together intelligence officers from Iran and Iraq for the first time since the two nations had fought a horrific war, and Iran announced that it would end its ten-year blockade of Iraq.

HASSAN AL-TURABI IN AMERICA—In May 1992, Turabi arrived in North America for a tour that would highlight his position as an important intellectual power broker. Little suspecting that his life was about to take a dramatic turn, he began by attending a scholarly roundtable at the University of South Florida. Lecturing on "Islam, Democracy, the State and the West," some of his statements seemed so divorced from reality that they left many participants speechless. Completely ignoring the ongoing civil war, he declared, "In Sudanese society ethnic minorities tend to disappear," and added "the Sudanese are Arab in culture. . . . There is no Arab–African divide anywhere in the Sudan." He called the worldwide Islamist movement "highly democratic. . . . Islam shuns absolute government, absolute authority, dynastic authority and individual authority." He called the 1991 Gulf War "a blessing in disguise because Islamist movements around the world were "turned into mass movements" and were "radicalized." Confronted with accusations that the Sudanese government practiced torture, Turabi, rather than deny the charge, shrugged it off and stated that "This behavior is typical of police around the world."

Turabi moved on to Washington, D.C., where he appeared before the Africa Subcommittee of the House of Representatives and repeated his opinions, leaving many committee members bewildered. In an interview with *New Perspectives Quarterly*, he again contradicted reality by intoning, "We have no interest in terrorism. . . . Islam can have nothing to do with terrorism." Flushed with his rhetorical successes, Turabi flew to Toronto, where he was scheduled to have meetings with government officials and representatives of the oil industry.

HASSAN AL-TURABI'S UNFORTUNATE ENCOUNTER—On the morning of May 25, 1992, Turabi flew to Ottawa to meet with functionaries in the

Department of External Affairs. His appearance was met by a demonstration of Sudanese exiles protesting the policies of Turabi and Bashir. That evening, one of the protesters, thirty-five-year-old Hashim Badr el Din Mohammad, was dropping off a friend at the airport when he noticed Turabi sipping coffee with two companions. A Sufi who was infuriated by the impositions of Turabi's intolerant brand of Islam, Hashim rushed toward Turabi yelling, in English, "Murderer, murderer, slavemaster! Terrorist in Canada! Fascist in Canada! Slavemaster in Canada!" And in Arabic, "Stop. Where are you going to? I will never let you go." Unfortunately for Turabi, Hashim was not just another oppressed Sudanese; he was a six-foot-eight-inch karate coach with a seventh-degree black belt. One of Turabi's companions, a Muslim minister from Chicago named Ahmed Osman Makki, lunged at Hashim, who knocked him to the floor. Turabi tried to hold off Hashim, but the latter smashed him in the side of the head and sent him flying through the air. Turabi spent the next four weeks in an Ottawa hospital and could not speak or control his movements. Although Turabi eventually made a full recovery, the second PAIC General Assembly, scheduled for the autumn, had to be cancelled. As for Hashim, a sympathetic jury acquitted him on the charge of assault on the basis that Makki and Turabi had struck him first.

CARLOS THE JACKAL—Illich Ramírez Sánchez, better known as Carlos the Jackal, was an anti-Israeli Venezuelan Marxist who became the most notorious terrorist of the 1970s and mid-1980s. His most famous act was a 1975 attack on OPEC headquarters in Vienna, during which he and five accomplices took more than sixty hostages. Sometimes working on a for-hire basis, Carlos organized a variety of bomb attacks, most of them in France. He also shot to death an informer and two Parisian policemen who had come to arrest him. By 1990, Carlos was considered over-the-hill and inactive. However, he was still wanted for the crimes he had committed when he was younger. After being expelled from Syria, he was given refuge, in August 1993, in Sudan, where he was welcomed by Bashir and Turabi. However, as he settled into life in Khartoum, it became clear that Carlos did not exactly pursue a lifestyle that was consistent with Islamist ideals. In fact, he was an alcoholic and a womanizer; but he had an even worse strike against him: he was being tracked by the Western world's leading spy agencies. The CIA informed French intelligence that it had pinpointed Carlos' location in Sudan. The French confirmed the identification at the PAIC General Assembly in December 1993. Initially, Bashir's government refused to acknowledge that Carlos was in the country. However, the French produced photographs of Carlos engaged in behavior that did not reflect the regime's values and threatened to reveal to the Islamic world that Sudan was harboring a debauched Marxist terrorist. Bashir capitulated and turned over negotiations to Turabi, who agreed to hand over Carlos to the French. In exchange, France gave Sudan mili tary equipment, police training, a desalination plant, a grant to Sudan Airways, and access to aerial photographs of SPLA troop positions in the south. The French also agreed to publicly praise Hassan al-Turabi for his role as a mediator with Algerian Islamists.

In August 1994, Carlos checked into Ibn Khalmud hospital for minor surgery relating to a low sperm count. While he was recovering, security personnel informed Carlos and his wife that his life was in danger and he had to be transferred to a military hospital. From there he was moved to a private villa and then, in the middle of the night, he was snatched by French agents and flown to Paris, where he was tried for the murder of the French policemen, convicted, and sentenced to life imprisonment; and it is in prison that he remains today.

The success of this deal would inspire Bashir and Turabi to offer for trade another terrorist to whom they had granted sanctuary: Osama bin Laden.

OSAMA BIN LADEN IN SUDAN—It would appear that bin Laden first met Hassan al-Turabi during a visit to Sudan in 1984. Four years later he opened an air charter company in Khartoum and in late 1989, after the coup that brought Omar al-Bashir to power, bin Laden established the Wadi al-Aqiq holding company and deposited $50 million in a previously minor bank in Khartoum. Before long, bin Laden started investing that money. He opened thirty businesses, including a trucking company, a furniture manufacturer, and a bakery. He also exported from Sudan fruits, vegetables, sesame, wheat and cotton, and imported into Sudan honey, sweets, farm equipment and, oh yes, arms. He arranged to send Sudanese cotton to the Taliban in Afghanistan in exchange for weapons that were supposedly captured from Soviet troops. Coming from a family that made its fortune in the construction business, it was not surprising that he also received the contract to build an airport at Port Sudan and to construct the road from Port Sudan to Khartoum. Some of the deals between Bashir and bin Laden may have helped the Sudanese government, but they were damaging to the people. When the government could no longer pay for the roadwork bin Laden's company was doing, it gave him instead a million acres of farmland in the Gash River Delta on the Eritrean border. Bin Laden then hurt the area's poor farmers by overplanting watermelons and driving down the price, and hurt the rich farmers by gaining a monopoly on sesame exports. In fact, he brokered a deal that sent the entire Sudanese sesame crop to Russia in exchange for arms. Bashir also granted bin Laden tax exemptions on all his businesses. And bin Laden took Hassan al-Turabi's niece as his third wife in exchange for duty-free importation of construction equipment and vehicles.

Of course, Osama bin Laden had other interests besides making money. After Saddam Hussein invaded Kuwait in 1990, bin Laden wrote a ten-page letter to Saudi defense minister Prince Sultan offering to use the skills he learned fighting the Communists in Afghanistan to train Saudis to defend themselves. He even offered the use of his family's construction equipment to dig trenches along Saudi Arabia's border with Iraq. The Saudi royal family, wary of giving the popular bin Laden too much power, instead hired the United States and its allies to defend the country. By 1991, Osama bin Laden was no longer welcome in his native Saudi Arabia. After sojourning in Pakistan, he arrived, at the invitation of Turabi, in Sudan, assuring himself the best of Sudanese hospitality by donating $5 million to Turabi's National Islamic Front.

In March 1990, Bashir announced that all "Arab brothers" could enter Sudan without a visa. Bin Laden knew how to exploit this ruling. He established a "farm" on the Blue Nile south of Khartoum that was actually a group of training camps to teach the use of weapons and explosives. There were twenty-three camps for Islamists who had fought in Afghanistan; three camps for al-Qaeda; and training courses for terrorist groups from Egypt and Algeria, insurgents from Yemen and Eritrea, Palestinian fighters for Hamas and Hezbollah, and anti-Qaddafi Libyans. Bin Laden donated $2.5 million to operate the Port Sudan airport in exchange for the right to use it to ship arms to sympathetic groups in Somalia and Yemen. He also funded a program that, under the auspices of the NIF, provided forced military training of university and secondary students.

In 1994, bin Laden was stripped of his Saudi citizenship and settled in Sudan. By 1996, however, Bashir and Turabi concluded that bin Laden was too hot to handle. Considering how much they had gained by their betrayal of Carlos the Jackal, they decided to try to make a similar deal for Osama bin Laden. First they tried to extradite bin Laden to Saudi Arabia, but the Saudi royal family refused to take him. Then they asked the Saudis to act as go-betweens for a deal with the United States. In fact, a representative of Bashir, Al-Fatih Urwah, did meet with the CIA in Virginia. However, the Clinton administration, noting that in the United States bin Laden was only an unindicted co-conspirator in the 1993 bombing of the World Trade Center, and distrustful of the Sudanese government, turned down the offer to negotiate for bin Laden. On May 18, 1996, bin Laden left Sudan at the request of the Sudanese government and moved to Afghanistan. A bitter bin Laden claimed that the Sudanese owed him millions of dollars, and he characterized the Bashir–Turabi leadership as "a mixture of religion and organized crime."

SUPPORTING TERRORISM—It was nice to have Osama bin Laden's money, but Hassan al-Turabi was perfectly capable of supporting terrorist groups without it. The second PAIC General Assembly, delayed because of Turabi's Canadian injury, was finally held in December 1993 and brought together a veritable who's who of terrorist groups. Turabi would boast, "I am close to . . . every Islamic movement in the world, secret or public." In 1992,

Dr. Ayman al-Zawahiri acquired funding from Iran to establish three training camps in Sudan, including one in Omar Bashir's childhood hometown of Shendi. While people in Sudan were trying to cope with food shortages, the PAIC sent a thousand tons of food and medicine to Somalia's Islamic Unity Party. When, in October 1994, a bus bomber killed twenty-two Israeli civilians in Tel Aviv, Turabi called it "an honorable act." As a matter of record, this was a year and a half after he organized a conference on religious tolerance.

With the end of the Cold War, the U.S. government no longer saw a need to support the Sudanese extremist government. One month after the inauguration of President Bill Clinton in 1993, terrorists bombed the World Trade Center in New York, killing six people and injuring about a thousand. Four months later, U.S. authorities arrested a member of the Sudanese delegation to the UN and charged him with planning another attack. They caught redhanded bombmaker Siddiq Ibrahim Siddighli, who had been Turabi's bodyguard during his 1992 visit. The U.S. State Department added Sudan to its list of states supporting terrorism, a group that Turabi referred to as "a list of honor." In addition to supporting terror in the United States, the government cited the fact that Sudan provided sanctuary for, among others, Hamas, Hezbollah, the Popular Front for the Liberation of Palestine, Islamic Jihad, the Algerian FIS, and terrorist groups from Egypt, Tunisia, and Yemen.

In 1995, Bashir and Turabi almost went too far when they tried to assassinate the dictator of Egypt, Hosni Mubarak. On June 24 of that year, Mubarak was in Addis Ababa, Ethiopia, for a meeting of the Organization of African Unity when two Egyptian assassins based in Khartoum fired at his limousine. They were themselves shot to death, as were three accomplices. Another three were arrested and three more escaped. An Ethiopian investigation determined that the assassins were staying in a house rented by a Sudanese citizen and that their weapons were delivered by Sudan Airways. The incident led to two days of fighting between Egyptian and Sudanese forces. Eventually, the United Nations Security Council imposed sanctions on Sudan for refusing to extradite the three escapees. By this time, Bashir had alienated almost every other government in the world. Out of the entire community of nations, Sudan's only remaining allies could be counted on the fingers of two hands: Iran, Iraq, Afghanistan, China, Syria, Yemen, Qatar, and Malaysia.

On August 7, 1998, terrorists bombed the U.S. embassies in Kenya and Tanzania, killing 263 people, including 12 Americans, and wounding 4,000. In retaliation, two weeks later, President Clinton ordered missile attacks against Osama bin Laden's al-Qaeda training camps in Afghanistan. For reasons not fully known, he also bombed the Al-Shifa Pharmaceutical Industries plant in Sudan, claiming that it was financed by bin Laden and that it produced precursor chemicals used in the manufacture of VX nerve gas. The owner of the plant, Salih Idris, denied involvement in the making of weapons, invited foreign journalists to visit his plant, and hired a U.S. firm to prove that he had no connection with Osama bin Laden.

In May 1999, the U.S. government quietly released the $24 million of frozen funds that Idris had invested in U.S. accounts.

After the terrorist attacks of September 11, 2001, Omar al-Bashir came to the conclusion that terrorism was the new equivalent of Communism and that one could gain the support—and money—of the United States by offering to become its ally in the War on Terrorism.

THE SECOND CIVIL WAR—For all the time and effort that Bashir and Turabi put into transforming Sudan into an extreme Islamist state, they still had to deal with a monster of a problem: the growing rebellion among non-Muslims in the south. The second civil war had broken out in 1983 and it was dissatisfaction with the conduct of the war, and with the threat of negotiations, that led to Bashir's ascension to power in 1989. Once Bashir gained control of the nation and its military, he had to match his words with action. The southern rebel groups had no intention of waiting for Bashir to get himself organized. In October, the SPLA defeated government forces at Kurmuk and threatened the Roseires Dam that supplied the electricity for much of the north. Muammar al-Qaddafi sent weapons and military supplies to shore up the Sudanese armed forces in exchange for the freedom for Libya to use the borderlands in Darfur to support rebels who were fighting Qaddafi's enemies in Chad. Saddam Hussein also gave Bashir military support. Bashir supported Saddam's invasion of Kuwait in August 1990, but this decision backfired. Iraq no longer had weapons to share with Sudan, while Bashir lost the support of Saudi Arabia and the other wealthy Gulf states, which was a critical blow to the Sudanese economy because most of the 750,000 Sudanese who had been working in the Gulf states and sending money home were expelled. In addition, the Gulf nations stopped buying cereals and livestock from Sudan, which was forced to impose grain rationing at home. By this time, African Watch had reported that 500,000 Sudanese had died as a result of war or famine, and the group condemned both government and SPLA troops for gross human rights violations.

The SPLA was growing in strength, but in 1991 two unexpected developments would save Bashir's forces from collapse. In May, in Ethiopia, the government of Mengistu Haile Mariam, which had supported the southern rebels, was overthrown and replaced by a government that was sympathetic to Bashir. Almost overnight, the SPLA lost important bases and supply routes, and 200,000 refugees, who had been living in Ethiopia, were forced to return to Sudan. Bashir reacted quickly to this humanitarian crisis: he sent his air force to drop bombs on the refugees. The outside world was desperate to help the refugees, but Bashir and his government had a policy for dealing with this problem that they would follow forever. Their strategy was to burn down villages, force the inhabitants into camps, classify them as refugees, apply for disaster relief, and then distribute the relief goods to pro-government areas, giving it to displaced families only if they agreed to convert to Islam. Bashir would ultimately bungle his relations with the new Ethiopian government by boasting to the BBC that antirebel attacks were being launched from Sudanese bases in Ethiopia. This was true, but the Ethiopians had intended the fact to remain secret.

Fortunately for Bashir, the SPLA would soon receive another setback. John Garang may have been the military leader of an oppressed people but, despite his American education, he was a thug and a dictator, just like Bashir. He even modeled his internal security apparatus after that of the Sudanese army. In August he was "overthrown" by Riak Machar, a member of the second-largest southern tribe, the Nuer. Machar accepted weapons and supplies from Bashir's government, but when this became known, Machar lost credibility.

The split in the SPLA helped Bashir, but the war was drastically depleting the Sudanese economy. Military spending, which accounted for 4 percent of the national budget between 1985 and 1990, rose to 13 percent between 1990 and 1995. The per capita income of the average Sudanese was about $100, almost all of which was actually emergency aid.

In late 1991, the war spread to the Nuba Mountains, home to 1.5 million people who spoke fifty different languages and dialects. Although most of the Nuban tribes were Muslims, they followed Sufism and so, in the eyes of Turabi and Bashir, they were really anti-Islam. Bashir ordered the destruction of mosques in the Nuba Mountains and the prohibition of the use of local languages. The government seized land, sold it to Arab businessmen, and forced the local people into camps, which they called "peace villages." Almost one-third of the population was displaced. Non-Muslim men were circumcised and their children were forced to attend Quranic schools. According to Amnesty International, troops used civilians as human shields. In order to justify this jihad against fellow Muslims, Turabi arranged for the issuance of a fatwa that broadened the definition of apostasy: "An insurgent who was previously a Muslim is now an apostate; and a non-Muslim is a non-believer standing as a bulwark against the spread of Islam, and Islam has granted the freedom of killing both of them." Thus, people who had for generations identified themselves as Muslims found themselves redefined as the mortal enemies of Islam.

The National Islamic Front had created the Popular Defence Force (PDF) to supplement (and eventually replace) the regular armed forces. In fact, they were used as cannon fodder in the fighting against southern rebels. The PDF was made up of NIF volunteers, Arab tribal militias, and conscripted students and civil servants. In a 1993 radio broadcast, Bashir praised the PDF as "the school for national and spiritual education." He added that through the PDF, "the Sudanese citizen's mind can be remodeled and his religious consciousness enhanced." Bashir tried to boost the spirits of his army by declaring that soldiers who die in battle are martyrs who "irrigate the land of the south with their blood so the land may sprout dignity and honor," and he promised them that they would ascend directly to paradise. Just to be on the safe side, he allowed war booty to be divided among the soldiers, with officers being given double shares and bonuses given to anyone who impregnated a non-Muslim woman. As unpaid fighters, militia members were allowed to include as booty not just cattle and grain, but humans.

Still, the number of casualties on the government side was so high that the number of volunteers began to dwindle. Bashir declared all males aged eighteen to thirty draftable and then seized them off the streets and dragged them off buses. When some military leaders complained to Bashir that these tactics lowered the quality of the army, Bashir had the complainants arrested.

Bashir and Turabi also turned their wrath against Christians. Television commentators warned non-Muslims that they would go to hell. In February 1992, all Christian schools were nationalized. During the "Arabization" of Juba in Equatoria state, children were shot to death as they fled and their bodies were found floating down the Nile with their book bags still on their backs. In one particularly notorious case, a Christian pilot, Giorgis Yustus Butrus, who was the son of the Coptic bishop of Khartoum, was charged with possessing foreign currency. He was offered a pardon if he would convert to Islam. He refused and was executed. Thousands of Muslims joined with Christians in his funeral procession through Khartoum.

BASHIR CELEBRATES HIS 1996 ELECTION VICTORY BY DRESSING UP AS A SOUTHERN SUDANESE.
Raouf Mon/AP Photo

A CLASSIC DICTATORSHIP ELECTION—By 1996, the concept of democracy had spread around the world, and even dictators felt obligated to hold elections. Sudan actually had a history of elections going back more than forty years. Bashir and Turabi were wise enough to know that if a truly free election was held, the National Islamic Front would lose. So they concocted a strategy that assured their victory in 1996. There were 400 national assembly seats to be "contested," so that 201 were needed for a majority. The national congress of the NIF chose 125 of the assembly members. Elections in the south were cancelled because of the war, so Bashir personally selected the forty-six southern representatives. The government announced that the number of candidates for the remaining seats would be limited because competition in politics was damaging to the "cohesion of the community." Fifty NIF candidates ran unopposed, automatically giving the

NIF 225 seats—a majority—before the voting even began. To be on the safe side, security officials stored the ballot boxes in their office each evening and no records were kept of who voted. As for the presidential election, there were fifty candidates, but they were prohibited from campaigning in twenty-five of the twenty-six Sudanese states. Since the government had complete control of all aspects of the media, it was almost as if Omar al-Bashir was the only candidate. Not surprisingly, it was announced that he had won 75.7 percent of the votes. With the annoyance of democratic elections out of the way, Bashir could go back to ruling the country.

THE FINAL BATTLE . . . WITH HASSAN AL-TURABI—It was inevitable that conflict would eventually break out between Bashir and Hassan al-Turabi. Turabi, the Islamist theoretician and politician, had come so far, and only Bashir stood between him and his goal of becoming the official ruler of Sudan, free to speak not just at scholarly roundtables, but at the United Nations and other international forums. But Bashir was not about to step aside voluntarily. In his first two and a half years as leader of Sudan, he suppressed five separate coup attempts, including one in April 1990, to which he responded by arresting twenty-eight army and police officers. Within twenty-four hours they were all tried, convicted, executed, and buried. Bashir was not going to submit to Turabi's political ambitions without a fight.

In January 1993, Turabi pressed for the dissolution of the Revolutionary Command Council in a strategic attempt to weaken the power of the military. Bashir agreed to this nine months later, but installed himself as president of the new civilian government. While publicly maintaining an image of unity, Turabi and Bashir engaged in an ongoing series of chess-like moves. For example, as part of Turabi's campaign to crush Muslim groups with which he did not agree, in February 1994 he ordered an attack on a mosque belonging to Ansar al-Sunna, a puritanical sect related to Saudi-supported Wahhabism. Turabi's gunmen murdered twenty-six followers inside their mosque. Later that year, Bashir, in search of allies against Turabi and the National Islamic Front, allowed Ansar al-Sunna to resume activities. Once, in July 1995, Bashir was invited to speak at Khartoum University. His appearance was met by protests led by the NIF-controlled student union, leading to suspicions that the invitation had been a Turabi trick to publicly embarrass Bashir.

OMAR AL-BASHIR AND
HASSAN AL-TURABI
DURING FRIENDLIER TIMES
Reuters/Corbis

The Bashir–Turabi power struggle accelerated in 1999. Reaching out to exiled opposition leaders, Turabi met with Sadiq al-Mahdi (his brother-in-law) while Bashir invited Jaafar Nimeiri to return to Sudan and offered him a pension. In an attempt to reduce the power of the president (Bashir) and to put the military under civilian control, Turabi pushed through a law allowing the introduction of political parties and had himself elected secretary-general of the National Congress Party. He also offered to meet with leaders of the southern rebel groups—in Mecca. Since they were all followers of Christianity and traditional religions, they declined the invitation. Meanwhile, Bashir countered by returning confiscated property to the leaders of the major Islamic opposition parties.

Turabi instigated a debate in parliament to create a new constitution with a strong prime minister and a strong parliament. Bashir responded by dissolving parliament and declaring a state of emergency. He also closed all offices of Turabi's National Congress Party, whereupon Turabi created a new party, the Popular National Congress. In February 2001, Turabi and his new party signed an agreement with John Garang's Sudanese Peoples' Liberation Movement. After eleven and a half years of killing each others' supporters, Hassan al-Turabi and John Garang were suddenly partners. Bashir immediately had Turabi arrested and charged him with "communicating with the enemy." Exposed as a self-servicing hypocrite to hard-core Islamists, Turabi lost his power base and, languishing in prison and house arrest, he ceased to be an effective player in Sudanese politics. Observers who had viewed Bashir as nothing more than a front man for Turabi were forced to accept him as the undisputed dictator of Sudan.

OIL—When asked what could save Sudan, Hassan al-Turabi once replied, "God . . . and southern oil." Although exploration began in the 1960s, Chevron achieved its first significant strike, in South Kordofan, in 1980. Two years later another strike was made on the margin between Arab Sudan and black Sudan. In 1984, southern insurgents killed four Chevron employees, leading Chevron to withdraw from the country. Still, the lure of huge profits was too great to be ignored. Talisman Energy of Canada filled the void left by Chevron. Oil companies from China, Sweden, France, and Malaysia would also ultimately take their chances in Sudan. In November 1989, United Nations Human Rights Rapporteur Leonardo Franco reported that the Sudanese government had cleared the 100 kilometers surrounding the southern oil fields by using the Talisman airfield to launch fighter jets to bomb the villages near the oil fields. Similar actions were taken by the military and militia to clear out black Sudanese in 1992. The following year, Bashir's government used a more subtle tactic to gain control of oil fields in South Kordofan: they redrew the state boundaries to reposition oil-rich areas so that they would fall under the control of Arab-dominated regional governments. After much struggle and fighting, Bashir inaugurated an oil terminal south of Port Sudan in

August 1999, and a pipeline from the oil fields went fully operational at the beginning of 2000, reducing Sudan's dependence on Saudi Arabia and the other Persian Gulf oil states.

PEACE AS A TACTIC IN THE ENDLESS WAR—The immensity of the carnage in the Sudanese civil wars has been so great that periodically the international community has tried to interfere and promote a negotiated settlement to the fighting. For Omar al-Bashir, ceasefires have proven useful as a means to resupply and reposition troops and to plan the next offensive. The signing of peace agreements serves the purpose of pitting one rebel group against another and impressing foreign governments with his moderation (particularly in comparison with Hassan al-Turabi). This manipulation of the peace process reached its peak in 2005, when Bashir, less than four years after jailing Turabi for "communicating with the enemy," signed a peace agreement with John Garang that gave Garang the position of vice president of Sudan. Exhausted foreign diplomats hailed the agreement as a great step forward and there were mass celebrations in Sudan. However, a simple reading of the text of the agreement between Bashir and Garang revealed that it was as flawed as the one that ended the first civil war in 1973. To begin with, it made no provision for the removal of northern troops from the south. It did promise the southerners that they could vote for or against secession . . . in six years' time. Given Bashir's record, the chances for such an election actually taking place seemed slim. What's more, the agreement was only signed with Garang and did not include other southern rebel groups, much less groups fighting Bashir's government in the east and the west. Finally, Garang, a dictator himself, appeared to sell out his followers. After more than twenty years of fighting for the right of non-Islamic southerners to choose independence, upon assuming his role as vice president, he began speaking in favor of a united Sudan. Garang's intentions will remain forever unknown because, only three weeks after his inauguration as vice president, he was killed in a helicopter crash.

DARFUR—Bashir's pledge to end the civil war in the south appeared particularly insincere considering the horrific atrocities that his troops and associated militia were committing in the western state of Darfur, a region of more than 3.5 million people inhabited by non-Arabic Muslims.

For hundreds of years, from the fifteenth century until World War I, the region was ruled by the Fur Sultanate. It was finally incorporated into Sudan in 1916. The Fur and other tribes may have been followers of Islam, but to the Arab rulers of independent Sudan, they were black, just like the traditionalists and Christians in the south, and were thus subject in

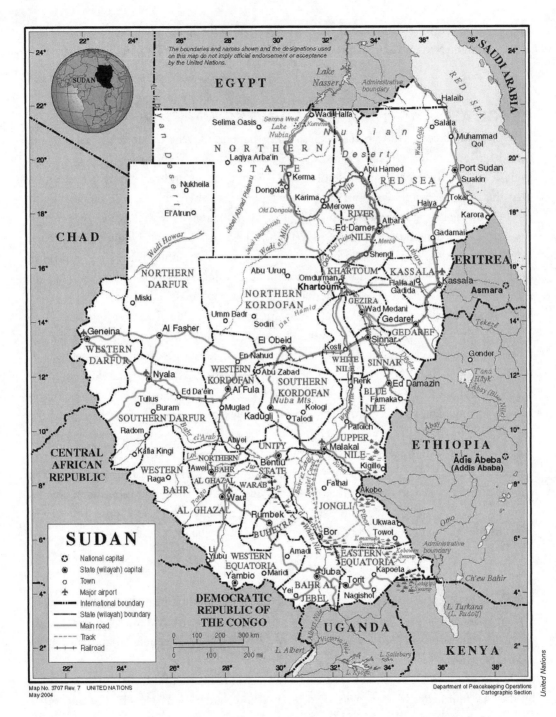

The boundaries and names shown and the designations used on this map do not imply official endorsement or acceptance by the United Nations.

SUDAN

✪	National capital
◉	State (wilayah) capital
○	Town
✈	Major airport
—··—	International boundary
—·—	State (wilayah) boundary
——	Main road
– – –	Track
+++	Railroad

Map No. 3707 Rev. 7   UNITED NATIONS
May 2004

Department of Peacekeeping Operations
Cartographic Section

United Nations

the best of times to disregard and in the worst of times to slavery and slaughter. A long drought that stretched from the mid-1970s into the early 1980s forced Arab cattle-herding tribes into the traditional territory of non-Arab tribes. Rather than mediate this problem, the Sudanese government sided completely with its fellow Arabs and even refused to acknowledge the ensuing famine, which so infuriated the governor of Darfur that he resigned in protest. By the time Bashir took power, slave-trading in Darfur was so widespread that the price of a slave boy had dropped from $90 to $10. (Cows went for $100.) Thousands of Fur were killed and locals who resisted the government troops and government-supported militia were dismissed as "bandits" and "outlaws."

By 2003, there were two major rebel movements operating in Darfur. To counter their influence, Bashir launched a ghastly campaign of destruction and ethnic cleansing. Government fighter jets and helicopters bombed villages, and minutes later government-supported militia, known as the Janjaweed, communicating by satellite phones, arrived on horseback and camel to murder, torture, and rape the villagers. The bombers targeted hospitals and schools and the Janjaweed burned crops and threw dead bodies into wells in order to contaminate the water supply. On February 9, 2004, in a George Bushian "Mission Accomplished" moment, Bashir declared the Darfur war finished, although in reality the killing continued. By the end of 2005, human rights groups estimated that 180,000 people had died and two million people were left homeless, while not a single Janjaweed member had been arrested for his crimes.

The United States has a hapless history of dealing with such Sudanese atrocities. On November 3, 1996, President Bill Clinton announced a ban on the importation of goods and services from Sudan. However, he made an exception for gum Arabic, of which Darfur is a major source, because it was considered vital to the manufacture of soft drinks, adhesives, and other products. On July 23, 2004, the U.S. Congress passed a joint resolution declaring the Sudanese government and the Janjaweed guilty of genocide in Darfur, but by then the invasion and occupation of Iraq had led to the loss of U.S. credibility and the United States was unable to find allies for action. In a sad commentary on the Darfur catastrophes, in July 2005, Andrew Natsios of the U.S. Agency for International Development declared that the burning of villages in Darfur had all but ended . . . because there were no more villages left to burn.

IN HIS WORDS:

"The ideal Sudanese woman should take care of herself, her children, her home, her reputation and her husband."

JANUARY 1990

"What we now apply in Sudan is God's will. We will never satisfy humans to displease the Almighty God."

SEPTEMBER 1992

"We will not relinquish power unless through the barrel of a gun."

SEPTEMBER 30, 1995

"We respect human rights in Sudan . . . Perhaps our understanding of human rights differs from your government's."

TO U.S. AMBASSADOR DON PETTERSON, NOVEMBER 10, 1992

2.

KIM JONG-IL—NORTH KOREA

THE NATION—The Democratic People's Republic of Korea occupies the northern half of the Korean peninsula. With a population of about 23 million, it has half the population of South Korea. Currently, North Koreans are more isolated than the people of any other nation in the world. The North Korean regime holds a special place in the history of dictatorships in that it is the first Communist government to pass on leadership from a father to his son.

THE CHOSUN PEOPLE—Although North Korea is viewed today as an extreme example of a Communist dictatorship, the roots of Korean authoritarianism begin deep in the peninsula's history. First mentioned in Chinese chronicles in the third century BC, Korea was known as Chosun, the land of "Morning Freshness." The Chinese conquered the Chosun capital in 108 BC, but active resistance forced them to give up all but one of their colonies by 71 BC. Korean history comes to life with the Three Kingdoms period. The first of the kingdoms, Koguryo, was established in what is now North Korea. The other two kingdoms were Paekche and Silla.

Buddhism and Confucianism arrived in Koguryo from China in AD 372, and it was Confucianism that would, more than 1,570 years later, form the basis of the repressive regime founded by Kim Il-sung and continued by his son, Kim Jong-il. Confucianism teaches a reverence for learning, respect for the past, and worship of ancestors. However, politically it emphasizes centralized authority. The emperor or king has a mandate from Heaven and he is expected to be virtuous and benevolent. His subjects are expected to be obedient and to pay him unconditional loyalty. The ruler has the exclusive right to deal with foreigners and to speak for his people. When Kim Il-sung and Kim Jong-il took control of North Korea, they used the concepts and references of Confucianism. The two Kims were "supreme and benevolent fathers of the nation," the Korean Workers' Party was known as the "Mother Party," and the country was referred to as one large revolutionary family. In deference to the Russian and Chinese Communists who established Kim Il-sung's regime, North Korea became Communist as well. However, in many ways, North Korea is less a Communist state and more a feudal kingdom that has adopted the terminology of Communism. In the hierarchy of power, the Confucian emperor has been replaced by the Kims, feudal vassals are now "party cadres," and the peasants have been transformed into the "masses."

The other historic factor that has permanently scarred Koreans is the seemingly endless threat from foreign invaders, particularly from the Chinese to the north and from the Japanese across the sea. In 612, the Koguryo army of 300,000 soldiers actually defeated a Chinese invasion force of 1,000,000 men. The Silla kingdom allied itself with the Chinese T'ang dynasty and, in the 660s, conquered Paekche and Koguryo. Then, in 676, with the support of Paekche and Koguryo, Silla pushed back the Chinese. The unification of the peninsula would last until 1945. The Koryo dynasty replaced Silla in 935. Koryo is the source of the English word "Korea." In 1259, the Mongols defeated Koryo after thirty years of fighting, and northern Korea was incorporated into the Mongol Empire. This was not a pleasant period for the Koreans. In 1254 alone, 206,000 men were captured and taken away. The Koryo princes were forced to live as hostages in Beijing and Koryo had to donate large numbers of virgins to the Mongols, who proceeded to use Korea as a base for attacking Japan.

The Ming dynasty began-in China in 1368. Twenty years later, the pro-Ming general Yi Song-gye seized control of the Korean government and ascended to the throne in 1392. The Yi dynasty, also known as the Chosun dynasty, lasted until 1910. Although it was the longest-lasting dynasty in Asian history, the government of Kim Il-sung and Kim Jong-il refuses to acknowledge it as a worthy predecessor because, for much of that period, the Chosun were only vassals of the Chinese.

In the sixteenth and seventeenth centuries, the Koreans were again caught in the middle of battling powers. The Japanese invaded Korea with 160,000 soldiers with the intention of moving on to invade China. The Koreans, using the world's first armor-plated warships, destroyed the Japanese fleets in 1592. The Japanese withdrew in 1598, but by that time the Korean peninsula had been laid waste and was swept by epidemics, famine, and peasant revolts. In a weakened state, the Koreans were ill-prepared for the next invasion, and were overrun by the Manchus, as the Chosun dynasty was reduced to a vassal state of the Chinese Ch'ing dynasty. In 1786, Christianity was banned and in 1866, 13,000 Catholics were executed.

By the nineteenth century, it was the turn of the Japanese to besiege and bully the Koreans. Beginning in 1876, the Japanese military forced Korea to open three ports to foreign trade, and by 1893, Japan accounted for 91 percent of Korea's exports and 50 percent of its imports. The United States also got in on the act, signing a treaty of friendship with Korea in 1882. However, when the USS *General Sherman* entered Korean waters in 1886 and refused to leave, the Koreans sank the ship, killing all twenty-five sailors aboard.

The current North Korean regime hails as one of the highlights of Korean peasant history the Tonghak Rebellion of 1894. Korean rebels occupied the southwestern quarter of the peninsula, challenging the Korean government and calling for the withdrawal of Japanese and Western influence. The Korean government asked for Chinese intervention and the rebellion was suppressed. However, this incident ignited the Sino-Japanese War, which took place on Korean soil and which ended in victory for Japan.

Now it was Russia's turn to pick on Korea. The Russian czarist government proposed that Russia and Japan divide the Korean peninsula at the 39th parallel. Instead, the two nations went to war in February 1904. When the dust and foam settled nineteenth months later, 150,000 people were dead and Japan was again declared the winner. As for Korea, it became a Japanese colony in 1910. The thirty-five-year Japanese occupation that followed was bitter and brutal. The Japanese took over 80 percent of Korean farmland, drove off the Koreans, and brought in almost 350,000 Japanese immigrants. Approximately 750,000 Korean farmers fled to Manchuria in China and to Russia. Another 125,000 migrated to Japan. The Japanese went to great lengths to suppress Korean culture. They banned the study of Korean history, forbade the use of the Korean language in schools, ordered that the Japanese religion of Shintoism be taught to schoolchildren, and ordered all Koreans to take Japanese names. When another Sino-Japanese War broke out in 1937, the Japanese forced Koreans to work in mines and munitions factories and then, in 1942, to fight in the Japanese army. Meanwhile, between 100,000 and 200,000 Korean women were forced to serve as "comfort women"—prostitutes—for Japanese soldiers. The Koreans did not take all this repression without fighting back. The largest pro-independence demonstration, involving an estimated 370,000 Koreans, took place in 1919. The Japanese responded by killing 6,670 of the demonstrators, wounding 16,000, and arresting at least 19,000.

The Sino-Japanese War was swallowed up by World War II, of which it became one of many fronts. At the Potsdam Conference in July 1945, the leaders of the United States, Great

Britain, and the USSR decided that once Japan surrendered control, Korea would be temporarily divided between the United States and the Soviet Union. The Soviets declared war on Japan six days after the conference ended and, a week later, Japan surrendered. The Soviet army occupied Korea north of the 38th parallel, while the Americans took over the south. A United Nations–authorized election in 1948 put Syngman Rhee in charge of South Korea. Rhee, who was seventy years old, had been educated in the United States at Princeton and Harvard. In the north, the Soviets installed Cho Man-sik, a popular non-Communist, as chairman, and Kim Il-sung, an anti-Japanese guerrilla leader, as head of the Korean Communist Party. Within six months, Cho had disappeared—never to be heard from again—and Kim was the undisputed ruler of North Korea.

THE GREAT LEADER—Kim Il-sung, aka The Great Leader, was born Kim Song-ju on April 15, 1912, in Mangyongdae near the current capital of North Korea, Pyongyang. His father, Kim Hyung-jik, and his mother, Kang Pan-sok, were Christians who were married at the ages of fifteen and seventeen, respectively. Kim operated an herbal pharmacy; Kang was a schoolteacher. The eldest of three sons, the future dictator of North Korea moved with his family to Manchuria when he was seven years old, spent two years in Pyongyang, and then returned to China at the age of thirteen. His ability to speak Chinese would come in handy later. Kim's father died when he was fourteen years old. When he was seventeen, Kim was arrested for helping organize the anti-Japanese Korean Communist Youth League. Imprisoned for several months, he endured the Japanese "Finger-Breaking Torture."

After his release from prison in the spring of 1930, Kim taught school for a while. His mother died when he was twenty-one years old, after which Kim joined an anti-Japanese guerrilla band and took the *nom de guerre* of a famous Korean resistance fighter: Kim Il-sung. He first gained a name for himself at the 1933 Battle of Dongning, when he and his band liberated a troop of Chinese soldiers who were surrounded by Japanese forces. The Japanese offered a reward for his arrest and once, thinking he had been killed, they actually paid the reward. However, Kim reappeared alive in a different region. Kim Il-sung's greatest guerrilla successes occurred in 1937. He beat back the Japanese in the snow at the Battle of Limingshui, and then he pulled off the exploit that he would later glorify to almost supernaturally heroic proportions. On June 4, Kim led 200 guerrilla fighters across the border from Manchuria into Korea and attacked the town of Pochonbo, destroying Japanese government offices, the police station, a school, and even the post office. The Japanese police pursued Kim's guerrillas across the Yalu River into China, but Kim defeated the Japanese. He then joined forces with another guerrilla leader, Choe Hyon, and attacked a Japanese timber camp and seized hostages.

Kim continued to fight the Japanese, but in 1941, Kim and the rest of the Korean fighters were forced to flee to Russia, where Kim settled into a camp near Khabarovsk.

It appears that Kim Il-sung's first wife, Kim Hye-sun, died in Japanese custody. In Russia he married Kim Jong-suk, the daughter of a poor farmer, who had joined the guerrillas when she was only sixteen years old. On February 16, 1942, she gave birth to Kim Jong-il, who would grow up to become North Korea's Dear Leader.

When Japan surrendered on August 15, 1945, Kim Il-sung was well-placed to take over the reigns of power. Both the Soviets and the Chinese approved of him because he had lived in their country and he spoke their language, and the North Koreans considered him a hero because he had fought bravely for independence and had evaded capture by the Japanese. In addition, most of North Korea's other prospective leaders traveled south to Seoul, assuming that Seoul would be the capital of Korea once it was reunified. Within a year, Kim had eliminated the opposition and consolidated his own power.

THE KOREAN CIVIL WAR—The Korean people had survived the Japanese occupation and World War II, but their ordeal was not over. Although separate governments were established in the north and in the south, both sides wanted reunification. The problem was that both Kim Il-sung of North Korea and Syngman Rhee of South Korea wanted reunification on their own terms. Both the Soviet Union and the United States withdrew their troops from Korea, leaving behind a few hundred "advisors" each.

Rhee was under great pressure politically. Although he called for an invasion of North Korea, he could barely keep together his own half of the country. Rebellions and uprisings were springing up, he had thrown about 14,000 political prisoners into jail and, on May 30, 1950, his party lost control of the National Assembly. Kim Il-sung, who had cut off power transmissions to South Korea only four days after Rhee's election in 1948, considered an invasion of the south a "Fatherland Liberation War" that would free South Korea from a foreign-dominated government. On January 12, 1950, the U.S. secretary of state, Dean Acheson, declared that Korea was outside the U.S. defense perimeter. Taking this to mean that the United States would not send troops to protect South Korea, and convinced that South Koreans would rise up to overthrow Syngman Rhee and would join his own forces, Kim Il-sung acted on his plan to invade the south. Cross-border skirmishes broke out in late June, and newspapers reported that South Korean forces had seized the North Korean town of Haeju. At dawn on June 25, North Korean troops drove across the 38th parallel. Unfettered by the internal dissension that Syngman Rhee's government was facing, and with an army twice the size of Rhee's, Kim Il-sung's soldiers had little trouble sweeping across South Korea. Within three days they had occupied Seoul and, by September 5, they controlled all of Korea except for a small beachhead in the south. However, the uprising that Kim Il-sung had expected did not occur, and his troops were not greeted as liberators as he had expected. What's more, despite Dean Acheson's assurance of neutrality in January, U.S. president Harry S. Truman considered the North Korean takeover a threat to U.S. interests.

On June 27, the United States went to the United Nations Security Council and asked for authorization for military action. The Soviet Union could have vetoed this proposal, but it had been boycotting Security Council meetings since January (over the issue of Chinese Communist representation at the UN). The proposal passed and, for the first time, the fledging United Nations created a military force. The UN army was led by U.S. general Douglas MacArthur, but included troops from fifteen additional nations, including Great Britain, Canada, Australia, Turkey, France, and, of course, South Korea. The UN forces landed at Inchon on September 15 and quickly cut the North Korean supply lines. They recaptured Seoul on September 28 and, on October 7, they crossed the 38th parallel and entered North Korea. MacArthur's forces seized Pyongyang on October 20 and reached the Yalu River that formed the border with China a week later.

The Chinese Communists, who had been in power less than a year, were alarmed by the unexpected arrival of enemy soldiers on their border, particularly after a few U.S. bombs "mistakenly" fell inside China. On October 25, the Chinese intervened on a massive scale. Usurping the power of Kim Il-sung, they took charge of the fight against the UN forces and sent about 300,000 troops into North Korea. General MacArthur was unprepared for the Chinese involvement and was forced to lead his troops on a difficult retreat. The Chinese and North Koreans expelled the UN forces from the north and reoccupied Seoul in January 1951. MacArthur and his men recaptured Seoul and by June the battle lines settled back at the 38th parallel, where the war had started.

Truce negotiations began in July, but they stuck on the subject of prisoner repatriation, and the fighting dragged on for two more years. An armistice agreement was finally reached on July 27, 1953, although Syngman Rhee refused to sign it. A four-mile-wide Demilitarized Zone was established between the north and the south, and the superpowers moved on to other issues and other conflicts. The Korean people, on the other hand, were left to recover from three years of war. Estimates of the number of South Koreans who died range from 500,000 to 1,000,000. In North Korea, the estimates ranged from 1,250,000 to 3,000,000. Eighteen of North Korea's twenty-two largest cities were at least half flattened. American bombers had destroyed the irrigation dams that provided the water for 75 percent of the nation's food production. Since 1952, most North Koreans had literally been living in caves and underground shelters.

THE KIM IL-SUNG ERA—Kim Il-sung survived in power throughout the Korean War and after and, indeed, for the rest of his life. Because U.S. troops had withdrawn from South Korea in 1949, and because Dean Acheson had declared South Korea outside the U.S. defense perimeter, Kim Il-sung considered American intervention in the war treacherous and made certain that every subsequent generation of North Koreans considered Americans to be murderous devils. This was an easy sell because the North Korean people had suffered so horribly from American bombs, napalm, bullets, and bayonets. Kim was also humiliated that he had had to rely on the Chinese and the Soviets to be saved. He took it out on his own people, purging all members of the military and the government whom he considered possible opponents.

However, Kim Il-sung was most obsessed with gaining revenge on the South Korean government. Despite the devastation it had suffered, North Korea entered the postwar period with distinct advantages over South Korea. The north had inherited the industrial infrastructure that the Japanese had created, while the south had remained primarily agricultural. In fact, 60 percent of South Korea's industrial facilities were destroyed during the war. North Korea, blessed with extensive natural resources, was able to rebuild with the help of aid from China and the USSR. For each year until 1974, the per capita income in North Korea exceeded that in South Korea.

In 1961, after Syngman Rhee won his fourth presidential election, the army in South Korea, led by General Park Chung-hee, seized power. Kim Il-sung launched a long-term program to destabilize Park, including an infiltration campaign that peaked in 1967–1968. The North Koreans eventually abducted 450 South Koreans, not to mention at least eleven Japanese. In January 1968, North Korean commandos attacked Park Chung-hee's office and residential complex. Two days later, the North Korean navy seized the *Pueblo,* a U.S. spy ship, and held its eighty-three-man crew for eleven months. The following year, the North Koreans shot down an American reconnaissance plane, killing thirty-one, and also hijacked a South Korean airliner. But Kim Il-sung's most outrageous anti-South acts were yet to come. On August 15, 1974, Kim's agents tried to assassinate Park Chung-hee. They missed Park, and killed his wife instead. Two years later, North Korean soldiers with axes and metal picks attacked a U.S.–South Korean tree-trimming crew, killing fifty-five Koreans and two Americans. In October 1983, two North Korean agents set off a bomb in Rangoon, Burma, killing seventeen visiting South Korean officials, including three cabinet ministers and the ambassador to Burma. And in November 1987, a North Korean agent placed a bomb on a Korean Airlines flight from Baghdad to Seoul, killing 115 people.

Of course, most of Kim Il-sung's energy was devoted to domestic affairs. In 1972, Kim, who once called Josef Stalin "The Godfather of the Korean People," pushed through a new constitution in which he gave himself complete power. He also developed for himself a record-setting personality cult. Among the many sobriquets that were used to refer to him in North Korean propaganda were:

> The Peerless Patriot
> The Ever-Victorious Iron-Willed Brilliant Commander
> The Red Sun of the Oppressed People of the World

and, needless to say,

> The Greatest Leader of Our Time

After his death, his son Kim Jong-il would declare him President for Eternity and the 1998 constitution referred to Kim Il-sung as "a genius ideological theoretician." (Kim Jong-il would become known as The Glorious Sun of the Twenty-First Century and The Leader of Steel.) Kim Il-sung did in fact create a political theory, muddled though it may have been. He called it *juche,* a term that foreign observers have had quite a bit of trouble defining. *"Ju"* translates as "main or fundamental principle" and *"che"* as "the body, self or foundation of something." Kim Il-sung explained that *juche* involved "solving for oneself all the problems of the revolution and construction in conformity with actual conditions at home," and added that man "desires to live and develop independently as master of the world and his own destiny" and to be "free from the fetters on nature and society." Somehow Kim Il-sung managed to apply this gibberish to every aspect of North Korean society, so that even today peasants have to grow their crops using *"juche* farming," according to which all decisions for planting, tending, and harvesting are made not by local farmers, but by the Korean Workers' Party. Kim Jong-il later renamed *juche* "Kim Il-sungism."

The glorification of Kim Il-sung reached something of a peak on his sixtieth birthday, in honor of which a 240,000-square-meter marble museum was opened to honor his life. Among the items on display were shoes, belts, and other pieces of clothing he had worn. Kim also turned his birthplace into a monument with markers to indicate where he used to sit on a swing, study, ride on a sled, go fishing. At one point, Kim Il-sung awarded himself a "double hero gold medal."

For all his absurd excesses, Kim Il-sung really was respected by most North Koreans, who were grateful to him for fighting for and saving their country. Of course, this impression was based on false and exaggerated presentations of his achievements. For example, his 1937 guerrilla raid of Pochonbo, although legitimately inspiring to an occupied people, was built up into an epic, history-making triumph. Likewise, the role of the Chinese and the Soviets in first defeating the Japanese and then driving the Americans out of North Korea was expurgated, and Kim Il-sung was portrayed in schools and history books as having led the fight against the Japanese and having given the U.S. Army its "first defeat since the War of 1812."

Kim Il-sung died of a heart attack on July 8, 1994. His son and successor, Kim Jong-il, spent an estimated $100 million to build a mausoleum to house and display his body. Out of respect for The Great Leader, his son, The Dear Leader, installed machines to air-blast the dust off the clothes of visitors and revolving brushes that cleaned the soles of their shoes.

THE DEAR LEADER—Few people dispute *when* Kim Jong-il was born—February 16, 1942—but *where* he was born is a subject of controversy. It would appear that Kim was born in a Soviet military camp near Khabarovsk in Siberia, where his parents, along with other guerrillas, were biding their time after being driven out of Korea by the Japanese. But since it just did not seem right to have The Dear Leader born outside of Korea, the North Korean propaganda machine came up with an alternative version of his birth. In this "official" version, Kim Jong-il was born at dawn on Mount Paekdu, at a secret camp inside North Korea. According to Kim Il-sung, his son was born "amidst the roar of gunfire on the battlefield" and "he grew up in clothes impregnated with powder smoke. . . . He grew up in the love of the guerrillas more than in my love." Kim Jong-il's official biography goes into greater, gushing detail: "In the blizzard-ridden secret camp of Mt. Paekdu, the mother had brought up her son under a rain of bullets, covering him with the hem of her uniform which smelt of powder smoke. . . . Ammunition belts were his playthings. The raging blizzards and ceaseless gunshots were the first sounds to which he became accustomed." This glorified account also serves the purpose of justifying the fact that, unlike his father, Kim Jong-il, the commander-in-chief of a million-man army, has no military experience.

Regardless of his alleged origins on Mt. Paekdu, Kim Jong-il grew up with a Russian

THE GREAT LEADER SHOWS THE WAY
TO THE DEAR LEADER
Alain Nogues/Corbis

name, Yura, which was a nickname for Yuri. He used the name Yura all the way through his high school years, and he is identified as Yura in his high school yearbook. When he was about five years old, Yura underwent a traumatic experience. He and his younger brother Shura were playing in a pond when Shura drowned. Kim Jong-il's responsibility in the tragedy is unclear. Kim also had a sister, Kim Pyong-il, but her story and whereabouts are unknown.

After the Japanese surrender at the end of

World War II, Kim Jong-il and his family moved back to North Korea and settled in Pyongyang. When he was seven years old, his mother died in childbirth. That same year, he entered the Namsan School for children of the privileged class. When the U.S.-led United Nations forces overran Pyongyang in 1950, Kim Jong-il and his sister fled to Jilin in Manchuria, a city with a large Korean population. They returned to Pyongyang after Chinese troops retook the city. North Korean propaganda portrays Kim Jong-il as an exceptionally precocious, wise, and intelligent child, while South Korean propaganda portrays him as a violent bully. Independent accounts of this period in his life are hard to come by. He graduated from Namsan Senior High School in 1960 and went on to Kim Il-sung University, from which he graduated in 1964 with a degree in political economy.

When you graduate from a university that bears your father's name, it is not difficult to find a job. Kim Jong-il was given a position in the propaganda and agitation department of the Korean Worker's Party Central Committee's Organization and Guidance Department. This department was run by Kim Jong-il's uncle, Kim Young-ju, a man who was considered a likely successor to Kim Il-sung until Kim Jong-il gained sufficient favor in his father's eyes to shunt aside his uncle. In 1973, Kim Jong-il's father appointed him director of the department, making him, at age thirty-one, the second most powerful person in North Korea.

When Kim Il-sung died in 1994 and Kim Jong-il ascended to power, most foreign observers predicted that his reign would be a short one. The theory was that the younger Kim was too weak and too weird to run a country, particularly one with a strong military and a strong Communist Party. But unbeknownst to the outside world—and to the vast majority of North Koreans for that matter—Kim Il-sung had secretly designated Kim Jong-il to be his successor as early as 1972 or 1973, and he had been training him ever since and gradually turning over to him the responsibilities of state. Kim Jong-il consolidated his power relatively quickly by seeking the support of his father's former partisan comrades who were now in influential positions. Those who were not receptive to Kim Jong-il's approaches paid the price. Vice-Premier Kim Dong-kyu ended up in a concentration camp, while Nam-Il, one of Kim Il-sung's earliest comrades, was run over by a large truck in the middle of the night. Having established his position, Kim Jong-il prepared himself for the power-grabbing that might accompany his father's death by gradually replacing thousands of party members at all levels with younger members who would be grateful to Kim Jong-il for their promotions and thus more likely to be loyal to him. It was not until 1980 that Kim Jong-il was publicly presented as the heir to the throne, and even then he was so infrequently seen in public that it was hard to take the designation seriously.

MAN OF THE ARTS—Kim Jong-il is unusually cultured for a dictator, most of whom have little time for such outside interests. He has written a book, *On the Art of Opera,* and another on journalism according to the precepts of *juche.* He plays the piano and the violin, and he has been known to conduct a chamber orchestra at his private parties. He is also interested in architecture. It is said that he has driven to high points above the city of Pyongyang and, if the view is inharmonious, he will order the construction of a building to fill in an awkward gap. But nothing compares to his real artistic love: the cinema. As early as the 1980s, Kim Jong-il possessed a personal collection of 20,000 films, and that was be-

KIM JONG-IL, AUTEUR
Tom Haskell/Sygma/Corbis

fore he began acquiring videocassettes and DVDs. He has boasted that he has seen every Academy Award winner, and he is a particular fan of James Bond films (except *Die Another Day,* which demonizes North Korea) and *Gone with the Wind.* He greatly pleased the North Korean masses by allowing American cartoons to be shown on television, including Bugs Bunny, Donald Duck, and Tom and Jerry. During the 1970s, he produced six films. This interest in filmmaking led to the most bizarre episode in Kim Jong-il's unusually bizarre life.

THE KIDNAPPING OF CHOI EUN-HEE AND SHIN SANG-OK—
Cinema fans would be hard-pressed to find a movie director with a stranger career than Shin Sang-ok. Born in South Korea, Shin directed his first film in 1952. Over the next twenty-five years he directed more than sixty films, specializing in romantic historical epics. From 1964 until 1975, he owned the largest film studio in South Korea. However, in 1976 life took a bad turn for Shin Sang-ok. He had been married to a famous actress, Choi Eun-hee, who had appeared in more than seventy-five films. But after twenty three years, the couple divorced, although they did remain close. Then Shin ran afoul of the South Korean government, which ordered that his films be subjected to strict censorship. When the censors ordered cuts to be made in his films, Shin replaced the deleted segments with black film so that his audiences would know that something was missing. South Korean dictator Park Chung-hee did not appreciate this gesture, and he ordered the revocation of Shin's license to make films. After decades of success, Shin found himself without a job and fearful that Park had worse punishments in store for him.

Meanwhile, Choi Eun-hee was also in search of employment. In January 1978 she traveled to Hong Kong, where a friend arranged a meeting with business associates to discuss the possibility of financing a film in which she would star. After the meeting, Choi was kidnapped and bundled onto a boat. After eight days on the ocean, the boat docked at Nampo in North Korea. Choi walked outside and discovered someone waiting for her on the pier— Kim Jong-il. He was charming and polite and treated her as if she had come of her own accord. Choi was taken to a luxurious villa. Kim Jong-il sent her flowers and began inviting her to parties at his own villas. In retrospect, it is possible that, although Kim Jong-il did admire Choi's acting skills, he was really using her as a lure to catch her ex-husband, Shin Sang-ok. If that was his intention, it worked.

All that anyone knew was that Choi Eun-hee had gone to Hong Kong and disappeared. Shin flew to Hong Kong himself, with the hope of finding Choi, but also in search of a way to resurrect his career in a country other than South Korea. Told that he might be able to obtain a passport from a South American nation, Shin got into a car with a man he thought was a friend. The car was stopped and surrounded by a group of Koreans who chloroformed him. Shin was so terrified that his attackers were agents of the South Korean CIA that he was actually relieved when he realized, by the dialect they spoke and by their use of the word "comrade," that they were really North Koreans.

Shin was also put on a boat and taken to North Korea, where he was told that Choi was dead. He was held for six months in Nampo, where he was forced to watch Marxist films and attend dull ideological lectures. Held in another villa, Shin twice tried to escape. After the second failed attempt, Kim Jong-il ordered Shin to be imprisoned. He spent three months in solitary confinement and four years behind bars. Eventually, he agreed to "repent." In 1983 he agreed to make films for North Korea. Released from custody, Shin was taken to a banquet hall, where he was introduced to Kim Jong-il and reunited with Choi Eun-hee. Shin and Choi, who later remarried, were given a mansion, servants, and matching Mercedes automobiles. Kim Jong-il ordered a film studio to be built and he gave them a $3 million-dollar-a-year budget. Shin directed seven films for Kim Jong-il, who allowed Shin to travel to film festivals in Communist nations, while Choi was kept in North Korea as a hostage.

In March 1986, Shin and Choi were given permission to travel together to Vienna. Seizing the opportunity, they bribed a taxi driver, enlisted the aid of a Japanese journalist who had been sent

CHOI EUN-HEE AND SHIN SANG-OK AFTER THEIR ESCAPE FROM FILMMAKING PRISON

Tim Clary/Bettmann/Corbis

to interview them, eluded their North Korean minders, and sought refuge at the U.S. embassy. The CIA was understandably skeptical of Shin and Choi's story, but the pair had brought with them a tape recording of Kim Jong-il discussing their kidnapping. The CIA flew Shin and Choi to Washington, D.C., debriefed them, and gave them a house in Reston, Virginia. They lived under CIA protection for three years, during which time they wrote a book that became a bestseller in South Korea. But Shin Sang-ok could not get the cinema out of his system. He wanted to make movies again and he wanted to do it in Hollywood. Shin changed his name to Simon Sheen, moved to Los Angeles, and tried to make deals. After a proposed project about Genghis Khan fell through, Shin had the Hollywood version of a brainstorm: *Home Alone* with martial arts. His idea was transformed into *3 Ninjas,* which grossed $29 million and led to three sequels, one of which, *3 Ninjas Knuckle Up,* Shin directed himself. It is not known if Kim Jong-il has added the *3 Ninjas* series to his collection.

LOVER AND FAMILY MAN—Kim Jong-il is five-feet-two-inches tall and weighs about 175 pounds. When he met Choi Eun-hee, he asked her, "Don't you think that I look like a midget's turd?" Despite being handsome-deficient, Kim Jong-il has had an active romantic life. When he was twenty-six years old, he began an affair with movie star Sung Hae-rim, who was divorced and five years older than Kim Jong-il. The two lived together throughout the 1970s and 1980s. Remarkably, they managed to keep this fact secret from Kim Il-sung, who, early in the 1970s, ordered his son to marry Kim Young-sook, the daughter of a military officer. Kim Young-sook presented her husband with a daughter in 1974. However, Kim Jong-il already had a son by Sung Hae-rim. Kim Jong-nam was born in 1971. He was raised in secret and was rarely allowed to leave the house. When he was eight years old, Sung Hae-rim's sister, Song Hae-rang, was brought in to live with Kim Jong-nam, and her two children were given the position of his playmates. All three eventually defected from North Korea and it is their accounts that provide the most reliable details of Kim Jong-il's private life. Kim Jong-nam grew up with a 990 square-meter playroom. He and his cousins were schooled at home and only allowed to go out after dark, in a car that they were not allowed to leave. When they grew older, they were permitted to leave the country to be educated in Geneva and Moscow. Sung Hae-rim died in Moscow in 2002. One cousin, Il-nam, was shot to death in South Korea in 1997. Kim Jong-nam was considered the frontrunner to inherit the kingdom of North Korea until an embarrassing incident sent his stock plunging. In 2001, Kim Jong-nam was expelled from Japan when he was caught trying to enter the country with a forged passport from the Dominican Republic. Jong-nam explained that all he wanted was to visit Tokyo Disneyland.

It is not known how many other mistresses Kim Jong-il has had, but he is believed to have had a daughter, born in 1969, with Hong Il-chon, and two sons in the 1980s with a Japanese-born Korean dancer named Ko Yong-hee, to whom he remained devoted until her death in 2004. Kim Jong-il appears to have been a reasonably attentive father, who enjoyed sitting on the floor and playing "Super Mario" with Kim Jong-nam.

THE KIM JONG-IL ERA—The 1970 edition of the *Dictionary of Political Terminologies,* published by the North Korean Academy of Social Sciences, denounced hereditary succession as "a reactionary custom of exploitative societies adopted by feudal lords as a means to perpetuate dictatorial rule." This definition was deleted from the 1972 edition of the dictionary. Still, the idea of introducing hereditary succession to a Communist nation was a bit delicate, so Kim Il-sung and Kim Jong-il propagated the theory of the unfinished or perpetual revolution that needed a "reincarnation" of Kim Il-sung to carry on the revolution after his death. Who better to take the role of Kim Il-sung's reincarnated spirit than his own son?

Kim Jong-il had the misfortune to begin taking over the reins of power just as North Korea's post–Korean War economic growth began to peter out. Considering that Kim Il-sung was a lifelong military man with no particular aptitude for economic policy, it is possible that, seeing the handwriting on the wall, he let his son do the hard work of governing while he played the elder statesman and toured the country enjoying the adulation of the people.

Unfortunately, Kim Jong-il, too, had no qualifications to oversee his nation's economy. By the 1990s, North Korea was in serious trouble. Despite large-scale food imports, there simply was not enough to go around. The government instituted a Two Meals a Day campaign and a One Foodless Day a Month campaign. Kim Jong-il allowed foreign ownership of businesses in special economic zones, but, in at least one case, he built a fifty-mile fence around a free economic zone to prevent contact between North Koreans and the foreigners. Russia and China demanded repayment of loans and refused to continue trade on the barter system, demanding hard currency instead. As if this wasn't bad enough, North Korea experienced major flooding in both 1995 and 1996, followed by a severe drought in 1997 that cut the important corn crop in half. All of these misfortunes were aggravated by Kim Jong-il's personal extravagances and massive military expenditures, which are estimated to make up 30 percent of the national budget. In 2004 there were 1.2 million people in the North Korean armed forces and 6 million in the reserves. Twelve percent of the male population between the ages of seventeen and forty-nine were in the armed services. In 1998, UNICEF reported that 63 percent of North Korean children were stunted and, according to a 2002 United Nations–European Union survey, the average seven-year-old boy in North Korea is 20 centimeters shorter than the average seven-year-old boy in South Korea and 10 kilograms lighter. Between 1995 and 2001, approximately 300,000 North Koreans fled to China, three-quarters of them women. Although exact figures are impossible to obtain, it is thought that between 500,000 and 1,000,000 North Koreans died from famine-related illnesses.

While the general populace was suffering, the North Korean military set up its own separate economy, selling Scud missiles and other weapons to Syria, Iran, Pakistan, Yemen, and other nations. In addition, Kim Jong-il created his own private business entity, "Division 39," the profits from which he tucked away in banks in Switzerland and Macao. Some of Division 39's businesses are legitimate, dealing in seafood, ginseng, gold, silver, and magnesium. But there is also evidence that Kim Jong-il has lined his pockets with the profits from counterfeiting U.S. dollars and from the smuggling of heroin and methamphetamines, which is reputed to gross $500 million a year.

RELATIONS WITH THE OUTSIDE WORLD—Kim Jong-il can be a bit testy, particularly when it comes to relations with South Korea. A couple of incidents illustrate this point. In November 1997, KBS-TV, South Korea's state-run television station, aired a mini-series that portrayed repression and corruption in North Korea. The North Korean government responded by issuing an official statement threatening to kill everyone involved in the production and broadcasting of the mini-series. In July 2000, the South Korean newspaper *Chosun Ilbo* published an article claiming that the 1950 Korean War had been ignited by North Korea invading South Korea. The North Korean response was to publicly threaten to "blow up" the *Chosun Ilbo* offices.

No aspect of North Korean policy has caused greater concern than its threats to build nuclear weapons. The USSR first supplied the materials for and oversaw construction of a small, 4-megawatt nuclear reactor in North Korea in 1962. In 1977, the North Koreans accepted International Atomic Energy Agency (IAEA) safeguards. During the 1980s the North Koreans built their own 30-megawatt reactor. Originally, this interest in nuclear reactors was nothing more than one component of Kim Il-sung's quest for energy self-sufficiency. However, Western nervousness about North Korea's nuclear capabilities led Kim Jong-il to realize that the threat of building nuclear weapons could be used as a bargaining chip, as could North Korea's development and sale of other weapons. For example, when a delegation of U.S. congressional staffers visited North Korea in August 1998, North Korean officials offered to stop the sale of ballistic missiles to Iran and other nations in exchange for $500 million a year.

Kim Jong-il did accept the presence of IAEA inspectors beginning in 1992 and in 1994 he agreed to freeze his nuclear program in exchange for U.S. fuel deliveries. On August 15, 1997, Kim Jong-il stunned the North Korean people by telling them that the United States was no longer an enemy. "They are our friends," he declared. This softening of relations with the outside world was furthered in 1998 when Kim Dae-jung, the newly elected president of

South Korea instituted his Sunshine Policy toward North Korea. In June 2000, Kim Dae-jung traveled to Pyongyang and met with Kim Jong-il, the first-ever summit between the leaders of North and South Korea. For the first time, Kim Jong-il admitted to the kidnapping of South Koreans and Japanese. Kim Jong-il also met with U.S. secretary of state Madeleine Albright and jokingly introduced himself as "the last of the Communist devils."

Kim Jong-il also made certain that other nations retained their fear of North Korea. As a reminder that he was not going soft, North Korea, on August 31, 1998, launched a missile test which happened to pass straight over Japan. Still, Japan, South Korea, and much of the rest of the world were feeling less worried about North Korea until George W. Bush took over as president of the United States. Bush ended fuel deliveries to North Korea, stopped negotiating with the North Koreans, and declared North Korea a member of his Axis of Evil and Kim Jong-il a "pygmy." Kim Jong-il responded by restarting his nuclear program, withdrawing from the Nuclear Nonproliferation Treaty, and reactivating his nuclear reactor. It is said that when George Bush invaded Iraq and overthrew Saddam Hussein, Kim Jong-il feared that he would be next. However, it is just as likely that Kim learned a different lesson: to survive the era of George W. Bush, build a nuclear bomb.

TOTAL CONTROL—The people of North Korea have never known freedom. After centuries of feudalism, they experienced Japanese colonialism and the Stalinism of Kim Il-sung and Kim Jong-il. Some of the elements of the system of social control in North Korea are almost silly. Cellphones are banned because they might be used to detonate bombs. The tuners on radios are fixed so that unauthorized channels cannot be accessed, and security officials make unannounced visits to people's homes to make sure no one is cheating. In 1978, the government introduced a new calendar based on the birth of Kim Il-sung in 1912, so that 2006 is now referred to as "Juche 95." In primary school, students spend one hour a week studying about the childhood of Kim Il-sung. In Korean language class, more than 60 percent of the time is spent reading about Kim Il-sung and Kim Jong-il. In all texts, the names of the two Kims are always printed in boldface. In arithmetic, word problems are based on computing how many American soldiers were killed in the Korean War or how many tanks the North Korean army destroyed.

But most of North Korea's repressive techniques are deadly serious. In a speech in 1970, Kim Il-sung publicly acknowledged a program that had begun in 1958, in which the authorities divided the entire North Korean population into three classes of "Loyalty Groups." The core class, made up of roughly a quarter of the people, are those whose families, in the pre-liberation era (before 1945), were soldiers, poor farmers, workers, or office clerks, as well as those families whose members were killed in the war. Members of the core class are given priority in housing, food, and medical care. The wavering classes, half the population, are pre-liberation merchants, farmers, and service workers, as well as immigrants from South Korea, China, and Japan, and families whose members left for South Korea, but stayed behind themselves. The third group is the hostile class, from families that were pre-liberation wealthy landlords or merchants, as well as religious scholars and those who have expressed dissatisfaction, even in private, with the Kims and their regime. Members of the

ONE MILLION NORTH KOREANS CELEBRATE THEIR NATION'S WITHDRAWAL FROM THE NUCLEAR NONPROLIFERATION TREATY.
Gong Yidong/AP Photo/Xinhua

hostile class are not allowed to live in Pyongyang. Needless to say, they receive the worst jobs, the worst housing, and the minimum of food rations. All citizens of North Korea are monitored by the Ministry of People's Security, which places informers in workplaces and neighborhoods to inform on anyone who criticizes the regime, even at home. Among the crimes for which one may be punished are disloyalty to The Great Leader and to The Dear Leader, an offense that includes allowing pictures of Kim Il-sung and Kim Jong-il to gather dust and allowing pictures of the Kims that appear in magazines or newspapers to be torn or folded.

Below the loyalty groups, like untouchables in the Hindu caste system, are the 250,000 people who are held in prison camps. It is not only people accused of crimes who are sent to these camps, but their families as well. Following the concept of *yongoje,* family purge, North Korean officials will round up and imprison, or at least banish, three generations of the family of a transgressor, including uncles, aunts, and cousins. Sometimes friends and work colleagues are punished as well. One case reported by Human Rights Watch is that of Kim Young. Kim was an official of the State Security Bureau when it was discovered that his father had been executed as a CIA spy thirty-six years earlier. Kim Young was immediately sent to prison, where he met his mother, who had been incarcerated since her husband was executed.

Accounts of the prison camps, which have been brought out by former prisoners, and even escaped guards, are harrowing. A 2003 report identified thirty-six forced labor camps, one of which is three times as large as Washington, D.C. There are reports of forced abortions, babies being killed, people sent to the "Discipline Department" for laughing or for looking at their reflection in a window, and informers staying awake through the night to report on what prisoners say when they talk in their sleep. A 1987 riot at Onsung Prison led to the killing of 5,000 prisoners. Prisoners work up to nineteen hours a day and products made by forced labor, including clothing, have been found to be "washed" through China and discovered on shelves in the United States. According to one prisoner, working with livestock is a good job because it is possible to steal the animals' food and to pick through animal dung for undigested grain. On the prison cell walls are slogans such as "adore the authorities of Kim Il-sung and Kim Jong-il with all your heart."

EXCESSES AND BIZARRE BEHAVIOR:

- In honor of Kim Il-sung's seventieth birthday, North Korea built a triumphal arch in Pyongyang that is a copy of the Arc de Triomph in Paris, but larger, and a Torch of Juche Idea monument made from 25,550 white granite blocks, one for each day of Kim Il-sung's life, that is one meter higher than the Washington Monument.

- Peeved by South Korea's coup in hosting the 1988 Olympics, Kim Jong-il spent $4.3 billion to prepare for the Thirteenth World Festival of Youth and Students held in Pyongyang in 1989. Large apartment buildings were built to house visitors, but without the use of construction elevators, which led to the death of more than 1,000 workers in three years.

- In 1996, Kim Jong-il suddenly took great interest in Pyongyang's female traffic police, who are known for their beauty. He ordered new uniforms for them with padded trousers to keep them warm.

- In 1974, Kim Jong-il decided that North Korean radio was not playing enough music. He personally listened to thousands of songs and then chose 330 to be played on-air. Three years later, he added another 1,177 songs.

- Kim Jong-il has never given a major speech or spoken to a large crowd. Although the government often stages mass rallies, at which up to one million North Koreans will march in columns fifty abreast, Kim's only known utterance at such an event was at a 1992 military parade, when he called out, "Glory to the heroic Korean People's Army."

- Every room in every building must display photographs of Kim Il-sung and Kim Jong-il, and special kits are distributed to clean the pictures.

- Every North Korean must wear a lapel pin with a photo of either Kim Il-sung or Kim Jong-il.

• Choi Eun-hee reported that at one of the parties she attended, Kim Jong-il served her a bottle of wine with a live snake inside.

IN HIS WORDS:

ADVICE FOR BROADCASTERS:

"Every word they speak before their microphone must grasp the hearts of the masses of people, inspire them strongly, scare the enemy like a bomb . . ."

FROM *THE GREAT TEACHER OF JOURNALIST: KIM JONG-IL*

ADVICE TO JOURNALISTS:

"It is advisable that the newspapers carry articles in which they unfailingly hold the President in high esteem, adore him and praise him as the great revolutionary leader."

DECEMBER 26, 1973

"The U.S. imperialists and their stooges are saying that we have no ideological freedom. . . . Our people have accepted the Juche idea . . . as their conviction of their own accord . . ."

MAY 5, 1991

"If we weaken the dictatorial function of the government . . . we cannot provide the people with democratic freedom and rights . . ."

JANUARY 3, 1992

POEM—According to an official biography, *Kim Jong-il: The People's Leader*, while a student in junior middle school, Kim Jong-il, worried because his father was working late, wrote this poem.

COULDN'T A SECOND BE AN HOUR?
Yesterday and today
In summer and in winter
A day has twenty-four hours.

There's no change
In the flow of time.

The hands of the table clock
In father's sleeping room
Are running so fast.
What's chasing them?

The night's already deep
But father isn't back yet.
Time flows mercilessly
And time for father's rest
Dwindles second by second.

Who ever understands
This uneasiness of mine?
You, clock, slow down your speed,
Couldn't a second be an hour
At least during father's rest? . . .

3.

THAN SHWE—BURMA

THE NATION—Burma, also known as Myanmar, is a Buddhist nation of about 55 million people, two-thirds of whom belong to the ethnic group known as Burmans. The other third of the population is divided among at least 135 ethnic groups, including the Shan, Karen, Rakhine, Mon, and Kachin. There are about two million Christians and an equal number of Muslims. A military junta has ruled the country since 1962 and many of the ethnic minorities have been fighting against government forces ever since. There are one million internally displaced persons and 700,000 Burmese (citizens of the country of Burma) who are legal refugees in other countries, most of them in Thailand and Bangladesh. Another two million Burmese work in Thailand.

Burma is rich in hardwoods and accounts for 75 percent of the world trade in teak. It is also the world's second-largest producer of illegal opium (behind Afghanistan). Thanks to free education provided by Buddhist monks, Burma has a long history of literacy, particularly among boys and men. However, the military government has all but destroyed the nation's intellectual tradition. In 2003–2004, only 1.3 percent of the national budget was devoted to education. Less than one-third of girls now complete primary school and the high school graduation rate for boys and girls has dropped to 2 percent.

There is a saying in Burma that one must be wary of five evils: fire, water (storms and floods), thieves, mean people, and—government.

BEFORE THE ARRIVAL OF THE EUROPEANS—Beginning in about AD 800 the Burmans migrated from eastern Tibet into the lowlands of present-day Burma. The Mon people were already settled in the fertile coastal area and the Shan were living in the northeastern hills. King Anawrata established his capital at Pagan in the eleventh century and was the first Burman king to promote Buddhism. He was also the first to build an empire. In 1057, he invaded the Mon kingdom in Lower Burma and captured monks and scholars, whom he brought to Pagan to teach Buddhism and to instruct village boys to read and write. In the late thirteenth century the Shan sought protection from the Mongol empire. The Mongol emperor, Kublai Khan, sent in a large armed force that completely destroyed the Burman kingdom. For the next 450 years the region was plagued by a series of civil wars.

BUMPING INTO THE BRITISH—Beginning in 1753, a new Burmese kingdom started reuniting various states. The Burmans also raided Thailand and fought off two invasions by China's Manchu dynasty. In the early nineteenth century, Burman forces moved west into Assam and ran into the British East India Company. European explorers and merchants had been around since the sixteenth century, but this was the first time the Burmans seriously clashed with the Europeans. What later came to be known as the First Burmese War broke out in 1824. British troops drove the Burmans out of Assam and then captured the coastal states of Arakan and Tenasserim. They continued up the Irrawaddy River until the Burmans surrendered. The Second Burmese War, in 1852–1853, ended with the British annexing Lower Burma. In 1878, King Thibaw attempted to lessen British influence by establishing trade relations with the French. The Third Burmese War began in 1885. The following year, the British annexed central and northern Burma, banished the king and his family to India, and put an end to Burman rule, ruling Burma themselves as a province of British India.

Many of the ethnic hill tribes were happy to have the British move in and protect them against the Burmans. In addition, the British allowed in Christian missionaries, who built hospitals and schools, and they placed members of some ethnic minorities in the civil service and in the colonial defense force. However, in making maps and creating governmental divisions, the British took some mountain areas that had never been ruled by the Burmans and mapped them into Burma.

To the British East India Company, Burma was basically a source of exploitable resources, in particular teak, oil, tin, and rubies and other gems. They built railroads and roads

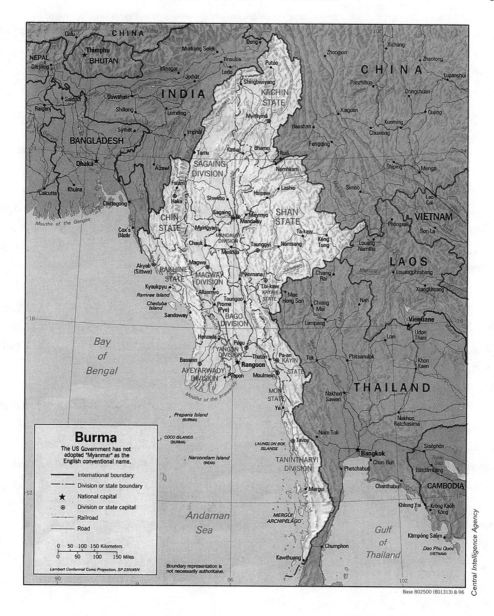

and developed river transport to get at what they wanted, and they brought with them Indians to work as clerks and farmers. They also opened Burma to Indian and Chinese merchants.

The Great Depression of 1929 reached Burma the following year. The price of rice plummeted and many Burmese farmers lost their land to Indian moneylenders. In 1931, anti-Indian and anti-Chinese riots broke out because it was easier to attack the Indians and

Chinese, who had taken money and jobs from the Burmans, than it was to attack the British, who had created the policies that benefited the immigrants. The Burmans, however, did occasionally rise up and this resistance came to a head in the 1930s. In 1930, an ex-monk named Saya San led a revolt in which thousands of armed peasants attacked colonial offices. The British brutally suppressed the revolt, displaying the severed heads of rebellious peasants, 10,000 of whom they killed, and hanging Saya San.

But in February 1936, an incident occurred that, although less violent, was to prove a harbinger of major changes ahead. The student magazine at the University of Rangoon published an article that specifically criticized a school administrator. When the editors of the magazine refused to reveal the name of the author of the article, the university expelled the editor and the head of the student union. This led to student demonstrations that spread to colleges and high schools around the country. The student editor, only twenty-one years old at the time, would soon become his nation's leader.

AUNG SAN—That editor, Aung San, did graduate from the University of Rangoon, after which he joined the Dobama Asiayone, the We Burmans Association. In 1937, under pressure, the British separated Burma from India and gave it a bicameral legislature, with one house fully elected and the other half elected. Of course the British governor retained veto power over the legislature and the new arrangement did little to alleviate Burman resentment of the British. In early 1941, Aung San and twenty-nine other nationalists, soon to be known as the Thirty Comrades, secretly traveled to Hainan Island in China to be given military training by the Japanese. With Japanese help, the Thirty Comrades created the Burma Independence Army and joined with the Japanese to drive the British out of Burma. Aung San took the position of minister of defense in the new puppet government. However, the Japanese occupation proved to be more brutal than that of the British. Aung San and his comrades formed the leftist Anti-Fascist People's Freedom League (AFPFL) to oppose the Japanese, with Aung San heading a guerrilla army. In March of 1945, they joined the Allies and helped create a road to bring supplies across Burma to China and then drove the Japanese out of Burma.

After World War II ended, the British tried to reimpose colonial rule, but widespread strikes and general resistance led them to give up the attempt. In January 1947, Prime Minister Clement Attlee agreed to grant independence to Burma. Elections were held for a transition government and the AFPFL won 196 of 202 seats. During the war, Burmans had fought against the armies of the Karen and Kachin ethnic groups, both of which had stayed on the British side throughout the war. Aung San reached out to these groups, incorporating ethnic troops into the national army and even appointing a Karen to be commander-in-chief. In February, Aung San and leaders of the Shan, Chin, and Kachin groups signed the Panglong Agreement that created the Union of Burma, based on a federal system with equality of the various states. The Karen did not sign the agreement because they thought, mistakenly, that the British would grant them independence separate from Burma. A new constitution created state councils for non-Burman ethnic groups and the Shan and Karenni were actually given the right to secede after ten years, if they chose to do so. The Kachin were not given this option because part of their territory had been controlled by Burmans, and the status and boundaries of the Karen remained unsettled.

Unfortunately, Aung San and six of his colleagues were assassinated on July 19, 1947, by order of a rival general, U Saw, who was arrested and executed. At the time of his death, Aung San, now revered as the father of his country, was thirty-two years old. He left behind three small children, one of whom, a two-year-old daughter, would emerge forty years later as the symbol of her nation's aspirations for freedom and democracy.

INDEPENDENCE—After the assassination of Aung San, his close friend, U Nu, took power and became Burma's first prime minister when independence was declared on January 4, 1948. Burman hopes were high. Prior to World War II, Burma had been the world's largest exporter of rice and, as the British colonialists had shown, the country was rich in diverse national resources. The newly independent nation had free speech, free education, independent newspapers, and a freely elected government. But in the borderlands, there was trouble on the horizon. Multiple ethnic insurgencies developed and, by 1949, the central government controlled little outside the capital of Rangoon. In addition, Burma was cursed by its proximity to China, where a civil war was coming to its conclusion. In June 1948, a Communist revolt erupted in the mountains, and in 1949 the Kuomintang army, covertly supported by the United States, fled the Maoist takeover of China and settled into Shan State in northern Burma. Both the Chinese and the Burmans sent troops to attack the Kuomintang.

Meanwhile, U Nu presented himself as the patron of Buddhism, something the Burmans had lacked since the British overthrew King Thibaw more than sixty years earlier. Once, in the midst of his reign as prime minister, U Nu left the government chambers and meditated for forty-five days on Mount Popa.

While U Nu was pursuing his own agenda, General Ne Win took over control of the army from the Karen commander and organized his troops to regain control of the land left to the Union of Burma by the British. By 1952, most of the country's population was back under government control.

NE WIN—Born Shu Waung in 1911, Ne Win dropped out of university when he was nineteen years old and worked as a postal clerk. Along with Aung San and U Nu, he was one of the Thirty Comrades who were trained by the Japanese during World War II. At the time he took over its leadership, the Burmese army had only a few thousand members. By 1988, Ne Win had expanded its size to 186,000. Under Ne Win, the army, known as the Tatmadaw, set up its own corporation, running shops, selling bulk goods and engaging in import and export.

By September 1958, Ne Win and two comrades, Maung Maung and Aung Gyi, had become sufficiently impatient with U Nu to stage a coup. Over the next eighteen months, Ne Win solved a border dispute with China and took advantage of splits among both the Shan and Karenni to keep either group from taking advantage of their right to secede.

Ne Win stepped aside to allow elections to be held in February 1960. U Nu won the election easily by pledging to make Buddhism the state religion. He then followed through with this promise, greatly upsetting the non-Buddhist minorities, whom Ne Win had just "pacified."

On March 2, 1962, Ne Win seized power again. This time, though, he had no intention of voluntarily relinquishing power, and he established a socialist military dictatorship that has ruled Burma ever since.

A THICK, DARK CLOUD DESCENDS—Ne Win established a seventeen-man Revolutionary Council of military officers and then formed the Burma Socialist Programme Party (BSPP), the name the junta would use for the next twenty-six years.

Ne Win took early aim at university students, whom he considered a potential political threat. He ordered the imposition of an 8:00 p.m. curfew for students living in dormitories. This led to demonstrations. On July 7, 1962, riot police stormed the campus of Rangoon University, seizing the student union and killing more than one hundred students. The next morning, the army blew up the student union, an attack that democracy advocates would not forget over the coming decades.

Over the next three years, Ne Win and his fellow generals transformed Burmese society. They nationalized all industries, banks, and large shops, 15,000 in all. The owners, many of whom were Indians and Chinese, lost everything, as military men took over the highest position in every enterprise. Ne Win also fired 2,000 civilian employees of the national administration and replaced them with members of the military. Trade unions were outlawed, private schools were nationalized, and a censorship board was established to review all publications. Foreign aid organizations were expelled and travelers' visas were limited to twenty-four-hour stays. The judicial system was replaced by a national network of three-man panels.

Each panel was chaired by a member of the military and filled out with two locals loyal to the government.

Most Burmese were farmers and Ne Win attempted to win their support by giving plots of land to many landless peasants. However, there was a catch. Farmers had to meet production quotas and they had to sell rice to the government at below-market prices. This led to hoarding and a growing black market. Between 1963 and 1968, Burma's annual rice exports plunged from 1.8 million tons to 300,000 tons.

The military junta ordered all monks to register with the government. They refused. When monks in Mandalay, the nation's second-largest city, protested, government troops opened fire on them. After flurries of arrests, the registration of monks went ahead in 1965. Later, Ne Win himself would find religion—in his fashion. He adopted practices common to the people, including frequent consultations with fortune-tellers. He once shot his image in a mirror to avoid death and another time he ordered the building of 70,000 sand pagodas to protect the nation against danger. In 1970 he suddenly ordered all cars to drive on the right side of the road instead of the left because a spiritual advisor told him to move to the right to avoid attacks.

Ne Win's biggest accomplishment was his massive buildup of the military, which he funded with the help of a $1.2 billion loan from China. Before 1962, Burma exhibited a relatively high amount of social mobility. Thanks to free education, many students from poor families were able to attend university. After 1962, all opportunities for social mobility were dependent on joining the military.

As the Burmese economy disintegrated, due to corruption and mismanagement, Ne Win tried to redirect popular discontent against the Chinese merchants who dominated the black market in rice, the nation's staple. In 1967, mobs attacked Chinese-owned shops and homes, as well as the Chinese embassy.

U THANT'S FUNERAL—Internationally, the most famous Burmese citizen was U Thant, a diplomat who served as the secretary-general of the United Nations from 1961 through 1971. His achievements were a source of pride for the Burmese. U Thant died in New York City on November 25, 1978, and his body was shipped home to Burma. Ne Win ordered that no government official greet the body, which was to be transported by monks to an old race track. Thousands of people came to lay wreaths and pay their respects. On December 5, 1974, university students marched to the track and persuaded the monks to hand over U Thant's body. They drove the body to Rangoon University and installed it in a handmade mausoleum on the site of the student union that Ne Win's troops had blown up twelve years earlier. Thousands more visited the university grounds to pay homage to U Thant.

Ne Win closed all the universities in Rangoon and ordered all students from outside the city to return home. Then riot police attacked the campus, killing between eighteen and one hundred students and arresting 3,000.

As discontent with BSPP corruption grew inside the military, Ne Win uncovered a coup plot and dismissed 50,000 members of the party, which was more than half its membership.

FIGHTING THE ETHNIC ARMIES—Long gone were the days of Aung San and Burman respect for the autonomy of ethnic minorities. The Shan, the Karen, the Kachin, and the Mon had all organized thousands-strong armies that supported themselves through logging, mining, opium production, toll gates, and smuggling. There was also a Communist insurgency that was heavily supplied by China until the late 1980s, when the Chinese lost interest in the struggles of the Communist Party of Burma and aligned themselves with the Burmese military instead.

Ne Win divided the ethnic regions into white, brown, and black areas. White areas were under government control. In the brown areas, control was mixed. Black areas, controlled by one of the opposition groups, were considered free-fire, shoot-to-kill zones. In the mid-1960s, the government launched the Four Cuts Campaign, intended to cut rebel access to food, money, recruits, and intelligence. No one was allowed to be innocent or neutral. Each community, each village, each family had to support the Tatmadaw, fight against them, or flee. In the noncombat areas, government troops "recruited" young men by seizing them in the streets, in movie theaters, as they disembarked from ferries and buses, and sent them to the front lines to serve as porters. Over a thirty-year period, the Tatmadaw, in search of jade, gold, platinum, and coal, evicted and relocated 100,000 Kachin alone. Some of the groups in mountainous areas had never been under Burman control and they had no intention of cooperating with the invading national army. In 1976, several of the ethnic armies formed the National Democratic Front, but each army remained autonomous and sometimes they fought each other for resources and territory.

Meanwhile, Ne Win and nineteen other members of the ruling junta made a superficial attempt to achieve legitimacy by resigning from the military and transforming themselves into a civilian government. In 1981, Ne Win even announced that he was abdicating the presidency. However, he retained his role as head of the BSPP and nothing really changed.

1988: THE YEAR OF FREEDOM WITHIN REACH—On September 1, 1987, the Burmese government announced what appeared to be a major economic reform. Farmers were now free to buy and sell rice and eight other grains to traders on an open market. Four days later, the BSPP dropped another bombshell. They declared worthless all bank notes above the value of 15 kyat (about $2.20), which accounted for 70 percent of the currency in circulation and wiped out most people's savings overnight. They then replaced 50- and 100-kyat bills with new 45- and 90-kyat denominations because nine is a lucky number and 4+5=9 and 9+0=9.

Because Ne Win and other government leaders refused to hear bad news, production figures were invented to reflect stated goals instead of reality. By 1988, the annual debt equaled three-quarters of the gross national product.

On March 12, 1988, at a teashop in Rangoon, a brawl broke out between a group of university students and a group of locals. The instigator, the son of a BSPP official, was detained, but quickly released, while several students remained in custody. Other students staged a spontaneous protest in front of the police station, whereupon riot police killed a student named Phone Maw. Student demonstrations were organized. On March 16, in what became known as the Red Bridge Massacre, unarmed students in the midst of a protest march found themselves blocked by soldiers in front of them and riot police behind them. On their right was Inya Lake and on their left a neighborhood of large homes with high walls. The soldiers and police attacked. Some students were beaten to death, while others drowned in the lake. Forty-one students suffocated to death inside a prison van. Within two days, the size of the demonstrations grew beyond 10,000 people. The government closed the universities for two months. When they reopened in June, the students in Rangoon voted to support the overthrow of one-party rule. The next day, June 21, riot police stopped a student march. A battle ensued, leaving eighty civilians and twenty riot police dead. Two days later, seventy more demonstrators were killed in the city of Pegu. In the towns of Taunggyi and Prome, violence broke out between Buddhists and Muslims.

On July 23, the BSPP convened an emergency conference. Ne Win, who was now seventy-seven years old, proposed holding a referendum in which the Burmese people could choose between one-party rule and a multiparty system. Having stated his case, he resigned as leader of the party. He was replaced by General Sein Lwin, a choice that was not exactly intended to placate the student demonstrators. As the head of the riot police, Sein Lwin had been in charge of blowing up the Rangoon University student union in 1962, cracking down on the students and others following the death of U Thant in 1974, and organizing the Red Bridge Massacre only four months earlier.

8888—During a BBC radio interview, students called for nationwide demonstrations on August 8, 1988, 8-8-88 being an auspicious date. On August 3, the government imposed martial law in Rangoon. Undaunted, at 8:08 a.m. dock workers in Rangoon launched the day of protest by walking off the job. There were large street demonstrations in which people carried signs with photographs of Aung San and students displayed the flying peacock banner that symbolized the student union that the military government had destroyed in 1962.

Almost 3,000 people died over the next four days, most of them marchers shot by soldiers. There were demonstrations in the tens of thousands as far away from Rangoon as Shan State and Karen State. In some places, villagers killed suspected members of military intelligence. On August 12, the BSPP removed General Sein Lwin from his post as president. A week later he was replaced by a friend of Ne Win, Dr. Maung Maung, a civilian legal scholar best known for having written the 1982 law that deprived Indians and Chinese of citizenship. Maung Maung lifted martial law and ordered all troops to return to their bases.

Almost overnight, dozens of newspapers and magazines appeared on the streets and there were public burnings of BSPP membership cards. Around the country there was looting of government property. As government control deteriorated, so did the distribution of food, and local committees were rapidly formed to handle food shortages and security. The students called for a nationwide strike on August 26. That morning the government opened the prisons, adding thousands of criminals to the crowds in the streets. Demonstrations were held in 250 cities and towns.

THE LADY APPEARS—Daw Aung San Suu Kyi was born in 1946. She was two years old when her father, Aung San, was assassinated. At fifteen she moved to New Delhi when her mother, Khin Kyi, was appointed Burma's ambassador to India. Later she studied at Oxford University. After graduating with a degree in philosophy, politics, and economics, she worked for almost three years at the United Nations in New York City while U Thant was secretary-general. Inspired by the philosophies of Mahatma Gandhi and Martin Luther King, she became an advocate of nonviolence. "It's hate that is the problem," she would say, "not violence. Violence is simply the symptom of hate."

In 1972, Aung San Suu Kyi married Michael Aris, a British scholar specializing in Tibetan Studies. They settled in Oxford and she gave birth to two sons. Prior to their marriage, she wrote these words to her future husband: "I only ask one thing, that should my people need me, you would help me to do my duty by them." For the next sixteen years, Aung San Suu Kyi lived a reasonably normal life, raising her children and continuing her academic studies. In April 1988, she received word from Burma that her mother was gravely ill, and she returned to Rangoon to care for her.

Suu Kyi watched the developments of August 1988, the demonstrations and the killings, with growing concern, and she saw that many of the demonstrators carried signs with pictures of her father. Finally, she agreed to speak at the August 26 rally in Rangoon. More than half a million Burmese gathered in front of the city's famous Shwedagon Pagoda, curious to see the daughter of their national hero. Recalling her father's assassination, she said, "People have been saying I know nothing of Burmese politics. The trouble is, I know too much." She concluded by referring to the current crisis as "the second struggle for independence." Articulate and charming, Suu Kyi won over the huge crowd. Overnight she was transformed from an Oxford academic and housewife to the symbol of the Burmese peoples' struggle for freedom and democracy. The Burmese dubbed her The Lady.

AUNG SAN SUU KYI WITH A
PHOTOGRAPH OF HER FATHER
NLD/epa/Corbis

After speaking with foreign embassies about the possibility of forming an alternative interim government, student leaders and politicians held a series of meetings with U Nu, Aung San Suu Kyi, and disaffected generals. The students wanted to form a government within forty-eight hours, but U Nu proved to be an obstacle because he insisted on being made the leader. On September 15, a crowd gathered, intent on attacking the Ministry of Defense. However, retired Brigadier General Aung Gyi persuaded them to disperse. Two days later, when demonstrators did take over the Ministry of Trade, the army did not intervene.

The next day, however, troops appeared everywhere, attacking strike centers and killing at will. Among the victims were 600 monks. The government used photographs to identify strike leaders and then went door-to-door making arrests. Almost 10,000 students fled the cities and headed to the borderlands, where most of the various minorities took little interest in the upheaval, considering it nothing more than another Burman civil war.

A new military junta took charge, calling itself the State Law and Order Restoration Council, which became better known by its unpleasant-sounding acronym, SLORC. The chairman of the new junta was General Saw Maung, but it was widely assumed that Ne Win was still calling the shots behind the scenes, particularly as the commander-in-chief of the army was seen visiting him twice in the twenty-four hours before the coup. Military control was reestablished in only two days. SLORC promised to give all civil servants their back pay if they would return to work.

On September 23, Saw Maung spoke to the nation and claimed that he did not intend to "cling to state power for long." He announced national elections and encouraged the creation of political parties. The BSPP registered as the National Unity Party, while the main opposition, including Aung San Suu Kyi, registered as the National League for

Democracy (NLD). The junta would later declare Aung San Suu Kyi ineligible to run for office because she was married to a foreigner. This decision forced one of the leading generals, Khin Nyunt, to publicly disown his son after the young man married a Singapore Airlines air hostess.

Three million people joined the NLD. Aung San Suu Kyi, along with NLD leader U Tin Oo, toured the country and gave more than 1,000 speeches. She and U Tin Oo even campaigned in the minority states, just as Aung San had done back in 1947. Suu Kyi spoke about Buddhist values, such as loving-kindness, tolerance, and self-control. Meanwhile, SLORC was busy changing the name of the country from Burma to Myanmar and declaring various activities to be unpatriotic. For example, it announced that eating cheese was un-Myanmar.

As the long election campaign stretched through 1989, it became clear that the SLORC junta had made a terrible mistake (from its point of view) by allowing free, democratic elections. Although the government controlled all media, and all campaign literature had to be cleared by the censors, the popular appeal of the NLD was overwhelming. On the evening of April 5, 1989, after a day of campaigning in Danubyu in the Irrawaddy Delta, Aung San Suu Kyi and a group of NLD organizers were stopped and ordered off the road by government soldiers. Suu Kyi waved the others away and kept walking toward the soldiers. "It seemed so much simpler," she later explained. "to provide them with a single target." A captain ordered six of his soldiers to raise their rifles and shoot her. At the last second, a major ran forward and overruled the captain.

In July 1989, the SLORC generals sent thirty NLD leaders, including U Tin Oo, to prison, and they put Aung San Suu Kyi under house arrest. She did not see her children again for two and a half years and she remained in detention for six years. By November 1989, about 6,000 pro-democracy Burmese had been arrested and 2,992 public employees had been fired because of their political views.

THE ELECTION—The national parliamentary election was finally held on May 27, 1990. Ninety-three parties fielded slates and there were also eighty-eight independent candidates. The NLD captured 60 percent of the popular vote and won 392 of the 485 seats. The government's National Unity Party finished fourth with only ten seats. The NLD even won in districts dominated by military barracks. The Shan Nationalities League for Democracy gained twenty-three seats and the Arakan League for Democracy eleven. The remaining seats were divided among twenty-three other parties, most of them representing various ethnic minorities.

The military junta seemed stunned by the results, which was a good indication of how out of touch they were with the people they were ruling. General Saw Maung began to stall. About two months after the election, the NLD tried to form a parallel government. SLORC sent out forces to arrest all concerned, but twelve members of the parliament-elect escaped to the Thai border and formed a government-in-exile tasked with the responsibility of pleading the cause of Burmese democracy to the world. Unfortunately, the outside world showed little interest. Meanwhile, Saw Maung announced that the parliament could not convene until a constitution could be written and that a constitution could not be written until a National Convention could be held to create the rules for writing a new constitution.

On August 8, 1990, the monks in Mandalay held a commemoration of the second anniversary of 8-8-88. Soldiers shot into the crowd, killing two monks. At that time, there were about 300,000 Buddhist monks and novices in Burma, as well as 20,000 nuns. On August 27, they began a religious boycott of all soldiers and their families. The monks refused to accept alms from soldiers and their families, refused to attend ceremonies at their homes, and refused to attend their funerals. Two months later, the military disrobed and arrested 300 monks in Mandalay and then raided more than 100 monasteries and forced an end to the boycott. Meanwhile, the army continued to hunt down and arrest as many MP-elects as they could find.

SLORC opened Burma to foreign trade and investment, mostly through joint ventures with military-owned companies, and primarily in the fields of oil, gas, mining, and lumber. To help its foreign partners, it used forced labor to build roads, bridges, and canals.

In 1991, Aung San Suu Kyi was awarded the Nobel Peace Prize. Her son Alexander accepted the prize on behalf of all the Burmese people.

In April 1992, Saw Maung was ousted by the junta. General Maung Aye, who once walked on a Karen flag on national television, was named commander-in-chief of the army and Lt. General Khin Nyunt, a protégé of Ne Win, was put in charge of military intelligence. Senior General Than Shwe took the positions of chairman of SLORC, head of state, secretary of defense, and commander-in-chief of the armed forces.

THE SENIOR GENERAL—Than Shwe was born February 2, 1933, in Kyaukse, near Mandalay. After graduation from high school he worked as a postal clerk and then enlisted in the military when he was twenty years old. He graduated from Officer Training School in Hmawbi and in 1958 he was attached to the Psychological Warfare Department in the wars against the Shan and the Karen. He was promoted to captain in 1960, lieutenant colonel in 1972, and colonel in 1978. In 1983, after thirty years in the army, he was given command of the military district that included the Irrawaddy Delta in the southwest. Than Shwe's patience paid off in 1985 when he was promoted to brigadier general, Vice Chief of

Staff of the Army, and Vice-Minister of Defense. The following year he moved up to major general and he gained a seat on the ruling party's Central Executive Committee. At the time of the 1988 pro-democracy demonstrations, Than Shwe was serving as the chairman of the BSPP's Regional Committee in Irrawaddy Division. Considered General Saw Maung's right-hand man, he was one of the twenty-one founding members of SLORC, subsequently replacing his mentor in 1992.

On his way up the ladder, Than Shwe was considered a simple, honest, obedient soldier. He read *Time* magazine, chewed betel nut, and played golf. He was married to Daw Kyoing Kyoing, a member of the Pa-O ethnic group in Mon State. Unlike the other generals, he sent his children to school in an army truck instead of a luxury sedan. Sullen, slow-moving, and given to long, boring speeches in which he railed against neocolonialists, Than Shwe was seen as a figurehead. Although it is true that other generals did more work than he did, Than Shwe would eventually prove himself much worse than a mere figurehead.

DEALING WITH THE ETHNIC MINORITIES: WARS AND CEASE-FIRES—Khin Nyunt was in charge of dealing with the multiple insurgencies around the country and he signed ceasefire agreements with seventeen different groups. On the surface, this ceasefire strategy seemed like an effort to achieve peace, but in practice he turned many of the ethnic armies into subsidiaries of the national army, giving them government approval to exploit the locals in their area, sometimes in brutal fashion, in exchange for an agreement to not attack outside their region. When the Karen National Union, which had been fighting the government since 1953, split into Buddhist and Christian factions in December 1994, Khin Nyunt arranged for the national army to support the Buddhist faction, which was able to torture and kill Christians who refused to convert to Buddhism. When ceasefires didn't work, the military junta used other tactics. Between 1996 and 2004, they emptied 2,500 villages, forcibly relocating more than half a million people, including 300,000 in Shan State alone. In 1998, Khin Nyunt formed the Dam Byan Byaut Kyu, Guerrilla Retaliation Units made up of five to ten soldiers who would enter villages, seize a suspected opponent, and execute and decapitate him.

BURMA'S COMPULSORY VOLUNTARY ORGANIZATION—On September 15, 1993, Than Shwe became the patron and chairman of the newly formed Union Solidarity Development Association (USDA), which was meant to be a political organization for the masses. It wasn't difficult to convince people to join because members earned an exemption from forced labor, as well as passes that allowed travel around the country. Just to be on the safe side, all civil servants were required to join, as were teachers and students.

THE LADY REAPPEARS—In 1995, Than Shwe met with Aung San Suu Kyi at her home, after which she was released from a six-year house arrest. There were rumors that her release was a precondition for Japanese development aid. On January 4, 1996, the NLD held an Independence Day celebration at Aung San Suu Kyi's home. Two comedians, U Par Par Lay and U Lu Zaw, performed a pantomime that satirized the regime. They were arrested and sentenced to seven years in prison. Aung San Suu Kyi tried to attend the trial in Mandalay, but was stopped at the Rangoon train station. In May, the NLD announced that it would hold a meeting in honor of the sixth anniversary of its 1990 election victory. SLORC responded by arresting hundreds of MP-elects and their supporters. Suu Kyi held informal rallies at the gate of her compound every weekend, where she and other NLD leaders would speak and answer questions. But in December 1996, the military junta banned her meetings and also closed the universities in Rangoon and Mandalay, while arresting 2,000 peaceful demonstrators.

On November 15, 1997, SLORC changed its name, which was too evil-sounding, to the softer State Peace and Development Council (SPDC). By this time, Maung Aye, in charge of military offensives, was overseeing a major acceleration in the construction of military bases and barracks, as the Tatmadaw increased its public presence across the country. Khin Nyunt, meanwhile, was still in charge of harassing NLD members and their families and breaking up and buying off ethnic armies.

On the eighth anniversary of its election victory, the NLD asked for recognition of the 1990 election results. The SPDC responded by arresting hundreds of NLD supporters. It also prevented Aung San Suu Kyi from leaving Rangoon, twice confining her in her car. In early 1999, her husband learned that he was dying of prostate cancer. The SPDC refused to grant him a visa to visit his wife, insisting that Aung San Suu Kyi go visit him in Oxford. Fully aware that if she left Burma she would not be allowed to return, she refused. Whenever she tried to speak to her husband on the telephone, the government cut the line. Michael Aris died, without seeing his wife again, on his fifty-third birthday, March 27, 1999.

In October 1999, Burmese students occupied the Burmese Embassy in Bangkok. The Thai government showed sympathy to the students, outraging the generals in Rangoon, who shut down the border between Burma and Thailand. After the two governments reconciled and the border was reopened, the Burmese erected on their side of the border two statues of King Bayinnaung, who was famous for invading Thailand (then known as Siam) in the mid-sixteenth century.

Aung San Suu Kyi and U Tin Oo were again put under house arrest in September 2000. Suu Kyi was released on May 6, 2002, and soon began traveling outside Rangoon again. Wherever she went, she was greeted by large crowds. On her sixth trip, in December, the authorities used fire hoses to disperse a gathering of 20,000 NLD supporters.

THE DEPAYIN INCIDENT—On May 6, 2003, Aung San Suu Kyi, accompanied by U Tin Oo and ten male NLD youth, set out on her eighth trip, this one to Kachin State, northwest of Mandalay. On May 24, the government put all armed organizations, including the army and the police, on a state of emergency. The next day, 100 members of Than Shwe's USDA attacked Aung San Suu Kyi's motorcade with bricks, slingshots, knives, and sticks. That same day, the government released prisoners from Mandalay Prison, paid them 300,000 kyat each, and taught them how to attack the NLD. Local authorities also paid 3,000 recruits 500 Kyat a day and free meals to protest against Suu Kyi as she passed through their district.

At 6:30 p.m. on May 30, Aung San Suu Kyi and her motorcade of twenty cars and twenty-five motorcycles left Butalin Township for Depayin Township. Some of her support-ers tried to follow her on motorcycles, but, unbeknownst to the NLD motorcade ahead, they were stopped and beaten by the police, who killed a monk and a student. Two hours later, the motorcade was three miles short of Depayin when they found the main road blocked by logs and they were forced to take an alternate route through a forest. Thousands of villagers came out and a monk asked Aung San Suu Kyi to give a speech. She declined because of the late hour. Suddenly, several hundred USDA members attacked the motorcade from behind and the NLD representatives found themselves under attack from all sides by police, soldiers, prisoners, and USDA members dressed as monks carrying guns, sharpened bamboo sticks, slingshots, and steel and iron pipes. Eleven people were killed and Suu Kyi, attacked in her car with sticks, was injured on the right side of her face and on her shoulder. Her driver man-aged to reach Depayin, where the villagers chanted "Long live Daw Aung San Suu Kyi." Nonetheless, Suu Kyi and eighteen other NLD members were arrested and placed in "protec-tive custody" in Yemon Military Camp outside of Rangoon. There she was held incommuni-cado for four months.

The Depayin attack signaled an ominous shift in tactics for the military regime, as well as a power struggle between two factions in the junta leadership. The so-called pragmatists, led by Khin Nyunt, believed in dealing with the ethnic armies by pitting them against each other, and with the pro-democracy opposition by placating foreign governments with super-ficial gestures and drawing out the process of writing a new constitution for as long as possi-ble. (By 2006, this process had been going on for thirteen years and the National Convention in charge had not yet gone through half of the provisions to be discussed.) It says a lot about the state of human rights in Burma that Khin Nyunt, the brutal head of military intelligence, is considered a moderate. Yet, relatively speaking, it is true because the other faction, the hardliners led by Than Shwe, believed in simply crushing the pro-democracy movement and the ethnic armies.

THAN SHWE TAKES CHARGE—The Depayin attack on Aung San Suu Kyi was a sign that Than Shwe intended to impose his will on the country. On October 19, 2004, Than Shwe had Khin Nyunt arrested, and he promoted Lt. General Soe Win, the presumed planner of the Depayin attack, to prime minister. To a certain extent, Than Shwe's coup-within-a-coup had more to do with money than political power. Than Shwe abolished Khin Nyunt's National Intelligence Bureau and confiscated all the businesses owned by military intelligence, including mines, farms, hotels, karaoke bars, massage parlors, and the border trade with China and Thailand. Than Shwe fired two Supreme Court justices who refused to provide advice in favor of convicting Khin Nyunt, and he reportedly even ordered the detention of Khin Nyunt's personal astrologer. He cleaned out military intelligence, sending 2,500 intelligence agents to the army infantry and replacing them with untrained soldiers and police officers.

THE TATMADAW—Than Shwe's armed force, the Tatmadaw, is run separately from the rest of the country. It is a self-perpetuating elite that operates its own health care system, its own educational system, its own housing, and even its own private banks. By incorporating Khin Nyunt's holdings into the Ministry of Defense, Than Shwe created a financial empire that rivals that of Burma itself. For years, between a third and a half of Burma's budget has gone to the military. Yet in 1998, rations for soldiers were cut so far that military units in the field were ordered to pursue a Self-Reliance Program in which they would provide their own food, either by growing it, buying it from villagers or, more often than not, by confiscating it from the local population. In conflict areas, the Tatmadaw forces villagers to build and maintain army barracks and makes them supply the materials for building. The villagers are not compensated. Government troops often exploit villagers shamelessly. For example, in December 2004, troops guarding a pipeline built by the French oil company Total in southern Burma extorted money from two villages for the right to conduct Buddhist ceremonies. In January 2005, Muslim Rohingyas in Arakan State were forced to pay for permission to conduct Eid-ul-Adha prayer services. Locals, including young girls and boys, are routinely raped by troops. A 2002 report by the Shan Women's Action Network and the Shan Human Rights Foundation concluded that one-quarter of rape victims in Shan State were murdered by the soldiers who raped them. A similar study in 2004 in Karen State came up with the same results.

It is estimated that 20 percent of the Burmese armed forces are underage children. At least nineteen armed opposition groups also use children. In the case of the government, they have been known to seize orphans and street children and to snatch other children on their way to school, sometimes changing their names to prevent their families from finding them.

THE CULTURAL ZOO—In 2004, the government forced the Salon Sea Gypsies of Tennaserim Division out of their boats and transported them to islands, where the Sea Gypsies were turned into a tourist attraction.

ASEAN: MIXED MESSAGES—In 1997, The Association of Southeast Asian Nations (ASEAN) accepted Burma as a member. The Burmese generals were so thrilled by this sign of legitimacy that they ordered a song to be written about it. In 2005, it came to be Burma's turn to host the annual ASEAN Summit and chair the organization. The ASEAN nations account for 50 percent of foreign investment in Burma and the military regime enthusiastically prepared for the event, constructing apartments for the delegates and upgrading hotels and the airport. But there was such an outcry that allowing Burma to host the summit would be an embarrassment that, after tense negotiations, Than Shwe was forced to lose face by giving up the chairmanship of ASEAN and allowing the summit to be moved to Malaysia.

CAPITAL FLIGHT—In October 2005, Than Shwe's government raised gasoline prices 900 percent and bus fares 500 percent. He dealt with rising discontent with his policies in a novel manner. He announced on November 26 that the nation's capital, which had been Rangoon for 120 years, would be moved to Pyinmana, a town of 30,000 people 245 miles to the north, known primarily for its cultivation of sugar cane and bamboo shoots. Than Shwe was not the first world ruler to move his capital, but the way he went about it was unusual. Along with the unexpected announcement, he gave all civil servants forty-eight hours to leave their families behind and move to Pyinmana. Because government employees in Burma are not allowed to resign without per-

A MILITARY CONVOY MOVES EQUIPMENT, PEOPLE, AND EVEN OFFICE FURNITURE TO THE NEW BURMESE CAPITAL.
AP Photo

mission, they had no choice but to drop everything and leave immediately. When they arrived in Pyinmana, they discovered that the new capital was still under construction, with Chinese companies hard at work. Although residences and facilities for Than Shwe and other government leaders had already been completed, the civil servants were forced to sleep in shells of uncompleted buildings or outdoors. Foreigners were barred from entering the area, and foreign governments were informed that space would be provided to them to build new embassies—in late 2007.

FORCED LABOR—One abusive practice that distinguishes Than Shwe and the Burmese generals from most other dictatorships is their extensive use of forced labor, both for infrastructure projects, such as roads, bridges, and airports, and in support of the military. Typically, military officers call a village meeting and explain how many villagers they need for a project and the village headman is expected to supply the personnel. Because men are needed in the fields, families are often forced to send women and children instead. There is a Buddhist tradition called *loh ah pay,* which is voluntary labor performed to gain merit, such as cleaning a temple or pagoda. The Burmese military leaders claim that forced labor is really *loh ah pay* and that, in the words of Soe Nyunt, the director-general of the Labor Department, if forced labor was eradicated, Burma would "suffer a loss of culture."

FORCED LABOR TASKS—Among the many tasks that villagers are expected to perform without pay are clearing brush and grass in and around military camps, building fences, cutting firewood, carrying water, cooking, cleaning barracks, constructing sentry posts, and delivering messages to other camps. Villagers are also expected to give up cropland to the army and to cultivate rice and other crops for the soldiers. The Tatmadaw also forces villagers to serve as "operation porters," sometimes for weeks at a time, carrying supplies for the soldiers. Men are expected to carry 49 kilograms, women 33, and children 16. In war zones, villagers are sometimes forced to walk in front of the troops, acting as human minesweepers. Female operation porters can be forced to submit to sex by the soldiers at night.

In order to deflect the criticism of the International Labor Organization and human rights groups, the Tatmadaw has taken to using prisoners for forced labor and as human minesweepers and shields. When not enough prisoners are available, the authorities arbitrarily arrest villagers for borderline or nonexistent crimes, converting them from civilians to prisoners overnight.

The Burmese generals also practice forced conscription. After the 2003 Depayin Incident, all civil servants and all males aged eighteen to forty were compelled to undergo military training. Both soldiers and police are not allowed to leave at the end of their term unless they have recruited three or four replacements.

HOLDING FOREIGN COMPANIES RESPONSIBLE—In 1996, the French-Belgian oil company Total paid compensation to 463 victims of forced labor in Burma. Six years later, more lawsuits were filed against Total in both Belgium and France. This time, Total executives were charged with paying Burmese army battalions and encouraging forced labor. EarthRights International also filed suit in 1996 against the California oil company Unocal on behalf of Burmese villagers who had been forced to work on the Yadana gas pipeline project in Tenasserim Division and who had experienced rape and murder at the hands of the Burmese military. In a landmark ruling in June 2004, the U.S. Supreme Court ruled 6–3 that the Alien Tort Claims Act could be used by foreigners to file lawsuits in the United States about abuses committed abroad. In response, in December 2004, Unocal settled the suits that had been filed against it in both California and federal courts before they went to trial.

JUSTICE, BURMESE STYLE—Prisoners in Burma can be held three years without trial. Torture has been documented since 1962 and is used by the police, the army, ethnic armies and, especially, by military intelligence. Torture techniques include electrocution, sleep deprivation, covering a prisoner's head with plastic and pouring water on him, kneeling on glass, hanging by the arms or feet, and putting bullets or pencils between the fingers and squeezing hard. Political activists are often beaten as soon as they arrive at the prison gate. Most political trials take place behind closed doors and the defendants are not allowed legal counsel, nor are they allowed to call witnesses.

CENSORSHIP—According to the Reporters Without Borders 2005 World Press Freedom Index, Burma ranked 163rd out of 167 nations. Even though the government controls all media, the Press Scrutiny Board examines every publication and prohibits "any incorrect ideas and opinions which do not accord with the times." Among the many forbidden topics are AIDS, human rights, drugs, the arrest of Khin Nyunt, and natural disasters, including the December 26, 2004, tsunami (because earthquakes are considered a harbinger of governmental change). All e-mail is monitored and all Internet search engines are blocked.

WOMEN IN GOVERNMENT—Although Burma has a National Women's Affairs Committee, half of the thirty-two members are men, including the chairman and vice-chairman.

THINGS THAT ARE ILLEGAL IN BURMA—

- According to the 1950 Emergency Provisions Act, which is still in force, it is illegal to engage in an act that "causes or intends to disrupt the morality or behavior of a group of people or the general public," punishable by seven years in prison. It is also illegal to make a written or verbal statement that could "cause misunderstanding among the people."

- In 1997, MP-elect Dr. Tin Min Htut was charged with violating the 1947 Foreign Currency Exchange Act because his son was caught playing with two coins from Singapore in a tin cup.

- James Nichols, the honorary consul representing Scandinavia, died in prison in 1996 while serving three years for unauthorized use of a fax machine.

- After the 2004 arrest of Khin Nyunt, one of his spokesmen, Colonel Hla Min, was charged with possession of a service revolver and "living beyond his means."

- In 1996, Than Shwe issued an order making it illegal, subject to twenty years' imprisonment, to criticize the National Convention in charge of creating a new constitution or to draft an independent version of a constitution.

- In December 2004, NLD members were prosecuted for failing to register overnight guests and sentenced to seven years in prison.

- Fourteen NLD members were arrested on December 6, 2004, for "conspiring to celebrate the National Day" without permission.

- In October 1997, MP-elect Dr. May Win Myint was sentenced to seven years in prison for traveling with Aung San Suu Kyi inside Rangoon. After he completed his sentence, he was kept in prison anyway.

- A video shop in Sittwe, in Arakan State, was raided in January 2005, and the shop owners were arrested and fined for renting out tapes of the December 26, 2004, tsunami and its aftermath. The tapes were copies of news broadcasts from CNN and the BBC.

- In February 2005, the magazine *Han Thit* (New Style) was suspended for two months for carrying an advertisement that mentioned St. Valentine's Day.

- The current affairs magazine *Khit-Sann* was closed down in September 2004 for being too "pro-American."

- In November 2003, three men were sentenced to death for charges that included possessing the business card of an officer of the International Labor Organization (ILO) and possessing ILO documents. Two of the three were released after fourteen months.

- In 2004, numerous people were arrested for "hiding in the dark," including some who were seized in broad daylight.

- On January 19, 2004, twenty-six monks were sentenced to eighteen years in prison for refusing to accept donations from military authorities.

- In December 2003, Ko Thet Lwin, a forty-six-year-old man employed by the Canadian firm Ivanhoe Mines Ltd., was sentenced to seven years in prison for accompanying a foreign colleague to the home of Aung San Suu Kyi.

- Women caught possessing a condom can be charged with prostitution. Abortions are illegal (although approximately 750,000 are performed each year).

- In September 2004, four Rohingya Muslims were given sentences of five years for repairing a village mosque.

- In July 2003, Zaw Thet Htwe, the editor of a sports magazine, was arrested after he wrote an article questioning the government's use of a $4 million grant to develop football (soccer). He was charged with plotting to assassinate military officials and sentenced to death. After a year and a half of international pressure, he was released.

- In September 2004, in Ye Township, the Thein Kabar Tea Shop was fined for "creating conflict" by playing the Burmese version of BBC radio's World Service.

- In June 2004, the government declared it against the law to possess a CD of the Burmese exile hip-hop group Myanmar Future Generation (MFG).

(Claudia Daul/Reuters/Corbis)

4.

ROBERT MUGABE—ZIMBABWE

THE NATION—Zimbabwe is a mineral-rich country in southern Africa. Its population of about thirteen million consists primarily of the Shona (75 percent), who live in the eastern two-thirds of the country, known as Mashonaland, and the Ndebele, also known as the Matebele, (18 percent), who live in the west in Matabeleland. The average life expectancy for Zimbabweans is only thirty-nine years. In 2006, Zimbabwe had the world's highest inflation rate (more than 1000 percent), unemployment stood at 80 percent, and one-third of the population had AIDS. During most of the colonial period, the country was known as Southern Rhodesia and from 1964 through 1979 as Rhodesia. The name Zimbabwe is derived from the Shona phrase "dzimba dza mabwe," meaning "houses of stone." Robert Mugabe's life is a tragic tale of a man who had the opportunity to be a leader of postcolonial democratic Africa, but who chose instead to be a vindictive and murderous dictator.

PRECOLONIAL ZIMBABWE—The original inhabitants of present-day Zimbabwe were Bushmen whose language, with its unusual clicking sounds, fascinated early European academics. However, when settlers arrived, they found it difficult to befriend the reticent Bushmen and so hunted down and killed them instead. The current population of Zimbabwe has its origins in the Bantu people of the Niger/Congo region who, over a period of 2,000 years, spread throughout sub-equatorial Africa. By the tenth century, the Karangas, Shona-speaking descendants of the Bantu, had colonized present-day Zimbabwe, Malawi, and the lowlands of Mozambique. The Karangas discovered and worked with gold, tin, and copper and built the royal palace of Zimbabwe in the eleventh century. They also established a trade in gold and ivory, which they transported to Mozambique, from whence Arab merchants shipped it as far away as India and China. In the fifteenth century, the Rotsi, a Shona-speaking people from the south, took over the royal palace of Zimbabwe. The Portuguese, lured by the gold and ivory, colonized Mozambique and replaced the Arabs as the Rotsi's trading partners.

In 1834, Moselekatse, a Zulu general, broke with the chief he had been serving and fled north, forcing the Rotsi to retreat to the west. Moselekatse and his followers settled in the Matopos Hills and became known as the Matabele: "those who blend easily with the bush." The Rotsi, or Shona, became subjects of the Matabele.

THE UNAVOIDABLE WHITES—The Dutch began colonizing southern Africa in the early 1600s and the British in the early 1800s. When, in 1833, the House of Commons outlawed slavery in all British dominions, the Dutch settlers, known as Boers or Afrikaners, who were dependent on slaves, migrated north in the "Great Trek." Fighting their way through the Zulus, they established their own republics, the Natalia, the Orange Free State, and the Transvaal.

THE RHODESIAN—Cecil Rhodes was born in Hertfordshire, England, in 1853. Suffering from tuberculosis, he was sent, at the age of seventeen, to the British southern African colony of Natal, where his older brother was already running a cotton plantation. When diamonds were discovered in the Orange Free State, Rhodes moved there and formed a business selling excavating equipment. In 1880, he founded the De Beers Diamond Mining Company. When gold was discovered in the Transvaal, Rhodes invested in the fields and, in 1887, established the Goldfields of South Africa Company. In 1888, he sent his partners north and they made contact with the king of the Matabele, Moselekatse's son, Lobengala. Lobengala signed away the mineral rights to his kingdom for 1,000 rifles, 10,000 bullets, a steamboat, and £1,200 a year. The following year, the British government granted Rhodes a royal charter for his British South Africa Company (BSAC).

Reports of gold having been discovered in Mashonaland was sufficient motivation for

Cecil Rhodes to order an expedition to the area. One hundred eighty adventurers, all under the age of twenty-five, accompanied by hundreds of armed militia, set off on a 400-mile trek to Mashonaland under the guidance of elephant hunter Frederick Courteney Selous. Dubbed the Pioneer Column, they left on June 28, 1890, with the promise of a farm each and gold claims. When it turned out that there were no significant deposits of gold, many of the Pioneers left. Those who stayed were the first white colonizers of Mashonaland. A BSAC administrator, Dr. Leander Starr Jameson, encouraged more British to emigrate and, without bothering to consult with the Mashona who were already living there, parceled out land to the white settlers. Within ten years, the whites had seized one-sixth of the land—sixteen million acres. They had also disrupted the economy of the Matabele, who had long been collecting tribute from the Mashona. Jameson then demanded that the Matabele vacate the area. When they refused, the Matabele War broke out in 1896. The British used Maxim machine guns to push back the Matabele and went in search of King Lobengula, who took his own life. The British named the country Southern Rhodesia in honor of Cecil Rhodes.

In Transvaal, gold really was discovered, which, naturally, attracted Rhodes' attention. Hoping to overthrow the Boer government, Rhodes sent Jameson to invade Transvaal in January 1896. The invasion failed and Rhodes was forced to resign as both the managing director of the BSAC and as prime minister of Britain's Cape Colony.

The Boer victory proved to the Matabele that the British were not invincible. In March 1896, they rose up against the Europeans, as did the Mashona, killing more than 10 percent of the European population. Cecil Rhodes managed to negotiate a peace settlement and the fighting came to an end in October 1897. The following year, the Native Reserves Order in Council created reserves for the blacks on low-quality land, while the whites were promised a degree of self-government.

On the eve of World War I, there were 836,000 blacks in Southern Rhodesia and 28,000 whites, yet the whites owned three-quarters of the land. The British and the Boers had already fought against each other in two wars and tensions between the two were rising again when World War I broke out and the Europeans were distracted by their fight against the Germans. In a referendum in October 1923, the whites in Southern Rhodesia voted for self-government rather than joining the thirteen-year-old Union of South Africa. The Land Apportionment Act of 1930 allotted 49 million acres to Southern Rhodesia's 50,000 whites and 29 million acres to its black population of 1.1 million. It also prohibited black Africans from owning land in white areas.

THE MAN—Robert Mugabe was born February 21, 1924, at the Katuma Jesuit Mission, fifty miles west of Salisbury (now Harare), on land donated by the British South Africa

Company because Jesuits had accompanied the Pioneer Column in 1890. Robert was the third of six children born to Gabriel Mugabe, the Mission's carpenter, and his wife Bona, both of whom were Roman Catholics. Robert was a bookish child who took advantage of the good education offered by the Jesuits. In 1934, Father Jerome O'Hea was appointed head of the Jesuit mission. A native of Ireland, he was keenly aware of his own people's struggle against the British and he was a strong advocate of black education. O'Hea added to Katuma a technical college, a teacher-training college, and a hospital. He preached equality of the races and spoke out against the racial discrimination that poisoned the rest of the country.

Two of Mugabe's older brothers died of disease while he was still a child. When Robert was ten years old, his father deserted the family, leaving Robert and his remaining siblings to be raised by their mother and their grandparents. Recognizing his intelligence, Father O'Hea enrolled Robert in the Katuma teacher-training college. When he was seventeen years old, he took a job as a primary school teacher in order to support his mother and his siblings. Three years later, his father reappeared, after a ten-year absence, with a new wife and three more children. His father died shortly thereafter and Robert had six children to support. When he was twenty-one years old, Mugabe left Katuma to take a teaching position and met the Reverend Ndabaningi Sithole, who, decades later, would play an important role in Zimbabwe's political development.

In 1949, Mugabe earned a scholarship to the all-black University of Fort Hare in Cape Province, South Africa. It was at Fort Hare that the African National Congress (ANC) had been founded in 1912 and from which Nelson Mandela had been expelled for leading a student strike in 1940. Mugabe joined the Youth League of the ANC and met several important political activists including Oliver Tambo of the ANC, the South African Zulu leader Mangosuthu Buthelezi, and Leopold Takawiri, who introduced him to Marxism. But for all his interest in politics, Mugabe was a serious student who did not smoke or drink and who earned degrees in history and English literature.

Mugabe returned to Southern Rhodesia in 1952, taught school, and earned another degree in education. At the time, 90 percent of blacks in Southern Rhodesia were literate, yet apartheid (the Afrikaans word for "separateness") had been the official racial policy since 1933. The white minority referred to all black males as "Boy" regardless of their ages. In Gwelo, the town where Mugabe lived, "WHITES ONLY" signs were posted in front of the library, department stores, the swimming pool, and elsewhere. Blacks on tobacco plantations worked up to eighteen hours a day, six days a week. In 1953, the British combined Southern and Northern Rhodesia with Nyasaland to create the administrative entity of Rhodesia and Nyasaland. In 1958, Garfield Todd, the prime minister of the Federation, was removed from office for being too sympathetic to the black population.

THE DAWN OF THE LIBERATION MOVEMENT—In 1957, Ghana was about to become the first British African colony to achieve independence. Its soon-to-be-president, Kwame Nkrumah, invited Africans from other countries to come to Ghana to teach and to study and to spread the movement for African liberation. Mugabe was one of the idealists who responded. In Ghana, he soaked up the rhetoric and the spirit of activism. He would later explain, "I wanted to see what it would be like in an independent African state. Once there, I began to develop definite ideas. You could say that it was there I accepted the general principles of Marxism." It was also in Ghana that, at the age of thirty-five, he met the woman he would later marry, a Ghanaian teacher named Sally Heyfron.

Back in Rhodesia, the African National Congress was launched as a national party, led by Joshua Nkomo, who was chosen for his moderate image. Nkomo and the ANC tried not to scare the white population and emphasized goals that would be viewed as reasonable, such as abolition of discriminatory laws and the extension of the right to vote. At the time, the right to vote was based on income, so that only 560 black Africans were included in the list of 52,000 eligible voters. The ANC touched a nerve in the black population and quickly grew into a mass movement that called for redistribution of land. Some ANC members began guerrilla attacks. The Rhodesian government declared a state of emergency on February 26, 1959, banned all political parties advocating African nationalism, and imprisoned hundreds of their leaders. In 1960, nationalists launched a more radical group, the National Democratic Party (NDP), that demanded not just land redistribution but political power for the black majority.

Mugabe returned to Rhodesia in May 1960, in order to introduce Sally to his family before they married. He intended to return to Ghana to complete his teaching contract there, but nationalist friends of his asked him to stay and to join their cause. In July, police arrested three NDP leaders, one of whom was one of Mugabe's closest friends. Mugabe joined a 7,000-strong demonstration outside the prime minister's office. Riot police opened fire on the crowd. The day after the "March of the 7,000," half of the black workforce did not show up for work and the number of demonstrators swelled to 40,000. Mugabe spoke to the crowd and presented his vision of a future Zimbabwe that would be African-ruled, like Ghana. The unrest spread and the British colonial government passed the Law and Order (Maintenance) Amendment Act. This law gave the government a free hand in curbing freedom of speech, assembly, movement, association, and privacy. The police were given unlimited powers to arrest and detain anyone without trial. Anything that seemed to encourage the violent overthrow of the colonial government was deemed "an act of terrorism," punishable by life imprisonment. The white chief justice of Rhodesia, Sir Robert Tredgold, resigned in protest, publicly stating, "This bill outrages every basic right. . . . It will remove the last vestige of doubt about whether Rhodesia is a police state."

Mugabe gave up his teaching post in Ghana, married Sally, and was elected publicity secretary of the NDP. In 1961, the British government held a conference to decide Rhodesia's future. Joshua Nkomo, as president of the NDP, headed a nationalist delegation that took part in the conference. Nkomo agreed to the creation of a constitution that gave blacks token representation in a parliament. Mugabe and other NDP members were outraged by Nkomo's capitulation, and Mugabe's own rhetoric turned more harsh. "Europeans must realize," he told one rally, "that unless the legitimate demands of African nationalism are recognized, then racial conflict is inevitable." He urged the crowd to remove their shoes and socks as a symbol of their rejection of European civilization. In December 1961, he told an NDP meeting, "If European-owned industries are used to buy guns which are aimed against us, we must withdraw our labor and our custom, and destroy those industries." Six days later, the government banned the NDP. The nationalists simply formed a new party, the Zimbabwe African Peoples Union (ZAPU). Mugabe was again named publicity secretary and Nkomo returned as party president.

The more violent nationalists began attacking white schools and churches, burning crops and forests and sabotaging railway lines. After nine months, the government banned ZAPU, arrested Mugabe and other leaders, and restricted them to their home districts for three months in an attempt to calm the situation in the capital of Salisbury. When Mugabe returned, he was arrested for giving a speech in which he referred to the Law and Order Act as "the legislation of murder." His wife Sally was also arrested when she accused Great Britain of abandoning black Africans and said, "The Queen can go to Hell."

Joshua Nkomo told Mugabe that other African leaders had recommended that ZAPU's executives leave the country and establish a government-in-exile in Dar es Salaam, Tanganyika. Mugabe reluctantly agreed, but when he and Sally arrived in Dar es Salaam they discovered that Nkomo had lied to them to get Mugabe and other nationalist opponents out of the country. Mugabe now found himself stuck outside Zimbabwe with a pregnant wife and new charges against him for breaking bail when he left.

Back in Salisbury, his colleagues formed an anti-Nkomo nationalist party, the Zimbabwe African National Union (ZANU). Mugabe's old friend, Reverend Ndabaningi Sithole, was chosen president and Mugabe, in absentia, was elected secretary-general. In Matabeleland, the armed wings of ZAPU and ZANU went to war against each other, which did not encourage the Rhodesian whites about the prospects for black rule.

A DECADE IN PRISON—In December 1963, Mugabe sent his wife and three-month-old son, Nhamodzenyika, to Ghana and returned to Zimbabwe where he was immediately arrested. Sentenced to twenty-one months in prison in March 1964, he was placed in a maximum security prison in Salisbury. In August, the new right-wing leader of Rhodesia, Ian Smith, banned ZAPU and ZANU and sent Nkomo to prison with a ten-year sentence.

Mugabe made the most of his years of incarceration, earning three more degrees through correspondence with the University of London and creating a school for his fellow prisoners. When his son died of cerebral malaria in 1966, Ian Smith personally rejected Mugabe's request to attend the funeral. That same year, ZANU guerrillas killed a white farmer and his wife. This led the government to transfer ZANU's leaders, including Mugabe, to Salisbury's Central Prison, where he shared a communal cell with Reverend Sithole. Mugabe would remain in this prison for eight years.

FREE AT LAST—In 1974, outside events caused a chain reaction that led to Mugabe's release from prison. Far away in Portugal, General António de Spínola staged a coup and announced plans to withdraw Portuguese troops from Angola and Mozambique and to grant independence to both nations. Faced with the prospect of two hostile, black-ruled nations on his border, the white president of South Africa, John Vorster, pressured Ian Smith to make peace with ZANU and ZAPU in Rhodesia. In November 1974, Smith released Mugabe, Nkomo, and Sithole from prison. Having been incarcerated for ten years and four months, Mugabe was Africa's second-longest-held political prisoner. Only Nelson Mandela of South Africa spent more time in prison.

Fearing rearrest, Mugabe left for Mozambique, which achieved independence two months later. Mozambique's president, Samora Machel, offered Mugabe and his wife a villa, and they lived there for the next four years. With black rule in their own nation increasingly possible, Zimbabwe's nationalist leaders, Mugabe, Sithole, Nkomo, and Bishop Abel Muzorewa, tried to set aside their differences and work together against Ian Smith and the white Rhodesians. In November 1975, the military wings of ZANU and ZAPU joined forces to form the Zimbabwe People's Army. However, their rivalry could not be hidden. When the Soviets who were supplying arms to the army insisted that Mugabe recognize Nkomo as the movement's leader, Mugabe turned to the Chinese for weapons. Later he would also reach out for aid to the Soviet Union, North Korea, Cuba, and Vietnam.

Alarmed by the growth of Communist involvement in the guerrilla struggles in southern Africa, U.S. president Gerald Ford sent his secretary of state, Henry Kissinger, to the region to protect American interests. With Kissinger's support, Ian Smith announced that he would accept black majority rule in Zimbabwe as long as the whites retained control of the army and the police. In October 1976, Mugabe and Nkomo issued a joint statement flatly rejecting the proposal. Over the next three years, the nationalist parties, their armies, and their leaders maneuvered for position in preparation for the increasingly inevitable assumption of power by the black majority. White farmers were driven from their homes in the east; ZANU

ROBERT MUGABE AND JOSHUA NKOMO,
RELUCTANT PARTNERS IN 1979
Hulton-Deutsch/Corbis

blew up Salisbury's largest fuel depot, destroying a month's fuel supplies; Muzorewa briefly led a superficial transitional government; and then, in October 1979, Mugabe and Nkomo agreed to the creation of a new constitution. The Lancaster House Agreement declared Zimbabwe a sovereign republic and all political parties were allowed to campaign for a February 1980 election for a bicameral legislature. The House of Assembly would consist of eighty black members and twenty white members. The Senate would have forty members, fourteen black, ten white, ten to be elected by the Council of Chiefs, and six to be nominated by the president on the recommendation of the prime minister.

The ZANU Manifesto, approved by Mugabe, stated, "ZANU wishes to give the fullest assurance to the white community, and the Asian and coloured communities, that a ZANU government can never in principle or in social or government practice, discriminate against them." After five years in Mozambique, Mugabe returned to Zimbabwe and, at a press conference, told the country, "The State of Zimbabwe must be truly democratic." However, the election campaign was punctuated with violence. There were two assassination attempts on Mugabe, including one in which a grenade was thrown at his house. His supporters retaliated by bombing two churches in Salisbury. When a leftist paper described Mugabe as "a psychopath suffering from paranoia," their printing press was bombed. On election day, ZANU guerrillas intimidated voters at polling stations. The election results were announced on March 4, 1980. Mugabe's party won fifty-seven seats in the Assembly, a majority. Nkomo's party gained twenty seats and Muzorewa's party three seats. Mugabe offered Nkomo the ceremonial post of president, which he refused, eventually settling for the minister of home affairs, which gave him control of the police. Robert Mugabe took over as the first prime minister of independent Zimbabwe.

THE HONEYMOON—On the day of the announcement of his victory, Robert Mugabe told the nation, in a nationally televised acceptance speech, "There is no intention on our part to use our majority to victimize the minority." He included two white men in his cabinet and appointed a white military officer, Lt. General Peter Walls, supreme commander of the armed forces. When the British flag was replaced with the flag of Zimbabwe, he tried to reassure the white population by pledging that "The wrongs of the past must be forgiven and forgotten." Despite all these gracious words, many of the 170,000 whites in Zimbabwe were edgy. Statues of Cecil Rhodes were removed and Cecil Square in the center of Salisbury was renamed Africa Unity Square. In 1982, the name of the capital city itself was changed from Salisbury to Harare. The future of the whites was unclear. Six thousand white farmers owned two-thirds of the most productive lands. They employed 300,000 people, a third of the labor force. They also dominated the economy, including banking, industry, and trade. Zimbabwean television, black-controlled for the first time, began to broadcast references to "racist whites." By the end of the year, 10 percent of the white population had left the country, most of them moving to South Africa, which was still white-ruled.

If most whites inside Zimbabwe were cautiously willing to give Mugabe a chance, outside the country he was being hailed as a hero. Here was a leader with a sellable story. Mugabe was an intelligent black African who had been born into a common family, earned multiple university degrees, served more than ten years in prison because he championed the rights of his people, helped lead the liberation of his country from colonial rule, and won a democratic election to become his nation's first prime minister. Although he had previously aligned himself with Communist regimes, he knew that it was the Western countries that had the money he needed to build a new Zimbabwe. "I think we were never really hostile to Britain as such," he said. "When we fought the war here, of course we said we were fighting colonialism and imperialism. But we were never really hostile to the British people." The British people responded with military assistance and with financing of a land distribution program. The United States offered a three-year, $225 million aid package. In its first year of independence, Zimbabwe garnered pledges of almost $2 billion.

THE HONEYMOON ENDS—But there was trouble on the horizon. Lt. General Walls revealed on television that he had appealed to British prime minister Margaret Thatcher to cancel the election results, and Mugabe ordered Walls to leave the country. In the summer of 1980, one of Mugabe's closest friends, Edgar Tekere, accused the Anglican Church of being "an instrument of oppression" and then led an attack on a white farmhouse in which an elderly white farmer was murdered. Tekere was tried for the crime, but acquitted. Problems developed between the black Zimbabwean government and the white South African government. The South Africans tried to destabilize Zimbabwe by establishing a network of spies, informers, and saboteurs inside the military and the police. In July 1982, South African raiders destroyed thirteen aircraft at Zimbabwe's main air force base. The police arrested six air force officers, charging them with collaborating in the raid, and then tortured them until they signed confessions. At their trial, a black judge, Enoch Dumbutshena, acquitted the men on the basis that their confession had been obtained by torture. The accused were still embracing their family members when Mugabe's forces had them rearrested.

In November 1982, Mugabe ordered Ian Smith's passport to be withdrawn because, during a trip to Great Britain and the United States, he had criticized the Zimbabwean government, which Mugabe considered "political bad manners and hooliganism." By the end of the third year of independence, 70,000 whites, more than 40 percent, had emigrated. When Ian Smith's party won fifteen of the twenty Assembly seats reserved for whites at the 1985 election, Mugabe declared, "Those whites who have not accepted the reality of a political order in which the Africans set the pace will have to leave the country." Then he added, in the chiShona language, "We will kill the snakes among us; we will smash them completely."

THE MASSACRES IN MATABELELAND—Mugabe continued to draw support abroad, including in Africa, for his frontline stance against the remnants of white racism and imperialism. But that changed with his stunning and barbaric attacks on his own countrymen in Matabeleland beginning in 1983.

Mugabe saw his two main enemies as the government of South Africa, which was in fact training a dissident army, and Joshua Nkomo, who had retained a 20,000-man army rooted in Matabeleland. In October 1980, Mugabe secretly signed an agreement with Kim Il-sung of North Korea to have more than one hundred North Korean advisors train a brigade of Zimbabweans to deal with internal dissidents. At a 1982 party rally, Mugabe compared having Nkomo in his cabinet to having "a cobra in the house," and he added, "The only way to deal effectively with a snake is to strike and destroy its head." He kicked Nkomo out of his government and seized his property. Then he turned his sights on Nkomo's base, Matabeleland. Instead of concentrating his wrath on Nkomo and his supporters, Mugabe treated all the Ndebele people of Matabeleland as his enemies. Portraying Nkomo as an ally of South Africa, Mugabe warned, "An eye for an eye and an ear for an ear may not be adequate in our circumstances. We might very well demand two ears for one ear and two eyes for one eye." In January 1983, he deployed the North Korean–trained 5 Brigade to Matabeleland and launched a campaign of arson and murder against the civilian population. Going from village to village, Mugabe's men killed at least 2,000 civilians in the first six weeks. Tens of thousands more were beaten. Villagers were forced to sing songs in the chiShona language and to dance on the mass graves of their recently buried family members. During one four-month period in 1984, 8,000 people were processed through an interrogation center known for torture. The 5 Brigade dumped another 8,000 bodies down an unused mine only to have the bodies float to the surface when it rained.

The government-controlled press did not report that any of this was happening, and much of the international community chose to ignore the reality of the stories that were coming out of Matabeleland. Faced with repeated assassination attempts, Nkomo fled the country. However, he returned for the 1985 election and his party won all of the fifteen seats contested in Matabeleland South. As a matter of survival, he signed a Unity Accord, merging his party with Mugabe's in exchange for amnesty. Mugabe never acknowledged the Matabeleland massacres. As he put it, "If we dig up history, then we wreck the nation."

CENTRALIZING POWER—In 1987, Mugabe abolished the position of prime minister and made himself executive president, which meant that he was head of state, head of the government, and commander-in-chief of the armed forces. He abolished the clause in the constitution that reserved twenty Assembly seats for whites, and every six months he renewed the state of emergency that gave the government the authority to detain people without trial.

WHO OWNS THE LAND?—At the time of independence in 1980, the 6,000 white commercial farmers owned 39 percent of the land, 8,000 black commercial farmers owned 4 percent, and the communal lands where four million Zimbabweans lived made up 41 percent of the land. The remaining 16 percent was national park land. By 1990, under the terms of the Lancaster House Agreement and funded by Great Britain, 416,000 people had been resettled on 6.5 million acres formerly owned by whites. Unfortunately, a good deal of the best land was given to politicians and members of the military and the police who had no farming experience. In 1990, Mugabe amended the constitution to allow the government to confiscate land at any price it deemed to be fair. He also seized the land of his political opponents, including his former ally and cellmate, Reverend Ndabaningi Sithole. In 1994, the news broke that the government had forced a white farmer to sell his 3,000-acre farm, allegedly to house thirty-three homeless peasants. In fact, the land was given to the minister of education.

In 1997, the War Veterans' Association, which had long complained of governmental neglect of veterans, engaged in street protests and even marched into a meeting between Mugabe and African-American investors and denounced Mugabe. Mugabe agreed to pay each veteran a lump sum and provide them with land, free education, and free health care. This satisfied the veterans, but it caused a massive drain on the already bankrupt economy.

With national elections on the horizon, Mugabe played the race card, ordering full-scale invasions of white farms on February 26, 2000. Although the attacks were coordinated by the War Veterans' Association, the veterans actually hired unemployed youth to do most of the dirty work. In less than two weeks, about 400 farms had been invaded and the farmers, in many cases, beaten, tortured, and even murdered. Black laborers suspected of supporting an opposition party were given the same treatment. Although the war veterans had been paid by Mugabe's party, Mugabe pretended the attacks were a spontaneous uprising. Finally, he told the nation, "We want the whites to learn that the land belongs to the Zimbabweans," and that he did not consider whites to be citizens of the country. A High Court judge ruled that the farm occupations were illegal, but Mugabe ignored the ruling and the attacks continued. When 7,000 blacks and whites joined together for a peace march on April 1, 2000, war veterans attacked them with clubs. When a policeman arrested three squatters for almost beating to death a white farmer, he himself was murdered. Some of Mugabe's own cabinet members objected to the land confiscations, but Mugabe ordered the farm invasions to continue. He considered the black farm workers and their families who lived on the white-owned farms to be his enemies. They were beaten and the women raped and their homes destroyed. By May 15, 1,400 farms had been invaded. On May 24, Mugabe signed a decree allowing the seizure of 800 farms without the payment of compensation. Mugabe's response to criticism of his actions, which came from African leaders like Nelson Mandela, was, "Where was the rule of law when our land was seized by the Rhodesians?" By the time of the election, at least thirty-seven people had been killed, although the figure was probably much higher considering that reporting cases of abuse and violence was itself dangerous.

ELECTIONS MUGABE STYLE—One of Mugabe's longtime friends, Edgar Tekere, accused Mugabe of leading the country toward dictatorship and challenged Mugabe in the 1990 presidential election. Tekere was hardly a democratic alternative, having been even more violent toward both whites and the supporters of Joshua Nkomo than Mugabe. Tekere attracted only 17 percent of the votes, as Mugabe gained his third five-year term. Prior to the 1990 parliamentary elections, students demonstrated against corruption, which was widespread. Police fired tear gas grenades at the students and the universities were shut down for the first time. Church leaders and trade union leaders spoke out against the unnecessarily brutal handling of the student protests. Morgan Tsvangirai, the secretary-general of the Zimbabwe Congress of Trade Unions, accused Mugabe of trying to suppress public expressions of discontent over poverty and unemployment. Mugabe had Tsvangirai arrested three times, as the courts kept releasing him. Shortly before the election, Mugabe increased the number of seats in the parliament from 100 to 150, including 20 that would be appointed by the president (Mugabe) and 10 by the council of chiefs, the members of which were also chosen by Mugabe. Candidates from six major parties contested the election, but in the end Mugabe's party miraculously won 117 of the 120 contested seats. In the 1995 election, they improved to 118 of 120 seats. In preparation for the 1996 presidential election, Sithole was charged with terrorism, arms possession, and conspiracy to murder Mugabe. He was released pending appeal and challenged Mugabe in the election, as did Muzorewa. It was announced that Mugabe won 92.7 percent of the vote. Sithole fled the country, traveled to the United States, and died three years later in Philadephia.

In 1999, the Zimbabwean Electricity Supply Authority, riddled with corruption, ran out of money, as did the state oil company, causing fuel shortages. Mugabe played his always reliable blame-the-whites card, claiming that white farmers had bought all of the fuel and hidden it in large drums on their farms. Morgan Tsvangirai organized a series of strikes against the corruption of Mugabe's rule and formed a new party, the Movement for Democratic Change (MDC). Mugabe accused the party of being a front for whites and the vehicle Great Britain would use to recolonize Zimbabwe. Following this fanciful theory, he branded Tsvangirai and other party leaders traitors. In February 2000, with inflation running at 58.5 percent and basic food products in short supply, Mugabe held a referendum to allow him to run for two more five-year terms and to make Great Britain responsible for paying for land reform. Although advertisements for the "Vote No" campaign were banned, the referendum was defeated 55 percent to 45 percent. Mugabe's supporters claimed they had lost because whites had come into the country from South Africa to vote, but Mugabe made the best of the situation by saying that his loss proved that Zimbabwe was a democracy.

He then tried to find new tactics to ensure that he would win the parliamentary elections in June. The main one was to blame the whites for all the problems in the country and to physically attack white farmers and the blacks who worked for them. Several farms were turned into "reeducation centers" where workers were forced to sing songs in praise of Mugabe's party, the ZANU-PF. His supporters also beat teachers in Matabeleland accused of supporting Tsvangirai and the MDC. By late May, 250 schools were forced to close and 7,000 teachers fled their homes. MDC activists were also seized and tortured. It was in this climate that the election was held. When the results were announced on June 27, it turned out that despite all of the violence and intimidation, Mugabe had only scored a narrow-victory. His ZANU-PF won sixty-two seats and the MDC fifty-seven, with one seat going to an independent. Actually, more people had voted against Mugabe than for him, but his party won anyway. Because thirty parliamentary seats were appointed, Mugabe ended up with a clear majority of seats, ninety-two to fifty-eight.

SMOTHERING THE OPPOSITION—Having narrowly escaped defeat despite all his thuggish machinations, Mugabe immediately began preparing for the 2002 presidential election. In speeches, he claimed that the MDC was fronting for a conspiracy against him organized by the old Rhodesian white leaders and supported by Great Britain and the United States. When the Supreme Court continued to rule against the land confiscations, Mugabe declared, "Whatever the courts might say on the matter, the land is ours and we will take it." His party demanded that all white judges be removed and the white chief justice, Anthony Gubbay, who had been appointed by Mugabe, was threatened by a mob. One independent newspaper, the *Daily News,* ran a front-page headline calling for Mugabe's impeachment. It was harassed, bombed, and finally closed.

In 2001, Mugabe changed the rules for voter eligibility by requiring that voters show rental agreements for their housing. Because many MDC supporters were poor and lived in makeshift shacks, they did not have rental agreements and lost the right to vote. As the Zimbabwean economy, riddled with corruption and incompetence, disintegrated, the government defaulted on its foreign loans and the vital tourism industry collapsed. Meanwhile, AIDS spread rapidly while hospitals ran out of drugs. In February 2002, the European Union and the United States issued sanctions prohibiting Mugabe and his cohorts from entering their territory, a development that Mugabe used to his favor in his election campaign. Again playing the race card, he declared, "Our party must continue to strike fear in the hearts of the white man, our real enemy." Meanwhile, Morgan Tsvangirai was gaining support among military officers and even among the war veterans. One month before the election, Australian television broadcasted a video that appeared to show Tsvangirai discussing the desirability of Mugabe's death. On February 25, sixteen days before the election, Mugabe had Tsvangirai arrested on charges of treason. Mugabe won 56 percent of the vote and Tsvangirai 42 percent, but the election was widely considered to have been rigged, with huge discrepancies in some areas between the number of votes cast and the number of eligible voters. In September, Tsvangirai, rhetorically addressing Mugabe at a rally, said, "If you don't go peacefully, we will remove you violently." Invoking the same law that the British colonial government had used to imprison him, Mugabe had Tsvangirai charged with "an act of terrorism," encouraging the violent overthrow of the government. Zimbabwe's Supreme Court acquitted Tsvangirai in October 2004.

THE SECOND WIFE—After Sally, his wife of more than twenty-five years, was diagnosed with kidney cancer, the sixty-three-year-old Mugabe began an affair with his twenty-three-year-old secretary, Grace Marufu, who was married and a mother. Mugabe and Grace had two children, a girl born in 1988 and a boy in 1990. Sally died in 1992 and Mugabe was free to remarry, which he and Grace did in 1996. Grace bore Mugabe another son in 1997. Unlike first wife Sally, a politically active intellectual, second wife Grace has earned a reputation as an expensive woman who enjoys shopping and furnishing large mansions. Once she turned a huge profit in an illegal land scheme, building a mansion in a wealthy suburb and selling it to Muammar al-Qaddafi, the dictator of Libya.

MUGABE WITH HIS SECOND WIFE, GRACE, AT THEIR WEDDING CEREMONY
Joao Silva/AP Photo

CLEAN THE FILTH—On May 19, 2005, Mugabe launched Operation Murambatsvina (Clean the Filth) in which, according to United Nations estimates, 700,000 Zimbabweans were forcibly removed from their homes or businesses. Mugabe's government claimed this was done to "restore order and sanity," but many locals suspect that the real motivation was to forestall demonstrations as the nation's economy continued to deteriorate.

WATCH YOUR WORDS IN ZIMBABWE—Among the many repressive laws enforced by Mugabe is one that makes it a crime for any citizen to make an "abusive, indecent or obscene statement" about Mugabe even if the speaker is not in Zimbabwe. In a recent case that demonstrates the absurd side of this law, a Zimbabwean named Arnold Bunya told his brother, while the two were riding a bus, "Do not be thickheaded like Mugabe." Overheard by a government security agent, Bunya was sentenced to two weeks in jail.

5.

ISLAM KARIMOV—UZBEKISTAN

THE NATION—The most populous country in Central Asia, Uzbekistan was of little interest to the outside world until, in the days following the terrorist attacks of September 11, 2001, the United States was attracted to its 85 mile border with Afghanistan. Although 80 percent of the population of 26 million are Uzbeks, there are significant minorities of Russians and Tajiks. Uzbeks themselves also live in neighboring countries, such as Turkmenistan and Kyrgyzstan, where they make up 13 percent of the population, and Tajikistan, where they account for almost a quarter of the population. There are also two million Uzbeks in Afghanistan.

Uzbekistan is a weirdly shaped nation, the product of the Stalinist equivalent of gerrymandering. In fact, there are four parts of Uzbekistan that are surrounded on all sides by Kyrgyzstan. Besides the capital of Tashkent, Uzbekistan includes the ancient Silk Route cities of Samarkand and Bukhara, part of the ecologically ruined Aral Sea and, in the east, most of the densely populated and politically volatile Fergana Valley.

Most Uzbeks are Sunni Muslims and 99 percent are literate. Uzbekistan is the world's second-largest exporter of cotton (behind the United States), and it is one of the only nations in the world that is self-sufficient in oil.

United Nations

HISTORY—Samarkand was founded at least 2,500 years ago. The area that is now Uzbekistan was conquered by Darius the Great of Persia and, in 328 BC, by Alexander the Great. Islamic Arabs took over in the eighth century AD and Genghis Khan ruled the region in the thirteenth century. In the 1380s, another conqueror, Tamerlane, gained control and established the headquarters of his empire in Samarkand, which he turned into a cultural center as well. When Uzbekistan gained its independence 600 years later, the new government, headed by Islam Karimov, found itself short of historical heroes and chose to exalt Tamerlane (known locally as Amur Timur). Although Karimov's supporters would characterize Tamerlane as a kind, well-educated, and devout Muslim, among historians he is better known as a brutal tyrant who killed millions of people, ordered his troops to launch severed heads at cities they were attacking, and left behind pyramids made of skulls as a warning, including a pile of 90,000 in Baghdad alone.

Uzbek nomads did not appear in present-day Uzbekistan until the Shaybani Uzbeks invaded from the north in 1501. By 1510, they had completed their conquest of Central Asia.

The Persians invaded again in the eighteenth century, but it was the next group of invaders who would shape modern Uzbekistan.

THE RUSSIANS RUSH IN—While Central Asian warlords were preoccupied with fighting each other, Europeans were beginning to show an interest in their region. To the south, British forces were conquering Afghanistan, while Russian merchants and settlers from the north moved into Uzbek territory. Once Russian troops completed their conquest of the Caucasus Mountains in the 1850s, the Russian government began turning its focus onto Central Asia, particularly when the civil war in the United States disrupted their supply of cotton. In 1864, Russian forces began attacking the khanates that ruled the Uzbek people. Tashkent fell in 1865, Bukhara in 1867, Samarkand in 1868, Khiva in 1873, and, finally, Kokand in 1876, thus completing the Russian takeover of present-day Uzbekistan. By the turn of the century, the Russian railway system had extended into the area, which was now under the control of the Ministry of War. During World War I, Central Asians were exempt from military conscription, but when the Russian government cancelled this exemption in the summer of 1916, violent demonstrations broke out in the eastern Uzbek territory.

COMMUNISM—While the Bolsheviks were fighting to take over the Russian Empire and to establish the USSR, they actively excluded Muslims from positions of power. When the local people set up their own government in Kokand in the Fergana Valley, the Red Army dismantled it. They also put down a revolt after the Russian Civil War ended, eventually conquering Khiva and Bokhara in 1920. In 1924, the Soviet government created the Uzbekistan Soviet Socialist Republic, which also encompassed ethnic Tajik regions. In 1929, the Tajiks were given their own republic, leaving behind the borders of present-day Uzbekistan.

Communist rule had its good points, such as the spread of literacy and the emancipation of women, but for the most part, the effects were overwhelmingly negative. In a land of farmers, agriculture was collectivized. Josef Stalin decided that the purpose of the Uzbek SSR was to provide cotton, and the Soviet machine forced the Uzbeks to stop growing food crops and replant their land with cotton. In the post-Stalinist era, it was the diversion of rivers that fed the Aral Sea that caused its destruction. Since 1960, the Aral has lost 60 percent of its water and the water level has dropped fifty feet. The Soviet reliance on Uzbek cotton led to one of the great scandals of the Communist period. Faced with unrealistically high cotton quotas, Sharaf Rashidov, the first secretary of the Communist Party of Uzbekistan from 1959 until

1982, colluded with high central government officials to falsify production figures. When this long-lasting scam was finally exposed, the name Uzbekistan became synonymous with corruption, and Rashidov was posthumously viewed as a hero by the Uzbek people.

Stalin, suspicious of non-Russians in the USSR, arrested and executed all Uzbek nationalists in the 1930s. When the power of the Communist Party started to break down in the 1980s, a careful opposition developed in Uzbekistan. A group of intellectuals, Birlik (Unity), advocated saving the Aral Sea, diversifying agriculture, and making Uzbek the state language. When ethnic fighting broke out in the Fergana Valley in 1989, the national government chose an Uzbek from a different part of the republic to be first secretary of the Communist Party of Uzbekistan. His name was Islam Karimov.

THE BOSS—Islam Abduganivich Karimov was born in Samarkand on January 30, 1938. It would appear that his father was an Uzbek and his mother a Tajik; however, the details of his childhood are foggy. For example, his most recent official biographies state that his father was an office worker, but that he was raised in an orphanage. However, a 1995 biography, also authorized, claimed that he grew up in a poor family, the sixth of seven children, and that his father was a day laborer and his mother a housewife. At any rate, Karimov did study mechanical engineering at the Central Asian Polytechnic Institute before moving on to the Tashkent Institute of National Economics, where it took him three tries to pass the bookkeeping exam.

Karimov began his work career as an assistant foreman and technologist foreman at the Tashkent Farm Machinery Plant. Then he became an engineer at the Chkalov Tashkent Aircraft-Making Plant, which manufactured cargo planes for the USSR. In 1966, Karimov settled in at Gosplan, the state planning committee, gradually moving up the bureaucratic ladder from senior scientific specialist to first deputy. Karimov was appointed Finance Minister of Uzbekistan in 1983. In 1986, his patience with the Communist system paid off, as he gained the positions of Chairman of the State Planning Committee, Deputy Chairman of the Government of the Republic, and First Secretary of the Kashkodar Section of the Communist Party. In 1989 he was promoted to First Secretary of the Uzbekistan Communist Party Central Committee and, in March 1990, the Uzbek parliament elected Karimov president of the republic.

Karimov is married to Tatyana Akbarovna, formally a researcher at the Institute of Economics at the Uzbekistan Academy of Sciences. The couple has two daughters, one of whom, Gulnara, later developed a power base of her own. Speaking to the *Washington Post* in 2004, Gulnara's husband (by then ex-husband), Mansur Maqsudi, provided a rare insight into Karimov's private personality. "When you argued with him," explained Maqsudi, "the loudest would win the argument. It wasn't about facts; it wasn't about arguments. It was about who could shout the loudest." Maqsudi also described an office next to Islam and Tatyana's bedroom that included a five-foot-tall safe. One day, according to Maqsudi, he passed by the office and saw Mrs.Karimov sitting on the floor in front of the safe counting cash.

TAKING POWER—Karimov was fortunate to be the leader of Uzbekistan at the time that the Soviet Union collapsed. He sat on the fence during the August 1991 putsch that tried to restore Communism. When it failed, the Supreme Soviet of Uzbekistan declared independence on August 31. Karimov banned all activity by the Communist Party. However, two months after independence, he changed the name of the Communist Party of Uzbekistan to the People's Democratic Party of Uzbekistan, allowing all the people who had ruled the republic under Communism to remain in power.

Islam Karimov prides himself on being an intellectual and he has written numerous boring and pretentious works on economics. Upon finding himself the president of an independent nation, he was indeed wise enough to identify the forces that were most likely to threaten his goal of holding on to power as long as he wanted. These forces were (1) Russia, (2) the secular opposition, and (3) the Islamic opposition.

Even before independence, Karimov pushed through four laws that squelched potential critics of his regime. The Law on Protecting the Honor and Dignity of the President outlawed criticism of Karimov. The Law on Public Associations in the Uzbek SSR limited the right to register organizations, including NGOs. The Law on Mass Media squashed free speech, and the Law on Freedom of Conscience and Religious Opposition barred opposition groups from appearing in state media.

As if these laws did not adequately set the tone for Karimov's reign, the new constitution that went into effect in December 1992, closed a few more potentially democratic loopholes. Among other provisions, it allowed Karimov to appoint and dismiss all judges and it gave him the right to dissolve parliament in case of "insurmountable difficulties" between parliamentary deputies and the president. For good measure, it also abolished the office of vice president, lest any individual achieve a position that could challenge Karimov. Finally, the constitution gave Karimov the right to appoint and dismiss all regional administrators, known as *hakims*. Traditionally, local affairs, such as family disputes and real estate transactions, were overseen by councils of elders, called *mahallas*. The Communists had inserted their own appointees, the *hakims*, to deal with the *mahallas*. By taking charge of the appointment of all *hakims*, Karimov extended his personal power down to the most local levels, while at the same time appearing to align himself with the traditional elders. In addition, the new constitution allowed the *hakims* the right to nominate 45 percent of the members of the parliament (the Oly Majlis), which meant that instantly Karimov chose almost half of the members of the legislature.

THE SECULAR OPPOSITION—Before full independence was achieved, two non-Communist parties emerged in Uzbekistan. Birlik was created in 1988 and the Erk (Freedom) Democratic Party in 1990. Since both concentrated on promoting Uzbek culture and the Uzbek language, Karimov responded to their growth by giving a series of public lectures on "The Uzbek Way." Weak as Birlik and Erk were, Karimov decided to take no chances with them. In 1993 he banned both parties and arrested their leaders, charging them with "conspiracy to overthrow the elected government" and "defaming the honor of President Karimov." It would be another ten years before Karimov felt sufficiently unthreatened by Birlik and Erk to allow them to hold party congresses. In the meantime, in order to appease international opinion, Karimov grudgingly allowed the formation of the Human Rights Society of Uzbekistan (HRSU). Unfortunately, Karimov's true attitude toward this group was starkly revealed by an incident that took place in the summer of 2000. Tajik herdsmen in Surkhandarya Province informed troops of the Uzbek army that Islamist guerrillas had moved into their mountain grazing lands. Instead of praising the herdsmen for this tip, Karimov's government accused them of aiding the guerrillas and drove them out of their homes, causing some to die of cold and hunger. One of the herdsmen, Khazratul Kodirov, gave an interview to BBC World Service in which he described the displacement of his people. The Uzbek army seized Kodirov, tortured him, and killed him. The HRSU representative in charge of monitoring the case, Shovriq Ruzimorodov, died in police custody July 7, 2001. The following year the chairman of the HRSU, Yoldash Rasulev, was convicted of "conspiracy to overthrow the constitutional order," although Karimov graciously pardoned him for his non-crime a few months later.

ELECTIONS—Having become the ruler of an independent nation as the result widespread international support for the spread of freedom and democracy, Karimov was well aware of the symbolic importance of direct elections. In December 1991, he ran for president against poet Muhammad Solih, founder of the Erk Party. Karimov won 86 percent of the vote and gained what was supposed to be a five-year term. Parliamentary elections were scheduled for 1994 and this time Karimov faced the international expectation of a multiparty election. Not to worry. Karimov simply created some new parties, ordered various supporters to join them, and then arranged for the vote to take place. Since his party only won a minority of the seats, Karimov was able to brag to other countries that he ran a democracy, which, of course, ignored the fact that he controlled every seat in the parliament. Karimov's term as president was due to end in December 1991, but nine months earlier he staged a referendum that extended his term until 2000. The year 1999 saw another parliamentary election in which all parties pledged their loyalty to Karimov. Karimov himself was reelected president in January 2000. He gained more than 90 percent of the votes, which was not surprising considering that his opponent, Abduhafez Jalalov, publicly announced that even he had voted for Karimov. Two years later, another referendum extended his term until 2007. By the time of the next parliamentary election on December 26, 2004, international tolerance of Karimov's electoral shenanigans was wearing thin. Taking no chances, Karimov refused to register legitimate opposition parties and banned independent observers from all polling places.

THE ISLAMIC OPPOSITION—The success of the Afghan mujahedin in driving Soviet troops out of their country in 1989 brought great pride to those Uzbeks who felt themselves more Muslim than Communist, and especially so because fighters of Afghanistan's Uzbek minority had actively contributed to the victory. As the USSR began to fall apart, Muslim missionaries rushed into Uzbekistan from Pakistan, Egypt, and, especially, Saudi Arabia. In 1989 there were 170 mosques in Uzbekistan, all of them registered with the government. By 1995, there were approximately 5,000 mosques, almost half of which belonged to unregistered congregations, whose members came to be known as "independent Muslims."

The Islamic Renaissance Party (IRP) held its founding congress in January 1991. Since Uzbek law prohibited parties based on religion, its leaders were arrested. The IRP's prime mover, Haji Abdullah Otaev, disappeared in late 1992, never to be seen again, and the IRP never recovered.

Karimov was keenly aware that most Uzbeks viewed the revival of Islam with pride and enthusiasm, and he weaved together this pride with a sense of nationalism and tried to present himself as its symbol. During the December 1991, presidential campaign, Karimov, who had spent twenty-five years as a Communist Party bureaucrat and leader, exclaimed, "Islam is the conscience, the essence of life, the very life of our countrymen." He also placed his hand on the Quran when he was sworn in as president, and he peppered his speeches with phrases like "Allah's wishes."

Meanwhile, in the town of Namangan in the Fergana Valley, two men, Juma Namangani and Tahir Yuldosh, acquired Saudi funding to build a mosque. Namangani (born Juma Khojoev) had been conscripted into the Soviet army in 1987 and served as a paratrooper in Afghanistan. While there, he gained respect for the mujahedin, both as soldiers and for their

Islamic activism. Yuldosh, an unofficial mullah, was the leader of the Adolat (Justice) Party, which professed a fundamentalist interpretation of the Quran. In a rare interview with Voice of America in 1998, Yuldosh explained, "We want the model of Islam that has remained from The Prophet, not the Islam in Afghanistan or Iran or Pakistan or Saudi Arabia."

When the pre-independence mayor of Namangan refused to issue a construction permit for the Saudi-financed mosque, Islamic idealism and political discontent fused. Unemployed youth seized the office of the Communist Party of Uzbekistan and set up a crude version of Islamic rule in the town. Karimov was so preoccupied with the upheaval in the USSR that he had no choice but to tolerate this development for the time being. Finally, in April 1991, he paid a visit to Namangan, presumably to show his support for the revival of Islam. But, unexpectedly, he found himself forced to sit quietly while Tahir Yuldosh lectured him and demanded, among other things, that Karimov turn Uzbekistan into an Islamic state in which mosque attendance would be compulsory. Karimov gritted his way through this display of disrespect for his authority, but back in Tashkent he unleashed his fury, ordering mass arrests in Namangan. The following year, Karimov banned the Adolat Party and imprisoned its leaders.

Juma Namangani slipped across the border into Tajikistan and joined the Islamic opposition forces fighting in what would develop into that nation's five-year civil war. Islam Karimov had a different reaction to the war in Tajikistan. He offered military hardware to the anti-Islamist forces and ordered Uzbek jets to bomb opposition strongholds.

The sense of alarm that Karimov felt about Islamists holding their own in the war in Tajikistan was exacerbated in September 1996 when the government of another of Uzbekistan's neighbors, Afghanistan, fell to the forces of the radical Islamist Taliban. What was worse, the Taliban forces, after taking Kabul, pushed north into areas occupied by ethnic Uzbeks, where they clashed with Uzbek fighters led by General Abdul Rashid Dostum and drove them out of the city of Mazar-e Sharif into Turkey. Dostum recaptured the city the following year. If the aggressive behavior of Islamist armies on his borders unnerved Karimov, he was still able to use the fighting in Afghanistan for his own purposes. "While war is in progress there," he commented in April 2000, "how can we seriously engage in matters of renovation and democratic transformation?"

Back in Uzbekistan, Karimov was already engaged in a campaign against Islamic religious leaders. In August 1995, Sheikh Abduwahi Mirzoev, the chief prayer leader of the city of Andijan in the Fergana Valley, disappeared on a flight from Tashkent to Moscow, the first of several religious leaders to vanish over the next three years.

In Namangan, on December 2, 1997, anti-Karimov activists beheaded an Uzbek army captain and displayed his head outside his office. In the following two and a half weeks, a former collective farm chairman and his wife were beheaded and three policemen were killed in a shoot-out. Government forces responded by arresting more than 1,000 people.

THE VIOLENT ISLAMIST OPPOSITION—In 1998, Juma Namangani and Tahir Yuldosh came together again and formed the Islamic Movement of Uzbekistan (IMU), and called for the resignation of the Karimov government. While fighting in Tajikistan, Namangani, who was again receiving Saudi funding, established a military camp in Tavildara. After the formation of the IMU, Namangani would use the camp against Karimov. By this time, Namangani had acquired a reputation as a heroic guerrilla leader, sort of an Islamic Che Guevara.

On February 16, 1999, six bombs went off in Tashkent, killing 19 people and wounding 128. Not surprisingly, Karimov blamed the IMU, although he did take the opportunity to also blame his former presidential opponent, Muhammad Solih, and to sentence him to death in absentia. Five weeks after the Tashkent bombing, Karimov threatened to arrest any father whose son joined the IMU.

In August, a Namangani unit raided villages in Kyrgyzstan and exchanged hostages for ransom. Outraged, Karimov bombed IMU villages in Kyrgyzstan, killing civilians in the process. On another raid, the IMU took four Japanese geologists hostage and demanded the release of political prisoners. The geologists were freed five weeks later amid rumors that the Japanese government had paid the IMU $2 million.

During the year 2000, the IMU killed at least twenty-four Uzbek soldiers and launched a particularly audacious attack on the Uzbek army only eighty miles north of Tashkent. During the winter of 2000–2001, Karimov cut off gas supplies to the capitals of Kyrgyzstan and Tajikistan in order to pressure the governments of those two countries to crack down on IMU bases. He also lined the borders of Kyrgyzstan and Tajikistan with mines and barbed wire.

THE NONVIOLENT ISLAMIC OPPOSITION—In addition to the IMU, Karimov cracked down on another group, Hizb ut-Tahrir (Party of Liberation), commonly known as HT, whose aim was to restore Islamic rule in all Muslim lands. Unlike the IMU, the HT supported democracy and opposed religious wars, ethnic favoritism, and discrimination against women. None of this stopped Karimov from convicting twenty-two HT members in connection with the Tashkent bombings and, despite the lack of any evidence, sentencing six of them to death. For the record, although the HT has never been connected to an act of violence, they do make one exception to their prohibition against killing.

According to HT doctrine, violence is allowed in conflicts already under way in which Muslims are fighting oppressors. Specifically, they approve of Palestinians killing Israelis. In fact, one of the insults used by HT leaders against Karimov was to call him "a Jew."

RELATIONS WITH THE UNITED STATES—From the very beginning of his reign as the dictator of Uzbekistan, Islam Karimov was almost obsessively pro-American. In no way did he admire or agree with American values. Rather, he saw the United States as a counterweight to the Russian behemoth to his north, which he feared would recapture Uzbekistan or, at the very least, enslave it economically.

For its first decade of independence, Uzbekistan voted with the United States on almost every issue at the United Nations, even when it dealt with Israel and Palestine. In 1992, Uzbekistan became the first Central Asian nation to recognize Israel and, in 1998, Karimov actually visited the Jewish state. Karimov supported President Clinton's 1995 trade embargo of Iran, and that same year U.S. and Uzbek forces engaged in their first joint military exercise. At the same time, a U.S. company, Newmont Mining, began processing low-grade stockpiles of gold in Uzbekistan. Starting in 1997, trade between the United States and Uzbekistan jumped from $50 million a year to $420 million. Newmont wasn't the only American company interested in Uzbekistan. In his introduction to the U.S. edition of his book *Uzbekistan: Along the Road of Deepening Economic Reform* (published in Houston), Karimov bragged about establishing a joint venture with Enron to prospect, explore, and develop gas fields. At the urging of Enron head Ken Lay, the then-governor of Texas, George W. Bush, met with the Uzbek ambassador to the United States. The deal, like so many of Enron's plans, fell through.

In June 1996, Karimov paid his first visit to Washington, D.C. President Clinton felt uneasy about Karimov's already appalling human rights record, but agreed to meet with Karimov if the Uzbek leader pledged to release eighty-nine political prisoners. Karimov agreed to the deal, although, in the end, only five of the prisoners were actually confirmed to have been released. If Karimov received a cool reception at the White House, he was greeted more enthusiastically at the Pentagon, where William Perry, the secretary of defense, praised Uzbekistan as "an island of stability." This tension between Uzbekistan's economic and geopolitical value on the one hand and its embarrassing record of human rights abuses on the other has colored U.S.–Uzbek relations ever since.

In September 2000, the Clinton administration declared the IMU a terrorist group, citing its connection with Osama bin Laden, its involvement in the drug trade, the killing of civilians, and its kidnapping of four American mountain climbers (who later escaped). This declaration delighted Karimov. However, five months later, the U.S. State Department lambasted Karimov's government for torturing prisoners by beating them with blunt objects and asphyxiating them with gas masks.

9/11: A DREAM COME TRUE—On September 11, 2001, Islamist terrorists using hijacked airplanes killed almost 3,000 people in the United States. This tragic event saddened people around the world. But for Islam Karimov, it was a stroke of luck beyond his wildest dreams. He was in the midst of an armed struggle with the al-Qaeda–affiliated IMU and feeling the pressure of the Taliban on his doorstep. For years he had been groveling for U.S. support and all he got in return was Enron, a couple of joint military exercises, and a lot of complaints and lectures about human rights and democracy. Suddenly, literally overnight, the administration of now-U.S. president George W. Bush was his new best friend. High-ranking American officials streamed into Tashkent and offered him money and friendship. U.S. defense secretary Donald Rumsfeld made multiple visits to Karimov without saying a word about nasty subjects like torture and human rights. Secretary of State Colin Powell assured the world that "President Karimov wants to bring through a new generation that understands democracy." Powell was as wrong about that one as he would later be about Saddam Hussein having weapons of mass destruction. Others saw right through Karimov. Reacting to Powell's meeting, the *Washington Post* editorialized that the Bush administration was sending the message that "If you play ball with the United States in Afghanistan we will look the other way as a decade of democratization efforts is ground to dust."

Within two weeks of 9/11, 200 U.S. soldiers had already arrived in Uzbekistan and Karimov turned over his military base in Khanabad to the United States. The Americans rushed military supplies to Uzbek General Dostum and then began bombing Afghanistan. The Taliban was driven from power and the IMU was destroyed. Juma Namangani was reportedly killed during the U.S. bombing of Mazar-e Sharif in November. For Karimov, the defeat of his Islamist enemies was cause for celebration, but he was to reap even more benefits in the aftermath of 9/11. The number of U.S. forces in Uzbekistan would eventually surpass 5,000. As the Russian newspaper *Nezavisimaya Gazeta* lamented, "The arrival of every American soldier in Uzbekistan chips away at Russia's influence in the region." This was exactly what Karimov had hoped for. The Islamist guerrilla forces were gone and Russia's influence was diminished. And yet there was even more good news for Karimov. In one year, U.S. aid to Uzbekistan jumped from $85 million to $300 million, some of it, no doubt, ending up in that safe next to Karimov's bedroom. And when President Bush painted his War on Terrorism as a battle between good and evil, he could have taken his words directly from one of Karimov's speeches, since that was exactly how Karimov had been portraying his fight against the IMU. Now it was easy to read the Americans. Instantly, Karimov discovered previously hidden links between all of his opponents and Osama bin Laden, and even members of Hizb ut-Tahrir were arrested for having alleged connections with al-Qaeda.

Dozens of members of the U.S. Congress visited Karimov in Tashkent and in March 2002, Karimov had tea in the White House with President Bush. As late as 2004, some members of Congress were so gullible or self-deluding that they continued to praise Karimov. For example, during a visit to Tashkent in March of that year, Representative David Dreier of California gushed that he was "very encouraged from the reports that we have been seeing in the area of human rights." In the executive branch, confusion reigned. In July 2004, the State Department declared that Uzbekistan's human rights record was so poor that it cut off the $18 million in aid it was supposed to receive. The following month, however, the Department of Defense pledged $21 million in assistance to the Uzbek military.

THE UZBEK PRINCESS—At her nineteenth birthday party in Tashkent, Islam Karimov's elder daughter, Gulnara, met a twenty-four-year-old Afghan-American from New Jersey named Mansur Maqsudi. The couple met one more time and then married in November 1991. They celebrated one wedding in Tashkent and then another in New Jersey. Maq-

sudi was given the post of manager in Uzbekistan's Coca-Cola bottling plant, as well as part ownership of the business, and the couple had two children. Nonetheless, the marriage was a rocky one. Mansur was particularly concerned about Gulnara's spending habits. During a visit to London, she wanted to buy $230,000 worth of jewelry. When Mansur refused to pay for it, Gulnara reached into her bag and purchased the jewelry with cash that her mother had given her.

One day in July 2001, Gulnara, accompanied by her bodyguards, took her son Islam and her daughter Imam to the Six Flags Great Adventure amusement park in New Jersey. But when she tried to pay for their tickets, she discovered that her husband had cancelled her credit

GULNARA KARIMOVA,
THE UZBEK PRINCESS

cards. Back home, the couple got into a shouting match that continued until her bodyguards intervened. The next day, Gulnara left Mansur a note suggesting that he watch the 1989 film *The War of the Roses,* about an ugly divorce. Then she took the kids and returned to Uzbekistan. Mansur never saw his children again. An Uzbek judge granted Gulnara a divorce and a New Jersey judge gave one to Mansur. Because arrest warrants were filed with Interpol for each of them, neither was able to travel to Europe. In Tashkent, security forces raided the homes of Mansur's family; took twenty-four of his relatives at gunpoint, including an eighty-five-year-old grandmother who was an Uzbek citizen; drove them thirteen hours to the Afghan border, and dumped them on the other side. The Uzbek government seized Mansur's share of the Coca-Cola bottling plant and claimed that he owed $9 million in back taxes. Gulnara, on the other hand, came away from the divorce with 20 percent of Uzbekistan's wireless telephone company (worth $15 million), a $13 million Uzbek resort, $11 million in bank and investment holdings in Geneva and Dubai, a $10 million retail complex, a recording studio and spa worth $5.5 million, Tashkent nightclubs worth $4 million, a house in Tashkent, and $4 million worth of jewelry.

HUMAN RIGHTS . . . FOR ONE HUMAN—In 2003, Karimov ordered the parliament to pass a law that made him and all members of his family immune from prosecution forever. Later he made it illegal to refuse to praise him and his policies during religious services. Actually insulting him was punishable by up to five years in prison. He also criminalized placing loyalty to Islam above loyalty to the nation's leaders. For good measure, Karimov banned the study of Arabic, which was being used by students and scholars to read the Quran in its original language.

TROUBLE WITH A CAPITAL T—In October 2002, without warning or explanation, Karimov's government shut down all billiard halls.

TORTURE—Upon the issuance of a United Nations report on torture in Uzbekistan in December 2002, UN Special Rapporteur Theo van Boven told reporters that "torture, as far as I can see . . . is not just incidental, but systemic in nature." According to Human Rights Watch, at least 7,000 political prisoners are held in Uzbek custody at any given time. Many of them are subjected to "psychiatric treatment." Another group at risk in Uzbekistan is journalists. In 2002, in one of his periodic gestures to please the outside world, Karimov magnanimously announced an end to media censorship. Actually, media censorship had been outlawed by the 1992 constitution. But there had never been much need for official censorship since the threat of beatings and torture had always been enough to encourage self-censorship. In June 2002, the Committee to Protect Journalists declared Uzbekistan the only country in Europe or Central Asia that imprisons journalists "for carrying out their professional duties."

One typical case of torture in Uzbekistan was that of Muzafar Avazov, a thirty-five-year-old father of four, who, along with a companion, Husnidin Alimov, died while incarcerated in Jaslyk prison. When his body was released to his family, it was covered with heavy bruising, his fingernails were gone, and more than 60 percent of his body was burned, leading observers to surmise that he had been scalded in boiling water. Relatives of other prisoners have reported that their family members are forced to sign statements begging Karimov for forgiveness and admitting that they are terrorists. Karimov bragged that fifty to sixty people were sentenced to death in 2004. Neither the prisoners nor their families were informed of the dates of their executions and, in some cases, even their burial sites were kept secret. Karimov, as a point of information, had designated 2004 the Year of Kindness and Mercy.

Although the U.S. State Department repeatedly condemned Uzbekistan's use of torture to extract confessions (real or imagined) from prisoners, the CIA took advantage of Karimov's brutal methods. During the three years after the terrorist attacks of 9/11, the Bush administration airlifted dozens of prisoners from the U.S. prison camp at Guantánamo Bay and other sites to Tashkent so that Uzbek security personnel could take care of them. In July 2004, Craig Murray, the U.K. ambassador to Uzbekistan, wrote a memo to the British Foreign Office accusing the CIA of using the program to violate the United Nations Prohibition Against Torture. The Foreign Office responded that it was all right to use information gained by torture as long as the torture was not performed by British interrogators.

THE ANDIJAN MASSACRE—Until 2005, the worst excesses of Islam Karimov's regime had taken place behind closed doors. But on May 13, 2005, Karimov ordered a mass killing that could not be ignored.

Akram Yulashev was a mathematics teacher from the town of Andijan in the Fergana Valley who came from a family of math and chess experts. But Yulashev was also interested in spiritual matters. In 1991, after two years of work, he completed a forty-four-page handwritten work called *Yimonga Yul* (Path to Faith). Distributed as a pamphlet the following year, it presented twelve lessons that stressed that spiritual values were more important than material values. One admirer of the pamphlet, an entrepreneur named Bakhrom Shakirov, donated land to Yulashev's followers to start businesses that included a bakery, a restaurant, a shoe factory, and a hair salon.

Although Yulashev did not advocate the overthrow of the government, Karimov felt threatened by the movement, which his government dubbed Akramia after Yulashev's first name. In 1998, Yulashev was convicted on a phony drug charge, released as part of a presidential amnesty, and then rearrested almost immediately following the 1999 Tashkent bombings.

Meanwhile, a group of businessmen and community leaders in Andijan, unable to obtain credit from government banks, began to pool their capital to help each other. They established a minimum wage that was higher than what the government paid and they paid their employees' medical expenses. By 2004, they were employing thousands of workers in a wide variety of industries and providing consumer goods, such as furniture and clothing, at prices that undercut the government monopolies. In June of that year, Karimov had twenty-three of the businessmen arrested. Twenty-two of them were charged with organizing a criminal group, attempting to overthrow the constitutional order of Uzbekistan, membership in an illegal religious organization, and possession or distribution of literature containing a threat to public safety. The other defendant was a government employee who was charged with abuse of power.

The trial of the twenty-three began on February 11, 2005. The nonlawyer who tried to present their defense quit because the judge would not allow him to question the witnesses. As the verdict was expected to be delivered on May 13, government security officers arrested some friends and relatives of the accused. During the night of May 12–13, fifty to one hundred young men who were friends, relatives, and supporters of the businessmen attacked a police station and a military barracks and stole AK-47 rifles, grenades, a military truck, and other weapons. In the process, they may have killed four policemen and two soldiers. After midnight, the attackers used the truck to ram down the gate to the prison and they freed the twenty-three businessmen, as well as more than 500 other prisoners, whom they told, "Now you are freed from injustice. Please go out." After a one-hour gun battle at the building housing the National Security Service, the attackers and some of the freed prisoners moved on to the center of town and took over the local government building *(hokimiat).*

Using cellphones, they called for a mass protest in Bobur Square. They also distributed a hastily produced leaflet that said, "We are unjustly accused of membership in Akramia. . . . If we don't demand our rights, no one else will protect them for us. . . . Let the region's governor come and representatives of the President too, and hear our pain. . . . If we stick together, they will not harm us."

By morning more than 10,000 people had gathered in the square, including lots of women and children. The attackers gave speeches about poverty, corruption, the lack of jobs, and the unfair trials. Some of the freed prisoners described their prison conditions and their trials. Then the loudspeaker was turned over to anyone who wanted to speak, and ordinary citizens voiced their complaints, including government employees who had not been paid in four months. Meanwhile, the more aggressive of the protestors took hostage men in uniforms. Later they freed the soldiers, but kept the policeman, as well as the head tax inspector, the city prosecutor, and two government officials, who were forced to "confess" to the crowd. The prosecutor gave to one of the protest leaders, Abduljon Parpiev, the phone number of the Uzbek interior minister, Zokirjon Almatov. Parpiev demanded the release of political prisoners, including Akram Yulashev, and he asked Almatov to send a government representative to the square to listen to the peoples' grievances.

A false rumor spread that Karimov himself was coming and the crowd cheered because many of them naively believed that their problems were caused by local officials and that the president would overrule their decisions. Instead, Karimov sent the army. By 4:00 p.m. the crowd realized that military armored personnel carriers had blocked all the roads around the square and that no one could leave. At 5:20 the troops opened fire on the crowd. One route was left open and people rushed forward in an attempt to escape. But the route was actually a shooting gallery with government snipers on rooftops and behind sandbags. Hundreds of people were killed, including all but four of the hostages.

More than 600 survivors tried to walk the thirty-five miles to the Kyrgyz border, although not all of them made it because they were ambushed along the way. Back in Andijan, the wounded lay untreated and dying. The next morning, soldiers executed the wounded. Water cannons were used to wash away the blood, the dead bodies were taken away, bullet holes in buildings were painted over, and broken windows replaced. All that remained was the bodies of seventeen muscular men, which were shown to journalists as proof that all the deaths had been caused by these seventeen attackers.

When the U.S. government rejected Karimov's version of events and condemned the massacre, Karimov became so furious that, on July 29, 2005, he ordered the United States to evacuate the Karshi-Khanabad air base it had been using since 9/11. He then signed a treaty with Russia that increased its military ties with Uzbekistan. In September, following the usual torture-induced confessions, fifteen Andijan demonstrators pleaded guilty to various crimes after which they went on trial. Karimov's government claimed that, as part of an Islamic holy war, Akram Yulashev had directed the uprising using a mobile phone hidden in his maximum security prison cell. Six of the defense lawyers asked forgiveness for representing the defendants. Between November 2005 and January 2006 at least 230 other people were convicted in seventeen related trials, all of which were closed to the public.

KARIMOV SPEAKS:

> *"At a certain stage of historic change, you need a strong will and a certain figure . . . and you have to use some authoritarian methods at times."*
>
> JANUARY 28, 2002

> *Speaking to the Uzbek parliament about the followers of Juma Namangani:*
> *"Such people must be shot in the head. If necessary, I will shoot them myself."*
>
> MAY 2, 1998

"I am prepared to rip off the heads of two hundred people to sacrifice their lives in order to save peace and calm in the republic . . . If my child chose such a path [the IMU], I myself would rip off his head."

APRIL 2, 1999

AN OBSESSIVE TENNIS FAN, ISLAM KARIMOV
POSES WITH YEVGENY KAFELNIKOV AND MARAT
SAFIN AT THE 2001 PRESIDENT'S TENNIS CUP
TOURNAMENT IN UZBEKISTAN.

Anvar Ilyasov/AP Photo

(Fritz Reiss/AP Photo)

6.

HU JINTAO—CHINA

THE NATION—With a population of 1.3 billion, China contains one-fifth of the world's population. For every person who lives in the United States there are four in China. Luo Gan, a member of the nation's ruling Politburo, suggested this solution to China's overpopulation problem: "We have too many people. We should encourage our people to leave and settle abroad. There are a lot of nice places to live in the world." Almost all Chinese are members of the Han ethnic group. The fifty-five recognized non-Han minorities make up only 8 percent of the population, but China is so big that that 8 percent translates to more than 100 million people, a number larger than all but ten countries in the world. Although China shares borders with fifteen different nations, the vast majority of Chinese live far away from any of them.

Since 1949, China has been ruled by a single party, the Chinese Communist Party (CCP). Party members hold all important positions in the government and the military. The highest authority is the twenty-four-member Politburo of the CCP and its nine-member standing committee. Because of its size and its enormous economic potential, many of the world's governments have tended to ignore or pay lip service to the fact that China is a repressive authoritarian state.

ROOTS—China's recorded history is so long and so rich that it is difficult for most Westerners to grasp. For example, the first comprehensive history of China, the *Shiji*, was written by Sima Qian between 105 and 84 BC. Although the Communists did not take charge of China until after World War II, the roots of the Chinese brand of nonroyal authoritarianism run deep. As far back as the Shang dynasty, which began in about 1766 BC, the king considered himself to be the earthly instrument of Heaven's design. This same mandate of Heaven was claimed by the Zhou dynasty (1122–256 BC). In 651 BC, the rulers of the central states held a conference to deal with what would be a recurring problem in Chinese history: foreign invaders, in this case non-Chinese tribes from the north. This period saw the inauguration of standing armies with professional career soldiers, as the military gained an increasingly important role in society. Wars, which previously had been viewed as something of a sport by the aristocracy, became more serious and were now fought to gain territory and resources. Military conscription became common and some of the larger states raised million-strong armies.

The Zhou period saw the development of several important philosophical schools that addressed the subject of governance. The most famous philosopher, Confucius (551–479 BC), promoted the concept that rulers should be *junzi*, which is usually translated as "gentlemen," and that their behavior should be guided by principles of moral virtue. Confucius believed in centralized authority and he agreed with earlier thinkers that an emperor or king had a mandate from Heaven. The ruler's subjects were expected to be unconditionally loyal and obedient and to accept the ruler's right to speak on behalf of his people. Mo-tzu (480–390 BC), the first great critic of Confucius, argued that the concept of *junzi* was an excuse for maintaining social inequalities. Mencius (372–289 BC) agreed that the founders of the Zhou dynasty, by their virtue, had been granted the approval of Heaven and, with it, the right to rule, but he also taught that the people had the right to rebel if the ruler neglected or oppressed the people because such treatment was not the will of Heaven. The Legalists, of whom the most famous was Han Fei (280?–234 BC), were a group of thinkers who believed that the state should be ruled by laws and institutions and that rulers should be judged not by their virtues or morals, but by the effectiveness of the results they produced. The Legalist view is still important in present-day China.

In 359 BC, Shang Yang, a minister in the western frontier state of Qin, began a series of reforms that included the creation of administrative districts known as *hsien*. Eventually, this system led to civil servants who were representatives of the central power taking over the control of administrative functions that had previously been run by the local nobility. Shang Yang also burned books, massacred scholars, instituted a system of government surveillance, and pursued the strategy that if you made the law severe enough no one would violate it. When his patron, Duke Zhao, died in 340 BC, Shang Yang's opponents had him drawn and quartered.

In 230 BC, the Qin prince Cheng began a series of military campaigns that, within nine years, unified China proper under a centralized, nonhereditary bureaucratic system for the first time. The Qin dynasty was overthrown after only fourteen years, but the Han dynasty that followed lasted from 206 BC until AD 220. The Han emperor Wu Ti, who reigned for fifty-four years (141–87 BC), expanded the Chinese empire to its greatest size yet, stretching from Central Asia in the west to Korea in the east and from Inner Mongolia in the north to Vietnam in the south. Wu Ti introduced civil service examinations for government posts, opening the civil service to those who were talented instead of only to those who were well connected.

One early ruler who would later be cited by the Communists as a forerunner of their own philosophy was Wang Mang, who served as regent from AD 1 to 6 and then seized power in AD 9. Wang Mang abolished private ownership of land and "nationalized" all estates and the slaves who worked on them. His measures managed to alienate both the gentry and the peasantry and he was overthrown after a series of peasant uprisings.

By the end of the fourth century, much of the North China Plain was controlled by non-Chinese dynasties of the Toba tribal federation. The Toba instituted a land equalization program that was similar to that of Wang Mang. Under the Toba, all land belonged to the state. Every free citizen was allowed to farm a certain amount of land, but after he or she died, the land was returned to the state to be redistributed. In 581, Yang Jian (known posthumously as the Wendi) changed the land distribution system by charging a land tax and requiring each adult male to give twenty days of labor to the state. He also ordered government bureaucrats to work in regions other than those of their birth, a system which, for the most part, is used today for important government positions.

In the seventh century, the Chinese empire stretched to its greatest size ever, from the border with Iran in the west to Pyongyang, the capital of present-day North Korea, in the east. In 751, Chinese forces were defeated by an Arab army in the Battle of Talas in Kyrgyzstan, initiating a steady, centuries-long decline in China's power. The Mongol armies, first led by Genghis Khan and later by Kublai Khan, gradually conquered China in the thirteenth century, establishing the Yuan dynasty in 1271. Mongol rule of all of China would last less than a century.

The founder of the Ming dynasty, Zhu Yuanzhang, rose from being a beggar to the emperor of a unified China in less than twenty years. Upon formally ascending the throne in

1368, he took the name of Hongwu. Distrustful of his advisors to the point of paranoia, Hongwu tried and executed 1,500 people in 1380, including one of his oldest companions. Six centuries later, observers would compare the founder of the Chinese Communist regime, Mao Zedong, to Hongwu, in that he rose from humble origins, unified China, and purged anyone who could be remotely considered a possible opponent.

The Manchu people, a non-Han ethnic group, moved out from the northern province of Manchuria to overthrow the Ming and establish the last Chinese dynasty, the Qing, in 1659. It was the Manchus who were the first rulers of China to have to deal seriously with the European powers.

THE WHITE MONGOLS ARRIVE—Catholic missionaries, primarily Jesuits, began arriving in China in the thirteenth century. The Portuguese were the first of the European colonial powers to arrive, followed by the Spanish, the British, and the French. During the eighteenth century, Europeans and Americans acquired a taste for certain Chinese products, in particular tea, silk, and porcelain. However, the Chinese had little interest in anything that the West had to offer. The British tried to remedy this imbalance by taking raw cotton and opium from India and sending it to China. The Qing government did not mind the cotton, but was alarmed by the spread of the debilitating effects of opium. In 1839 it passed laws prohibiting the opium trade, seized the opium owned by Chinese traders, and destroyed 20,000 chests of British opium. The British government sent a punitive expedition that ended with the defeat of the Chinese forces in 1842. What came to be known as the First Opium War concluded with the Treaty of Nanjing, which gave the island of Hong Kong to the British and granted British citizens resident in China exemption from Chinese laws. The Treaty of Nanjing, along with two more treaties with the French, were known popularly in China as the "unequal treaties."

JESUS CHRIST'S YOUNGER BROTHER—In 1847, a poor village teacher from Kwangtung Province named Hung Hsiu-chuan founded the Association of the Worshippers of God, a group that was influenced by Protestant ideology. Within three years he had recruited about 30,000 members who were soon known as the Tai Ping. Merging with other anti-Manchu groups and inspired by tales of Wang Mang and other ancient leaders, they confiscated large estates and redistributed the land to local farmers, without allowing them to actually own the land. Hung Hsiu-chuan announced that he was Jesus Christ's younger brother and that he was driven by divine inspiration. In 1851 he founded the Kingdom of the Heaven of the Great Peace and he proclaimed himself the King of Heaven. He banned slavery, opium smoking, arranged marriages, and foot binding. Unnerved by the

growing popularity of the Tai Ping, the Western powers threw their support behind the Qing, and the Tai Ping Rebellion was crushed in 1865.

Meanwhile, the European powers were on the move. Russian czarist troops invaded Manchuria and Chinese Turkestan (present-day Xinjiang), the French established colonies in Cochin China in present-day Vietnam and in Cambodia, and the British took over Burma and acquired a ninety-nine-year lease of Kowloon, across from Hong Kong. When Japan defeated China in the Sino-Japanese War in 1895, China was forced to give up Taiwan and the Penghu Islands and to recognize Japanese control of Korea. The United States, which had not taken over any Chinese territory, proposed in 1899 that there should be an "open door" policy in which all foreign powers would be granted equal access to all Chinese ports. With the exception of Russia, they all agreed. In 1900, an antiforeign movement of secret societies, known in China as the Tihetuan and in the West as the Boxers, began burning down facilities built by missionaries and killing Chinese Christians. In June they attacked foreign-held areas in Beijing and Tianjin. The Qing declared war on the foreign powers, who invaded China, crushed the Chinese forces, and occupied northern China. To many Western historians, the Western occupation was a major turning point in Chinese history, but to the Chinese, with their longer view of their own history, the Westerners were just another set of foreign invaders and their occupation lasted barely as long as that of the Mongols.

SUN YAT-SEN—Acknowledged as the founder of modern China, Sun Yat-sen was born November 12, 1866, in Guangdong Province. At the age of thirteen he moved in with his older brother in Honolulu and attended missionary school. Four years later he moved to Hong Kong to study medicine, returning to Honolulu when he was twenty-eight. When China lost the Sino-Japanese War in 1895, he returned to Guangdong. In 1905 he founded a revolutionary movement that was based on his Three Principles of the People: nationalism, democracy, and people's livelihood. By nationalism he meant that the only way to overthrow foreign imperialism was to think and act as a nation rather than as a region or a clan. Sun believed in republican Western democracy, including the right to referendums and recall elections, but as time went on, he leaned more toward traditional Chinese village democracy. In promoting "people's livelihood" he emphasized raising the population's standard of living and allowing farmers and workers to own the land and the means of production.

The republican revolution broke out in Wuchang, the capital of Hubei Province on October 10, 1911. Because the existing dynasty, the Manchus, was non-Han, the revolution was not just republican, but nationalist. Within seven weeks, fifteen of the twenty-four Chinese provinces had overthrown Qing authority. In December, Sun Yat-sen returned to China from a fundraising trip in the United States, and on January 1, 1912, he was inaugurated as the provisional president of the Chinese republic. However, by this time, the commander-in-chief of the imperial army, Yuan Shikai, had already seized power in Beijing and Sun was forced to allow Yuan to take his place as president on March 10. Throughout most of the country, warlords were running the provinces and were content to let the government in Beijing deal with China's foreign affairs.

In August 1912, one of Sun Yat-sen's associates, Song Jiaoren, formed a new political party, the Kuomintang (National People's Party), which was often referred to as the Nationalist Party. National elections for a new bicameral parliament were held in February 1913, and were won by the Kuomintang. Undeterred by this detail, the increasingly dictatorial Yuan Shikai had Song Jiaoren assassinated. That summer seven provinces revolted against Yuan, who successfully put down the rebellions and intimidated the parliament into electing him president of the Republic of China. Yuan banned the Kuomintang and ordered its members to leave parliament. Finally, he simply dissolved parliament and, through a new constitution, declared himself president for life. In late 1925, Yuan went even farther, announcing that he would reinstate the monarchy with himself as emperor. Rebellions broke out all over the country and several warlords declared independence. In the end, Yuan died of kidney failure in June 1916, leaving the country in chaos.

Fighting on the Allied side in World War I, Japan occupied the German-held Chinese territory of Shandong Province. In 1917, the Beijing government declared war on Germany, but the following year it signed a secret agreement with Japan acknowledging the Japanese claim to Shandong. During the 1919 Paris Peace Conference, this deal was made public, which led to widespread student demonstrations against the government and against Japan. These demonstrations developed into a national reawakening known as the May Fourth Movement. In 1917, Sun Yat-sen joined with southern warlords to create an alternative government and he revived the Kuomintang in 1919. Sun appealed to Western democracies for aid, but they were not interested, so in 1921 he turned to the newly forming Soviet Union. Soviet advisors arrived in China in 1923 and set about reorganizing the Kuomintang along the lines of the Communist Party of the USSR. In 1922 the Chinese Communist Party (CCP) had only 300 members, while the Kuomintang had 150,000. Nonetheless, the CCP was admitted into the Kuomintang in 1924.

CHIANG KAI-SHEK—Chiang Kai-shek was born to wealthy parents in Zhejiang Province on October 31, 1887. After spending one year at a Chinese military academy, he went to Japan, where he continued his military education and served in the Japanese army from 1909 until 1911. When he heard about the uprisings against the Manchus, he returned home. He joined the Kuomintang in 1918 and in 1923 he was sent to the USSR for several months of military and political training. When Chiang returned to China he established the Whampoa Military Academy near Guangzhou with himself as the head. Sun Yat-sen died of cancer in March 1925. Chiang dismissed his Soviet military advisors and in the summer, as the commander-in-chief of the National Revolutionary Army, set out on the Northern Expedition. Over the next nine months, he defeated one warlord after another and conquered half of China. After Sun's death the Kuomintang was ruled by a collective leadership, but in March 1926, Chiang emerged from a power struggle as the party's only leader.

MAO ZEDONG—One of the most important figures of the twentieth century, Mao Zedong was born December 26, 1893, in Hunan Province in the village of Shaoshan, where 75 percent of the residents were surnamed Mao. The oldest of four children, he began attending school at the age of eight. But when he was thirteen, his father, who had raised himself to moderate wealth through hard work, pulled him out of school and made him work in the fields by day and manage the account books by night. When he was fifteen years old, Mao ran away from home and went to live in the neighboring county with his maternal uncle, who enrolled him in the local primary school even though he was six years older than the other students. When he was seventeen, Mao took a steamer to the city of Changsha and enrolled in middle school. He was a voracious reader and would later say that he gained his real education from reading newspapers. When he heard about the anti-Manchu Wuchang Uprising of October 10, 1911, he joined the army and served six months as a common soldier. After being discharged, he spent six months reading in a library and then became a teacher, a profession he pursued for five years. He published his first article, "A Study of Physical Culture," in 1917. In it he fused nationalism with bodybuilding, explaining, "If our bodies are not strong, we will be afraid as soon as we see enemy soldiers."

Mao worked in a library in Beijing and then returned to Changsha after the beginning of the May Fourth Movement in 1919. A prominent local spokesman for anti-imperialist, anti-warlord forces, he was forced to flee Changsha after the failure of a student strike. However, he returned in the summer of 1920, won the position of principal of a primary school, and married Yang Kaihui. He organized a Marxist study group and, in January 1921, he told his friends that he was a Communist. In July 1921, he led the Hunan delegation to the First Congress of the Chinese Communist Party in Shanghai. Upon his return, he assigned Communist representatives to organize mine workers, railroad workers, and even barbers. The local warlords put an end to this activity in early 1923. That same year, Mao was elected to the Central Committee of the CCP and he worked diligently to align his party with the Kuomintang. Attacked by both the left and the right, he became ill. Still, he pressed on and, in October 1925, he was appointed acting head of the Kuomintang's propaganda department. He was already expressing the strategy that would put him at odds with both the Kuomintang and with the orthodox Communists: that the strength of China was the peasantry and that peasants should own their own land and not work the land of others.

The CCP–Kuomintang alliance collapsed in June 1927 and Chiang Kai-shek launched a vicious anti-Communist repression. Mao led an armed rural insurrection in Hunan, the Autumn Harvest Uprising, but it was defeated after only ten days. Captured, he managed to bribe his way out. Fleeing with 1,000 men, he joined with bandit leaders and organized peasant uprisings while also fighting against warlords and the leadership of the Communist Party. He was finally expelled from the CCP Politburo because of his insistence on organizing peasants. Mao and another revolutionary military commander who shared his viewpoint, Zhu De, created the slogan that would become famous and would inspire guerrilla groups around the world: "If the enemy advances, we retreat; if the enemy halts and encamps, we harass; if the enemy tires, we attack; if the enemy retreats, we pursue." Somewhat less well known were Mao and Zhu De's Three Rules of Discipline: "Obey orders, don't take anything from the workers or the peasants, turn in anything taken from the landlords or the gentry." They also created Eight Additional Rules that included: put back the doors you use for bed boards, replace the straw borrowed for bedding, speak politely, pay fairly for what you buy, return everything you borrow, pay for anything you damage, don't bathe in the sight of women, and don't search the pockets of captives.

CIVIL WAR, PART ONE

CIVIL WAR, PART ONE—In April 1927, Chiang Kai-shek's troops massacred 5,000 Communist supporters in Shanghai and Changsha. Mao Zedong also faced problems with warlords in Hunan, who executed Mao's sister and his ex-wife, and with the Communist Party itself, which, in February 1929, ordered Mao and Zhu to attack the cities despite the fact that two-thirds of the Communist Red Army troops were peasants. Chiang, meanwhile, was becoming increasingly dictatorial. In an attempt to eliminate not just the Communists but all non-Kuomintang political parties, he enacted the Speedy Punishment of Crimes Endangering the Republic law, which was modeled after a similar law being used by the Fascists in Italy. In 1932, Chiang created the Blue Shirts, a party within the party that he never publicly acknowledged. With a membership of more than 10,000 that was dominated by army officers, Chiang used the Blue Shirts to maintain control of the military.

In September 1931, the Japanese took advantage of the chaos in China to invade Manchuria in the north, installing the last Qing emperor, Puyi, as the head of a puppet government in 1932. After consolidating their control of Manchuria, the Japanese pushed south. Despite this foreign invasion, Chiang remained obsessed with fighting the Communists. He designated Communist-controlled areas "Bandit Suppression Zones" and ordered his Kuomintang troops to engage in "Extermination Campaigns" against the Communists. Both sides experienced tumultuous infighting. For example, in the December 1930 Furien Incident, Mao ordered the execution of 2,000 people he claimed were collaborating with the Kuomintang. On the other side, in January 1932, the 20,000-man Twenty-Sixth Nationalist Army deserted en masse to the Communists. Using guerrilla warfare, the Communists fought off four attempted encirclements by the Kuomintang. For the fifth campaign, which was launched in October 1933, Chiang, aided by German General Hans von Seeckt, com-

mitted one million troops, a huge arsenal, and 400 airplanes. Many of the Kuomintang soldiers were upset that they were fighting their fellow Chinese instead of repelling the Japanese invaders, and Chiang had to take a pause in the fighting to control his own troops. It is estimated that one million civilian peasants died as a result of fighting between the two sides. After a year, the Kuomintang finally broke the Red Army's resistance and on October 16, 1934, Mao and about 90,000 Communist troops set out on what would be immortalized as The Long March.

MAO ZEDONG IN 1936
Bettmann/Corbis

THE LONG MARCH—Unlike most historical events that have been glorified by dictatorial regimes, The Long March really was an extraordinary achievement. Actually, Mao himself started the "march" on horseback because of a bout with malaria. In the course of the following year, the Red Army executed a series of spectacular and heroic escapes, as it faced a wide range of obstacles ranging from Kuomintang bombing campaigns to mosquito-infested marshes. During one period, unable to make fires, they survived on raw grains and vegetables. At another point they defeated an army of Tibetan fighters and stole their clothes (despite the high-minded resolutions of the Eight Additional Rules) in order to survive the cold. After criss-crossing about 6,000 miles (some say it was "only" 3,700), less than 10,000 survivors arrived safely in the town of Wuchichen in the northern Shensi Soviet area. Another branch of the Red Army, led by Chu Teh, lost 15,000 soldiers in August 1936 while crossing the Yellow River, including a women's regiment of 2,000.

CIVIL WAR: THE INTERMISSION—In 1936, Chiang Kai-shek ordered the Manchurian warlord Chang Hsueh-liang, popularly known as The Young Marshall, to deploy his 15,000-man army against the Communists. Like most Chinese soldiers, The Young Marshall preferred to fight the Japanese. So he arrested Chiang on December 11 and forced him to negotiate with a representative of Mao Zedong named Zhou Enlai. So nine years of civil war ended not with a victory by one side, but with a mutiny. The number of battle deaths was variously estimated to total between 400,000 and 1,275,000. Once the Kuomintang and the CCP called a truce, the Chinese gradually turned the tide against the Japanese. However, beginning in 1940, clashes between the two reluctant allies became more frequent. Even before World War II ended, the CCP–Kuomintang conflict was annexed by the nascent Cold War. The United States began aiding Chiang Kai-shek in late 1941. U.S. troops arrived in China in mid-1943, reaching a peak strength of 113,000 in late 1946. At the Yalta Conference in February 1945, the Allies agreed to allow Soviet troops to enter Manchuria to fight against the Japanese. When the Japanese were forced out of the country, the Soviets invited the CCP to move in and seize the weapons left behind by the 594,000 Japanese and 75,000 Manchurian troops. In August and September of 1945, Chiang Kai-shek's American chief of staff, General Albert Wedemeyer, arranged for 500,000 Kuomintang troops to be transported by air and sea to central and north China. In August, the U.S. ambassador to China, Patrick Hurley, accompanied Mao Zedong to Chungking to meet with Chiang Kai-shek. The talks ended unsuccessfully after two months, but the Americans continued to try to prevent a resumption of the civil war. On January 14, 1946, U.S. special ambassador General George A. Marshall managed to arrange a truce, but it did not include Manchuria and even then it broke down after six months. The United States withdrew its troops in early 1947, but continued to give Chiang Kai-shek massive amounts of aid.

CIVIL WAR, PART TWO—Full-scale civil war resumed in July 1946. Over the next three years it would claim more lives than both the Korean War and the Vietnam War. The Kuomintang began with three million troops and the Communist People's Liberation Army (PLA) with about 1.3 million. However, the PLA, with its strategy of appealing to the masses, grew quickly, tripling in size by the spring of 1948. The PLA finally captured all of Manchuria after winning the Battle of Mukden on November 2, 1948. Four days later, the climatic battle of the civil war, the Battle of Hwai Hai (aka the Battle of Suchow) pitted 600,000 PLA troops against 500,000 Kuomintang. The fighting went on for two months, during which 100,000 soldiers lost their lives and the Communists took 300,000 prisoners. The PLA moved on to take Beijing on January 23, 1949. On December 7, Chiang Kai-shek fled to the island of Taiwan with 5,000 soldiers (and $300 million). Another Kuomintang general, Hu Tsung-nan, led a retreat into the wilds of Sinkiang Province in the west and then into Burma. By the time all fighting ended in June 1950, 4,500,000 Kuomintang soldiers had been taken prisoner and 1,775,000 had defected to the Communists. During the four years of the second half of the Chinese Civil War, 1,200,000 Chinese lost their lives in battle.

THE DAWN OF THE COMMUNIST DYNASTY—The People's Republic of China was established on October 1, 1949, with its capital in Beijing. Mao Zedong defined the new government as a "people's democratic dictatorship," to be led by the Chinese Communist Party, the "vanguard of the working class." The CCP had 4.5 million members, 90 percent of whom were peasants. Mao was the chairman of the Party and Zhou Enlai took the position as premier and head of state. Zhou tried to negotiate with the United States, but the administration of President Harry Truman was not interested. In December 1949, Mao traveled to Moscow and spent nine weeks negotiating with the Soviet dictator, Josef Stalin. In February, the two Communist governments signed a thirty-year treaty of friendship. The Chinese Communists soon found themselves embroiled in the civil war in neighboring Korea, but this did not distract Mao from transforming China into his version of a Communist paradise. In June 1950, the Communists began confiscating land from landlords and redistributing it to the poor. This change was undertaken with such haste and lack of long-term planning that an estimated two million people died in the process. The Communists cracked down on "enemies of the state" and engaged in an ideological cleansing of scientists, university professors, artists, writers, and others that included public trials and public confessions. Unrealistically confident that this cleansing had succeeded, Mao announced, "Let a hundred flowers bloom, let the hundred schools of thought contend." Much to his chagrin, almost all of the "hundred schools of thought" criticized the Communist Party. CCP leaders accused their critics of being "bourgeois rightists" and punished them in an Anti-Rightist Campaign.

ECONOMIC BUNGLING—Following the USSR model of stressing heavy industry, in 1953, Mao and the CCP initiated the First Five-Year Plan. They centralized all government administration, abolished private enterprise and nationalized banking, industry, and trade. By 1956, 90 percent of China's farmlands had been collectivized. Mao followed this further disruption of the Chinese economy with his 1958 Great Leap Forward. A direct attack on the institution of the family, the Great Leap Forward created 23,500 people's communes of about 22,000 people each. Each commune was supposed to be self-supporting with communal kitchens and mess halls. The program was an utter disaster and led to an estimated 27 million deaths due to starvation and disease. Mao was forced to resign his government leadership position, although he remained the chairman of the CCP. Deng Xiaoping, the general secretary of the CCP, led an economic recovery movement. Threatened by Deng's success, Mao began purifying the Party in 1962. He forced intellectuals to do manual labor, forced professionals to put the goals of the Party ahead of the needs of their fields of expertise, and generally purged the Party of his opponents.

GOVERNMENT-APPROVED CHAOS—Having already subjected the Chinese

people to the failures of the First Five-Year Plan and the Great Leap Forward, Mao Zedong embarked on an even worse program in 1966: the Great Proletarian Cultural Revolution. Convinced that the CCP was filled with "capitalist and bourgeois obstructionists," Mao and his third wife, Jiang Qing (his second wife, He Zizhen, bore him six children but they divorced after eleven years of marriage), promoted Mao's ideas, in the form of the *Quotations from Chairman Mao,* as a holy text and they sent out high school and university students, known as Red Guards, to punish anyone they decided was not ideologically pure. Before long, the Party had collapsed, the economy was in chaos, Red Guard factions were fighting one another, and the average Chinese citizen was afraid to express even the mildest opinion. In mid-1968, Mao was finally forced to admit that things had gone too far. The only institution that had remained unscathed by the turmoil of the Cultural Revolution was the People's Liberation Army. Mao allowed the PLA, led by Lin Biao, to crack down on the Red Guards. By the time the situation was under control, between 400,000 and a million Chinese had been killed. In September 1971, Lin Biao attempted to overthrow Mao, but his coup failed. He fled in an airplane, but his plane crashed in Mongolia and he died. As for Mao, his health was declining and he made his last public appearance in 1973. However, he still retained enough power as late as 1976 to remove Deng Xiaoping from all of his public posts and to appoint his chosen successor, Hua Guofeng, acting premier and first vice-chairman of the CCP.

THE YEAR OF TRANSITION—For China, 1976 was the year of transition. Three

of the nation's most powerful leaders died, beginning with Zhou Enlai in January and then Zhu De in July. On July 26, the city of Tangshan in Hebei Province was hit by a massive earthquake that killed hundreds of thousands of people. In fact, the Tangshan earthquake is regarded as the deadliest earthquake in modern history. According to Chinese tradition, such a disaster was viewed as a withdrawal of the mandate of Heaven and it presaged a great change. Thus, it did not come as a surprise when Mao Zedong himself died six weeks later, on September 9. With Mao gone, Jiang Qing and three others were denounced as the Gang of Four and Jiang Qing eventually died in prison. Athough Hua Guofeng assumed all important positions, in July 1977, Deng Xiaoping was reinstated and an intraparty struggle gradually led to the rehabilitation of most of the Party leaders who had been denounced during the Cultural Revolution. In March 1979, Mao was officially deemed no longer infallible and in

1981 the Party announced that in his later years Mao had made mistakes by deviating from his own sacred Thought.

MONEY TALKS—In December 1978, the CCP Central Committee adopted Deng Xiaoping's strategy of emphasizing economic development over Maoist class struggle. To promote his goals, Deng managed to reduce Hua Guofeng to a figurehead by putting two of his own protégés in positions previously held by Hua. Hu Yaobang, a liberal by Chinese Communist standards, was made general secretary of the CCP and Zhao Ziyang took over as premier. The number of small businesses in China grew from 100,000 in 1978 to six million in 1983. Special Economic Zones were created to attract foreign investment. By 1982, 90 percent of farming had been decollectivized. Each household was required to pay its commune in cash or kind for the right to lease farmland and then to turn over a percentage of its harvest. However, whatever was left over, the farmers could sell and keep the profits. Grain production rose 5 percent a year in the early 1980s, but later the prices paid by the government did not keep pace with the inflation rate and production stagnated. In 1985, Deng Xiaoping published *Building Socialism with Chinese Characteristics,* which formally presented his approval of private enterprise while at the same time maintaining strict control of the economy through central planning.

The 1982 Twelfth Party Congress signaled a significant development in the leadership of the Communist Party: the rise of the technocrats, men who had been trained in a technical science, pursued a professional occupation, and held a Party leadership post. As the old guard of Mao's generation faded away, they were replaced by these technocrats. In 1982, none of China's provincial governors were technocrats; by 1997, 77 percent were technocrats. In 1978 only 23 percent of Politburo members were college-educated. By 1988 the figure was 67 percent and by 1998, 92 percent.

THE TIANANMEN MASSACRE—By 1988, the official inflation rate was 18 percent and economic anxiety was widespread. When Hu Yaobang, the liberal, died in April 1989, the government refused to honor his memory. This sparked demonstrations in Beijing's Tiananmen Square that mushroomed into protests against inflation, corruption, and nepotism and then into calls for the resignation of Deng Xiaoping and the institution of freedom of speech and democracy. Soon the crowds grew to more than 100,000 people. Some workers, inspired by the Solidarity movement in Poland, started independent trade unions. When the government cracked down, these workers were punished more severely than the students who had initiated and led the protests. On May 15, there were pro-democracy demonstrations in 132 Chinese cities. Four days later, the government put

BILLBOARDS PORTRAY THE SAINTS OF THE
CHINESE COMMUNIST RELIGION: MAO ZEDONG,
DENG XIAOPING AND JIANG ZEMIN.
Michael Reynolds/epa/Corbis

Beijing under martial law. Considering local army troops too sympathetic to the protestors, they brought in troops from outside the city. On June 3 and 4, the troops assaulted the demonstrators, killing about 500 of them. Chinese embassies abroad were ordered to collect videotapes of foreign television coverage of the demonstrations. The tapes were sent back to Beijing and used to identify and then arrest the demonstrators.

After Tiananmen, the CCP increased its control over the People's Liberation Army and the PLA was encouraged to build up its business interests. By the early 1990s the PLA operated more than 10,000 businesses, including joint ventures with foreign partners, international hotels, and foreign trade. PLA representation on the CCP Central Committee also rose to 25 percent. The collapse of the USSR in August 1991 rattled the Communist leadership. At the 1992 Fourteenth Party Congress, the CCP added Deng Xiaoping to the pantheon of Communist Gods, alongside Marx, Lenin, and Mao. "Deng Thought," especially his promotion of a socialist market economy, was canonized as the official guide to government policy. Respect for Confucianism was revived and Western democracy was criticized as being contrary to Confucianism and to Chinese traditions. Deng's strategy of liberalizing the economy while maintaining strict control of all political institutions and refusing to allow freedom of expression would come to be known as the "Chinese model" and would be emulated by dictators around the world.

THE MAN—Hu Jintao's ancestors were tea merchants from Anhui Province in central China, who then moved to the city of Taizhou in Jiangsu Province northwest of Shanghai. Hu's father sold tea in Shanghai and that was where Hu was born on December 21, 1942. His mother died when he was a child and he and his two younger sisters grew up with his grandparents in Taizhou. His father became an accountant and Hu himself worked briefly as an accountant for a company that sold household equipment. When he was sixteen years old, Hu passed the entrance examination for Qinghua University in Beijing, China's elite science and technology school. Qinghua had been founded by Americans in 1911. Beginning a trend that would continue throughout his life, Hu was the youngest student in his class. He was a member of the student dance team and was known to dance solo at parties, although this detail of his life was deleted from his official biography in the 1980s. Known for his pho-tographic memory, Hu was identified as a potential leader in his sophomore year. After earn-ing a degree in riverine hydropower generation in the hydraulic engineering department in 1964, Hu stayed on at Qinghua to do postgraduate research and to serve as a "political trainer," in charge of ideological indoctrination. The president of Qinghua University, Jiang Nanxiang, accepted Hu as a probationary member of the Communist Party in 1964, and the following year he was made a full Party member. At Qinghua, Hu met and married fellow student Liu Yongqing. The couple has a son and a daughter. Their daughter is rumored to be living in the United States under an assumed name. In the autumn of 1968, during the Cul-tural Revolution, Hu was sent to do manual labor, building housing, in the remote north-western desert province of Gansu. After the political climate in China calmed down, Hu was allowed to work as a technician during the construction of the Liujia Gorge Dam, which was completed in 1974. During this time he also managed Communist Party affairs for the local Ministry of Water Resources and Electric Power. In 1974, Hu was transferred to the provin-cial capital of Lanzhou, where he served as the deputy chief of the Project Design Division of the Gansu Provincial Construction Commission. Two years later he led the Gansu construc-tion team's efforts in its relief work following the Tangshan earthquake.

In the late 1970s, Hu Jintao made the contact that would lead to his comparatively rapid rise in the Communist Party power structure. Hu met, and became a protégé of, Song Ping, a fellow Qinghua University graduate. Song, the chairman of the Gansu Provincial Revolu-tionary Commission and the first secretary of the Gansu branch of the CCP, was well-connected with the Zhou Enlai faction of the CCP and with Deng Xaioping. In 1980, Deng sent out a call to promote younger party cadres ahead of more senior officials. Song re-sponded by sending Hu Jintao to Beijing to attend the Central Party School's inaugural training class for middle and young cadre. The executive vice president of the school hap-pened to be Jiang Nanxiang, the former president of Qinghua University whom Hu had de-fended against the Red Guards during the Cultural Revolution. Jiang introduced Hu to the Party General Secretary, Hu Yaobang. In 1981, Song Ping was promoted and sent to Beijing to serve as vice-chairman (and later chairman) of the Party's Central Planning Committee. In 1982, Hu was selected as an alternate member of the CCP Central Committee. At thirty-nine, he was its youngest member. Having already, thanks to Song Ping, moved up the ranks in the hierarchy of the provincial branch of the Communist Youth League (CYL), Hu was transferred to Beijing to become president of the All-China Youth Federation. In November 1984, he gained the highest position in the CYL. As part of his responsibilities, he was in charge of the CYL newspaper and he ordered the paper to criticize a hardliners' campaign against Western ideas. In so doing, he alienated two members of the "Princeling Party," sons of Party leaders, who complained about him to Hu Yaobang. Because Hu Yaobang liked Hu

Jintao, he eased him out of this confrontation by sending Hu Jintao to serve as Party secretary in the impoverished southwestern province of Guizhou. At the age of forty-three, Hu became the youngest provincial Party secretary in the history of the People's Republic of China. Three months later, Hu was made a full member of the CCP Central Committee. Arriving in Guizhou in July 1985, Hu soon made himself popular. Although he never moved his family to Guizhou, he lived in a modest fashion, and he visited every one of the province's eighty-six county-level administrative units and familiarized himself with the people's problems. He ordered tuition waivers for poor students to help them attend university and he worked to improve economic conditions. By the end of 1987, Guizhou's economic output had more than doubled and per capita income had almost tripled in comparison to pre-1985 levels. Far from the political turmoil in Beijing, such as the downfall of Hu Yaobang in 1987, Hu Jintao maintained a clean record, free from enemies.

HU JINTAO'S TIBETAN ADVENTURE—Because of its exotic culture and its spiritual component, Tibet has long held a special fascination for Westerners. China invaded Tibet on October 7, 1950. The Tibetan army was small and ineffective, but the Chinese did face resistance from various mountain tribes, in particular the Khampa of eastern Tibet. China annexed Tibet in May 1951 after losing 2,000 soldiers in battle. Another 2,000 Chinese froze to death, 3,000 died of disease, and 3,000 were declared missing. About 5,700 Tibetans were killed and 2,000 were imprisoned. Tibetan guerrillas continued to fight against the Chinese. In May 1956, they ambushed and massacred 2,000 Chinese soldiers. The Chinese responded by bombing a monastery in Batang in eastern Tibet, killing 2,000 monks and pilgrims. For the next seventeen years, the CIA supported the Khampas in their struggle against the Chinese. On March 10, 1959, 20,000 rebels, armed only with swords and old muskets, revolted in the Tibetan capital of Lhasa. During a week of heavy fighting, Chinese forces killed 65,000 Tibetans. The leader of the Tibetans, the Dalai Lama, fled Lhasa with eighty supporters, arriving in India two weeks later. The Indian government offered sanctuary to the Tibetans in Dharamsala, which has been home to the Dalai Lama ever since.

While Hu Yaobang was general secretary of the CCP, he visited Tibet and issued an apology to the Tibetan people. However, when he lost power in 1987, Chinese policy toward Tibet turned more repressive once again. As the thirtieth anniversary of the Chinese occupation neared, the Chinese government knew that it would face major protests in Lhasa. In June 1988, the new head of the Communist Party, Zhao Ziyang, following a suggestion from Song Ping, proposed that Hu Jintao be chosen to replace the current Party secretary in Tibet, who was considered too soft on repression. From October 30 until November 20, Hu accompanied Yan Mingfu, the Communist Party's head of propaganda for minority areas, on an inspection tour of Tibet. On December 9, Hu was officially appointed Party secretary for Tibet. The next day, International Human Rights Day, police fired into a crowd of protestors in Lhasa.

For Hu Jintao, this new appointment was a test of his willingness to follow the policies of whichever faction was in power in China. Vaguely associated until now with reformist elements, Hu was expected instead to take a hard line. Once again leaving his family behind in Beijing, Hu arrived in Lhasa January 12, 1989. He met with Party leaders and told them, "With the powerful PLA and armed police as our backing," he and the leaders would "do our work well." The sympathy with the locals that Hu had shown during his assignments in Gansu and Guizhou did not reappear in Tibet. It is not clear whether this was a result of racist attitudes that he harbored toward the Tibetans or whether he simply wanted to do whatever it took to toe the party line. On January 23, Hu traveled to Shigatse, Tibet's second-largest city, for the reopening of a rebuilt Buddhist stupa that had been destroyed during the Cultural Revolution. At the ceremony, he shared the podium with the Panchen Lama, the second-ranking member of the Tibetan hierarchy, who had spent most of the previous twenty years under house arrest in Beijing. Speaking to the assembled crowd, the Panchen Lama criticized the Chinese presence in Tibet and described the damage it had done to the Tibetan people and their culture. Five days later, the Panchen Lama was declared dead, reportedly as the result of a heart attack. Rumors spread that he had been poisoned and, although it was never substantiated, this version of his death was widely believed. On February 7, large crowds paraded through the streets of Lhasa displaying the banned Tibetan exile flag. After speaking directly with General Secretary Zhao Ziyang, and with the occupation anniversary coming closer, on February 20, Hu ordered armed Chinese troops to march through the city. On March 5, a demonstration in Lhasa turned into a riot. Police shot to death ten Tibetans and one policeman was killed. Forty more Tibetans would die over the next few days. Martial law was declared on March 7 and all foreigners were given two days to leave Lhasa. Tibetans without residence permits for the city were ordered to leave within two weeks. Tibetans suspected of having separatist thoughts were investigated, as were those "who are suspicious for the need for investigation." In September 1989, Hu succumbed to "fatigue" and began making increasingly frequent medical visits to Beijing, finally moving there permanently in the summer of 1990. He did, however, retain his title as secretary of the Party Committee for the Tibetan Autonomous Region for two more years.

CLIMBING TO THE TOP—Back in Beijing, Hu Jintao, having proved himself in Tibet, continued his steady rise in the Communist Party. In the spring of 1992, Deng Xiaoping made him his point man in the organizing of the fourteenth Communist Party

Congress. Deng announced that he wanted to put men under the age of fifty on the Polit-buro Standing Committee, China's highest authority. Song Ping nominated Hu as one of four candidates. Of the four, two were disqualified when it was discovered that they would turn fifty before the Congress opened in October. Hu got the job and, at age forty-nine years nine months, he became, as usual, the youngest member of the Standing Committee. With Song Ping's approval, he replaced Song as the man in charge of Party personnel. Hu, proba-bly recalling his run-in with the Princelings, banned nepotism and established performance standards for promotion. In March 1993, he was appointed president of the Central Party School, which gave him contact with every rising Party leader in every province. Under Hu's control, the school began teaching courses in comparative politics and Western economics and management. Hu was now affiliated with the three main sources of Party leaders—Qinghua University, the Chinese Communist Youth League, and the Central Party School—and was now viewed as the heir apparent to China's number-one position. When Deng Xiaoping died in February 1997, his ashes were scattered into the Bohai Sea. Hu was the only Politburo member to accompany Deng's family and bodyguards at the ceremony. The leader of China, Jiang Zemin, appointed Hu state vice president in March 1998. Al-though this was a largely ceremonial post, it was Hu's first major position outside of the Party. Once again, he was the youngest vice president in the history of the People's Republic of China. He was put in charge of an important program: overseeing the closure of businesses owned by the army and transferring the assets to local authorities. Meanwhile, Hu began making trips abroad, including representing China at the ASEAN Summit in Hanoi in December 1998. In November 2001, he toured Europe for the first time, visiting Russia, Germany, France, the United Kingdom, and Spain, and then, accepting an invitation from Vice President Dick Cheney, he visited the United States in 2002.

In 1999, Jiang Zemin awarded Hu the post of vice-chairman of the Central Military Commission and in May of 1999 he gave Hu his first public role: addressing the nation on television after the United States bombed the Chinese embassy in Belgrade, killing three journalists. In a carefully worded speech, Hu exploited the patriotic feelings of the Chinese people, lambasting the Americans for their "brazen" attack. But he also reminded his viewers that they must "guard against overreactions."

Over the next couple years, Hu accumulated more and more important state and Party positions, and in 2004 succeeded Jiang Zemin as chairman of the CCP Central Military Commission and head of the army. When he finally achieved full power, it marked the first time that an heir apparent in Communist China had survived the usual internecine struggles and actually taken charge of the country—and he did so without developing any serious enemies.

INHUMAN RIGHTS—Hu Jintao inherited a system that was based on repressing free speech, freedom of assembly, freedom of religion, and democracy in general. Because of his mixed record during his long climb to the top of the Communist hierarchy, many observers hoped that Hu might introduce reforms relating to civil liberties and political expression. Unfortunately, this has not been the case. To begin with, Hu has made it clear that the Chinese army should be loyal not to the state, but to the Communist Party. In 2004 he reportedly advised Party leaders to study North Korea and Cuba as models for maintaining order.

- **TIBET**—Tibetans have been arrested for speaking with foreigners, possessing the autobiography of the Dalai Lama or video-and audiocassettes of his speeches, preparing a list of casualties of Chinese crackdowns, and advising friends to wear traditional Tibetan costumes on the Chinese national day. In 2005, two monks were sentenced to eleven years in prison for hoisting the banned Tibetan flag. Incommunicado detention is routine. Torture is the expected form of interrogation. There is no right to trial in an open court; defense is permitted for mitigation of punishment, not for pleading innocence. Tibetans call judges "sentencing officers." The Chinese government vets all applicants for the monkhood and prohibits the performance of traditional rites. In July 2005, the Chinese chairman of the Tibetan Autonomous Region announced that China would choose the next Dalai Lama. The boy the Dalai Lama identified in 1995 as the next Panchen Lama (#2 in the Tibetan hierarchy) has been under virtual house arrest, probably in Beijing. The Chinese government chose a different boy and, in June 2005 in Sichuan, ordered monks to publicly greet him.

- **CRIMINAL JUSTICE**—According to statistics compiled in 2003, only 1 to 5 percent of trials in China have witnesses. The conviction rate in criminal trials is 99.7 percent. The criminal code names sixty-eight crimes that are punishable by death, including embezzlement, counterfeiting, bribery, pimping, stealing gasoline, and selling harmful foodstuffs. Exact annual figures for the number of executions in China is not known, although it appears to be in the thousands. Amnesty International's cautious estimate for 2005 was 1,770. The majority of the world's executions take place in China. In March 2004, the government introduced traveling "execution vans."

- **FORCED LABOR CAMPS**—According to Chinese government statistics, there are 260,000 people being held in 300 "reeducation through labor" camps throughout the country. The reform through labor system, known in Chinese as *Laogai,* was borrowed from the Soviet Union and begun in China in the 1950s. Originally created to "reeducate" class enemies of Communism, the Chinese have broadened its usage to include petty criminals, drug users, political dissidents, members of the Falun Gong spiritual group, and personal enemies of local officials. The Chinese justification for the labor camps is that criminals exploit society and that through work they will absorb the Communist ideology and become proper members of the proletariat. Under the system, local police and others can send anyone to the camps for three years without a trial. The inmate population of these camps has tripled in the last twenty years. Since the days of Deng Xiaoping, the Chinese government has tried to make the reeducation camps operate at a profit. According to official documents, at least 200 *Laogai*-made products are exported to other countries, including a quarter of China's tea, a majority of its rubber-vulcanizing chemicals, steelpipe, hand tools, and cotton. According to the Washington, D.C.–based Laogai Research Foundation, prisoners in the labor camps mine asbestos without protective gear, work with battery acid with no protection for their hands, often work fifteen hours a day, and are subject to torture.

- **TORTURE**—According to a United Nations investigation, among the methods of torture used by Chinese police and in prisons to extract "confessions" and to maintain discipline are immersion in sewage, ripping out fingernails, sleep deprivation, burning with cigarettes, and beatings with electric prods. Although China outlawed torture in 1996, its definition of illegal acts—those leaving physical marks—is so narrow that interrogators can employ a wide range of methods contravening UN standards. Suspects can also be manacled in contorted positions, some of which are given names like gymnastics moves, such as "reversing an airplane," where a victim must remain standing, bent double, with arms splayed upwards and backwards.

- **RELIGION**—China has tried to deflect criticism of its suppression of religion by legalizing controlled worship. For example, the government sponsors its own version of the Catholic Church that does not recognize the authority of the pope. Evangelical Christians have been arrested for "praying for world peace." In June 2004, Jiang Zongxiu was beaten to death by police after she was arrested while distributing Bibles in a marketplace in Guizhong Province. In March 2005, the government passed the Regulations on Religious Affairs. This directive requires all congregations, mosques, temples, churches, and monasteries to register to be legal. According to the law, all religious bodies must "safeguard the unification of the country, the unity of the nationalities and the stability of society." This wording has proved sufficiently vague to give the government control of all religious teaching. The Chinese authorities have used this carte blanche to particular effect in Buddhist Tibet and in Xinjiang Province against the Muslim Uighur people. In Xinjiang it is illegal to teach religion to children under the age of eighteen and schoolchildren may not even sing traditional songs. It is also forbidden to publish anything about Islam that does not "uphold the Marxist point of view of religion," and the government has destroyed thousands of books about Uighur history and culture. In Xinjiang, almost half of the prisoners in the area's labor camps are there for religious reasons.

• **FALUN GONG**—Falun Gong is a meditation- and exercise-based spiritual group, whose belief system, although strange, is peaceful and seemingly harmless, except, that is, to the Chinese Communist Party. Falun Gong was outlawed in China on July 22, 1999, its publications banned, and thousands of its followers arrested and even executed. The harsh government action followed an unexpected incident three months earlier when 10,000 Falun Gong adherents staged a day-long silent protest outside the Zhonggnanhai compound where the nation's leaders live in Beijing. Even though it seems bizarre that powerful government officials like Hu Jintao and the Politburo of the CCP should feel threatened by such an innocuous group, from the Chinese Communist point of view, the Falun Gong are suspiciously similar to the Tai Ping of the nineteenth century and other sects that have served as rallying points for mass discontent.

• **THE GREAT FIREWALL OF CHINA**—The Chinese government spent $800 million to create the Jin Dun (Golden Shield) Project, a broadband network that incorporates a system for automatically policing Internet gateways, blocking foreign websites, filtering content and key words, invading computers, sending out viruses, and connecting with the monitoring systems of the Public Security Bureau. The system is run by a 50,000-person Internet control department. China is the only country in the world whose laws include the concept of a "Web political criminal." Publishing articles on the Internet can be deemed "committing an offense." According to Reporters Without Borders, China is "the biggest jailer in the world for cyberdissidents." Of course, according to the Committee to Protect Journalists, China is also "the world's leading jailer of journalists," and in China there are no privately owned television or radio stations. In creating its Internet control system, China has benefited from lots of help from foreign friends, including Cisco, Yahoo, Microsoft, and Google. Cisco, which has annual revenues in China of $500 million, sells the Chinese routers with censorship capability built in. It also sells surveillance technology to the Chinese Public Security Bureau and other law enforcement agencies. It has also been accused of selling network equipment to the Chinese government for its so-called Policenet, which allegedly gives the police direct access to a citizen's Internet history and e-mails. In July 2002, Yahoo signed a voluntary self-censorship pledge written by the Chinese government. Yahoo agreed to filter its search results so that a search for "Free Tibet" in Chinese yields no Web pages. In 2005, Yahoo admitted to providing the Chinese government with information leading to the arrest of journalist Shi Tao, who was subsequently sentenced to ten years in prison for e-mailing a copy of a government warning about the fifteenth anniversary of the Tiananmen Square massacre to foreign Web sites.

- **FAMILY AFFAIRS**—In six of China's thirty-one provinces, government permission is needed for a married couple to have a first child. Some provinces practice forced abortion and sterilization. In rural areas, where two-thirds of the population lives, a couple is usually given permission to have a second child if their first child is disabled or a girl. In most of the country it is illegal for a single woman to have a child. Zhou Jiangxiong, a thirty-year-old farmer in Hunan Province, was detained in May 1998 by officials at a local birth-control office who wanted him to reveal the whereabouts of his wife who was suspected of being pregnant without permission. They hung him upside down, beat him, burned him with cigarette butts, and castrated him. He later died.

- **IT'S YOUR HOME UNLESS WE WANT IT**—According to the Centre on Housing Rights and Evictions, the Chinese government has evicted more than forty million citizens since 1985. It has also forced people in cities to leave their homes, including 2.5 million in Shanghai alone and, according to government figures, at least 400,000 in Beijing in preparation for the 2008 Olympics. In March 2005, Chinese authorities announced that, in advance of the 2010 World Expo, another 500,000 families would be moved from their homes in Shanghai to the outskirts of Beijing. They said this was being done "to protect the environment." The Ministry of Public Security reported that in 2005 there were 87,000 cases of "disturbances of public order." Most of these protests and demonstrations were in response to land seizures and evictions, although some were inspired by cases of local corruption and environmental pollution. On December 6, 2005, security forces shot to death at least twenty demonstrators in Dongzhou village in Guangdong Province who were protesting inadequate compensation for land expropriated for construction of a power plant. This was the first known killing of protestors since the Tiananmen Square Massacre in 1989.

- **COAL MINING DEATHS**—Workers in China are not allowed to form autonomous unions. According to official figures, sixteen million enterprises are considered "toxic." In 2005, 5,986 workers died in coal mining accidents. This may seem shocking in comparison to the much lower number of mining deaths in other countries, but, in fact, this was the first time in four years that the figure dropped below 6,000 deaths.

FRIENDLY DICTATORS—Unlike the Soviet Union in the days of the Cold War, China pursues its foreign policy without any regard whatsoever for ideology. All that matters is business and the Chinese will do business with any country, Communist or capitalist, democratic or authoritarian. In its quest for resources and markets, the Chinese government has embraced dictators who are the worst of the worst. Kim Jong-il has no better ally than Hu Jintao's China. Less than two weeks after Uzbek troops massacred hundreds of civilians in May 2005, Uzbekistan's dictator, Islam Karimov, was welcomed in Beijing with a red carpet and a twenty-one-gun salute. China is now the leading trading partner of Omar al-Bashir's Sudan. In October 2004, China signed a $70 billion oil deal with the dictators of Iran. China is so friendly with Robert Mugabe of Zimbabwe that the Chinese government paid for the roof of Mugabe's presidential palace and for T-shirts used in his election campaign. They also magnanimously trained Zimbabwean censors in the best methods to control the Internet.

HU JINTAO ON TAIWAN:

> *"Taiwan affairs should be decided by the Taiwan people. . . . This does not mean they can hold a referendum and then declare independence."*

(Harish Tyagi/epa/Corbis)

7.

KING ABDULLAH—SAUDI ARABIA

THE NATION—Saudi Arabia occupies two-thirds of the Arabian Peninsula. It is a mostly desolate land with no rivers, no lakes, and no perennial streams. Less than 1 percent of the land is arable and it is possible that all of the nation's water may run out in thirty years. In the south of Saudi Arabia lies the Rub' al-Khali, the Empty Quarter, the world's largest stretch of sand. Still, the population of Saudi Arabia, which has tripled since 1973, stands at roughly 25 million, one-third of whom are noncitizen foreign workers. It is illegal for a Saudi citizen to follow a religion other than Islam. Ninety percent of Saudis are Sunnis and 10 percent Shiites.

Contained within the borders of Saudi Arabia are two important elements that have transformed the country into a major player in the world scene. In the western region of Hijaz are the two holiest cities in the Islamic world: Mecca, the site of the Grand Mosque and Mount Arafat, where Mohammad preached his last sermon, and Medina, site of The Prophet's tomb and shrines to Islamic heroes. One of the duties of the world's 1.5 billion Muslims is to try to visit Mecca at least once in a lifetime. About two million Muslims make this pilgrimage (hajj) every year. In Hasa, in the east of the country, in the region occupied by the Shi'a minority, is the nation's other great asset: oil. Saudi Arabia contains 25 percent of the world's oil reserves and accounts for 11 percent of the world's production. The Ghawar field, which provides half of the nation's output, is the largest oil field in the world.

This nation of spiritual and material riches is ruled by the Saud family, a king and several thousand princes whose ruling style is a fusion of medieval feudalism and the Mafia. They follow a rigid, uncompromising version of Islam known to the West as Wahhabism. However, their devotion to ideology is balanced by a keen sense of self-preservation.

MUHAMMAD AND THE BIRTH OF ISLAM—Muhammad Ibn Abdullah was born in about 570 in Mecca which, at the time, was a commercial center that contained the Kaaba, a temple that was the destination of an annual pilgrimage. In his youth, Muhammad traveled extensively with his merchant uncle and was exposed to the monotheistic religions of Judaism and Christianity. When he was forty years old, Muhammad was meditating in a cave when he had a vision of the Angel Gabriel, who taught him various verses that were later transcribed and became the Quran. Muhammad gradually developed followers and, by 622, the Muslim community was large enough to be considered a threat to the local authorities. So Muhammad and his followers fled to the nearby oasis of Yathrib, which they renamed Medina. Cut off from their own tribes and without land of their own, Muhammad and his followers began raiding caravans on their way to Mecca. In 623, fighting broke out between the Meccans and the Muslims, but by 630 Muhammad's forces were so strong that they were able to conquer Mecca without a fight. They destroyed the town's idols, but kept the black stone of the Kaaba and transformed the annual pilgrimage into a Muslim one. Muhammad died in 632, having spread his faith over all of the Arabian Peninsula. His followers then carried Islam around the world.

The Muslim leaders who succeeded Muhammad were known (in English) as caliphs. The fourth caliph, Ali, moved his capital from Medina to Iraq and the Arabian Peninsula reverted to tribalism. The Ottoman Turks took power in Arabia in the sixteenth century, and it was also during this period that the Saudi extended family settled in the area.

THE PARTNERSHIP—Sheikh Muhammad bin Saud was just another tribal leader in the central Arabian region of Nejd when, in 1744, he provided shelter for a local preacher and judge named Sheikh Muhammad bin Abd al-Wahhab. Under the rule of the Ottomans, Islam, having already split into factions, lost its fervor. Wahhab's message was that Islam needed to be cleansed. Although they are known to much of the world today as Wahhabis, the followers of Wahhab called themselves Unitarians (*muwahaddun*). Wahhab believed that

there should be no distinction between religion and the state; that all conduct, including government, should be based on the original, unadulterated rules set down in the Quran and interpreted by the first three generations after Muhammad. He taught that all Muslims were equal, regardless of their class, nationality, or ethnic or tribal origin. Nonbelievers, on the other hand, were subject to punishment, and his punishment for adultery exemplified his view of women. The man was reprieved, but the woman was stoned to death.

Wahhab's teachings were not particularly popular, but they did attract Saud, and together they formed a powerful combination of military power and religious proselytizing. To this day, the descendents of Muhammad bin Saud control the government of Saudi Arabia and the descendents of Muhammad bin Abd al-Wahhab control its religious affairs. It is this same combination of sword and God that has allowed the Saud family to establish kingdoms in Arabia three times.

THE FIRST SAUDI KINGDOM (c1744–1819)—Saudi forces captured Mecca and Medina and, eventually, almost one million square miles. While the Ottoman Turks were busy dealing with the Napoleonic Wars, the Wahhabis destroyed all traces of the Turks, including shrines and mosques they had built. In 1811, the Viceroy of Egypt, Muhammad Ali, launched the Ottoman counterattack. In 1818, his son, Ibrahim Pasha, conquered Mecca and then continued another 500 miles to Nejd, the center of Wahhabism. His troops also destroyed the Saudi capital of Diriya. Ibrahim Pasha was not a compassionate conqueror. His troops took all the food they could find and they sent the Saudi ruler to Constantinople (Istanbul) where he was beheaded.

THE SECOND SAUDI KINGDOM (1824–1891)—The grandson of Muhammad bin Saud, Turki, and his son Faisal established a new Saudi capital at Riyadh and set about reconquering the lands they had lost and reconverting the populace to Wahhabism. Their efforts received a setback in 1871 when the Turks occupied the eastern Arabian province of Hasa and gave their support not to the Saudis, but to a rival family, the Rashid. The loss of Hasa was a heavy blow to the Saud family because it was the source of the dates and pearls that they used to bribe the tribes of central Arabia. The Rashidis gained control of all of the Saudi domains and the Saud family were reduced to figurehead leaders with no power. In January 1891, the Saudis, led by Abdul Rahman, abandoned Riyadh and went into exile. After two years on the road, they sheltered in Qatar and then settled in Kuwait, from which they began to launch raids against the Rashidis. When Muhammad bin Rashid died in 1897, clan infighting broke out, opening a window of opportunity for the Saudis.

THE FOUNDERS—Abdul Aziz bin Abdul Rahman Al Saud, the son of Abdul Rahman, was ten years old when his family fled Riyadh. When he married for the second time at age eighteen (his first wife had died), the Sauds were too poor to pay for the wedding and a local merchant had to fund the festivities. But the family had not forgotten their past glory and had not given up the hope of rising again.

The 1902 recapture of Riyadh has been raised to such a mythic level in Saudi Arabia that it is difficult to sort out the facts from the legend. It appears that in late September of 1901, Abdul Aziz left Kuwait with a fighting force of forty men. Their numbers grew to about 200, but many drifted away as it became clear that the opportunities for plunder were slim. Armed with daggers, swords, pistols, rifles, and short-shafted spears, there were fifty or sixty warriors left when they reached the outskirts of Riyadh in January 1902. Scaling the walls of the Masmak battlements in the middle of the night, they waited until morning. When the governor, Rashid Ibn Ajlan, emerged from prayers, Abdul Aziz and his men launched their attack. A melee ensued and Abdul Aziz's cousin killed Ajlan. Abdul Aziz appeared on top of the battlements holding Ajlan's head and then threw it down to the anxious crowd below. When the Saud family returned to Riyadh, Abdul Aziz tried to hand over control of the city to his father, but Abdul Rahman, following tribal tradition, handed authority back to his son because he was deemed more fit for the job. Only twenty-one years old, Abdul Aziz, who came to be known internationally as Ibn Saud, was the leader of a family that had twice controlled most of Arabia.

While in Kuwait, Ibn Saud had been impressed by the way that nation's leader, Sheikh Mubarak, had escaped Turkish control by cultivating the British and he tried to do the same. However, whereas Kuwait had a harbor, Riyadh had nothing that the British wanted. In fact, the Western powers had so little interest in the region that their cartographers did not even know the latitude and longitude of Riyadh. Left to his own devices, Ibn Saud and his warriors managed to fight off a counterattack by the Rashidis, but their resources were so depleted by their effort that in February 1905, Ibn Saud, in exchange for control of Nejd, had to accept the official role of district commissioner for the Ottoman Turks. The Saudis needed another four or five years to completely eliminate the Rashidi threat.

THE HASHEMITES—The Saudis also faced another regional challenger, the Hashemites, who would later rule modern Syria and Iraq and who still rule Jordan. The House of Hashim had ruled Mecca since 1073. In December 1908, the Turks appointed Sharif Hussein, the leader of the Hashemites, the emir of Hijaz. In 1910, Sharif Hussein captured Ibn Saud's brother and kept him hostage until the Saudis paid a ransom. At this point the British decided to foment an Arab revolt against the Turks and looked for a leader among the Arabs. Given the choice between Ibn Saud and Sharif Hussein, the British chose Hussein because he had lived in Turkey and was familiar with modern politics, because he was a descendant of Muhammad, and because his home base, Hijaz, was more important than Ibn Saud's home base of Nejd. In addition, Wahhabism was not popular outside of Nejd.

Nonetheless, Ibn Saud was still fighting for territory. In 1913, Saudi forces invaded Hasa on the Persian Gulf. Enlisting the aid of the local Bedouin, they defeated the Turks. This victory gave the Saudis date palms and access to the sea. It also earned them vast stretches of sand under which, unbeknownst to them at the time, was something that would prove far more valuable: oil.

Soon the Turks and the British were engaged in a chess match, searching for the right Arab allies to serve as surrogate armies in their larger struggle. For their part, Ibn Saud and Sharif Hussein sought protection from these stronger powers in their local battle against each other. In the spring of 1914, Ibn Saud accepted the Turkish title of *wali* (governor). Two years later, when British troops captured Basra in Iraq, they discovered a secret treaty in which the Saudis had promised the Turks not to grant concessions to the British. On December 26, 1915, however, Ibn Saud signed a ten-year treaty with the British in which he would be recognized as the ruler of Nejd and its dependencies under British protection. In exchange, he agreed to not attack any neighboring sheikhs. In fact, this was what he had asked of the British back in 1902.

In June 1916, Sharif Hussein also made a deal with the British, who gave him arms to fight the Turks. Sharif Hussein also convinced the nobles of Mecca to proclaim him "King of the Arabs," a presumption that did not sit well with the vast majority of Arabs. Finally, the Ottoman Turks lost control of the Arabian Peninsula forever.

Ibn Saud soon learned that he had to be careful aligning himself with the British. In November 1917, the Bolsheviks, having taken power in Russia, published the Sykes-Picot Agreement which revealed that Great Britain and France had promised independence to the Arabs only to create an Arab revolt against the Turks, and that they had no intention of allowing the Arabs to keep control of any land beyond the peninsula. In addition, a letter from Arthur Balfour, the British foreign secretary, to Lord Rothschild, the president of the British Zionist Federation, gave approval for the establishment of a Jewish homeland in Palestine. The British hoped that the Jews would help protect the Suez Canal. Many British leaders also wanted to rid Europe of the Jews, whom they viewed as dangerously revolutionary.

When the Saudis defeated the Hashemites at the Battle of Turabah in May 1919, the British switched their main Arab allegiance to Ibn Saud. Two months later they invited Ibn Saud to visit Great Britain. The Saudi leader declined the invitation, but instead sent his fourteen-year-old son, Faisal, who thus became the first member of the House of Saud to visit Europe.

THE IKHWAN—The Ikhwan (Brotherhood) were desert evangelicals who took the Quran as the literal Word of God and wanted to revive the severe restrictions of Wahhabism. They punished Muslims who did not attend mosque services and they threatened Christians. They opposed anything that smacked of affectation, including silk, gold, long mustaches, and trimmed beards. They also opposed anything that did not exist during the time of Muhammad 1,300 years earlier, including tobacco, telephones, and telegraphs. But they did allow one exception: rifles. Ibn Saud made an alliance with the Ikhwan, and together, in 1921, they defeated the remaining forces of the House of Rashid, one of whose leaders, Saud, died in battle, leaving behind three widows. Ibn Saud gave one Rashidi widow to his brother, one to his own son, Saud, and kept the third one, Fahda bint Asi Al Shuraim, for himself. In 1924, Fahda gave birth to Abdullah, the current king of Saudi Arabia.

The Rashidis were no longer a threat to Ibn Saud, but he still had to contend with the Hashemites and their increasingly bizarre leader, Sharif Hussein. As a result of the Uqair Conference in November 1922, Ibn Saud gained a disputed strip of land claimed by Kuwait, but lost other land to Iraq. With British support, the Hashemites created Transjordan (present-day Jordan) to the north and assumed the throne of Iraq, which meant that Ibn Saud was practically surrounded by Hashemites. Sharif Hussein, desperate for money, doubled the price of entrance for pilgrims to Mecca. In late 1924 he banned the Ikhwan from participating in the hajj. The Ikhwan responded by attacking Mecca and overthrowing Hussein. His forces surrendered Medina the following year and, thanks to the military prowess of the Ikhwan, Ibn Saud was declared King of Hejaz.

Although Ibn Saud already controlled his home territory of Nejd, as well as Hasa, the former domain of the Rashidis, it was his takeover of Hejaz and the holy cities of Mecca and Medina that transformed him from a local tribal leader to a ruler of international importance. He put an end to 850 years of Hashemite rule of the holy cities and was now in charge of the hajj.

But Ibn Saud still had to deal with the Ikhwan, who were also supported by the Bedouin nomads. In 1927, he held a conference with 3,000 Ikhwan, who voiced their complaints to him: they did not approve of the introduction of telegraph lines; they did approve of young Faisal's visit to England; they wanted him to punish the Shiites for their interpretation of Islam; and they wanted the Muslim "infidels" from Iraq and Transjordan to stop using Saudi grazing land. As sympathetic as Ibn Saud was to many of the positions of the Ikhwan, he recognized that they were a threat to his personal power. As he formed a new government, he drastically centralized authority and he filled almost all of the most important government posts with members of his own family. The Ikhwan revolted, but, with the help of the British, who now looked to Ibn Saud as their man in the region, he defeated them. Over the next four years, Ibn Saud's forces put down a series of revolts and successfully consolidated his rule.

THE KINGDOM OF SAUDI ARABIA—On September 18, 1932, Ibn Saud, at the age of fifty-two, declared himself the King of Saudi Arabia. Actually, the concept of a king had never been accepted in central Arabia, where tribal tradition supported less centralized leadership, but Ibn Saud was inspired by European royalty and so a king he would be. He ran his new country like the Mafia. Cousins by marriage became lieutenants, half-brothers were given areas to rule, and non-Saudis, if they proved their loyalty, were treated like adjuncts to the family.

Pursuing Wahhabist doctrine, Ibn Saud took the position that there should not be a division between religion and the state. He claimed that his absolute authority was sanctioned by Allah and that disobedience to him was heresy. He used the ulema (religious leaders) to issue fatwas (written judgments) to justify his policies. He tried to expand his kingdom by invading Yemen, but the Yemenis successfully resisted and Ibn Saud had to settle for a peace treaty. Internationally, he flirted with the Soviets, who loaned him oil, and with the Nazis, who gave him German-made rifles and built him an arms factory in Riyadh. Basically though, Ibn Saud leaned toward Great Britain through most of World War II. On February 14, 1945, after the Yalta Conference, Ibn Saud met for the first time with a non-Muslim leader: the president of the United States, Franklin Delano Roosevelt. Roosevelt, who died two months later, agreed to help the Jewish people only in ways that were not hostile to the Arabs. Ibn Saud also met with Winston Churchill, who irritated him by smoking. By the end of the war, Saudi Arabia had turned away from Great Britain and embraced the United States. Ibn Saud also managed to declare war on Germany in time to be invited to join the United Nations.

ALLAH'S GIFT—Oil was discovered in southern Persia (Iran) in 1908. The following year the British formed the Anglo-Persian Oil Company. By the time of World War I the British navy had switched from coal to oil. The British government bought 51 percent of Anglo-Persian in 1914, eventually changing its name to Anglo-Iranian in 1935 and British Petroleum in 1954. In Saudi Arabia, Ibn Saud granted his first drilling concession in 1923 to a New Zealander named Major Frank Holmes. Nothing came of the deal. In 1928 the world's five leading oil companies, Standard Oil of New Jersey (now Exxon), Standard Oil of New York (now Mobil), Anglo-Persian (now BP), Royal Dutch Shell, and Compagnie Francaise des Petroles, concluded five years of negotiations by divvying up the old Ottoman Empire. Left out of the deal, Standard Oil of California went directly to Ibn Saud and, in exchange for $175,000 in gold and a couple of loans, obtained the exploration rights to 360,000 square miles in Saudi Arabia. It finally struck oil in Hasa on March 20, 1938. Exploitation of the find was delayed by World War II.

After the war, the Saudis renegotiated their oil contracts. Although they lost quite a bit of money to American accounting practices, what was left made Ibn Saud an extremely wealthy man. Despite the severe restrictions of Wahhabism, he managed to father more than sixty children, and a common joke was that the only way that Ibn Saud united the Arab people was in bed.

PASSING THE TORCH—As early as 1933, Ibn Saud designated his eldest surviving son, Saud, crown prince, meaning that he was the successor to the throne. Ibn Saud also groomed his second-eldest son, Faisal, as a successor. By 1950 the founder's health was deteriorating and he handed over authority to Crown Prince Saud. Saud and Faisal were very different, and the tension between them would color the politics of Saudi Arabia for the next fourteen years. Faisal was well-educated, well-traveled, and sophisticated, while Saud was a man of the desert who spoke no foreign languages and who preferred remaining in the Saudi home base of Nejd. Saud strengthened various religious prohibitions and expanded the reach of the religious enforcers, the Society for the Encouragement of Good and the Prevention of Evil. His strict Wahhabist beliefs made him unpopular in Hejaz. Faisal, on the other hand, gained popularity by legalizing football (soccer) in 1951, which had previously been banned because men exposed their thighs in public and because the ulema considered football a cover for subversive activity. Ibn Saud died, at one of Faisal's palaces, on November 9, 1953. The fifty-one-year-old Saud became Saudi Arabia's second king and Faisal moved up to crown prince.

KING NUMBER TWO: SAUD—Saud ibn Abdul Aziz was born the day that his father captured Riyadh in 1902. Outdoing Ibn Saud, he would eventually father fifty-two sons and fifty-five daughters. Saud's reign was characterized by widespread corruption, conflict within the royal family, and the necessity of dealing with the populist, antimonarchist rise of Egypt's Gamal Abdul Nasser, who led the overthrow of the Egyptian monarchy in 1952. Saud also outlawed strikes and the teaching of political science.

Nasser preached an appealing line: the Ottoman Turks had oppressed the Arab people and then the Western powers had divided them. Now it was time for all Arabs to unite and take control of their own destiny. At first Saud the king and Nasser the nationalist formed an odd couple, brought together by their opposition to the pro-British Hashemite monarchies in Jordan and Iraq. Saud gave money to Nasser to help him spread his message. But soon he came to view the Egyptian as a threat. When Nasser visited Saudi Arabia in 1956 to ask for oil, he was so popular that he was greeted by the largest demonstration in the nation's history. In July of that year, Nasser nationalized the Suez Canal, and he did so without consulting Saud. As angry as that made Saud, it was nothing compared to his reaction when Great

Britain, France, and Israel attacked Egypt in October. Saud broke relations with the British and the French, and halted oil shipments to both countries. It was Saudi Arabia's first oil embargo, but it would not be the last. Saudi oil revenue fell by 40 percent, but there was a silver lining in the uproar: U.S. president Dwight Eisenhower, immersed in a Cold War, anti-Communist crusade, decided to make Saud his representative in the Arab world.

Not all Americans were so enthusiastic about supporting the House of Saud. When King Saud visited New York in January 1957, the city's Catholic mayor, Robert Wagner, refused to welcome him. Wagner cited Saud's anti-Semitic remarks, his refusal to allow Jewish soldiers to participate in the U.S. Training Mission in Saudi Arabia, his banning of Christian ceremonies, and the fact that Saudi Arabia still practiced slavery. Senator Wayne Morse of Oregon put the case bluntly. "Here we are . . . pouring by way of gifts to that totalitarian state, Saudi Arabia, millions of dollars of the taxpayer's money to maintain the military forces of a dictatorship. We ought to have our heads examined." None of this mattered to Eisenhower, who increased U.S. aid to Saudi Arabia by $180 million in exchange for five-year use of the Dhahran military base.

The following year, the nine leading brothers in the Saudi royal family, increasingly concerned about King Saud's overspending and alcoholism, asked Crown Prince Faisal to return from the United States, where he was recovering from surgery. Faisal cracked down on corruption using tactics such as giving each family member a personal allowance and banning the import of private automobiles. By 1962, he had cleared the national debt. Saud tried to return to power in December 1960, forming an unlikely alliance with a group of liberal half-brothers led by Finance Minister Prince Talal. Talal ventured the radical proposal that Saudi Arabia should have a constitution. However, the ulema declared that the nation already had a constitution: Islamic Shari'a law. Saud dismissed Talal and revoked his passport.

Meanwhile, the Saudi conflict with Nasser was continuing to fester. Nasser and Saud traded assassination attempts (both officially denied). In 1958, Egypt and Syria merged to form the United Arab Republic, but three years later Saud managed to convince the Syrians to withdraw from the union by slipping $12 million to the Syrian royal family. Nasser's popularity was growing throughout the Arab world, but then he made a fatal mistake. On September 26, 1962, revolutionaries overthrew the royal family of Yemen. The House of Saud was naturally alarmed to see a royal family right across its border lose all their power, particularly when the Egyptian army arrived in Yemen to help the new government. Furthermore, the new U.S. president, John F. Kennedy, did not buy the argument that the Saudi royal family was a legitimate bastion against Communism. But he did agree to give the Saudis military exercises if they would initiate reforms. So in November 1962, Faisal announced a ten-point reform program that included the abolition of slavery. At the time there were about 30,000 slaves in Saudi Arabia; the government bought 4,000 of them.

Faisal shared responsibilities with three of his younger brothers. He put future King Fahd in charge of reforms; he put future king Abdullah in command of the mostly tribal National Guard, which was responsible for domestic security and political repression; and he gave command of the Yemeni war against Egypt to future crown prince Sultan. Of course, it was necessary for the brothers to coordinate their activities. For example, when Fahd opened schools for girls, Abdullah's National Guard had to be called out to enforce the decision.

In the spring of 1963, the republican revolutionaries in Yemen announced their intention to reclaim the province of Asir, which the Saudis had taken in 1920. The Egyptian military, using Soviet arms, bombed three southern towns in Saudi Arabia, killing many people including thirty-six patients in a hospital. President Kennedy sent fighter jets over Saudi cities to draw the line on Nasser's aggression.

In December 1963, Saud again demanded that he be given power and he retired to his palace along with 1,500 troops. Three months later, seventy princes of the House of Saud met in what they called a Council of Those Who Bind and Loose. King Saud told the princes, "I am not Queen Elizabeth. Arabian kings are kings or nothing." The princes agreed. The ulema declared Saud unfit to rule and the princes gave the kingdom to Faisal.

KING NUMBER THREE: FAISAL—Faisal ibn Abdul Aziz was proclaimed king November 2, 1964, and his brother Khalid was promoted to crown prince. By this time Gamal Abdul Nasser was increasingly preoccupied with his conflict with Israel, and the war in Yemen was draining the Egyptian coffers. In June 1967, Israel crushed the Egyptian-led Arab forces in the Six-Day War and doubled its size by conquering land that belonged to Egypt, Syria, and Jordan. Nasser could not continue the war in Yemen. He met with King Faisal and agreed to withdraw Egyptian troops from the country. After five years, Faisal had emerged victorious over Nasser.

The Six-Day War destroyed Arab illusions about their power. But for Saudi Arabia it had a positive aspect because it left the Saudis as the strongest Arab nation. It also increased Faisal's hatred of Israel, which now controlled Jerusalem, Islam's third-holiest city behind Mecca and Medina. He blamed a "Zionist-Bolshevik" conspiracy.

Domestically, Faisal put an end to the period of reform in 1965. He initiated a witch hunt, ordering the arrest of anyone who was even remotely pro-Nasser. He put the Grand Mufti, Saudi Arabia's most respected religious leader, in charge of the nation's education. He ordered all government officials to join in group prayers. Sex segregation was formally imposed at the age of nine, at which time a girl also had to start wearing a veil. He forbade the installation of direct-dial telephones because men and women might talk together in a lewd manner. Instead, all calls had to go through operators. Faisal also forbade the use of Cadillacs because they were associated with ex–King Saud. He did allow the introduction of television, although it was heavily censored. Even scenes of Mickey Mouse and Minnie Mouse kissing were excised. After the Grand Mufti died, Faisal created a Ministry of Justice to take control of the religious courts, and he took from the new Grand Mufti the responsibility of interpreting Shari'a law. He also co-opted the ulema by creating a seventeen-member Council of Senior Ulema which was answerable to his rule.

In 1969, Saudi Arabia's only Arab allies were other monarchies. But Faisal smoothed relations with more countries, including Egypt after the death of Nasser in 1970. By 1971, Saudi Arabia's only Arab enemies were Yemen and Iraq. Still, the Saudis were nervous. When Muammar al-Qaddafi in Libya and the Ba'athist regime in Iraq nationalized the operations of British Petroleum in January 1972, King Faisal offered the United States unlimited oil in exchange for military protection.

On October 6, 1973, during the holiest day of the Jewish calendar, Yom Kippur, Egypt and Syria—seeking to recapture the land they lost in 1967—attacked Israel. The U.S. president, Richard Nixon, ignoring pleas from the oil industry, gave $2.2 billion in emergency aid to Israel. Back in 1960, Saudi Arabia, along with Iran, Iraq, Kuwait, and Venezuela, had created the Organization of Petroleum Exporting Countries (OPEC), whose members represented 80 percent of the world's oil production. The day after Nixon's 1973 announcement of support for Israel, OPEC declared that, for the first time, the producers would set the price of oil, and they immediately cut production by 10 percent and threatened to cut 5 percent more each month until the Israeli-Palestinian problem was settled. King Faisal announced that a holy war had begun. He stopped all oil shipments to the United States and he vowed to continue the embargo until he could "pray in Jerusalem under an Arab flag." Unfortunately for Faisal, Saudi Arabia provided only 4 percent of the American oil supply and Iran, Iraq, and Libya were happy to keep pumping and make up the deficit. Only sixteen days after the beginning of the Yom Kippur War, the United States and the USSR helped negotiate a ceasefire. Faisal's vow to punish the West until the Arabs controlled Jerusalem fell flat. However, as in 1968, a war against Israel turned out to be a blessing in disguise for the Saudi royal family. The world needed more and more oil. Faisal ended the embargo on March 19, 1974, after President Nixon agreed to sell to Saudi Arabia sophisticated fighter aircraft, as well as tanks and naval vessels. As soon as the embargo was lifted, Saudi wealth mushroomed. Between 1973 and 1974, the price of oil more than tripled, from $2.70 a barrel to $9.80 and oil exports skyrocketed from $5.9 billion in 1973 to $32.5 billion in 1974. The Saudis had no problems spending their jackpot. Car imports tripled in a year and real estate prices rose dramatically.

FAISAL VS. FAISAL—On March 26, 1975, King Faisal was shot to death by one of his nephews, twenty-six-year-old Faisal ibn Musaid. Saudi security forces interrogated the younger Faisal and then, before three months had passed, they beheaded him. The official Saudi line was that the interrogators could not find any motive for Faisal's act and that he was on drugs and crazy. In fact, it was not difficult to surmise a motive. Ten years earlier, Faisal's older brother had taken part in a violent protest against a television station in Riyadh. King Faisal ordered an assault against the protesters and Faisal's brother was killed. Faisal had studied at the University of California, Berkeley, and had been exposed to the radical politics of the time. His uncle was not only a well-known tyrant, but the king had killed his own brother.

KING NUMBER FOUR: KHALID—Khalid ibn Abdul Aziz was sixty-three years old when he assumed the throne of Saudi Arabia. But Khalid was not an ambitious man and was satisfied with a ceremonial role. The new crown prince, his younger brother Fahd, took charge of the nation's most important decisions. Still, Khalid's reign coincided with a tumultuous time in the region's history. In February 1979, the pro-Western Shah of Iran was overthrown and Ayatollah Ruhollah Khamenei turned Iran into an Islamic Republic run by Shiites. This inspired the Shiite minority in Saudi Arabia, and the government used force to put down violent rioting.

On November 20, 1979, about 700 armed members of a messianic Wahhabi group seized control of the Grand Mosque, one of the holy sites in Mecca. Their leader, Juhaiman al-Utaibi, demanded the overthrow of the Saud family, the expulsion of all foreigners, and an accounting for the nation's wealth that the royal family had wasted. It took Saudi troops, with support from Great Britain, France, and Jordan, two weeks to flush out the rebels, by which time almost 300 people had been killed, including twenty-five pilgrims and twenty hostages. Of the 143 rebels who were taken prisoner, sixty-three were publicly beheaded.

Three weeks later, Soviet troops invaded Afghanistan. The Saudi regime was shaken by these threats both inside and outside the country. But U.S. president Jimmy Carter pledged to protect the Saudi royals and their oil fields. "Any assault on the Gulf," he declared, "will be regarded as an assault on the vital interests of the United States."

KING NUMBER FIVE: FAHD—When Khalid died in 1982, Fahd moved up to king and Abdullah, the longtime commander of the National Guard, ascended to crown prince. Back in the 1950s, Fahd had served as Saudi Arabia's first minister of education, and later, for thirteen years, as King Faisal's interior minister. Fahd Ibn Abdul Aziz was a high liver in the tradition of his father, Ibn Saud, and his older brother, Saud. He loved food, women, gambling, and luxury. When he visited Monte Carlo and France, paparazzi caught him in front of casinos and brothels. As late as 2003, when he was eighty years old, he brought with him on a vacation in Marbella, Spain, 350 attendants, fifty black Mercedes, and a 234-foot yacht. Fahd's regime saw a rise in corruption, with kickbacks reportedly going as high as 30 percent in the armaments and construction industries. Fahd did put some of the nation's oil profits to good use, providing new highways, free water, and a free modern hospital system.

The early years of Fahd's reign marked the beginning of deficit spending, as 25 percent of the gross national product was spent on defense and Saudi Arabia became the world's leading importer of advanced weapons. There was also a marked growth in foreign labor, even while Saudi unemployment remained high. Fahd allowed women to take jobs in all-female beauty salons, schools, banks, and services, but this led to an increased presence of the religious police on the lookout for forbidden interaction between the sexes.

In 1986, Fahd gave himself the title of Custodian of the Two Holy Mosques, but it was this role that brought him into conflict with the supporters of Iran's Islamic Revolution. Iranian-inspired rioting left 400 dead during the 1987 hajj. Fahd approved the reduction of Iran's pilgrim quota from 150,000 to 40,000, whereupon Iran boycotted the hajj.

King Fahd also used his nation's oil largesse to fund foreign wars, but two of these projects would come back to haunt him. He had given major support to the mujahedin fighting the Soviet invaders in Afghanistan, and he had encouraged and paid young Saudi men to go there and fight. When the Soviet troops finally left Afghanistan in 1989, the Saudi mujahedin returned home to an economy that was short on jobs. But now they were militant Islamists and they were well-trained military fighters. In the years to come, these returning mujahedin, and younger men to whom they would pass on their ideology, would become a dangerous threat to the Saudi royal family.

During the 1980–1988 war between Iraq and Iran, the Saudi government gave $25.7 billion in aid to Saddam Hussein on the assumption that he was the lesser of two evils. Having spent massively to upgrade its own military, the Saudi royal family exuded confidence. On April 27,1990, Defense Minister Prince Sultan boasted, "There are no foreign troops in the Kingdom of Saudi Arabia. This is because the Kingdom's policy is to rely on Allah and the arms of its sons in defending itself and its holy places." Three months later, Iraq invaded Kuwait and easily overran the country. Fearful that the Iraqis would cross the border into Saudi Arabia, King Fahd panicked. Osama bin Laden proposed to use the battle-hardened mujahedin to defend the country, but Fahd viewed bin Laden as a threat to his own power. Instead, Fahd, without consulting Crown Prince Abdullah or other members of the family, decided to accept U.S. president George H.W. Bush's offer to defend the kingdom. More than 500,000 American troops poured into Saudi Arabia along with more than 200,000 troops from other, mostly Arab nations. The presence of the Americans was humiliating to many citizens of Saudi Arabia, who were disgusted at being protected by "Jews and women." Saddam Hussein's forces, although numerous, were weak, poorly trained, and easily defeated. When this became clear, it exposed the weakness of the Saudi regime, which had wasted billions of dollars on its military and yet was unable to defend itself. (Actually, it has never been proved that Saddam Hussein ever intended to invade Saudi Arabia.) The war was over by the end of February 1991, but King Fahd and the royal family still had a heavy price to pay, both literally and figuratively. Saudi Arabia reimbursed the United States and other coalition members to the tune of $65 billion, and then laid out another $50 billion to buy more weapons.

Discontent with the regime mildly emboldened opponents of the royal family to submit petitions for reform. One such Letter of Demands, signed by hundreds of ulemas, academics, and lawyers, called for an end to privilege for the royal family, a requirement that state officials be competent, an end to usury and taxes, and the safeguarding of individual rights. The royal family rejected the demands, and the Senior Ulema Council ruled that Saudi citizens did not have the right to publicly petition the king. King Fahd did propose in 1992 that Saudi Arabia adopt its first written constitution, and he also appointed a ninety-member consultative council, the Majlis al-Shura, which had no power.

Since it was obvious that the royal family had no intention of giving up even a tiny piece of power, it was not surprising that a violent opposition soon developed. Overwhelmingly, the Saudi people believed that the United States had used Saddam Hussein's invasion of Kuwait as an excuse to establish a permanent military presence in their country. There was a civilian insurrection in the town of al-Bureida, followed by hundreds of arrests. On November 13, 1995, a bomb attack on a U.S. military mission in Riyadh killed five people and wounded sixty. Four Saudis were ultimately beheaded for the crime.

Two weeks after the Riyadh bombing, Fahd suffered a stroke. Although he continued to be king, his duties were gradually turned over to Crown Prince Abdullah.

KING NUMBER SIX: ABDULLAH—Although he did not officially take over as king of Saudi Arabia until Fahd's death in 2005, Abdullah had been the de facto ruler of the country since Fahd's stroke ten years earlier. Born Abdullah bin Abdulaziz al-Saud in Riyadh in 1924, his mother was the eighth wife of Ibn Saud. Like his brothers, Abdullah was educated at the Princes' School at the royal court. "I train my own children to walk barefoot," Ibn Saud once said, "to rise two hours before dawn, to eat but little, to ride horses bareback." Like all of Ibn Saud's sons, Abdullah spent time at his father's daily majlis and observed the way he dealt with the problems brought to him by Saudi male citizens. Meeting another requirement, he spent time in the desert with the Bedouins, an experience he apparently took to more comfortably than most of Ibn Saud's sons.

ALONG A HIGHWAY IN RIYADH, A LITTLE REMINDER
OF WHO IS IN CHARGE
Lynsey Addario/Corbis

In 1962, Abdullah's older brother, Faisal, put him in charge of the newly formed National Guard, which was primarily made up of Bedouins, and which was given the responsibility of maintaining security in the cities, a task that became increasingly important as Saudi Arabia transformed into an overwhelmingly urban society. Beginning in the 1970s, Abdullah represented his nation at international conferences and at meetings with world leaders. During his visits to the United States, he met with President Gerald Ford, Vice President George H. W. Bush, President Bill Clinton, and President George W. Bush. Despite his familiarity with U.S. leaders, Abdullah was skeptical of Fahd's decision to allow U.S. troops in Saudi Arabia. After meeting with American officials in 1990, he is said to have remarked, "By God, they will never leave."

Abdullah has four wives, seven sons, and fifteen daughters. He speaks English and three of his sons attended the University of California, Santa Barbara, while another went to England's Royal Military Academy, Sandhurst. Abdullah breeds horses and was the founder of the equestrian club in Riyadh. He is also the patron of the annual Crown Prince's Camel Race. He established libraries in Riyadh and Casablanca, Morocco, and since 1985 he has been chairman of the Jenadriyah National Culture and Heritage Festival.

On June 26, 1996, four weeks after the beheading of the men found guilty of the Riyadh bombing, a truck carrying 5,000 pounds of explosives blew up near the barracks of the U.S. Air Force base at Khobar, killing nineteen people and wounding more than 500, most of them Americans. This incident shook the royal family and clouded U.S.–Saudi relations. But it was another terrorist act that really confused the partnership.

FIFTEEN SAUDIS ATTACK THE UNITED STATES—The Saudi royal family did not know quite what to make of George W. Bush during the early months of his presidency. They considered his father a good friend and George W. himself had been in the

oil business. Yet in August 2001, the new President Bush infuriated Abdullah by publicly stating that the violence between Israel and Palestine was the fault of the Palestinians. Previous presidents had shown at least a little sympathy for the Palestinian plight and had occasionally rebuked the Israelis for one excess or another. Abdullah passed on his displeasure through diplomatic channels, stating in a letter to Bush that because of U.S. support for Israel, "It is time for the United States and Saudi Arabia to look at their separate interests." Abdullah was delighted when Bush responded with a letter reversing his position.

On September 11, 2001, terrorists using hijacked planes attacked New York's World Trade Center, the symbol of U.S. economic power, the Pentagon, the symbol of U.S. military power, and were thwarted in their attempt to attack the White House, the symbol of U.S. political power. The U.S. government quickly revealed the identities of the nineteen, fifteen of whom were citizens of Saudi Arabia. The mastermind of the attacks, Khalid Sheikh Muhammad, was also a Saudi, as was Osama bin Laden, the godfather of al-Qaeda, the organization that oversaw the planning of the attacks. Many Saudis could not accept the fact that their own citizens could have committed such a horrific crime. The Saudi interior minister, Prince Nayef Ibn Abd Al-Aziz, blamed the 9/11 attacks on "Zionists," and Crown Prince Abdullah himself refused to acknowledge the existence of al-Qaeda in Saudi Arabia until more than eighteen months later.

In the days following 9/11, when all commercial flights were grounded, the Bush administration allowed 140 Saudis, mostly members of the royal family and relatives of Osama bin Laden, to leave the United States without being questioned by the FBI. Although the vast majority of these fortunate Saudis were innocent of any connection to al-Qaeda, there were some who might have provided crucial information about bin Laden's actions and, particularly, about al-Qaeda's funding. Later investigators were especially interested in one person who was allowed to leave: Prince Ahmed bin Salman, who died in his sleep ten months later at the age of forty-two. In August 2002, 600 family members of 9/11 victims filed a $1 trillion lawsuit against the House of Saud and other Saudis alleging that they had funded terrorism, either directly or by laundering money through questionable wings of legitimate charities. When the U.S. Congress released its report on the 9/11 attacks in July 2003, the Bush administration blocked the release of twenty-eight pages dealing with Saudi Arabia, claiming that their publication would jeopardize ongoing investigations into terrorist funding. They remain classified today.

In the immediate aftermath of 9/11, Crown Prince Abdullah and his family went to great lengths to smooth over relations with the United States. They paid $17.6 million to lobbyists and public relations firms, most notably Qorois Communication and Patton Boggs, to spread the message of Saudi–U.S. friendship in a campaign that included 1,541 television ads in two weeks. In November 2001, the Saudi government awarded a $140 million contract to develop an oil field to Halliburton, the company formerly run by Vice President Dick Cheney and in which he still held stock options. The Saudi public relations efforts did not sway the American people who, according to polls, overwhelmingly considered Saudi Arabia more of an enemy than an ally. The feeling was mutual. A Zogby International poll showed that 87 percent of Saudis had an unfavorable opinion of the United States. But if the people of the two countries were mistrustful of each other, their leaders felt just the opposite. President Bush would gush about the "eternal friendship" between the United States and Saudi Arabia. When Abdullah visited Bush's ranch in Crawford, Texas, in 2002 and again in 2005, the two made a point of kissing and holding hands in front of the cameras. Reports of their meetings have revealed some awkward moments. For example, during the first visit in 2002, Bush took Abdullah's hands and tried to lead him in a Christian prayer.

FOREIGN AID—Like most wealthy families, the House of Saud has used some of its excess funds to help causes it supports. For example, over the years Saudi Arabia has donated money to Idi Amin, the dictator of Uganda; Said Barre, the dictator of Somalia; and Mobutu Sese Seko, the dictator of Zaire (Congo). In fact, the Saudis paid Moroccan troops to put down an anti-Mobutu revolt. They were the principal financial supporters of Yassir Arafat in Palestine, Jonas Savimbi and his UNITA rebels in Angola, Muslim rebels in Bosnia and Azerbaijan, and the mujahedin in Afghanistan. They gave $25.7 billion to Saddam Hussein; they supplied oil to the apartheid regime in South Africa to help it survive an international boycott; and they were the leading backers of the terrorist-supporting Taliban in Afghanistan. Members of the Saudi royal family contributed to Ronald Reagan's presidential campaign in 1984 and, when the U.S. Congress made it illegal to give money and weapons to the Contra rebels in Nicaragua, the Saudis stepped up and donated $32 million to the Contra cause. They also helped finance U.S covert operations in Lebanon. Good friends with the first President Bush, royal family members gave a $2 million painting to the White House, $1.1 million to the George Bush Presidential Library, and $500,000 to the George Herbert Walker Bush Scholarship Fund at Phillips Academy.

The Saudi royal family has also aggressively tried to convert Muslims around the world to Wahhabism, which, because of its austerity and intolerance, has always been a hard sell. Since 1975, the House of Saud has spent more than $70 billion financing mosques and Islamic centers, distributing Qurans, and building Islamic schools, such as the *madrasahs* in Pakistan and the *pesantren* in Indonesia. According to a March 2002 article in *Ain al-Yaqeen*, an official Saudi magazine, the Saudi royal family had fully or partially funded 210 Islamic centers, 1,500 mosques, 202 colleges, and 2,000 schools in countries where Muslims are not a majority. This program has included more than $300 million spent in the United States, where the vast majority of Muslims studying religion in Arabic do so using Saudi textbooks. Some of the textbooks that are used in Saudi Arabia contain alarming content. An eighth grade school book claimed that Allah cursed Jews and Christians and turned some of them into apes and pigs. According to a ninth grade text, Judgment Day will not come "until the Muslims fight the Jews and kill them." In the tenth grade, Saudi students could read that Muslims should not befriend non-Muslims and that "it is forbidden to show happiness during the holidays of the infidels." One text actually included a section on "ways to show hatred to the infidels." The Saudi government claimed to have deleted this particular chapter after 9/11.

ELECTIONS SAUDI STYLE—One of the best ways to understand the depth of repression in Saudi Arabia is to take a look at the "reforms" that the royal family promotes as evidence of their liberalization. In 2005 the Saudis actually held an election. Of course, it was not for a national government, but rather for municipal councils. Not only were women not allowed to run for office, they could not even vote. In fact, only 400,000 men (in a nation of 25 million people) were considered eligible to register. The election was irrelevant anyway because only half the council seats were up for election. The other half were appointed by Abdullah and the royal family. As King Fahd once said, "If we were to have elections . . . the winners would be rich businessmen who could buy the votes."

JUSTICE SAUDI STYLE—According to Amnesty International, police in Saudi Arabia routinely use torture to extract "confessions." The accused are held in incommunicado detention until after they have been interrogated and often until after they have confessed. Even then, they are not allowed to discuss their case with visitors. If, in court, a defendant renounces his confession, he is returned to prison for more sessions of "interrogation." A noteworthy case from 2004 illustrates Saudi practices. The authorities arrested twelve nonviolent dissidents for holding a public gathering in favor of establishing a constitutional monarchy. All twelve confessed, but in court three of them, university professors Abdullah al-Hamid and Matrouok al-Falih and poet Ali al-Damaini, renounced their confessions. One of their lawyers was imprisoned without charge after he spoke about the case on television. At the beginning, the trial was public, but then the doors were shut and it was held in secret. The defendants were sentenced to six to nine years in prison.

FLOGGING AND OTHER PUNISHMENTS—The Saudi authorities have something of an obsession with flogging, which is imposed for a variety of transgressions, including alcohol-related offences and traffic violations. The record for the most lashes imposed on a prisoner is 4,750, for having sex with his wife's sister. Although it is not known if he survived, his wife's sister got sixty-five lashes as well, even though she was the one who reported the incident. Teenage boys are publicly flogged for talking to a young woman or whistling at one. There have been incidents of floggings being announced through public address systems at shopping malls to give shoppers a chance to watch. In March 2001, a military officer was given twenty lashes for using a mobile phone during a flight. Flogging victims can be suspended with chains and lashed with a flexible metal cable.

As awful as flogging is, it is mild in comparison to Saudi punishments for more serious crimes. A convicted thief can have his right hand cut off, while highway robbers are punished by cross-amputation, the loping off of their right hand *and* their left foot. Then there is Qisas (retaliation) punishment which means an eye for an eye—literally. In 2000, for example, an Egyptian national was convicted in Medina of throwing acid in the face of another Egyptian and damaging his left eye. The guilty party, Abdel Moti Abdel Rahman Mohammad, was sentenced to forcible removal of his left eye.

WOMEN: NOT SEEN, NOT HEARD—In Saudi Arabia, a woman cannot appear in public with a man who is not a relative, cannot travel without a male relative's permission, cannot drive, and cannot work with men. In court, a woman's testimony is equal to half that of a man and, whereas a man can divorce his wife by just saying so, it is almost impossible for a woman to divorce her husband. Women are required to completely cover their bodies in public and they must wear veils. Ibn Baz, a famous Grand Mufti, forbid women to wear high heels. "The wearing of high heels," he decreed, "is impermissible because it may lead the woman to fall . . . and it shows the stature of the woman and her behind more prominently." Some Saudi women have expressed satisfaction with the restrictions in their country. However, from the point of view of human rights, the problem is that those Saudi women who would like to live a freer life have no choice. The strict suppression of women is not voluntary, but obligatory.

Domestic violence against women is deeply rooted in tradition. Ibn Saud, a national hero, was notorious for his physical abuse of slaves, servants, concubines, and wives. The issue finally surfaced publicly in April 2004 when a well-known television presenter, April Rania al-Baz, was beaten by her husband because she answered the telephone. He dumped her unconscious at a hospital, where she was discovered to have thirteen facial fractures. Because she was famous, her husband was imprisoned and she was able to obtain a divorce and retain custody of her two sons. Unfortunately, her case is the exception, and most beaten wives have no choice but to suffer abuse.

The Mutawa'een religious police are on constant patrol, watching for transgressions of the rules of sexual segregation. One particularly shocking case occurred in Mecca on March 11, 2002. A fire broke out in a girls' school. As the girls rushed out of the building, the Mutawa'een forced them back inside because they were not wearing headscarves and because they were not accompanied by male relatives. When male bystanders tried to enter the school to save the girls, the Mutawa'een stopped them because they were not relatives. In the end, fifteen girls died because of the intervention of the religious police.

FOREIGN WORKERS—The Saudi royal family has, for decades, imported foreigners to do unpleasant jobs. Yemenis serve as servants and street sweepers; Thai women as nannies; Filipino men as waiters; Korean men as construction workers; and Somalis, Ethiopians, Indians, and Sri Lankans as servants and manual laborers. These foreigners, particularly those women who work inside private homes, are subject to physical abuse and sexual violence. Eighty percent of prison inmates in Saudi Arabia are non-Saudis and about half of those prisoners who are executed are foreign nationals.

BASIC FREEDOMS—It almost goes without saying that in Saudi Arabia freedom of speech, freedom of assembly, and freedom of religion are nonexistent. All Saudi citizens are required by law to be Muslims. In 2004, Brian O'Connor, a Christian citizen of India, was beaten and deported for owning a Bible and other Christian literature. It is illegal for schools to teach Western philosophy or religion other than Islam, and classrooms are monitored by informers.

SAUDI DESIGNER AMRO ABDELLATIF (RIGHT) AND ONE OF HIS MODELS DISPLAY CLOTHING BEARING THE IMAGES OF KING ABDULLAH AND THE WORDS "THE FALCON OF THE ARABS."
AP Photo

The Ministry of Information, created in 1982, has the right to license, restrict, and close all newspapers. The Supreme Information Council, created in 1981, monitors books, magazines, movies, and other media. All radio and television stations are owned by the government, and censorship is so extreme that statistics on automobile accidents are kept out of the media because they might be construed as a criticism of the king or the government. Even sermons in mosques are pre-censored. The Saudi royal family would not allow the Internet into the country until 1999, and all websites are banned until they have been individually approved. All phone calls are recorded and in 2004 the government banned mobile phones with cameras. In September 2004, they passed a law prohibiting public employees from "engaging in dialogue with local and foreign media."

The highlight of Saudi Arabia's struggle with the issue of human rights took place in October 2003 when the government actually hosted an international human rights conference. Hundreds of Saudis took advantage of this unusual occurrence to stage a public protest. They were all arrested. About eighty of the protestors were held for several months and others were flogged.

Ibn Saud kept control of the people he conquered through a combination of force of arms, intermarriage with more than thirty tribes, and the imposition of Wahhabism, which transcended and disempowered tribal hierarchies. He and his successors viewed nepotism and corruption as natural methods of wealth distribution. Later, the Saudi royal family used their oil profits to buy the loyalty of the population by providing free education and health care and subsidized services. When the world demand for oil has stagnated and Saudi profits have dropped, dissent has grown. But with the demand for oil growing, particularly in China, the Saudi royal family has regained the power and influence that their wealth can buy.

(Richard Wayman/Sygma/Corbis)

8.

SAPARMURAT NIYAZOV— TURKMENISTAN

THE NATION—Turkmenistan is a remote ex-Soviet republic in Central Asia. Three-quarters of the country is desert and only 3 percent is arable. Despite its physical isolation, Turkmenistan has attracted international interest because it sits atop large reserves of natural gas and oil and because it is strategically located, with borders on, among others, Afghanistan, Iran, and the Caspian Sea. According to the most recent census, 77 percent of the population are Turkmen. The two largest minority groups are Uzbek (9.2%) and Russian (6.7%) although, since the breakup of the Soviet Union, almost half of the Russians who once lived in Turkmenistan have fled north. The total population is pushing five million.

HISTORY—Traditionally, the Turkmen are nomadic herdsmen, for whom tribe and clan are more important than nation or religion. The land that is now Turkmenistan has been occupied by a seemingly endless succession of conquerors: the Persians, Alexander the Great,

Scythians, Sassanians, Huns. Arabs arrived in the late seventh and early eighth centuries and brought with them the Islamic faith. Then came the Ottoman Turks and the Mongols. In 1221, Genghis Khan's youngest son, Toloi, razed the Turkmen city of Merv and is said to have killed up to one million people. The Khans were followed by Tamerlane. The next few hundred years were marked by war and poverty and rebellions against the Muslim shahs and Persian shahs who held sway.

In the 1860s the Russian government sent troops to help the Turkmen rebels and then annexed the area. At first the Turkmen agreed to the annexation, but soon they viewed the Russians as just another set of occupiers. Fighting broke the back of the Turkmen resistance at the Battle of Geok-Tepe in 1881. By 1885, Russia controlled all of present-day Turkmenistan. In the chaos of the Russian Revolution, the Turkmen managed to establish their own government, but after gaining control in the more populated regions of what would become the Union of Soviet Socialist Republics, the Communists returned to Central Asia. In 1924 they created the Turkmen Soviet Socialist Republic and set the borders that still exist today. In fact, tribal loyalties were so strong that few of the inhabitants saw themselves as Turkmen until the Communists imposed the identity on them. Another rebellion broke out in 1927, but in 1932, Stalin's troops regained control of Turkmenistan and executed thousands of people, including the republic's president and premier. The Communists set about transforming Turkmenistan, converting the Turkmen from nomadic herdsmen into settled farmers, and forcing them to produce high-quality cotton. By the 1950s, much of Turkmenistan was closed to outsiders and the republic had become the most isolated and obedient of the Soviet republics. The Soviet government ran Turkmenistan as a colony of Russia, using it as a source of natural gas, oil, and cotton, which made up 80 percent of the republic's revenues. When the Soviet Union collapsed in 1991 and Turkmenistan became an independent nation, the Turkmen unemployment rate was 18 percent.

THE MAN—Saparmurat Niyazov was born in Ashgabat on February 19, 1940. He was a member of the Tekke tribe, Turkmenistan's largest. In his book *Rukhnama,* Niyazov says that his grandfather, Annanyyay Artygy, was sent into exile during the Stalinist crackdown of 1932 for the crime of owning a shop and having employees. At some point he returned and became a village chief, but in August 1937, he was arrested, declared an "enemy of the people," and executed. Niyazov's father, Atamyrat Annanyyay, was a teacher who joined the Soviet army during World War II and died in 1943 while fighting in North Ossetia in the Caucasus Mountains. According to Niyazov, when he himself was in his twenties he met an old friend of his father's who was a witness to his death. Atamyrat was one of six soldiers from Turkmenistan, five Turkmen and a Russian, who were taken prisoner by the Germans after a battle. As they waited to find out their fate, one of the Turkmen rolled a cigarette and passed it around. Another of the Turkmen objected to sharing the cigarette with the Russian, but Niyazov's father handed it to him anyway. The Germans ordered the prisoners to line up and called for all Communists to step forward. The Turkmen who had objected to sharing the cigarette with the Russian grumbled that Atamyrat might as well be a Communist. A German soldier pulled Niyazov's father out of the line and threw him together with other alleged Communists. He was then executed with a machine gun and thrown in a ditch. Back in Ashgabat, Niyazov's mother, Gurbanosoltan, was left a widow with three sons under the age of six, of whom the middle one was Saparmurat.

Saparmurat Niyazov was eight years old when he experienced the defining moment of his life. On October 6, 1948, a devastating earthquake de-molished the city of Ashgabat, killing an estimated 110,000 people. Among the dead were Niyazov's mother and both of his brothers. Stalin refused to acknowledge that the earthquake had taken place and the locals were left to dig out of the rubble by themselves. Niyazov was alone for six days before someone came to take away the bodies of his mother and his brothers. For Niyazov, it marked a premature end to his childhood. He was left with nothing but fond memories of his mother. He would later write, "When I encounter a difficulty, I re-member my mother's smile. That smile spreads through-out my soul and takes away the pain I have. It is as if a hand stretches out and takes the pain away." Such devo-tion to a dead mother is touching and admirable, but in Niyazov's case, it would lead to bizarre twists after he be-came a dictator.

THE FUTURE TURKMENBASHI
WITH HIS MOTHER

Niyazov spent most of the rest of his youth in a Communist Party orphanage. He seems to have lived for a time with relatives, but this was evidently an unpleasant experience and one to which he does not like to refer. He attended the Leningrad Polytechnic Institute and graduated in 1966 with a degree in power engineering. After graduation, he returned to Turkmenistan and worked at a power station near Ashgabat. In 1962, Niyazov joined the Communist Party. In Turkmen society, with its heavy emphasis on clan and kinship, Niyazov's lack of family was an enormous hindrance. But in the world of Communism, the opposite was true. As a genuine Turkmen, but without clan affiliation, he rose steadily in the Party hierarchy and by 1986 he had been chosen head of the Communist Party of Turk-menistan. At this time he showed no interest in Mikhail Gorbachev's *glasnost* and *perestroika*, but when the Soviet Union disintegrated in 1991, Niyazov was well-positioned to take charge of newly independent Turkmenistan.

Niyazov is married and has two children; however, none of his family members live in Turkmenistan. His wife, Muza, a Russian Jew, lives most of the year in Moscow with their daughter Irina. Their son, Murat, lives in Austria and justifies his existence by handling Turkmenistan's natural gas and oil concessions. Saparmurat Niyazov has a taste for Italian food and has publicly stated that smoking opium is good for one's health.

IN POWER—Saparmurat Niyazov insists that his countrymen refer to him as "Turkmenbashi": "Father of the Turkmen." He has gone to great lengths to intricately weave his personal history with the general national identity so that it is impossible to talk about one without talking about the other. Even before Turkmenistan became independent, Niyazov insisted that instruction in schools be carried out using the Turkmen language rather than Russian and he declared Turkmen the national language. When he took charge of Turkmenistan in 1986, his first decree was one that symbolized Turkmen nationalism without seriously threatening the government of the USSR, of which Turkmenistan was still a part. Traditionally, Turkmen had gained pride from the quality of their horses, the akhai-tekes. Soviet premier Nikita Khruschev had ordered the destruction of the akhai-tekes and insisted that farmers use tractors instead of horses. By 1986, there were only 1,250 akhai-tekes left in Turkmenistan. Niyazov ordered a halt to the slaughter of Turkmen horses.

When Turkmenistan gained sovereignty in 1990, an election was held to choose a president. Niyazov won 98.3 percent of the vote. Never again would Niyazov risk such a close contest. In 1992, he was reelected with 99.5 percent of the vote. Two years later, he staged a referendum to extend his term until 2002. The final count was Yes—1,959,408; No—212.

In December 1999, parliament amended the constitution to allow Niyazov to remain president for life. The following day Niyazov outlawed opposition parties for a period of ten years. In February 2001, in a magnanimous gesture, he announced that presidential elections would be held—in 2010. However, he also added that to be eligible, a candidate had to be resident in Turkmenistan for ten years, thus eliminating all of the major political figures he had forced into exile. Niyazov then created a 3,000-member forum, the *Halq Maslahaty,* to meet once a year. Their first act, in August 2002, was to endorse Niyazov as president for life after all.

Although Niyazov has repeatedly criticized Communism and the Soviet Union, he has shown a great affinity for Soviet methods of control and, in particular, for those of Josef Stalin. He has engaged in an escalating series of purges, which accelerated in the summer of 2001 and got so bad that the most qualified people for high-level positions turn down the promotions they are offered because accepting a high-level post means almost certain imprisonment down the line. Niyazov has also used public show trials and humiliated his enemies and imagined enemies on live television. On October 30, 2001, for example, during a live broadcast, he brought together the entire Turkmen diplomatic corps and denounced them one by one, culminating in the dismissal of two ambassadors. In 2003, senior Muslim cleric Nasrullah ibn Ibadullah, a member of the Uzbek minority, refused to publicly declare that Niyazov is "God's Prophet." Niyazov removed him from his office and replaced him with a more complacent cleric.

THE ASSASSINATION ATTEMPT—Niyazov's paranoia and megalomania

reached a head following an incident that occurred on November 25, 2002. He and his motorcade were driving through downtown Ashgabat at 7:00 a.m. when gunmen opened fire and tried to kill him. There is certainly no shortage of Turkmen citizens who would like to see Niyazov dead, but the confusing and contradictory details that the government released regarding the assassination attempt called into question whether it had really happened. First it was reported that there was one gunman in a truck. Eventually, the story grew until there were four gunmen in four vehicles and all four were shot to death during the incident. Were they killed by Niyazov's bodyguards? No. According to Serdar Durdyev, the chief of the International Information Department, the assassins shot each other. It seems that the bullets ricocheted off of Niyazov's armored Mercedes, bounced back and killed every one of the gunmen.

Whether or not there really was an assassination attempt became irrelevant. Niyazov used the alleged incident to engage in an orgy of repression. He ordered the arrests of hundreds of political opponents and, in a breach of international protocol, his forces raided the embassy of Uzbekistan. When the Uzbek ambassador lodged a formal complaint, Niyazov expelled him from the country. Among the most prominent figures to be arrested was former foreign minister Boris Shikhmuradov. Only five weeks after the incident, Shikhmuradov was convicted, sentenced to life imprisonment, and forced to make a public confession in which he acknowledged that Saparmurat Niyazov is "a gift given to the people from on high."

THE UNFORTUNATE AMERICAN—Leonid Komarovsky had the misfortune of

being in the wrong place at the wrong time. A former Moscow journalist, now a businessman in Newton, Massachusetts, Komarovsky happened to be in Ashgabat on a business trip on the day of the alleged assassination attempt, which he would later claim was actually a nonviolent protest by several dozen people holding up signs. The next day, Komarovsky was arrested and thrown into prison, where he was beaten and kicked by guards wearing steel-toed

A TEACHER OF ENGLISH IN ASHGABAT WRITES THE DATE
ON THE CHALKBOARD, THE MONTH OF JANUARY HAVING
BEEN RENAMED TURKMENBASHY AFTER NIYAZOV.

Burt Herman/AP Photo

boots. He was also drugged and forced to read a confession on state television. Then he was offered a deal. He would be released if he wrote two books. Kormarovsky agreed and spent twelve hours a day, watched by guards, writing, until he had completed the 250-page *Terrorist Attack in Ashgabat* about the assassination attempt, and *Turkmenistan: Truth and Lies,* a 350-page work praising Saparmurat Niyazov.

BIZARRE BEHAVIOR—Although Niyazov's Stalinist tactics would qualify him for any list of the world's worst dictators, what makes him stand out from the rest of the tyrants and thugs is the extreme weirdness of his decrees and, in particular, the personality cult that he has created. Among the most noteworthy manifestations are:

- He renamed the month of January "Turkmenbashi," after himself; April "Gurbanosoltan Edzhe" after his mother; and September "Rukhnama" after the book he wrote.
- He renamed all the streets in the capital with numbers and ordered all citizens to fly the national flag over their homes.
- He renamed the Caspian port city of Krasnovodok "Turkmenbashi."
- He banned ballet, opera, and circus for being alien to Turkmen culture and he shut down the Academy of Science.
- His face appears on every bank note.
- His image is permanently displayed—in gold—in the upper right corner of the television screen during all broadcasts.
- He ordered the erections of monuments of himself throughout the country including one of his mother holding him as a baby.
- He spent $7 million on a seventy-five-meter-high Arch of Neutrality on top of which is a twelve-meter statue of himself that revolves during the day so that he is always facing the sun.

- His face also appears on vodka bottles and tea boxes.
- He created two brands of cologne, one of which is named after himself and the other after his mother.
- In 2005, he banned car radios and lip-synching and forbade the playing of recorded music on television or at weddings.
- He ordered doctors to stop taking the Hippocratic Oath and instead swear allegiance to him.

Niyazov also built a $60 million gold-domed presidential palace made of white marble. In October 2004, he opened a $100 million mosque in his hometown of Gypjak. Large enough to accommodate 10,000 worshippers at a time, the interior walls are inscribed with quotations from the Quran and from his own works. Much of the revenue from the sale of natural gas goes to a special "presidential fund." It is estimated that he keeps more than $1.5 billion in personal overseas accounts. During his reign, he has instituted laws that forbid families and women under the age of thirty-five to travel abroad and he imposed a $50,000 fee for any non-Turkmen wanting to marry a Turkmen citizen. This later rule was aimed at Uzbeks desiring to marry ethnic Uzbeks in Turkmenistan. At various times, Niyazov has also banned the teaching of foreign languages, forbidden Turkmen to accept overseas scholarships,

AN INTOXICATING DICTATOR
Olga Homalova

monitored all foreign mail and phone calls, and ordered the army to abduct people from buses to help with the cotton harvest. Suspicions that Niyazov was engaged in the drug trade were raised following a 1997 incident in which a border guard, Major Vitaly Usaches, confiscated 400 kilograms of heroin at the Ashgabat Airport. Instead of being praised, Usaches was arrested and executed. Since independence, life expectancy in Turkmenistan has gone down, while the infant mortality rate has gone up.

TURKMENISTAN AND THE WORLD—Turkmenistan's relations with the outside world are centered almost entirely on the nation's reserves of natural gas and oil. The significant pipelines are operated by Russia, leaving Niyazov in the bitter position of being dependent on private Russian energy companies who can cut off his income at will and have

done so by raising transit fees. Niyazov did manage to build a small pipeline to Iran in 1997. In April 1998, Niyazov visited the United States and came away with Export-Import Bank credits to buy U.S.-made goods, agreements with Mobil and Exxon for exploration and extraction in western Turkmenistan, and $750,000 for a pipeline feasibility study. However, Niyazov is considered so erratic and untrustworthy that Western companies have been hesitant to commit to the building of pipelines that would compete with the Russian ones. Niyazov refused to participate in the U.S.-led invasion of Afghanistan in 2001, but immediately after the fall of the Taliban, with whom Niyazov was on good relations, he allowed humanitarian aid to pass through Turkmenistan. In 2002, the United States gave $18.1 million in aid to Turkmenistan, including $8 million for border security to combat the smuggling of drugs and weapons of mass destruction. Considering that it is Niyazov's government that controls smuggling, the aid was really little more than a bribe to keep on his good side.

NIYAZOV SPEAKS:

"I admit it, there are too many portraits, pictures and monuments. I don't find any pleasure in it, but the people demand it because of their mentality."

1995

"Our newspapers do not criticize me. There is no reason for such criticism."

1992

"There are not any opposition parties, so how can we grant them freedom?"

1998

"The silence that arises from the tongue of centuries rings in my ears."

2001

THE BOOK—Niyazov launched the publication of his book, *Rukhnama*, with a three-hour televised speech in which he compared his work to the Bible and the Quran. It is required reading at every level of the educational system and government employees must memorize excerpts verbatim or risk losing their jobs. *Rukhnama* is not a hate-filled rant like *Mein Kampf*. It is a mishmash of history, folktales, personal anecdotes, economic analysis, patriotic boosterism, and spiritual advice. The underlying message is that the Turkmen people are great and that it is Niyazov himself who brings out this greatness, as he fuses his own history with that of the nation. "When you go for a long journey," he says, "your mother prepares your food. I, however, have no mother, so I took the 'Turkmen' in place of food." Niyazov implies that all citizens must experience life as he does. As an orphan, he lectures his countrymen that "Nations are forever, but tribes are temporary. . . . Every member of the Turkmen nation must accept this principle." On March 20, 2006, Niyazov announced on national television that "Anyone who reads the *Rukhnama* three times will find spiritual wealth, will become more intelligent, will recognize the divine being and will go straight to Heaven."

IT IS THE TURKMEN

The real brave man, the gallant! Think, contemplate,
It is the Turkmen himself shall make this nation grand
Visit your past and take an excursion to the future
It is the Turkmen himself shall make this nation grand

The Turkmen boy is a lion, and a lion's son is a lion,
Unwillingness and avoiding duties are a shame
For those who run for the other, it is victory which accompanies them,
It is the Turkmen himself shall make this nation grand

Take lessons from the past and be an example for the future,
May all seven climates be proud when they see the Turkmen,
May the route the Turkmen take be the course the world follows,
It is the Turkmen himself shall make this nation grand

Try to be the equal of the learned Pyragy and Gorkut,
Try to be equal of the valiant Alp Arslan, Chagry Beg and Togrul,
For Oguz Khan people lagging behind does not suit
It is the Turkmen themselves who can make this nation grand.

(Hasan Sarbakhshian/AP Photo)

9.

SEYED ALI KHAMENEI—IRAN

THE NATION—Strategically located with borders on the Caspian Sea, the Persian Gulf, the Indian Ocean, and seven nations, Iran is one of the only countries in the world with an extensive history of both invading other countries and being invaded and occupied by foreign powers. It was the first Middle Eastern nation in which commercial quantities of oil were discovered (1908); the first in the region to have a revolution demanding a constitution (1905–1911); the first to have a parliament and the first to have a multi-party system (1941). It was also the first nation in the world to be the victim of a CIA-sponsored coup (1953) and the first Islamic nation to have a mass revolution in which millions of people took part (1979). Until the overthrow of Saddam Hussein in neighboring Iraq, Iran was also the only country in which the government was controlled by followers of Shi'a Islam. Although estimates vary, almost 90 percent of the population of more than seventy million are Shiites. There is a substantial Sunni population, most of whom are members of ethnic minorities, in particular Arabs and Kurds. The Shi'a have a long history of oppression. They inhabit areas under which are found the world's most important reserves of oil, yet they have rarely benefited from what should have been their good fortune. In both Iraq and

Bahrain, where Shiites are the majority, and Saudi Arabia and Kuwait, where they are the minority, the oil wealth has been exploited by Sunnis.

For most of its history, the people of the nation have referred to their country as Iran, while Europeans called it Persia. In 1935, the government asked foreigners to start using the term Iran, and gradually Iran replaced Persia in common usage, although the old name has lingered in certain cases, such as "Persian Gulf" and "Persian rug."

EARLY HISTORY—Settlements in what is now Iran date back to at least 8000 BC, and Iran has its own monotheistic religion, Zoroastrianism, which was founded in about 1000 BC. The first and probably greatest Persian dynasty was that of the Achaemenians, which lasted from 640 BC to 323 BC. In 550 BC, Cyrus the Great created an empire that stretched from Egypt and the Aegean Sea to the Oxus River, which divides Russia and Afghanistan. Cyrus is credited in the Bible with freeing the Jews from captivity and allowing their return to Jerusalem. Darius the Great, who reigned from 522 BC until 486 BC, earned recognition as the most famous Persian king because he invaded both Scythia (southern Russia) and Greece, where his army was finally defeated at the Battle of Marathon in 490 BC. Cyrus also ordered the construction of a 1,600-mile Royal Road that postmen could cover in six to nine days and a canal that connected the Nile River with the Red Sea. He built the Persepolis Palace, oversaw the creation of a banking system, and established an early system of coinage.

In 334 BC, Alexander the Great defeated the Persian army and destroyed Persepolis. Alexander died two years later. One of his generals, Seleucus, stayed on and founded the Seleucid dynasty. The Parthians came down from the steppes in the northeast, defeated the Greek Seleucids, and gained control of Persia and Mesopotamia. The Parthians would rule the area for 471 years. In 53 BC, they defeated the Roman army under Crassus at the Battle of Carrhae. Seventeen years later, they fought back an attempted invasion by Mark Anthony. In AD 116, Trajan became the first Roman emperor to reach the Persian Gulf, but even he was eventually forced back by the Parthians. The Parthian dynasty finally fell in 224, not to an invading force, but to a national uprising led by Ardeshir I. The Sassanians, a purely Persian dynasty, ruled from 224 until 642, during which time they revived Persian culture and Zoroastrianism. Among the most noteworthy Sassanian leaders was Khosrow I, who oversaw a cultural renaissance and whose chancellor, Bozorgmehr, is credited with creating the precursor of the modern game of backgammon. Between 629 and 632, the dynasty was ruled by two female monarchs, one of whom, Purandokht, signed a peace treaty with the Byzantines.

The seventh century would prove critical to Persian history. In 632, Muhammad, the founder of Islam, died. The next year, his Arab followers began to spread their faith through conquest, moving through present-day Kuwait to Mesopotamia. The last Sassanian king,

Yezdigird III, rejected Islam, calling the Arabs lizard-eaters and baby-killers. In 642, the Arabs defeated the Persians at the Battle of Nihavend, ending more than four centuries of Sassanian rule. Many Persians welcomed Islam because it taught equality and unity and was a relief from the feudalism of Zoroastrianism. In 661, the assassination of Muhammad's son-in-law, Imam Ali, led to a schism in Islam between the Sunnis and the Shiites. The Shiites believed in the divine right of the family of Muhammad through his daughter Fatima and her husband Ali and claimed that only someone who was a direct descendant of this couple could be fit to rule. Unlike the Sunnis, they also believed that Shiite leaders were infallible; a belief that still has a strong influence on Iranian life—and government—more than 1,300 years later. During a later dynasty, that of the Abbasids, three branches of Shi'a Islam developed. One of the branches, the Jaafaris (also known as Twelvers), has reigned in Iran ever since.

The Shi'a rejected as usurpers the Umayyad Caliphate that ruled the Islamic world between 661 and 750 and were glad to join the Abbasids in defeating the Umayyads. The Abbasid Caliphate, lasting from 750 until 1258, marked the pinnacle of Islamic power, and Iranians contributed greatly in the fields of science, medicine, and the arts. By shifting the capital of the caliphate from Damascus to Baghdad, the Abbasids brought about a cross-pollination of Semitic and Persian cultures. In the thirteenth century, Shah Ala ad-Din Muhammad II, a prince of Khiva, swept south and conquered Persia. In 1219 one of his governors murdered the members of a 500-man trade mission from the Mongol ruler Genghis Khan, who then sent a delegation to demand an apology and compensation. Ala ad-Din Muhammad had the leaders of the delegation beheaded. Genghis Khan responded by sending a 200,000-man army to destroy Ala ad-Din Muhammad and all his lands, which they did in brutal fashion. In the 1250s, Genghis Khan's grandson, Hulagu Khan, sacked Baghdad and executed the caliph, putting an end to the long-declining Abbasid Caliphate.

In the early sixteenth century, Shah Ismail I united Persia under a native leader for the first time in more than 800 years. Shah Ismail came from an important religious family. Although they were Sufis, they taught him Shi'a Islam. When he gained power, Ismail ordered Shiism to be the state religion and he went to great lengths to convert the Sunnis in his domain. Another leader of the Safavid dynasty, Shah Abbas the Great, defeated the Ottoman Turks and expanded his empire from the Tigris River to the Indus River. He was a brutal tyrant, but he was a skillful administrator and he made his capital, Isfahan, a center of art and architecture. In 1722, an Afghan chieftain, Mahmoud Khan, in bloody fashion, captured Isfahan and overthrew the Safavid dynasty. General Nadir Kuli expelled the Afghans and reinstated the Safavids, proclaiming himself shah, or king, in 1736. By this time, Persia was attracting the attention of the Europeans, and the rivalry between Great Britain and Russia actually helped preserve Persia's independence. In 1787, Aga Mohammad Khan proclaimed himself shah and by 1794 he had united Persia, beginning the Qajar dynasty that would last until 1925.

The Qajars signed treaties with the British, the Turks, and the Russians and conceded a good deal of territory, while modernizing Persia. Naser o-Din Shah also began granting commercial concessions to the British, beginning with a thirteen-year telegraph system project begun in 1859. Discontent with the shah's selling of the country to a foreign power peaked when he gave the British the tobacco concession in 1890, and he was forced to rescind the concession two years later. By 1905, Persians fed up with government corruption organized a general strike and demanded a constitution. On August 5, 1906, Mozafar o-Din Shah decreed the creation of a constitution and an elected parliament, the Majlis. The writing of the constitution was dominated by secularists, but the clergy ensured that Twelver Shiism was declared the state religion and that only Jaafari Shi'a could serve as shah, government ministers, and judges. The radical clergy took the position that sovereignty does not rest with the people because Allah delegated it to the *mujtahids,* religious scholars and leaders. A century later, it is this position that continues to limit the acceptance of democracy in Iran.

REZA SHAH—On February 21, 1921, Reza Khan, a common soldier who rose through the ranks to become a brigadier general, in secret collusion with the British, led a bloodless coup at the head of an army of 1,200 men. Reza Khan banned gambling and alcohol and made himself popular by reducing the price of bread. In 1925 he proclaimed himself Reza Shah Pahlavi, beginning the short-lived but ambitious Pahlavi dynasty. Reza Shah set out to curtail the power of the clergy. He limited the jurisdiction of the religious Shari'a courts, and the state took over many religious schools. In 1928 he pushed through the Uniformity of Dress Law that forced men to dress in Western clothes with round peaked caps. Only clerics and theological students were exempted. In 1934 he visited Turkey and was impressed by that country's modern ways. When he returned to Iran, he outlawed the wearing of veils by women and opened up to women all public places, including workplaces and schools. As for the men, he ordered them to replace their caps with European felt hats. In 1935 he formally asked the governments of the rest of the world to stop calling his nation Persia, a name chosen by the Europeans, and instead call it Iran, the name traditionally used by the Iranians themselves. Domestically, Reza Shah took away the power of the Majlis and eliminated free speech. An admirer of Hitler's nationalism, he invited German businessmen into Iran. Nevertheless, when World War II broke out, he tried to declare Iran neutral. However, the Allies were not interested in his position. They wanted to use the Trans-Iranian railway to move military supplies to the Soviet Union, so British and Soviet forces occupied the country in 1941. Reza Shah abdicated in favor of his twenty-one-year-old son, Mohammad Reza Shah, and he died in exile in South Africa in July 1944. Mohammad Reza would grow up to be a major player on the world scene and was commonly known internationally as The Shah.

THE SHAH—Mohammad Reza Shah was young, and it was difficult for him to assert power. The clergy tried to regain the power they had lost under Reza Shah, for example, by ordering women to wear veils while shopping. Still, when the war ended, the new shah did try to win support, in particular by annulling his father's ban on Iranians going to Mecca on the *hajj*. He blamed the British for his father's overthrow and he hated the Communists in the Soviet Union, so he moved his country closer to the United States.

NATIONALIZATION AND THE CIA—By 1950, Iranians were once again upset by the influence of foreign powers in their country and in particular the control of their oil industry by the Anglo-Iranian Oil Company. The Shah appointed General Ali Razmara prime minister in June 1950. Razmara opposed the growing movement to nationalize the Iranian oil industry and was assassinated on March 7, 1951. Eight days later, the Majlis voted to nationalize Anglo-Iranian. On April 28, the Majlis elected Mohammad Mossadeq prime minister. Mossadeq tried to negotiate with the British, but in the end he enforced the Oil Nationalization Act and seized Anglo-Iranian's assets. The Shah had no choice but to go along with what was clearly the will of the people. The British were furious and blockaded the Persian Gulf and prevented oil from leaving Iran. This caused the Iranian economy to collapse, but Mossadeq remained popular and the Shah was forced to give him increased powers. In 1953, the CIA launched Operation Ajax to remove Mossadeq from power. Through infiltration, they tried to drive a wedge between Mossadeq's secular and religious supporters. The Shah dismissed Mossadeq, but Mossadeq refused to give up his post and the Shah and his wife fled to Rome. Fighting broke out between pro- and anti-Shah forces. Funded by the CIA and MI6, the conflict climaxed with a nine-hour battle in front of Mossadeq's house that left more than 300 dead. Mossadeq was arrested and spent the remaining thirteen years of his life in prison and house arrest. General Fazlollah Zahedi declared martial law, the Shah returned to Tehran after less than a week away, and oil began to flow again.

The Shah became a really good friend of the United States, to whom he was beholden for his position of power. Between 1953 and 1960, the United States poured more than a billion dollars of aid into Iran and thousands of Americans began working there, particularly in the oil industry. In 1964, the United States gave Iran a $200 million loan in exchange for the granting of diplomatic immunity for all Americans in the country. The Majlis passed this highly controversial move in a close vote. The Shah agreed to join the Baghdad Pact with Turkey, Iraq, Pakistan, and the United Kingdom, and in exchange he was given the role of policeman of the Gulf. Between 1953 and 1969, the United States would give the Shah as much money in military grants as it gave all the other countries of the world combined. In

1960, the Shah returned the favor by donating millions of dollars to Richard Nixon's presidential campaign.

On January 6, 1963, the Shah instituted a White Revolution that allowed women to vote, promoted literacy, nationalized the forests, encouraged profit-sharing in industry, and ordered agrarian reform in which farmland was seized from landlords and taken over by the government. Having smashed his secular opposition, the Shah took aim at the radical clerics and, especially, the most popular of the clerics, Ayatollah Ruhollah Mousavi Khomeini.

AYATOLLAH KHOMEINI—Born Ruhollah Mousavi in either 1900 or 1902, he was only five months old when his father was murdered on orders of the local landlord. He began religious instruction at the age of six. After finishing his secular education at fifteen, his brother tutored him in Islamic studies for four years. He attended a seminary in Arak and then moved to the religious center of Qom. He graduated theological school in 1925 with a degree in Shari'a, ethics, and spiritual philosophy and became a teacher of ethics and philosophy. Khomeini's first book, *The Secrets Revealed,* which he published anonymously in 1942, attacked secularism while upholding private enterprise. In 1945, he graduated to the rank of *hojatalislam,* a step below ayatollah, which gave him the right to gather disciples. During the early 1950s, Khomeini was critical of Mossadeq because he considered him to be overly influenced by the Communist Tudeh Party, a view he shared with the Americans. But he was also critical of the Shah for his "plundering of the nation's wealth" by making deals with the U.S. government and with the Western oil companies, and he denounced the Shah's White Revolution.

On March 22, 1963, following a protest by theological students over the opening of liquor stores, paratroopers raided the school where Khomeini taught and killed several students. On June 3, Khomeini gave a major speech denouncing the Shah and two days later he was arrested. This led to large-scale rioting and the imposition of martial law. Officially, government troops shot eighty-six people to death, although the true figure was probably much higher. After two months in jail, Khomeini was transferred to house arrest. Released on April 6, 1964, he immediately resumed his anti-Shah speeches. On November 4, he was arrested again, but this time the Shah kicked him out of the country. Khomeini went first to Turkey, but then settled in rather comfortably in Najaf, a Shiite holy city in Iraq.

In 1967, the Shah imposed the Family Protection Law, which gave women the right to divorce without their husband's permission and required husbands to obtain their wife's permission before marrying a second wife. It also transferred family affairs from the Shari'a courts to secular courts.

The Shah signed a border treaty with Iraq in March 1971 that also gave Iran the right to send 130,000 pilgrims a year to visit Shi'a holy sites in the Iraqi cities of Karbala and Najaf. This part of the treaty had the secondary effect of giving Khomeini's followers the opportunity to visit him and to bring back to Iran tapes of his speeches.

By 1972, the year that President Nixon visited him in Iran, the Shah was becoming increasingly autocratic and megalomaniacal. He had taken over the appointment of government clergy and his National Security and Intelligence Organization (SAVAK), which was trained by the CIA, the FBI, and Mossad, was operating as a brutal political police force. Interviews showed that 90 percent of SAVAK prisoners were beaten, 80 percent were whipped, and a majority were burned with cigarettes. In August 1973, the Shah declared, "My visions are miracles that saved my country. My reign saved my country, and it had done so because God is on my side." In March 1975, he dissolved the multiparty system and created a single political party, his own. That same year, Amnesty International announced that Iran had the highest death penalty rate in the world. In 1976, the Shah boasted in an interview that he had 100 paid informers working inside the United States keeping an eye on the 60,000 Iranian students who were studying there. On November 15, 1977, the Shah visited President Jimmy Carter at the White House. His visit was met with large protests by Iranian students. Back in Tehran, more than 10,000 students marched in support of the students in the United States. One student was killed and many were arrested. When the arrested students were released on the authority of a *civilian* court, the growing Iranian opposition took heart that they were now less likely to be subjected to SAVAK torture. Opposition to the Shah was spreading to diverse sections of the population. In addition to the student movement, the bazaaris, the traditional merchants, had turned against the Shah because of his harsh campaign against profiteering. But it was the clerics who were leading the opposition. On October 7, 1977, masked religious students at Tehran University demanded that male and female students be segregated outside the classroom and handed out pamphlets to young women that said, "If you violate these guidelines, your lives will . . . not be safe."

In January 1978, the government published an article that accused Ayatollah Khomeini of being (1) involved with international communists, (2) a tool of colonialists, (3) of foreign origin, (4) of having worked as a British spy, (5) of having homosexual tendencies, and (6) of writing erotic poetry. This tactic of character assassination backfired. In Qom, the seminaries and the bazaars shut down in protest. Security forces shot to death seventy protesters, which led to the uniting of the opposition despite their deep philosophical differences. For the first time, street protests were accompanied by chants of "Death to the Shah," and some police changed into civilian clothing rather than follow orders to shoot the protestors. It finally dawned on the Shah that he was facing a major problem. In an attempt to appease the opposition, he increased the quota of pilgrims to go to Mecca; he banned pornographic films; he released the merchants who were in prison for overcharging; and he fired the head of SAVAK. But his efforts were undercut when media reports of Kermit Roosevelt's insider account of the CIA's role in the overthrow of Mohammad Mossadeq and the restoration of the Shah reached Iran. From Iraq, Khomeini told his followers to keep protesting until the Shah himself was overthrown.

On August 19, 1978, a fire broke out in the Rex Cinema in the oil port city of Abadan. The emergency doors were locked and 410 people died. Most of the public blamed SAVAK, and this event raised anti-Shah emotions to a higher level. The clergy issued a list of fourteen demands that included banning cinemas and casinos, releasing Islamic political prisoners, and allowing Ayatollah Khomeini to return to Iran. The Shah ordered the release of jailed

AYATOLLAH KHOMEINI IN PARIS, NEAR THE END OF HIS FOURTEEN YEARS IN EXILE
Diego Goldberg/Sygma/Corbis

clerics, closed the casinos, lifted censorship, and increased the pay of government employees and members of the military. But the protests continued, and on September 7 the Shah imposed martial law. On September 18, employees of the Central Bank of Iran released documents that showed that members of the ruling elite were transferring their savings abroad. On October 6, the Iraqi government, which was ruled by Sunnis and was worried that the events in Iran would spread to the majority Shiites in Iraq, expelled Khomeini, who continued his exile in Paris. From there, he urged the Iranian people to withhold payment of taxes and reminded his followers that it was the duty of the faithful to die if necessary in the fight against the Shah. However, he also stated that he opposed armed struggle because it led to a chain of revenge. On December 7, President Carter said that although he supported the Shah, it was up to the Iranian people to choose their own government. To the Iranians, this was a signal that the United States no longer supported the Shah. If fact, the Carter administration had already made contact with Khomeini, who promised to continue the flow of oil if the United States would help get rid of the Shah.

THE REVOLUTION SUCCEEDS—In January 1979, newspapers in Iran began running large pictures of Ayatollah Khomeini. On January 13, Khomeini established a

Council of the Islamic Revolution to form a provisional government and convene a constituent assembly to write a new constitution for an Islamic Republic. He also ordered the Council to negotiate directly with the military in order to avoid bloodshed. Three days later, the Shah left Iran, although he did not formally abdicate. Still, there were celebrations in the streets and people toppled statues of the Shah and his father and they cut the Shah's picture out of the center of paper money.

On February 1, Ayatollah Khomeini arrived in Tehran after fourteen years in exile. He was at least seventy-six years old. In the military, senior officers supported the Shah, middle-rank officers supported the revolution, and the rank and file were mixed. However, only the 30,000-strong Imperial Guards actually resisted. The revolutionaries captured the government television station, the Majlis building, and the military academy and overran the military bases. On February 11, the armed forces, down from 300,000 to 100,000 because of desertions, declared its neutrality, while the air force and armed civilians fought the Imperial Guards. The Shah was so unpopular that the opposition covered a wide range of movements and ideologies. There were Communists, radical students, mainstream social democrats, groups that promoted a fusion of Islam and Marxism, traditional Muslims, ethnic minorities, and Islamic extremists. But only Khomeini and his supporters were well financed. Khomeini received help from Muammar al-Qaddafi, the dictator of Libya, and from the Palestine Liberation Organization. But of more value to him, he was supported by the bazaaris, the traditional merchant class that the Shah had attacked. Within weeks the national army, now fully supportive of Khomeini, was fighting the Kurds in the north. On March 22, anti-Khomeini Islamic extremists assassinated Khomeini's first chief of staff.

Khomeini immediately set to work reshaping Iranian society and creating an Islamic Republic. Democracy, he said, "is a Western idea. We respect Western civilization, but will not follow it." He and his supporters argued that the centralization of power in the hands of a single man was not a form of dictatorship because he would rule according to divine will, not his own. Those who opposed the political leadership of the ulema, the leading clergy, were enemies of the Revolution. He created a system with an elected president who would serve a four-year term. The president would be responsible for signing and executing laws passed by the Majlis. All this seemed to fall within the parameters of a typically representative government. But Khomeini added a new element: the twelve-man Council of Guardians. Six of the Council members would be members of the clergy appointed by the *Rahbar*, the Leader (Khomeini), and the other six would be jurists appointed by the head of the judicial branch who was also appointed by the Leader. The Guardian Council would be allowed to exercise veto power over laws passed by the Majlis and approved by the president. Because the vast majority of Iranians were pleased to have Khomeini as their leader, this structure did not at first attract much attention. Khomeini banned co-education and required female government employees to wear veils. When women protested this decree in the streets, men threw stones at them. However, Khomeini responded to the women's position and allowed them to remain unveiled—for the time being. He promised freedom of the press—except for views deemed "detrimental to the fundamental principles of Islam or the rights of the public." As for political parties, they were "a fatal poison" and their leaders "soldiers of Satan." There was no need for such institutions because Allah would guarantee the national well-being. To be on the safe side, Khomeini banned political demonstrations of the sort that had brought him to power. On July 2, disaffected revolutionaries wrote a letter to Khomeini criticizing him for burning books, firing teachers, and controlling the media. They accused him of changing the slogan "unity of work [Iranians speaking with one voice] to "unity of following my words."

On October 22, President Carter allowed the Shah, who was dying of cancer, to enter the United States for medical treatment. This was the perfect excuse for Khomeini and his supporters to brush aside all dissent and rally the masses once again. On November 1, three million people marched in Tehran demanding that the United States extradite the Shah to Iran. Three days later, with Khomeini's tacit approval, 450 militant students attacked the U.S. embassy and took over the building after a three-hour struggle. They were looking for documents that demonstrated U.S. support for the Shah. American officials managed to shred many documents, but the students would later painstakingly piece them back together. The Iranian cabinet, which was more moderate than Khomeini, resigned in protest. Besides the documents and the building itself, the students also captured ninety people inside the building, including sixty-three Americans. They announced that they would release these hostages if President Carter would extradite the Shah. Carter refused. Eventually, the students whittled the hostages down to fifty-one men and two women. One hostage was released several months later for health reasons, but the rest were held captive for 444 days. On July 27, 1980, the Shah died in Egypt, removing the original reason the hostages had been taken. However, they were not released until the day that Carter left office and was replaced as president by Ronald Reagan, who, a few years later, would have his own embarrassing problems with the Iranians. In June 1981, it was revealed that some of those documents pieced together by the students showed that Abol Hassan Bani-Sadr, who had been president of Iran since February 4, 1980, had met secretly with the CIA. Khomeini removed him from office and he fled to Paris.

Meanwhile, Khomeini continued his attempts to impose his interpretation of Islam on the Iranian people. He banned chess, considering it a form of gambling. He banned the playing of music in public and shut down 420 movie theaters. He nationalized all banks and 450 major industrial businesses, and he made foreign trade a government monopoly. He closed the universities and did not reopen them until they had been purged and Islamicized. He ordered all female government employees to wear the chador. Tens of thousands of *komiteh,* revolutionary guards, were sent out to police the streets and enforce cultural restrictions, and citizens were urged to spy on and report on their neighbors and relatives. In December 1981, special judges were assigned to combat "impious acts," including homosexuality, adultery, gambling, and the catch-all, hypocrisy, not to mention showing sympathy for hypocrites and atheists. The death penalty was applied to a range of crimes, including rape, prostitution, and drug trafficking. As Khomeini put it on September 9, 1981, "When the Prophet Muhammad failed to improve the people with advice, he hit them on the head with a sword until he made them into human beings." In the three months following the dismissal of Bani-Sadr, 1,000 Iranians were executed, including at least 182 on September 18 and 19 alone. According to estimates by Amnesty International, during the first five years of Khomeini's reign 5,000 Iranians were executed. Many of Khomeini's policies were widely approved. For example, he raised the minimum wage and outlawed interest-bearing loans. In 1982 he also began to make concessions, declaring an amnesty for 10,000 political prisoners, ending his campaign against music, and allowing non-Muslims to consume alcohol.

THE IRAN–IRAQ WAR—Across the border in Iraq, that nation's dictator, Saddam Hussein, viewed the developments in Iran as both a potential threat and a potential opportunity. As a Sunni who ruled a population that was mostly Shiite, he was not pleased that a Shiite government had been created next door, and especially so because it had come to power as the result of a mass revolution. The Iraqi Shiites considered Ayatollah Khomeini their hero and Khomeini responded by urging them to overthrow Saddam and his secular Ba'athist Party. Saddam saw Iran as having been weakened by all the chaos, and if he could defeat Khomeini, he could expand his borders while at the same time crushing the Shiite hero. The Iranians also gave support to the anti-Ba'athist Kurds in the north of Iraq, while the Iraqis urged the Iranian Arabs in Khuzestan to sabotage oil installations and demand autonomy.

In June of 1979, Iraqi planes in pursuit of Kurdish nationalists bombed Iranian villages. The following month, only five months after the Ayatollah Khomeini's return to Iran, Saddam Hussein took over as the official head of state in Iraq. He deported 15,000 Iraqi citizens of Iranian descent and began executing Shiites suspected of being sympathetic to the Iranian Revolution. The border between Iran and Iraq was not officially drawn until 1913, and a dispute continued over control of the Arvand-Roud (known in Iraq as the Shatt al-Arab), a river formed by the confluence of the Tigris and Euphrates rivers that discharges into the Persian Gulf. In September 1980, Saddam abrogated a 1975 border treaty and claimed Iraqi control of the Arvand-Roud. On September 21, Iranian artillery fired on Iraqi ships in the Arvand-Roud. The next day the Iraqis dropped bombs on nine Iranian air bases, while the Iranians bombed seven Iraqi cities, including Baghdad and Basra. On September 23, Saddam

Hussein sent 33,000 Iraqi troops across the Iranian border along a 300-mile front. Saddam thought that the Sunni Arabs in Iranian Khuzestan would rally to his support, but he was wrong.

Both sides attacked each other's oil refineries and Iraq was able to take control of the Iranian oil port of Khorramshahr. On October 9, Iraq used surface-to-surface missiles for the first time, killing 110 civilians in Dezful in Khuzestan. In December, Iraq invaded Iranian Kurdistan, this time successfully hooking up with Kurdish rebels who were already fighting against the Iranian government. The armies of Iran and Iraq fought primarily on Iranian soil, trading attacks and counterattacks with heavy loss of life. By the end of the first year of fighting, 38,000 Iranians had been killed, along with 22,000 Iraqis. On March 19, 1982, Iran launched a massive counterattack. In eight days the Iranians were able to push the Iraqis back twenty-four miles and recover 800 square miles. In the process, they took 15,450 prisoners. The following month they won back another 500 square miles. On May 24, 1982, Iran regained the now ruined city of Khorramshahr, sweeping up a third of Iraq's forces as prisoners. Except for a few minor pieces, the Iranians had regained all of the land they had lost to the Iraqis in the first twenty months of the war. Khomeini twice rejected truce offers and, in his desperation to defeat Saddam Hussein, he quietly bought military equipment from Israel and sold oil to the United States. On July 13, the Iranian army made its first ground incursion into Iraq, but the attack failed and 10,000 Iranian soldiers were killed. In fact, the entire war bogged down, settling into a grim World War I–style stalemate. By the end of year three, 125,000 soldiers and civilians had lost their lives on behalf of a personal feud between Saddam Hussein and Ayatollah Khomeini.

In November 1982, the administration of U.S. president Ronald Reagan removed Iraq from the U.S. list of countries supporting terrorism (and put Iran onto the list) and restored diplomatic relations after an eighteen-year gap. Reagan began helping Saddam Hussein, beginning by turning over satellite photos of Iranian troops and then providing Saddam with hundreds of millions of dollars worth of agricultural credits that freed Iraq to spend its oil profits on its military. Much to the horror of the international community, Khomeini sent out human waves of 250,000 soldiers, many of them teenagers, leading to the deaths of 20,000 Iranians in one three-week period alone in early 1984. When Iran seized the Majnoon Islands in the marshes of southern Iraq, Iraqi troops stopped the Iranians with mustard gas and nerve gas.

On March 11, 1985, 60,000 Iranian soldiers tried to cross the Tigris River and attack Basra. Iraq repulsed the attack, but it took chemical weapons, 250 combat air sorties a day, and the elite Presidential Guard Division to do so. Iraq then retaliated by launching the War of the Cities, hitting Tehran with missile attacks. Iran bombed Baghdad. By the end of 1985, 200,000 Iranians had been killed and 45,000 had been the victims of chemical attacks. If anything, the war only got uglier in 1986, culminating, on December 24, in Iran's largest attack of the conflict, an attempt to take Basra. Over the next two months, 65,000 Iranian shells reduced the city to rubble, but they were unable to enter the city. Of the 200,000 Iranian soldiers who were part of the attack, 17,000 died and 45,000 were wounded. In November 1986, a Lebanese newspaper, *Al Shira* (The Sail) broke the news that while the Reagan administration had been supplying Iraq, it had also been selling weapons to Iran in exchange for the release of American hostages held in Lebanon. In early 1987, Iraqi SCUD missiles killed 3,000 civilians in 35 Iranian cities and injured another 9,000. Iran responded by shooting more missiles at Baghdad. That same year, the United States agreed to provide protection to Kuwaiti oil tankers operating in the Persian Gulf, drawing American troops into the conflict in a more direct manner. On May 17, the Iraqis mistook the U.S. frigate *Stark* for an Iranian warship and hit it with two missiles, killing thirty-six American sailors. The Reagan administration forgave the Iraqis since the two countries were allies, but it was not so forgiving of the Iranians. On April 14, 1988, a U.S. frigate hit an Iranian land mine, wounding ten sailors. Four days later, the United States destroyed two Iranian oil platforms, sank a guided missile frigate, and knocked out an armed speedboat. It was the biggest American naval encounter since World War II. On July 3, the USS *Vincennes* a $1.2 billion U.S. Navy guided missile cruiser, crossed into Iranian territory to chase a group of Iranian gunboats. In the midst of the exchange of fire, sailors on board the *Vincennes* spotted an Iranian airplane and shot it down. Unfortunately, it turned out to be a commercial passenger flight flying in its normal air corridor during a scheduled flight between Iran and Dubai. Two hundred ninety civilians from six nations were killed, including sixty-five children.

In March 1988, Iran made its last offensive against Iraq, attacking Kurdish areas in the north of the country. On March 16, the Iraqis, thinking the Kurdish town of Halabja was occupied by Iranian forces and Kurdish guerrillas, dropped poisonous gases on the town, killing thousands of Kurdish civilians. The Iraqis countered the Iranian offensive with a surprise attack on the Faw Peninsula in the south, in what would prove to be a decisive battle. On May 25, they cleared the approaches to Basra, thus recapturing almost all of the Iraqi territory that had been taken by Iran. Back in the north, in July, the Iraqis, along with a large force of anti-Khomeini Iranians, drove the exhausted Iranian army out of Iraqi Kurdistan. On the verge of defeat, the Iranian government agreed to a United Nations–sponsored ceasefire on August 20, 1988. When the eight-year war was all over, the border between Iran and Iraq was unchanged, but there had been more than a million casualties. On the Iranian side, 262,000 people had lost their lives, including 11,000 civilians. Of those, an estimated 25,000 had been killed by gas attacks. Another 600,000 Iranians were wounded and 45,000 had been taken prisoner. Meanwhile, more than 105,000 Iraqis died, 400,000 were wounded, and 70,000 were taken prisoner. Even though the war was over, the killing in Iran continued. On July 24, 1988, the radical anti-Khomeini Mujahedin-e Khalq Organization (MKO) attacked Iran from Iraqi territory. They were easily repelled, but back in Tehran the government sought its revenge by executing 4,400 MKO members and sympathizers who were already in prison, including many who had been sentenced for nonviolent crimes such as distributing literature and collecting funds for the families of other prisoners. The man in charge of the executions at Tehran's Evin Prison, Mustafa Pour-Muhammadi, was appointed Iran's minister of the interior in 2005.

KHOMEINI PREPARES FOR THE POST-KHOMEINI PERIOD—

As the Iran–Iraq War wound down, Ayatollah Khomeini, now well into his eighties, began to prepare Iran for life without him. Much to the surprise of many within his own regime, he softened many of his more repressive stances. In December 1987, for example, he refused to ban the showing of Western films on television even when they showed unveiled women, stating that they were religiously acceptable, and even sometimes educational . . . as long as they were not watched with lustful eyes. He also said that Shari'a law could be overruled if it was contrary to the interests of the nation or Islam. In August 1988, he legalized the selling of musical instruments (as long as they were used to play religious music) and even lifted the ban on chess. This outraged the conservatives who had always supported him. Khomeini countered their criticisms by telling them, "Based on your views, modern civilization must be annihilated and we must all go to live forever in caves and deserts." More important than these cultural changes were the revisions he instituted to the organization of the Iranian government. He established a thirteen-man Expediency Council to mediate the increasingly contentious disputes between the elected government and the Guardian Council. In April 1989, he created the Assembly for the Reappraisal of the Constitution which then eliminated the post of prime minister, increased the power of the president, and required the Leader to consult with the Expediency Council. Khomeini had been grooming a high-ranking cleric, Grand Ayatollah Montazeri, to take his place as Leader, but only five weeks before his death on June 3, 1989, Khomeini convinced the authors of the new constitution to lower the qualification requirements for the new Leader to make way for his new choice, a middle-ranked cleric named Ali Husseini Khamenei.

THE MAN—Ali Husseini Khamenei was born April 18, 1939, the second son of a religious family in the holy city of Mashhad in Khorasan Province. As a teenager, he was a disciple of Ayatollah Ruhollah Khatami, whose son, decades later, would be elected president of Iran. Khamenei studied in Najaf and then moved to Qom, where, in 1962, he became a student of Ayatollah Khomeini. When Khomeini was deported to Turkey, Khamenei returned to Mashhad and taught at a theological college. He was intensely involved in the movement to overthrow the Shah and was arrested six times, once spending two months in solitary confinement. In 1976 he went into internal exile, but returned to Mashhad when the revolutionary upsurge loosened the Shah's grip on power. When Khomeini returned to Iran and established an Islamic Republic, Khamenei was one of his first appointments to the Islamic Revolutionary Council. He also served as Friday Prayer Leader of Tehran and he was one of Khomeini's personal representatives on the Supreme Defense Council. On June 27, 1980, Khamenei was giving a sermon at the Abudhar mosque in Tehran, when a bomb, presumably planted by the MKO, exploded, causing Khamenei injuries to his lungs and his arm and forcing him to spend several months in a hospital. This and another bombing eliminated other leaders and in 1981 the Islamic Revolutionary Party chose him to be its candidate for president. Khamenei won with 95 percent of the vote. He also served in the Assembly of Experts that drafted a new constitution in 1982, and in 1985 he was reelected president. When Khomeini died, the Assembly of Experts, following his wishes, bypassed 200 ayatollahs and several grand ayatollahs and elected Khamenei Leader of the Revolution.

During the early years of his reign, Khamenei was not an aggressive leader and was satisfied to allow others to take charge of many of the responsibilities of governing.

RAFSANJANI—Like Khamenei, Ali Akbar Hashemi Rafsanjani was born into a religious family and studied in Qom, where he became a student of Ayatollah Khomeini. When Khomeini was deported, Rafsanjani handled Islamic charities on his behalf. Like Khamenei, he was active in the anti-Shah movement and was arrested and tortured by SAVAK. After the revolution, he was chosen to be the speaker of the Majlis, a position he held for nine years. In 1989, he was elected president of Iran and for the next several years he was the dominant force in Iranian politics. He improved relations with Europe, Japan, and the Soviet Union. When Saddam Hussein invaded Kuwait in 1990, Rafsanjani spoke out against the invasion, but when the United States led a coalition to oust Iraqi forces from Kuwait, he also opposed the presence of American troops in the region. Known as the Commander of Constructiveness, Rafsanjani tried to make Islam relevant to young people by providing for them a better material life. He also urged Iranian expatriates to return to the country. In December 1991, the Guardian Council ruled that all candidates for the 1992 Majlis election must be approved by the Council, whereupon they disqualified all leftist candidates. Rafsanjani was reelected president in 1993, but with, by Iranian standards, a modest 63 percent of the vote. As Rafsanjani's power waned, Khamenei shifted his support to the religious conservatives.

In 1989, Ayatollah Khomeini had issued a fatwa ordering the execution of the novelist

Salmon Rushdie because he considered Rushdie's novel, *The Satanic Verses,* blasphemous, and he offered a $3 million reward to anyone who killed Rushdie. Rafsanjani, while he was president, took a less militant position toward Rushdie and his novel, declaring, "an enlightened Muslim should not be afraid of a book." Nonetheless, Ayatollah Khamenei reaffirmed the death sentence as recently as 2005.

In summer 1995, the Majlis gave the Guardian Council increased power over elections. When the 1996 Majlis elections were held, the Council ensured a conservative victory, even annulling the results in sixteen districts. Still, the 1997 presidential election would change the image, if not the substance, of the government in Iran.

THE REFORMER—Muhammad Khatami was born into a wealthy family in Ardakan in Yazd Province in 1943. His father was a leading ayatollah, but he also listened to foreign radio and followed world affairs. When he was eighteen years old, the younger Khatami became a student of Ayatollah Khomeini in Qom. Unlike other theological students, he declined an exemption from the armed services and spent two years in the army. He earned a bachelor's degree in Western philosophy and did graduate work in the field of educational sciences. During the struggle against the Shah, he supplemented his religious studies by reading the works of leftist figures like Franz Fanon and Che Guevara. In 1978 the Association of Combative Clergy sent Khatami to Germany to head the Islamic Center in Hamburg. After the Islamic Revolution in Iran, he was elected to the first Majlis, and Ayatollah Khomeini appointed him head of the state publishing company. In 1982 he moved up to be Minister of Culture and Islamic Guidance, a position he retained for ten years. Khatami enforced strict censorship and oversaw passage of the restrictive Press Law of 1985. Once the Iran–Iraq War was over he began to relax censorship of the arts. Disliked by the conservatives for being too permissive, he was forced to resign in 1992. He then served as director of the National Library. He published a book of essays, *Fear of Waves,* that argued that Islam is superior to Western thought, but that it needed to deal with the modern need for freedom. With this freedom, he said, the West had acquired superior scientific, economic, and political powers. As he stated in 1997, "The strength of the Islamic Revolution stems from the freedom and individual rights that people hold under the Constitution." Ayatollah Khamenei gave Khatami permission to run in the 1997 presidential election, where he faced the conservative speaker of the Majlis, Ali Akbar Nateq-Nouri. In his campaign, Khatami appealed to women, to young people, and to the ethnic minorities, and he swept to victory with 69 percent of the vote.

After the election, U.S. president Bill Clinton rewarded the Iranians by placing the MKO on the U.S. government's list of terrorist groups. Khatami gave a three-hour interview to

CNN, and in February the U.S. wrestling team was allowed into Iran to compete in a tournament for the first time since the Islamic Revolution. But the fact that Khatami was the president of Iran and that he represented the will of the majority of the Iranian people did not mean he could successfully pursue a reformist agenda. In October 1998, an election was held for the Assembly of Experts that supervises the Leader. Khamenei announced that, for the first time, nonclerics, including women, would be allowed to run for the Assembly. Forty-six nonclerics, nine of whom were women, took up the offer and signed up to be candidates. Khamenei used the Guardian Council to reject all of them. In fact, the Council disqualified half of the candidates. Not surprisingly, conservative clerics won fifty-four of the eighty-six seats. In July 1999, university students protested restrictions on the press. Their protests mushroomed into general antiregime demonstrations and 750,000 Iranians staged a peaceful march in Tehran. Khamenei was careful in his response and praised the students as "valued members of the nation." As reasonable as Khamenei was in his words, his actions were a different story. *Neshat* (Vitality), the third-highest-circulation newspaper in Iran, published an article that challenged capital punishment and the Shari'a concept of eye-for-an-eye punishment. The government suspended the newspaper and sent its editor to jail for thirty months.

In the first round of voting for the sixth Majlis in February 2000, the reformists won two-thirds of the vote. Emboldened, the pro-reform press ran articles about corruption that were popular with the public. The second round of voting was scheduled for May 5. On April 17, the sitting Majlis outlawed criticism of the Leader and of the Constitution. Three days later, Ayatollah Khamenei told a crowd of 100,000 young people that, "Unfortunately, some of the newspapers have become the bases of the enemy. They are performing the same task as BBC radio and the Voice of America." The following week, the judiciary shut down fourteen reformist publications. Despite these restrictions, the reformists dominated the second round of voting. Again, Khamenei was measured in his verbal response. "The two factions," he said, "the progressive and the faithful, are as necessary as the two wings of a bird." But before the newly elected Majlis could meet, the Expediency Council ruled that the Majlis had no authority to investigate any foundation protected by the Leader. In June 2001, Khatami was reelected with 77 percent of the vote, but he seemed a reluctant candidate, resigned to his fate of being a figurehead with limited power.

When the 9/11 attacks took place in the United States, Ayatollah Khamenei condemned them and said that he would support United Nations–sponsored action against the perpetrators. For his domestic audience, he also condemned the U.S. air strikes against Afghanistan's Taliban regime, stating that "Terrorism is only an excuse. Why don't they announce their real intention, their motive for grabbing more power, for imperialism? Since when is it a norm to send troops to another country and hit its cities with missiles and aerial bombardment because of so-called terrorism in that country?" In reality, Iran had opposed the Taliban from the day it seized power and had consistently criticized the governments of Pakistan and Saudi Arabia for supporting the Taliban. When the Pentagon used Iranian air space during the bombing of Afghanistan, Khamenei and the Iranians did not lodge a protest. It was even reported that Iran had shared anti-Taliban intelligence with the Americans. After the Taliban was driven from power, Iran pledged aid to the new Afghanistan.

On January 29, 2002, U.S. president George W. Bush, in his State of the Union address, included Iran in his tripartite "Axis of Evil," accusing the Iranian government of building weapons of mass destruction and of exporting terrorism. The Iranians were shocked to be lumped together with their number-one enemy, Saddam Hussein, and with North Korea, and Bush's speech was particularly disheartening to the reformers in Iran who had been trying so hard to reestablish cordial relations with the West. When the United States invaded Iraq in March 2003, the Iranians were not pleased by what they saw as the beginning of a permanent American military presence to their west, complementing the U.S. bases to their east in Afghanistan. On the other hand, they were delighted by the removal of Saddam Hussein, the man they held responsible for the deaths of hundreds of thousands of their people. In addition, the Americans insisted that Iraq hold democratic elections, which meant that Shiites, being the majority in Iraq, would dominate the new government. At the very least, Iranian Shiites would have freer access to the Shiite holy places in Iraq. In April 2004, the Bush administration accused Iran of inciting unrest in Iraq. Ayatollah Khamenei was contemptuous of this accusation. "There is no need for incitement," he said. "You yourself are the biggest and dirtiest provokers of the Iraqi nation." When Shi'a uprisings broke out in Iraq, tens of thousands of Iranians marched in support of their fellow Shiites.

THE NONREFORMER—As the 2005 presidential election approached, Khamenei and the conservative clerics faced a challenge. They had successfully survived eight years of Muhammad Khatami's reformist rhetoric while preventing him from making any serious changes to society, and it was clear that they could continue to keep control as long as the Guardian Council and the Leader retained veto power over the actions of the president, the Majlis, and the judiciary. Yet it would be better if the president was a man who, although loyal to the conservatives, could appeal to young people and the poor in the same way that Khatami had. They chose Mahmoud Ahmadinejad, a relatively obscure politician, who was a protégé of Ayatollah Khamenei and a follower of the extremist Ayatollah Muhammad Taghi Mesbah Yazdi.

Born the son of a blacksmith in Garmsar in Semnan Province in 1956, Ahmadinejad attended the Iran University of Science and Technology, eventually earning a PhD in engineering and traffic and transportation planning. His involvement in the 1979 revolution is somewhat murky, but it is believed that he argued in favor of supplementing the takeover of the U.S. embassy with a simultaneous occupation of the Soviet embassy. During the Iran–Iraq War, he joined the Islamic Revolutionary Guards Corps and is alleged to have been involved in covert operations in Kirkuk, Iraq. He also served as an engineer in the army and as a *basiji,* one of the religious militia enforcing cultural restrictions. After the war, Ahmadinejad served the government in West Azarbaijan Province and in 1993 he was appointed governor of the newly created Ardabil Province in the northwest. In 2003, the city council of Tehran chose Ahmadinejad to be the city's mayor. He immediately set about imposing hard-line policies, such as creating separate elevators for men and women in city offices. As mayor, he was also in charge of the daily municipality-owned newspaper *Hamshahri.* When a *Hamshahri* journalist asked President Khatami about the existence of illegal parallel intelligence agencies, Ahmadinejad fired the journalist. Nonetheless, Ahmadinejad so angered Khatami that the president barred him from attending cabinet meetings, a privilege normally accorded to the mayor of Tehran.

Khamenei tapped Ahmadinejad to be the establishment candidate for president in 2005. His campaign motto was, "It's possible and we can do it." He pledged to put "the petroleum income on people's tables," a reference to the widespread belief that the nation's wealth was not filtering down to the common people. For the most part, Ahmadinejad sold himself as a man of the people who lived a modest life in a modest home. Relatively young for an Iranian leader, he did in fact cut into the youth vote that had previously supported reform. He finished second in the opening round of voting and then won the runoff. Assuming office on August 14, 2005, Ahmadinejad soon attracted the attention of the outside world

RUSSIAN-MADE ANTI-AIRCRAFT MISSILES ON DISPLAY IN FRONT OF A POSTER OF AYATOLLAH KHAMENEI DURING "SACRED DEFENSE WEEK" IN SEPTEMBER 2005

Vahid Salemi/AP Photo

with comments that played well inside Iran but sounded outrageous outside the country, particularly in the non-Muslim nations. For example, he called for Israel, which he referred to as a "disgraceful blot," to be "wiped off the map," a demand that he later moderated by suggesting that it be moved to "Europe, the United States, Canada, or Alaska."

Ahmadinejad gained domestic support when the West demanded that he shut down Iran's nuclear program. He claimed that his country was only interested in nuclear power and that nuclear weapons were "against our religion." "A nation," he explained, "which has culture, logic and civilization does not need nuclear weapons." Khamenei's reaction to Ahmadinejad was mixed. After all, it was Khamenei, not Ahmadinejad, who controlled Iran's nuclear policy, as well as all aspects of foreign relations. As long as Ahmadinejad did not develop too great a personal support base, Khamenei seemed satisfied to let him speak his mind and draw attention away from the real decision makers. Still, to be on the safe side, in September 2005, Khamenei expanded the power of the Expediency Council, which was still headed by ex-president Rafsanjani.

A SHORT GUIDE TO THE IRANIAN GOVERNMENT:

THE PRESIDENCY

The president is not entirely a figurehead, but he has limited power.

THE LEGISLATURE

The Majlis, also known as the Islamic Consultative Assembly, has 290 members who serve four-year terms. Like the president, their powers are limited.

THE JUDICIARY

The judicial branch is independent—except that the Leader can overrule anything it does.

THE COUNCIL OF GUARDIANS

Made up of twelve members and headed by the Leader, the Council screens all prospective candidates for all elected offices including members of the Majlis, the Assembly of Experts, and the president. Six of the members are appointed by the Leader and six are chosen by the head of the judiciary, who is himself appointed by the Leader.

THE ASSEMBLY OF EXPERTS

The Assembly selects and supervises the Leader. Its eighty-six members are elected by the public for eight-year terms.

(continued)

THE EXPEDIENCY COUNCIL
Consisting of twenty-five members, the Expediency Council mediates disputes between the Majlis and the Council of Guardians. The Leader sets its agenda.

THE LEADER
Known in Iran as the *Rahbar* and often, for effect, as the Supreme Leader, the Leader can overrule any decisions made by the president, the Majlis, or the judiciary.

EXECUTIONS—The Islamic Code of 1982 authorizes the death penalty for a range of crimes that includes rape, adultery, sodomy, and the habitual drinking of alcohol. The law was amended in 1989 to include death for possession of specific drugs, including thirty grams of codeine or methamphetamine. The Code goes into detail as to how executions are to be carried out. For example, it states, "In the punishment of stoning to death, the stones should not be so large that the person dies on being hit by one or two."

People convicted of premeditated murder are subject to the death penalty, but there is one exception. If a Muslim kills a member of a religious minority, his crime is not punishable by death. Most political executions are of minorities, usually Kurds and Baluchis. Apostasy, the rejection of Islam in order to switch to a different faith, is considered a capital crime. In one unusually outlandish case, an Iranian citizen, Mehdi Dibaj, was sentenced to death on December 3, 1993, for apostasy—forty-five years after he converted to Christianity. He was a minister in the Assemblies of God. After appeals from the United Nations and the Vatican, among others, Dibaj was released from prison, but he was found dead a few months later. The murders of other Protestant clergy followed.

During the 1990s, the Iranian government carried out dozens of assassinations overseas in a program run by Mustafa Pour-Muhammadi, the current minister of the interior. On September 17, 1992, an Iranian agent and four hired gunmen from Lebanon burst into the Mykonos restaurant in Berlin and shot to death four Iranian Kurds. Four and a half years later, a German court convicted the agent and his Lebanese accomplices of the murders. While no members of the Iranian government were charged in the case, the court concluded in its written opinion that the defendants had no personal motive for their crime and acted upon an "official liquidation order" issued by senior Iranian officials.

PUNISHING CULTURAL CRIMES—Created by Ayatollah Khomeini, the *basijis* are an irregular militia in charge of cracking down on cultural crimes. In 1989 and

1990, 5,200 young men and 3,500 young women were arrested in Tehran for such "crimes" as "illicit relations between boys and girls and married men and women." Some women were arrested for "exhibiting corruption on the streets," which is to say wearing makeup or sunglasses or not wearing a headscarf. In a typical case, *basijis* arrested twenty-eight young men and women between the ages of seventeen and twenty at a private party because they were in possession of videocassettes of "repulsive" (i.e., Hollywood) movies. They received fines and ten lashes and three were sent to prison. Mixed-sex wedding parties at which men and women celebrate in the same room, are also sometimes forbidden. In one notorious case in 1995, 127 of 128 guests at a wedding celebration were fined or flogged. The bride received eighty-five lashes and the father of the groom spent eight months in jail. The only guest who was spared was a child.

CENSORSHIP AND EXTREME CENSORSHIP:

- The bounty that Ayatollah Khomeini placed on Salmon Rushdie in 1989 for writing the novel *The Satanic Verses* became an international cause célèbre, but Rushdie is not the only novelist to incur the wrath of Iran's leaders. In 1990, the woman novelist Shammush Parsipur was charged with, among other things, writing a dialogue about virginity in her book *Women Without Men.*

- Satellite dishes were banned in March 1995, but their use is widespread anyway. Government-approved television is so religiously oriented that Iranians have nicknamed it "mullahvision".

- In July 1998, the Press Court revoked the license of the magazine, *Jame* (Association) because it published a photograph of young Iranian men and women dancing in celebration after Iran's victory over the United States in the World Cup soccer tournament.

- In November and December 1998, the Intelligence Ministry assassinated several writers and dissident politicians.

- On July 7, 1999, the Majlis amended the 1985 Press Law to allow the Press Court to overrule jury verdicts. The next evening, 500 Tehran University students were attending a meeting about the closure of newspapers when they were attacked with rubber clubs by 400 vigilantes, while members of the Law Enforcement

Forces watched. An off-duty soldier attending the meeting was killed. President Khatami was so incensed that he ordered the arrest of 100 of the perpetrators. Protests spread around the country, leading to 1,000 arrests, the closing of the university, and a journalists' strike. Khamenei blamed the United States for the entire affair.

WOMEN—After the 1979 revolution, Ayatollah Khomeini encouraged procreation and even lowered the marriage age for females from eighteen to nine. The drive to increase the population worked so well that in 1993 the government went in the opposite direction, decreeing an end to paid maternity leave for mothers who gave birth to more than two children. Couples were also required to attend contraception classes before getting married. Khomeini, who had drawn on the support of women before the revolution, turned against them after he took power. In addition to imposing a dress code, he declared that a wife must submit to her husband in all matters, including sex. In case of a divorce, which a husband could obtain by simply stating that he wanted one, the husband gained custody of the couple's children. The Family Law of 1998 eased some restrictions. Men had to go to court to obtain a divorce and if a man petitioned for a divorce without his wife's consent, she was entitled to half of the couple's property. However, women still had to sit in the back of buses; they could not travel without their husband's written permission; and in court their testimony was worth half that of a man.

KHAMENEI SPEAKS:

"Our importance around the world and in the eyes of other people is based on our standing up to America."

NOVEMBER 7, 1997

"The epoch of adhering to Western prescriptions has passed. The enemies of Islam are seeking to separate religion from politics. Using seductive Western concepts such as political parties, competitive pluralist political systems and bogus democracy, the Westernized are trying to present a utopic picture of Western societies and portray them as the only salvation for our Islamic society."

JULY 24, 1998

10.
TEODORO OBIANG NGUEMA—
EQUATORIAL GUINEA

THE NATION—Equatorial Guinea is a remote West African nation with a population of only 500,000. Despite its small size, it consists of two barely related halves that were joined politically by colonial powers. One part, Río Muni, is on the mainland of Africa. The other half is the island of Bioko (formerly Fernando Po) and several smaller islands. Bioko is actually closer physically to Cameroon than it is to the rest of Equatorial Guinea. The people of Río Muni are 80 percent Fang, while those of Bioko are Bubi and the Creole descendants of immigrants and liberated slaves, known as Fernandinos. The population is 80 percent Roman Catholic. One of the most overlooked nations in the world, Equatorial Guinea popped back onto the international scene after large reserves of oil were discovered there in 1995.

HISTORY—Portuguese sailors first stumbled upon Bioko in the fifteenth century, but did not pay serious attention to Río Muni until the twenteeth century. In 1787, Portugal ceded the rights to the region, and to its people as potential slaves, to Spain in exchange for claims in Brazil. Spanish settlers were quickly driven away by yellow fever. In 1827 the Spanish leased Bioko to the British, who used the island as a base to fight the slave trade. Spain reoccupied the island in 1844 and, ten years later, began establishing cocoa plantations. The local people, who were forced to give up their land, showed no inclination to work on the plantations, so the Spanish landowners brought in slaves and contract workers, first from Liberia and then from Nigeria. Beginning in 1879, Spain also used Bioko as a penal colony for Cuban prisoners it considered too dangerous to hold in Cuba. After the Spanish-American War of 1898, Spain named the territory Spanish Guinea and set the basic borders that are still used today. In practice, the Spanish showed so little interest in the area that, between 1865 and 1910, Spanish Guinea went through sixty-five governors, averaging a change every eight or nine months. It was not until 1939 that Spain began aggressively exploiting Río Muni, using it as a source of timber.

As the age of colonialism drew to a close, Spanish Guinea was renamed Equatorial Guinea in 1963 and became "self-governing." Bonifacio Ondo Edu, a mainland Fang, was chosen president of a transitional Executive Council and a constitution was enacted in 1967. The fact that the constitution was inspired by that of Spanish dictator Francisco Franco's should have served as a warning of the horrific nightmare into which the country was about to be plunged.

At the time of independence in 1968, cocoa accounted for 75 percent of the gross domestic product and 90 percent of it was grown on Bioko. A majority of the island's population, wary of the Fang leadership on the mainland, voted against the proposed constitution. Their slogan, "Independence yes, but without Río Muni," was ignored by Spain. The constitution was approved anyway. The election to decide Equatorial Guinea's first president was contested by three candidates. Ondu Edu, who, as transitional president had already developed a reputation for corruption and arrogance, received 37 percent of the vote. Atanasio Ndong Miyone, the founder of Equatorial Guinea's original nationalist party, picked up 21 percent of the vote, while Francisco Macías Nguema, who promised a return to "traditional Fang values," won 42 percent of the vote. Ondu Edu refused to join forces with Ndong Miyone, who then threw his support to Macías Nguema, thus giving him the presidency.

Most observers overlooked an ominous sign: Macías lost in his own district, which he had ruled for the past five years. Macías took office upon the declaration of Equatorial Guinea's independence in October 1968, but almost immediately a fact became apparent that should have been clear before the election: Francisco Macías Nguema was severely deranged. Over the next eleven years he would rule with a psychotic brutality that, since the days of Adolf Hitler, was matched only by Pol Pot of Cambodia.

THE UNCLE—Francisco Macías Nguema was born January 1, 1924, in Oyen in the Woleu Nteu province of Gabon, and was raised in the village of Mongomo in what later became Equatorial Guinea. His father was a well-known Fang sorcerer and Macías would later use this pedigree to his advantage in his political career. He was not an academic star and failed the basic civil service examination three times before passing on the fourth try. After working as a clerk, he gained a petty position in the forestry department, took four years off to work on his coffee plantation and then, in 1951, he gained a post as an assistant translator in the Racial Court of Mongomo. Whatever his intellectual deficiencies, Macías knew how to take advantage of his situation. He was adept at extracting bribes and kickbacks, exploiting the peasants who needed help, while crassly ingratiating himself to the Spaniards who were his superiors. He was appointed mayor of Mongomo in 1963 and, the following year, became minister of public works for Ondu Edu's transitional government. It was in this post that Macías attracted the attention of a Spanish lawyer and entrepreneur named Antonio García Trevijano, who saw Macías as the perfect front man for his own economic ambitions. After the election of October 1968, Ondu Edu fled to Gabon, but was forced back. Macías had him arrested. While in custody, Ondu Edu was tortured, mutilated, blinded, left without medical attention for a week and then, in January 1969, lynched in prison. His wife was also murdered. On February 25, Macías was traveling through the town of Bata, when he spotted Spanish flags flying over Spanish buildings. All of his suppressed rage over the condescending way the Spanish colonialists had treated him before independence boiled over and he ordered the Spanish consul general to pull down the flags. The consul general refused, so Macías sent bands of "Macías Youth" to attack expatriates. By March, all but a few hundred Spaniards had fled the country, leaving the management of the nation crippled.

Macías took out his wrath on the educated class. He closed all libraries, prohibited the use of the word "intellectual," and once fined his minister of education, Grange Molax, for using the word "intellectual" at a cabinet meeting. When the government director of statistics published economic estimates that were lower than expected, Macías had him dismembered. A militant atheist, he ordered his own photo to hang by the altar in every church and he forced all priests to publicly preach that "God created Equatorial Guinea thanks to Papa Macías," and that "Without Macías Equatorial Guinea would not exist." Not satisfied with imposing these humiliations, Macías eventually banned all religious meetings and funerals and forbade the use of Christian names. In 1972, he made the National Assembly name him "Grand Master of Education, Science and Culture" as well as "President for Life." Macías ultimately oversaw the murder of ten of the twelve members of his original cabinet and, in 1975, he had his vice president, Bosio Dieo, killed. His strategy of liquidating potential rivals extended beyond the political realm. Macías, who was sterile (fortunately), ordered the

FRANCISCO MACÍAS NGUEMA,
ONE OF THE WORST DICTATORS
SINCE ADOLF HITLER

execution of all of the former lovers of his third wife, as well as the killing of the husbands of women he desired.

Macías' most notorious atrocity took place in 1975 when he gathered together 150 political opponents in Malabo Stadium and ordered all of them killed in a mass execution while loudspeakers played the Mary Hopkins song "Those were the Days, My Friend."

But for all of his horrible acts, Macías' worst crime was his utter destruction of his nation's economy. By 1973, one-quarter of the citizens of Equatorial Guinea had fled the country, including everyone with any economic or political expertise, and most important posts had been given to members of his family. When ninety-five Nigerian contract workers demanded payment of their wages, Macías had them murdered. Finally, his treatment of foreign workers became so bad that the government of Nigeria evacuated 25,000 of its citizens who were still in the country. Macías forced Bubi on Bioko Island to work on the cocoa plantations, but their enthusiasm was not great and the cocoa industry almost ground to a halt. When he took office, Equatorial Guinea was producing 38,000 tons of cocoa a year; after ten years of Macías' rule, the annual harvest was down to 3,000 tons. The coffee crop was also diminished to one-tenth of what it had been.

By 1979, Francisco Macías had been responsible for the murder of at least 20,000 of his own citizens. Another 100,000, almost a third of the population, had gone into exile. It is thought that this marked the greatest refugee exodus by percentage of any country in modern history.

By this time, Macías, who had twice traveled to Spain for treatment of a brain tumor, was holed up in his village of Mongomo, where the troops protecting him were led by officers from Cuba and North Korea. In other parts of the country, security service officers had gone so long without being paid that a delegation of six officers traveled to Mongomo to try to collect the wages. This was necessary because Macías kept the national treasury in his home, with much of it stuffed in suitcases. Macías' bodyguards killed all six officers. It was this outrage that would finally lead to Macías' fall. One of the six officers was the younger brother of Teodoro Obiang Nguema, Macías' minister of defense, who was also Macías' nephew. Obiang gathered together relatives with military training and, with the support of the Spanish government and military aid from Morocco and Gabon, attacked Macías' forces. Macías was deposed on August 3, 1979, captured on August 18, put on trial September 24, and executed by firing squad on September 29. Members of the national army refused to take part in the execution because they were convinced that if they did so, Macías would return after death in the form of a tiger and hunt them down. In the end, troops from Morocco had to perform the deed. Two weeks later, Obiang declared himself president. Most of the few foreigners who followed events in Equatorial Guinea were relieved by the change of regime— but Equatoguineans knew better. At Macías' trials, his crimes were related in detail—except those committed after 1974, because Obiang was implicated in many of those that took place after that date.

THE MAN—Like his uncle, Francisco Macías, Teodoro Obiang Nguema Mbasogo was born (in 1942) in the district of Mongomo by the Gabonese border. And, like his uncle, he studied at the Spanish Military Academy in Zaragoza where he and other elite Equatoguinean youth were sent, in the words of one observer, "in an effort to temper dissatisfaction in the African colony." When his uncle was elected president in 1968, the twenty-six-year-old Obiang was appointed governor of Bioko and director of the infamous Black Beach Prison. He later became commander of the National Guard before taking over as secretary-general of the Ministry of Defense. In 1973, Obiang arrested and expelled Marceau Louis of the United Nations Development Program for refusing to turn over documents relating to the anti-Macías movement. On January 8, 1976, he ordered an attack on the Nigerian consulate that led to eleven deaths, and later that year he personally arrested more than 100 civil servants who had signed a petition of protest. Several of the unfortunate protestors were killed in prison.

IN POWER—After executing his uncle and seizing power in 1979, Obiang quickly dispelled any illusions that anyone might have had that he would open Equatorial Guinea to freedom and democracy. He declared an amnesty for refugees, which sent the message that being a refugee was a criminal offense. When some hopeful refugees returned, many of them were arrested and beaten.

Somewhat less bloodthirsty than his uncle, Obiang has nonetheless proved himself a more efficient tyrant. In the words of Gustav Gallon, of the United Nations Human Rights Commission, under Obiang torture is "a normal means of investigation." To be on the safe side, Obiang has made sure that his presidential guard is composed not of citizens of Equatorial Guinea, but of several hundred soldiers from Morocco. In 1991, Obiang wrote a new constitution that prohibited the impeachment of the head of state.

Justice under Obiang was symbolized by a 1986 incident in which thirty people were arrested for allegedly trying to overthrow the government. Obiang personally presided over the military tribunal that heard the case of legislator Eugenio Abeso Mondul, who was charged with heading the conspiracy. On the last day of the trial, Abeso Mondu was convicted and immediately executed by firing squad.

In an attempt to revive his nation's ruined economy, Obiang offered to return the cocoa plantations, which had been nationalized by Macías, to their original Spanish owners. However, there were few takers. Indeed, relations between Equatorial Guinea and Spain began to sour and Obiang looked to France for help. In 1982, Equatorial Guinea became the only non-Francophone member of the Franc Zone. When Spain granted asylum to Equatoguinean opposition leader Severo Moto Nsa in 1997, Obiang, in a bizarre fit of pique, changed the national language of Equatorial Guinea from Spanish to French.

In July 2003, state radio announced that Obiang "is in permanent contact with The Almighty" and that he "can decide to kill without anyone calling him to account and without going to Hell." Despite his alleged invincibility, Obiang, like many dictators, has tried to satisfy the concerns of foreign investors and governments by staging elections. However, in true dictator fashion, he has gone to great lengths to ensure his own victory. Six months before the election of December 15, 2002, Obiang had sixty-eight opposition leaders arrested and used torture to extract "confessions" from them, after which they were all sentenced to from six to twenty years in prison. Obiang won 97.1 percent of the vote.

OIL—Good fortune struck Equatorial Guinea in 1995—sort of—when large deposits of oil were discovered. Drilling began in 1996 and over the next three years the gross domestic product of Equatorial Guinea tripled. By 2003, oil represented 80 percent of the GDP as oil companies, particularly those from the United States, poured $5 billion into the country. Exxon, Mobil, Chevron, Texaco, Amerada Hess, and Marathon Oil turned Equatorial Guinea into the third-largest oil-producing nation in Africa. Under President Bill Clinton, the United States had protested Obiang's abuse of human rights by closing the U.S. embassy in Equatorial Guinea in 1995. Six years later, the oil-friendly administration of George W. Bush, quietly reopened the embassy. They also allowed the quasi-governmental U.S. Overseas Private Investment Corporation (OPIC) to fund a $450 million methanol plant and gave permission to a private firm, Military Professional Resources Incorporated (MPRI) of Alexandria, Virginia, to develop a coast guard to protect the oil fields in Equatorial Guinea. With the per capita annual income skyrocketing to $4,472, life for the average Equatoguineans should have improved dramatically, but, with Teodoro Obiang in power, such was not the case. In fact, 60 percent of the nation's citizens continued to live on less than $1 a day, while the huge bulk of the oil income went straight to Obiang, who declared that "there is no poverty in Guinea." Rather, "The people are used to living in a different way." The nation has little public transportation, no newspapers, and only 1 percent of government spending goes to health care. In addition, in 2001 it was estimated that only 43 percent of Equatoguineans had access to safe drinking water. On the other hand, Obiang deposited almost half a billion dollars into an account in the Riggs Bank in Washington, D.C. In a radio speech in 2003, he explained to the Equatoguinean citizenry that he felt compelled to assume full control over the national treasury in order to prevent civil servants from being tempted to engage in corrupt practices.

TEODORO OBAING, LIVING THE GOOD LIFE IN PARIS, 1998
Maher Attar/Sygma/Corbis

ALL IN THE FAMILY—Like his uncle before him, Teodoro Obiang has concentrated power and wealth within his own family. In 2004 seven of the nation's nine generals were his relatives and the other two were from his tribe. His brother-in-law, Teodoro Biyogo Nsue, served as ambassador to the United Nations before taking charge of family interests in the United States, which is to say, the oil revenue of Equatorial Guinea. Obiang's brother, Armenol Ondo Nguema, is the Director General of National Security. According to the U.S. State Department, Ondo Nguema ordered security forces to urinate on prisoners, slice off their ears, and cover them with oil to attract stinging ants. Ondo Nguema owns a house in Virginia, while Obiang himself owns two in Maryland. One of Obiang's sons, Gabriel Mbegha Obiang Lima, is the state secretary for oil, but it is another son, Teodorino, who has proved to be the most colorful member of the family. Teodorino is the Minister of Water and Forests, Fishing and Environment. He also owns the only private radio station in Equatorial Guinea and gained notoriety by becoming the first Equatoguinean to own a Rolls-Royce. Teodorino is attracted by the world of entertainment. In March 2001, he purchased a $5.8 million estate in the Bel Air neighborhood of Los Angeles. Settling into the Hollywood scene, he started his own rap music company, TNO Entertainment. The first artist he signed, Won-G, introduced his first music video with a dedication to Teodorino. The name of the song? "Nothing's Wrong."

(John Moore/AP Photo)

11.
MUAMMAR AL-QADDAFI—LIBYA

THE NATION—Libya is a North African nation of about 5,600,000 people of mixed Berber and Arab origin. Ninety-seven percent of the population are Sunni Muslims and 57 percent live in or near the three Mediterranean coastal cities of Tripoli, Benghazi, and Misratah. Libya, a mostly desert country, is a player on the world scene because of its high-quality petroleum reserves. Internationally, Libya is probably less well known than its leader, the notorious dictator Muammar al-Qaddafi.

HISTORY—The term "Libya" was first used by the ancient Egyptians to refer to a single Berber tribe. The Greeks used the name for most of North Africa. However, the term was not used for an actual political entity until well into the twentieth century. For most of its history, the story of Libya was really the history of three separate regions: Cyrenaica, nearest to Egypt; Tripolitania, where most of the population lives; and the Fezzan, a desert area dotted with oases. In the fifth century BC, the Phoenicians established, in Tripolitania, the greatest of their colonies: Carthage. In the third century BC, the Romans attacked Carthage and won

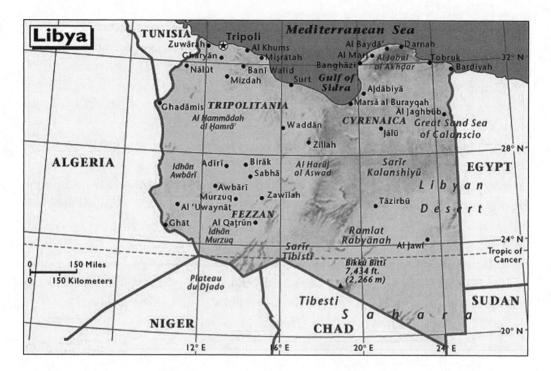

the two Punic Wars. They finally destroyed the city of Carthage and, eventually, Julius Caesar annexed Tripolitania and designated it a province of the Roman Empire. Meanwhile, the Greeks founded the city of Cyrene in Cyrenaica in 631 BC. The Greeks were driven off and the region was held by Persia and Egypt until it was conquered by Alexander the Great in 331 BC. Cyrene developed into a cultural center and the home of a school of philosophers, the Cyrenaics, who believed in moral cheerfulness. For more than 400 years, both Tripolitania and Cyrenaica existed as Roman provinces.

In AD 300 the word "Libya" was given its first official usage when Emperor Diocletian divided Cyrenaica into Upper Libya and Lower Libya. In 429, the Vandals made their capital at Carthage before moving on to sack Rome. Belisarius, a Byzantine general, drove out the Vandals in 533. In 642, an Arab general, Umribn-al-As, conquered Cyrenaica and then pushed into Tripolitania, bringing with him the religion of Islam. The native Berbers accepted Islam, but they found the Arabs brutal and arrogant. The Arabs, for their part, looked down on the Berbers as primitive. Although the conquering Arab soldiers married Berber women, the underlying clash between the two cultures would flare up 1,350 years later as Muammar al-Qaddafi tried to decide if Libya should align itself more closely to Arabs or to Africans.

In the ninth century, the Berbers revolted against Arab domination and in the 890s Shi'a Muslim missionaries converted many Berbers and then attacked and defeated the Sunni Muslims. A leader known as the Mahdi founded the Shi'a dynasty of the Fatamids. In 969, the Fatamids conquered Egypt and moved their capital to Cairo, leaving Tripolitania and Cyrenaica to be ruled by their Berber vassals, the Zirids, who led the Berbers back to the Sunni faith.

One of the worst periods in Libya history began in the eleventh century when the Fatamid caliph invited two nomadic Bedouin tribes, known collectively as the Hilalians, to migrate west into Cyrenaica and Tripolitania. An estimated 200,000 families swept into the region, "like a swarm of locusts," sacked Cyrene and Tripoli, and converted farmland to pasturage. In 1171, Saladin drove the Fatamids out of Cyrenaica, returning the area to the control of Egypt. However, the Egyptians generally neglected Cyrenaica, which reverted to the control of tribal chieftains.

The merchants of Tripoli declared it an independent city-state in 1460, but fifty years later Spain captured the city, razed it and, from the rubble, built itself a naval base.

In 1517, Turkish soldiers occupied Cyrenaica, which would remain part of the Ottoman Empire for most of the next 400 years. King Charles V of Spain turned over Tripolitania to the Knights of St. John of Malta, but they were driven off by the Turks in 1551. In the 1580s the Fezzan rulers also submitted to the Ottomans. However, in practice, the Turks had little interest in Cyrenaica and the Fezzan and left them alone. On the other hand, by the late 1600s, Tripoli had developed into an exotic city whose population included Turks, Moors, Jews, Moriscos (Muslims expelled from Spain), Europeans, and slaves of both Sudanese and European origin.

Ahmad Karamanli seized Tripoli in 1711 and established a hereditary Arab monarchy, which he financed through piracy. Ali Benghul restored Tripolitania to the Ottoman Empire in 1793. The grandson of Ahmad Karamanli, Yusuf ibn Ali Karamanli, ruled Tripolitania from 1795 until 1832, a period that saw increasing involvement with Western powers. Yusuf, for example, helped Napoleon Bonaparte during his Egyptian campaign.

TO THE SHORES OF TRIPOLI

The U.S. Marine Corps hymn begins, "From the halls of Montezuma to the shores of Tripoli." This refers to the first naval engagement of the newly independent United States. While America was a British colony, American ships were protected by the British navy, but when the United States won its independence, it lost British protection, and American merchant

When the Napoleonic Wars ended in 1815, France and Great Britain turned their attention to ending piracy in the Mediterranean. They also demanded that Tripolitania pay off all debts to European creditors. Yusuf was forced to raise taxes, which led to a civil war until Sultan Muhammad II sent in Turkish troops and, once again, reinstated Ottoman rule.

Meanwhile, in Cyrenaica, Muhammad bin Ali al-Sanusi, a popular religious leader, founded the Sanusi order, a school of Islam that taught an end to fanaticism and preached against voluntary poverty, demanding that all of its members work for a living. His son, Muhammad, also known as the Mahdi, brought all of the Bedouin tribes of Cyrenaica under control and then declared a holy war against the French.

When the twentieth century began, Tripolitania, Cyrenaica, and the Fezzan were nothing more than backwater provinces in a dying empire. In 1911, Italian troops captured Tripoli from the Turks. Distracted by the Balkan war that was looming on the horizon, in October 1912, the Turks signed a treaty that granted independence to Tripolitania and Cyrenaica, both of which Italy, anxious to make up for having missed most of the Age of Colonialism, promptly annexed. However, the Italians allowed the local sultan to retain religious authority, apparently not realizing that under Shari'a law that gave him control of the courts and the entire judicial system. This division of power led to twenty years of warfare. The first Italo-Sanusi War in Cyrenaica broke out in 1914 and soon turned into a front of World War I. When Italy joined the Allied Powers, the Sanusis automatically joined the Central Powers. In 1917, Idris al-Sanusi, who was pro-British, signed a truce with the Italians. But after World War I, the Allies gave their support to Italian control of Cyrenaica and Tripolitania. Opposition to colonial occupation was widespread, although it was divided into two main forces with differing goals: the educated urban nationalists hoped to create an independent centralized republic, while the Bedouin sheiks wanted power to be maintained by tribal states. In 1922 the Tripolitanian nationalists reluctantly agreed to allow Idris al-Sanusi to become amir of all regions of the future Libya. However, the Treaty of Lausanne, signed in 1923 by Italy and the Allies on one side and Turkey on the other, sanctioned the Italian annexation of Libya. In Cyrenaica, this set of the second Italo-Sanusi War.

By this time Benito Mussolini and the Fascists had taken power in Italy. Although the

ships fell prey to the Barbary pirates, which is to say the force controlled by Yusuf ibn Ali Karamanli. The pirates captured the ships and enslaved their American sailors. In 1803, U.S. president Thomas Jefferson sent the navy to blockade the harbor of Tripoli. Unfortunately, the USS *Philadelphia* ran aground. Its 308 sailors were forced to surrender and they were held hostage for nineteen months until the United States finally agreed to pay off Yusuf.

Italians were late to join the game of colonialism, they were quick to catch on to its spirit. In 1929, Rudolfo Graziani, the commander of the Italian forces in Cyrenaica, began an ugly and brutal war of attrition against the local population. Using Eritrean troops, he blocked wells, slaughtered livestock, herded the Bedouins into concentration camps, and executed 24,000 people. He also erected a barbed wire barrier that stretched 200 miles from the coast along the border with Egypt. Taking advantage of their larger army and their more advanced technology, the Italians overcame the last Sanusi stronghold in September 1931. They captured the Sanusi leader, Umar al-Mukhtar, and forced 20,000 Arabs to watch him hanged in public.

With their conquest complete, the Italians set about turning Cyrenaica and Tripolitania into an Italian province. They built highways and railways, expanded port facilities, and developed irrigation systems. In 1938 they supplemented this economic colonization with demographic colonization. Like the Zirids 900 years earlier, the Fascists flooded the region with more than 100,000 settlers, to whom they gave the best lands. Mussolini called the native Arabs "Muslim Italians," but in fact he did little to help them.

During this period, there were two important geographic developments. In 1934, after dividing Tripolitania and Cyrenaica into four provinces (the Fezzan remained a military territory), the Fascists named the colony Libya, resurrecting the name that Diocletian had used almost 1,500 years earlier. In 1935, Italy and France agreed to move the border between Libya and Chad 100 kilometers south across the Aouzou Strip; however, the French legislature never ratified the agreement. It would later turn out that the Aouzou Strip contained uranium and other minerals and, thirty-eight years later, the ambiguity regarding its possession would attract the attention of Muammar al-Qaddafi.

When Italy entered World War II on the side of Germany, Idris and the nationalist leaders joined the Allies. The Libyan Arab Force, known as the Sanusi Army, fought alongside the British and helped liberate Cyrenaica. In 1941 the Germans, led by Lt. General Erwin Rommel, retook Cyrenaica and continued into Egypt, where they were stopped at El Alamein and forced to retreat. The last Axis troops left Cyrenaica in February 1942 and Tripolitania in January 1943. Meanwhile, the Free French moved north from Chad and took control of the Fezzan.

At the conclusion of World War II, Libya, impoverished by Italian colonialism and with no apparent worthwhile natural resources, was not a major priority for the victorious allies. In 1947, the Four Powers, Great Britain, France, the United States, and the Soviet Union, sent a commission of investigation to determine what the Libyan people wanted. They discovered, not surprisingly, that a majority in each of the three regions wanted independence. The Four Powers declared that the Libyans were not ready for independence and, after much wrangling, proposed that for ten years Libya would be ruled as a United Nations trusteeship, with Great Britain in charge of Cyrenaica, Italy in charge of Tripolitania, and France in charge of the Fezzan. The Libyans were outraged and held huge demonstrations against the plan. Put to a vote at the United Nations in May 1949, the proposal fell one vote short when Israel and Haiti unexpectedly voted no. Finally, the big powers agreed to allow Libya to gain its independence by the beginning of 1952.

A National Constituent Assembly created a federal form of government with each of the three provinces having equal representation. This was a bitter pill for the people of Tripolitania, who formed a majority of the population and who also had to submit to the creation of a monarchy with Idris al-Sanusi, the grandson of the founder of the Sanusi sect, as king. King Idris I was given far too much power. Idris had the right to appoint half the members of the upper house of the legislature and all the members of the Supreme Court. He could dissolve the lower house, veto legislation, and unilaterally declare martial law. In fact, after the first elections were held in February 1952, Idris abolished all political parties.

When King Idris I proclaimed the United Kingdom of Libya on December 24, 1951, the newly independent nation was in a sorry state. An estimated 94 percent of the population was illiterate; the infant mortality rate stood at a shocking 40 percent; as a result of war and emigration, the population was a mere one million; and Libya's leading source of income was the sale of scrap metal scavenged from the battlefields of World War II. The Western powers were mildly impressed by Libya's strategic location, and Idris was able to lease military base rights to Great Britain and the United States, the most important being America's Wheelus Air Base near Tripoli.

The Libyans, who had been battered around and victimized by an endless succession of invaders and empires, finally caught a piece of luck: in 1959, Esso discovered major deposits of high-quality oil in Cyrenaica. Almost overnight, the outside world found Libya an interesting country. As the oil money poured in, the agricultural sector declined, while bribery and corruption boomed. For example, the Bechtel Corporation, which built Libya's first oil pipeline, established a cozy relationship with Prime Minister Mustafa Ben Halim, whose private firm managed to come away with at least 10 percent of the net profits on all projects. When Ben Halim fled the country after the 1969 coup, Bechtel helped him acquire a Saudi passport and citizenship.

The corruption and incompetence of Idris' government led to growing dissatisfaction and anti-Western agitation, while Idris, who dissolved parliament in 1964, made matters worse with his authoritarian decisions. In June 1969, the seventy-nine-year-old Idris left Libya for medical treatment and rest in Greece and Turkey. He would never return.

THE MAN—Muammar al-Qaddafi appears to have been born in 1942. His family were members of the Qathathfa tribe, Arabized Berbers who were exiled from Cyrenaica.

According to Qaddafi, his grandfather was killed fighting the Italians and his father was wounded during World War I. The family were Bedouin nomads who lived in tents and made their living growing barley and trading livestock. The youngest of six children and the only son, Muammar was the pet of the family, and he received an abundance of loving attention. When he was nine or ten years old, his father sent him to school for the first time in Sirte, a town of 7,000 people. He slept in the local mosque and went home to visit once a week, after traveling the thirty kilometers each way on foot. As one of only three or four Bedouin at the school, he was treated with contempt by some of the other students.

When Muammar was fourteen years old, his family moved to the Fezzan, where he attended the Sebha Preparatory School. It was here that he became best friends with Abdel Salam Jalloud, and the two would share a remarkable life's journey. During this period, Gamel Abdul Nasser of Egypt was promoting Arab pride and Arab unity, and the young Qaddafi was greatly moved by Nasser's message. His most prized possession was his copy of Nasser's *Philosophy of the Revolution.* Qaddafi was seventeen years old when he first began dreaming of leading a revolution in Libya. At school he led demonstrations to protest the assassination of Patrice Lumumba, to protest the French testing of atomic bombs, and in favor of the anticolonial revolution in Algeria. He was finally expelled from school for distributing photographs of Nasser. After attending school for two more years in Misratch, Qaddafi enrolled, in 1963, in the Military Academy in Benghazi. This was a calculated decision based on his realization that to achieve a successful revolution he needed to control the military. Qaddafi convinced friends of his, including Abdel Salam Jalloud, to enter the Academy as well. Qaddafi distrusted older officers and he concentrated on men his own age when he created the Free Unionist Officers, a group devoted to the goal of Arab unity. Qaddafi graduated in 1966 and then spent several months in Great Britain at the Royal Military Academy at Sandhurst.

THE 1969 COUP—By 1969, Qaddafi and his friends were ready to stage their coup. Qaddafi took advantage of the six weeks' leave he had accumulated and set the date for the takeover for March 12. However, it turned out that the legendary Egyptian singer Umm Kulthum was scheduled to perform that night. Her concerts lasted hours. All of Libya's political and military leaders would be there all night with their families. Out of respect for Kulthum and wishing to avoid the awkwardness of arresting the leaders in front of their wives and children, Qaddafi postponed the revolution. After another false start a couple weeks later, the coup was rescheduled for August 13, when the entire Army High Command would be together, attending a conference on the importance of air defense. However, Qaddafi's supporters felt they were not yet prepared to seize control of important army units in Tripoli, so the takeover was aborted again. Finally, on September 1, they were ready. At the time, Libya's army consisted of 6,000 men. There was also a small naval force, a small air force stationed at the Americans' Wheelus Field, and police and security forces numbering about 12,000 men.

At 2:30 a.m., Qaddafi and his followers made their move. By 4:30 they had successfully taken control of the military and the country without killing a single person. It says a lot about King Idris' lack of popularity that seventy young officers could overthrow the government in just two hours in a nearly bloodless coup.

A year later, Qaddafi and four of his associates celebrated the first anniversary of their coup by appearing on television and relating the details of their memorable night. Their tone was that of a bunch of fraternity brothers describing an elaborate prank, as they described stopping at an Italian-owned café for brioches and milk on their way to the revolution, losing control of one of their cars and running into each other, and so on.

IN POWER—At the age of twenty-seven, Muammar al-Qaddafi joined the ranks of world leaders. At 6:30 a.m. on September 1, 1969, he appeared on national radio and announced that henceforth Libya would be "a free, self-governing republic." Departing from his prepared text, he tried to reassure foreigners living in Libya that there would be no threat to their lives or property and that "our enterprise is in no sense directed against any state whatever." Qaddafi appointed himself commander-in-chief of the Libyan Armed Forces, while his best friend, Abdel Salam Jalloud, became deputy prime minister (within three years Jalloud would move up to prime minister). This was heady stuff for Qaddafi: to dream of leading a revolution at the age of seventeen and then pull it off only ten years later. And, unlike most coup leaders around the world, Qaddafi, thanks to Libya's oil reserves, had the resources to carry out some of his more fanciful plans.

Six weeks after seizing power, Qaddafi announced his five major goals:

1. *removal of foreign military bases*
2. *international neutrality*
3. *national unity*
4. *Arab unity*
5. *suppression of political parties*

By the end of his first year in power he had achieved four of those five goals. The bases were gone, he had staked out a position between the two superpowers in the Cold War, and he had most definitely suppressed all political parties. In a country with little history of political involvement, it was easy to achieve a rough approximation of national unity: Qaddafi nationalized the banks, raised the price of oil for foreign companies, and doubled the minimum wage. Achieving Arab unity was another matter, and it would prove to be a frustrating obsession that would dominate the rest of his life.

ARAB UNITY—Qaddafi had been deeply moved by what he viewed as a humiliating defeat of Arab armies by Israel in 1967. Inspired by the speeches of Nasser, he hoped to galvanize the support of other Arab leaders to gain revenge against the Jewish state. When Qaddafi made his first tour of Arab capitals in 1970, he was shocked that his calls for revenge met with tepid responses. Nasser himself was pleased to have a highly placed disciple, but he died only a few months later. The other leaders were annoyed that Qaddafi, a young upstart from a country far from the fighting, should lecture them as to what should be done. They found him not so much arrogant as naive. Yet Qaddafi was sufficiently piqued to support the Palestinians in their revolt against the king of Jordan. On February 21, 1973, Israel shot down a Libyan commercial airplane that strayed into the Israeli-occupied Sinai, killing 106 civilians. During the next war with Israel in October 1973, Qaddafi donated Libyan planes to the Egyptian air force. When Anwar Sadat, Egypt's president, agreed to a ceasefire with Israel, Qaddafi accused him of cowardice.

Between 1971 and 1980, Qaddafi made repeated attempts to unite Libya with various Arab countries. There was much talk of solidarity and occasionally papers were signed, but Qaddafi was always frustrated in his attempts to achieve a substantive union. In 1977 he actually fought a brief border war with Egypt, and in 1995 he threatened to expel 30,000 Palestinians from Libya to protest the Oslo Peace Accords signed by Israel and the Palestine Liberation Organization. (He suspended the program after expelling 1,500.) In 1984 he randomly laid mines in the Red Sea, disrupting traffic and severely damaging the Egyptian economy. Meanwhile, Qaddafi was showing increasing interest in Africa, a continent filled with leaders in need of the money Qaddafi was prepared to dole out. In 1998, Qaddafi changed the name of the national radio station from Voice of the Arab Nation to Voice of Africa. In 2003, at an Arab League summit to discuss the impending U.S. invasion of Iraq, Qaddafi engaged in a public exchange of name-calling with Saudi Arabia's Crown Prince Abdullah that was broadcast on television. Qaddafi announced that he was withdrawing from the Arab League and that Libya was "above all an African country."

GOVERNMENT BY CHAOS—When, in 1972, the Libyan parliament began pushing for democratic reforms, Qaddafi was not pleased. Declaring that "representation is fraud," he proposed that he would bring to the Libyan people a purer form of democracy than the ones available to citizens in the West. Vaguely inspired by China's Cultural Revolution, Qaddafi created a system of "popular committees." The idea was that in all institutions, including businesses with two or more employees, the workers would elect their own people's committee to run the show. "Everyone is on an equal level," said Qaddafi, "the director general with the simple worker." Commercial enterprises would also give up 50 percent ownership to the workers. Of course there was one catch to this new form of radical democracy. As Qaddafi explained, "I shall have the right . . . to tell the elected popular committees that they have not expressed the general will in a suitable manner, or they have not acted as they should in some way." In other words, Qaddafi retained veto power over every decision made by every popular committee.

Eventually, despite the restrictions, the popular committees became too independent for Qaddafi. In 1977 he created a new layer of control: the revolutionary committees, the members of which were chosen from zealots who responded to his speeches. Their job was to "guide" the popular committees and to identify for punishment anyone who engaged in "deviation" or "opposition."

In time, Qaddafi became dissatisfied with the revolutionary committees as well. He criticized them for being arrogant and corrupt—and for having long hair and wearing jeans. In 1995, Qaddafi added yet another level to his bureaucracy by creating 250 "cleansing committees" to weed out "counterrevolutionaries." Qaddafi's definition of counterrevolutionary is broad; at one point a cleansing committee arrested a Palestinian for selling "Israeli aphrodisiac gum."

CHAIRMAN OF THE UN HUMAN RIGHTS COMMITTEE—Respecting human rights has never been one of Muammar al-Qaddafi's strong points. At various times during his thirty-seven-year reign, he has:

- Redrawn administrative boundaries in order to disrupt natural tribal boundaries
- Imposed the death penalty for belonging to a political party other than his own
- Imposed the death penalty for speculation in currency, food, clothing, or housing
- Imposed the death penalty for alcohol-related crimes
- Expelled Italians and Jews and confiscated their property
- Launched a "Green Terror" against Marxists

- Held political trials in secret
- Forbidden the ownership of more than one private residence
- Shut down Islamic schools
- Punished those who refused to reveal the details of their personal wealth by having their hands chopped off
- Punished robbers by having their right hand and their left leg amputated

In 1997, Qaddafi ordered the People's Congress to pass a collective guilt and punishment law. According to this unusually appalling regulation, an entire family, tribe, village, or town can be punished if a single member helps, protects, or merely fails to identify a perpetrator of a "crime against the state." Included in the definition of such crimes are "practicing tribal fanaticism," possessing an unlicensed weapon, and the all-inclusive "damaging public or private institutions or property."

Considering this record of abuse, the United Nations hit one of the low points in its history when, in January 2003, Libya was chosen to chair the UN Human Rights Commission. How could this have happened? Qaddafi exploited a loophole in the Commission's rules, whereby each continent takes its turn in leading the Commission and the chair is chosen by the members of the continent itself. As the turn of Africa approached, Qaddafi went to great lengths to financially reward the leaders of African nations in order to win their votes. For good measure, he announced the release of political prisoners except "a group of heretics who are believed to have links with what is known as al-Qaeda and the Taliban." In a jab at the United States, he noted that these prisoners would be treated in the same manner as those the United States was holding in Guantánamo Bay. "These people do not have the right to defend themselves; we will never provide them with lawyers, nor will their human rights be respected."

TERRORISM—In 1979, Qaddafi warned opposition leaders living abroad that they must return home or face "liquidation." True to his word, over time Qaddafi would see to it that Libyan intelligence officers assassinated about two dozen Libyan exiles. During an anti-Qaddafi demonstration in front of the Libyan embassy in London in 1984, a Libyan intelligence operative mistakenly shot to death a policewoman named Yvonne Fletcher. Besides targeting his own opponents, Qaddafi gave money to various Islamic liberation and terrorist groups, most notably the Palestinian group headed by Abu Nidal. Still, when Ronald Reagan took power as president of the United States in 1981, Qaddafi was not an active participant in terrorism and even his support for terrorist organizations did not compare to that of Syria or, later, Iran.

Yet Reagan, almost from the day he took office, chose Qaddafi as his favorite enemy and set about provoking him. Reagan negotiated with Mikhail Gorbachev of the Soviet Union, provided arms to Iran, and turned a blind eye to Syria's support for terrorism. But for Reagan, it was Qaddafi who was the perfect enemy: he was obviously a tyrant, he was widely viewed as weird, and Libya, although wealthy, was a small country with an ineffectual military that lost a war to Chad. Since Qaddafi's actual behavior was often strange and erratic, it was easy to spread outrageous rumors about him. For example, in 1981, the Reagan administration declared that Qaddafi had outfitted "special assassination squads" to kill President Reagan and members of his cabinet, stirring a brief moment of national hysteria, although William Webster, the director of the CIA, said in an interview weeks later that the existence of such squads had never been confirmed. After his reelection in 1984, Reagan revved up his campaign against Qaddafi to include actual violence. The Americans prepared a plan called "Rose" that included an attack on Qaddafi's personal barracks. In March 1985, the U.S. military carried out maneuvers off the coast of Libya and challenged Qaddafi's version of the dividing line between Libyan and international waters. There was an exchange of fire and the United States sank two Libyan patrol boats in the Gulf of Sirte, killing seventy-two sailors. The Americans also conducted bombing raids against radar and missile installations. In December 1985, Abu Nidal launched terrorist attacks at the Rome and Vienna airports. The Reagan administration blamed Qaddafi for backing the attacks, although U.S. intelligence reports suggest that the Syrian government was more involved than the Libyans.

On April 5, 1986, a bomb went off at the La Belle disco in Berlin, a night spot frequented by U.S. soldiers. Three people were killed, two of whom were American soldiers, and 229 people were injured, including 79 Americans. A few days later, the U.S. government announced that it had intercepted communication that implied that the La Belle bombing had been organized by members of the Libyan secret service operating out of the Libyan embassy in East Berlin.

In the early morning hours of April 15, forty U.S. warplanes based in Great Britain flew over Libya and bombed a barracks in Benghazi, a naval academy, a frogman's training school, and a camp for training Palestinian guerrillas. However, it was the final site that the Americans bombed that attracted international attention: Qaddafi's personal compound at the Didi Balal naval base. Flying only 200 feet above the ground, the U.S. fighters dropped 2,000-pound laser-guided bombs on Qaddafi's residence. Remarkably, although they badly damaged his tennis courts, they missed Qaddafi, who was in his command center deep underground. The Americans did kill Qaddafi's eighteen-month-old adopted daughter and injured two of his sons. In all, 101 people were killed.

In a bizarre twist, supporters of Ronald Reagan would hail the attack as a high point of his presidency, a demonstration of how terrorists should be dealt with. To this day there are Reagan admirers who declare that, "we never had to worry about Qaddafi again after that." Unfortunately, the exact opposite was the truth. According to figures provided by the U.S. Department of State, in 1985, Libya was involved in fifteen acts of terrorism, twelve committed by Abu Nidal's group. In 1986, the number jumped to nineteen acts against non-Libyans, and Qaddafi for the first time began targeting Americans. A planned attack in New York in 1988 failed when a terrorist carrying bombs was stopped for a traffic violation in New Jersey. But then, on December 21, 1988, Qaddafi got his revenge against the United States when a bomb destroyed Pan Am flight 103 over Lockerbie, Scotland, killing 270 people. On September 19, 1989, Qaddafi also gained revenge against the French for their support of the Chadian military rout of Libyan forces by blowing up UTA flight 772 over the Sahara Desert, killing 171 passengers and crew.

The Americans and the French demanded that Qaddafi turn over the perpetrators of these two crimes. When he refused, the United Nations imposed an air embargo against Libya and then froze Libyan funds held in other countries. The UN also banned the sale of equipment to Libya that could be used for oil or natural gas operations, although the sale of petroleum was allowed to continue. These sanctions gradually took their toll on the Libyan economy. In 1996, Qaddafi agreed to let a French investigative judge come to Libya and search the offices of the Libyan intelligence services. Miraculously, the judge found a suitcase just like those used in the bombing. The French convicted six Libyans in absentia including Qaddafi's brother-in-law. In 1999, Qaddafi, in exchange for the lifting of UN sanctions, turned over to authorities two suspects in the Lockerbie case, Abdelbaset Ali Mohamed al-Megrahi and Al-Amin Khalifa Fhiman. A Scottish court, operating in the Netherlands, held an eighty-four-day trial that culminated in the conviction of al-Megrahi. Fhiman, on the other hand, turned out to be nothing more than an employee of Libyan Arab Airlines and he was acquitted. Qaddafi paid compensation to the families of the victims of both bombings, all sanctions were lifted, and oil companies and others enthusiastically recommended business with Libya. As for the La Belle disco attack, after a four-year trial, in November 2001, a German court convicted two Libyans and a German woman, Verena Chanaa, who was charged with actually planting the bomb. Qaddafi himself escaped prosecution because the U.S. and German governments refused to share intelligence with the prosecutors.

BIZARRE BEHAVIOR:

- Qaddafi has a long record of disappearing from public view without warning. The first instance occurred in 1971 when Qaddafi went missing for sixteen days and failed to show up for a meeting in Cairo of the Presidential Council of the United

Arab Republic. He suddenly reappeared and the meeting went ahead, although six days late. He also missed the celebration of the fourth anniversary of the Revolution, and the President of Tunisia, Hassib Bourguiba spoke in his place.

QADDAFI AND ONE OF HIS GREEN NUNS
Laurent Rebours/AP Photo

- Qaddafi is protected by a coterie of high-heeled female bodyguards known as the Green Nuns. One of them reportedly died when she took a bullet during a 1998 assassination attempt.

- In 1977, Qaddafi ordered all Libyans to raise chickens, even urban dwellers who lived in apartments.

- His speeches often include conflicting ideas, and the nation is forced to wait for written clarifications before policies can be carried out.

- He has been known to lie on the floor of his office, covered by a sheet, for up to two hours at a time.

- Qaddafi became so well known for making passes at female journalists that Western media outlets began sending their most attractive reporters to Libya in order to gain access to him.

- Imelda Marcos, the First Lady of the Philippines, made two trips to Tripoli to try to convince Qaddafi to stop funding Moro insurgents in the southern Philippines. The two got on well and, after Imelda's second visit, Qaddafi stopped the funding.

- Inspired by Mao Zedong's *Little Red Book,* Qaddafi compiled his philosophy into the *Green Book.* In the tent he used for entertaining guests, he had his favorite thoughts from the *Green Book* embroidered into the fabric of the walls.

- He also had his thoughts put to a disco beat and broadcast as music videos on Libyan television. Among the catchy lyrics from the song, "The Third Universal Theory":

The universal theory has seen the light,
Bringing mankind peace and delight,
The tree, oh, of justice, people's rule and socialism,
Completely different from laissez-faire and capitalism,
Based on religion and nationalism.

• Qaddafi invited IRA recruits to terrorist training camps in Libya. However, the recruits returned early to Northern Ireland when they discovered that they were being taught how to fight in the desert, a skill that was not terribly useful on the Emerald Isle.

• In the words of Jaafar Nimieri, former president of Sudan, Qaddafi "has a split personality . . . both evil."

QUOTES:

"We burned no books in Libya. We simply withdrew certain books from the libraries and bookshops."

1974

"The Libyan Arab people have existed for hundreds of years without oil and are capable, if necessary, of living without it for many more centuries."

1975

"American soldiers must be turned into lambs, and eating them is tolerated."

JUNE 15, 1986

"We must recognize that we are very far removed from the precepts of Christ, and that we are very close to the designs of Satan. . . . We need to read again the teachings of Christ and to find in them the voice which says to us, 'Give up Palestine, Southeast Asia, Ireland, Germany, and the African colonies . . . The World needs Christ again.' "

JANUARY 1, 1975

"Political struggle that results in the victory of a candidate with 51 percent of the vote leads to a dictatorial governing body disguised as a false democracy, since

49 percent of the electorate is ruled by an instrument of governing that they did not vote for, but had imposed upon them. This is dictatorship."

THE GREEN BOOK

"All of the great prophets of modern times have come from the desert: Mohammed, Jesus and myself."

OCTOBER 1988

MUAMMAR AL-QADDAFI (RIGHT),
MAN OF THE DESERT, PRAYING IN 1973
Genevieve Chauvel/Sygma/Corbis

(Siphiwe Sibeko/AP Photo)

12.
KING MSWATI III—SWAZILAND

THE NATION—Africa's last remaining absolute monarchy, Swaziland is smaller in size than New Jersey and has a population of 1.2 million. It shares a seventy-mile border with Mozambique, but is otherwise surrounded by South Africa. On a map, Swaziland appears like an ingrown polyp inside the body of South Africa.

The majority of Swazi citizens are peasant farmers who live on $1 a day. Swaziland has the dubious distinction of having the world's highest rate of HIV/AIDS: almost 40 percent. By 2004, the estimated average life expectancy had dropped to 37 years. Ten percent of Swazi households are headed by children. The government euphemistically refers to these households as "sibling families."

Swaziland's main export, sugar, is subsidized by the European Union, although the northern mountains produce marijuana that is bought by South African dealers and shipped to Europe.

ORIGINS—According to local tradition, before the sixteenth century the Swazi people migrated south into present-day Mozambique. Following violent clashes with another clan, the Swazi king, Ngwane II, led his people to northern Zululand in the mid-1700s. In the early nineteenth century, Ngwane II's grandson, King Sobhuza I, fled from the Zulus and settled his people in what is now Swaziland. Those families who accompanied him are known as "The Pure Swazi." Those who were already there, but who agreed to submit to Sobhuza I's authority, are called "The Found Ahead." Later immigrants, who now make up two-thirds of the population, are "Those Who Arrived After."

Sobhuza I's son, Mswati II, gained fame as a great fighting king who expanded his territory into Southern Rhodesia (Zimbabwe). Sobhuza I had had a vision that the white people would eventually come in large numbers and that the Swazis should not kill them. When the whites did come, in the form of Dutch Boer farmers and British traders, Mswati II, who reigned from 1839 until 1865, tried to accommodate them both. On the one hand, he asked for British protection against Zulu raiders, but he also sent his own army to help the Boers defeat a Sotho tribe in the north. He also signed his cross on two documents that gave most of his country to the Boers in exchange for 150 cattle.

After Mswati II's death in 1865, there was a fight over who would succeed him. His heir, Ludwonga, died mysteriously. A co-regent, Ludwonga's half-brother, was clubbed to death. Finally, a council of princes appointed Mbandzeni, a royal orphan, to rule along with Ludwonga's mother. When the two clashed, the queen mother fled, but she was captured and strangled to death. Mbandzeni brought peace to his nation, and in 1881 the Boers and the British signed the Pretoria Convention, which recognized Swaziland as an independent kingdom. Mbandzeni had no illusions about this independence being anything more than in name only. When he died in October 1889, he was convinced that because of the power of the whites, "the Swazi kingship ends with me."

Mbandzeni was succeeded by Ngwane V, better known as Bhunu, who was sixteen years old when he became king. In 1894, the Boers declared Swaziland a protected dependency of the South African Boer Republic. The Boers were not pleasant colonialists, and they imposed a hut tax on the Swazis in an attempt to force farmers to switch to cash crops or be driven into the labor market. When a Swazi councilor who was sympathetic to the whites was executed, the Boers charged King Bhunu with murder. He fled to Zululand and sought protection from the British, who negotiated with the Boers. After paying a £500 fine, Bhunu was reinstated as king. Bhunu died during the period of the Anglo-Boer War (1899–1902). When Great Britain won the war, the British reluctantly took control of Swaziland. Meanwhile, the Swazi royals chose one of Bhunu's widows, Lomawa, to be queen mother and her baby boy, Mona (Jealousy), to be the future king. Born July 22, 1899, he was renamed Sobhuza II.

KING SOBHUZA II—To this day, Sobhuza II is the longest-reigning ruler of any country in the world since the death of Emperor Franz Josef of Austria-Hungary in 1916.

While Sobhuza II was a minor, one of the nation's co-regents was his grandmother, Labatsibeni. She had seen her people subjugated by the Boers and the British and, after a lifetime of studying white people, she concluded that their power derived from money and books. She established a campaign to buy back Swaziland from the whites, and she introduced formal education to the country, including a school for princes. When Sobhuza II was sixteen years old, Labatsibeni convinced the council of princes to allow him to study abroad. Along with eight other Swazi boys and three girls, he was shipped off to Cape Province in South Africa, where he spent more than two years at Lovedale, a school run by the United Free Church of Scotland. Back in Swaziland, he was finally crowned king in 1921.

By the time the age of colonialism was coming to a close and the prospect of independence was spreading to every corner of Africa, Sobhuza II had been in power for four decades and he had learned a lot about dealing with the whites. In the first half of 1963, there were a series of labor strikes in Swaziland. The British Resident Commissioner asked Sobhuza II to enforce law and order, but the Swazi king refused to use force against his own people. The British flew in 600 soldiers from Kenya. Again Sobhuza held back his troops, this time rejecting the use of force against the foreigners. The British broke the strike and jumped to the conclusion that Sobhuza II was satisfied to be a powerless, ceremonial king, just like their own royals. Sobhuza II demanded that a referendum be held so that the Swazi people could vote for or against having him rule the country. The British authorities thought the idea absurd, but it fit in with their rhetoric about promoting democracy in their colonies, so they allowed the referendum to go ahead.

KING SOBHUZA II (RIGHT) WITH THE QUEEN'S
COMMISSIONER IN 1966
The Swazi Nation

Because 75 percent of the population were illiterate, Sobhuza II convinced the British to put animal symbols on the ballots instead of words: a lion to represent the king's position and a reindeer to represent the British position. What the British apparently failed to take into account was that the lion was considered a symbol of Swaziland, while the reindeer was seen as a foreign animal. When the referendum was held in January 1964 the lion won 122,000 votes, and the reindeer only 154. Three months later, an election was held for the newly created Legislative Council. All of the seats reserved for the whites were taken by a pro–South African, anti–United Kingdom party. Sobhuza II's party, the Imbokodvo National Movement, won all of the Swazi seats.

As independence came closer, another legislative election was held in April 1967. The Imbokodvo gained 79.4 percent of the votes and swept all of the seats. The whites, who owned 43 percent of the nation's land, began to worry about expropriation. For quite some time the South Africans had considered annexing Swaziland, but they gave up the idea because they were able to use Swaziland to set up subsidiaries of South African companies and thus get around the international anti-apartheid boycott against them.

On September 8, 1968, Swaziland declared its independence. Economically it remained dependent on South Africa. Even now, almost four decades later, Swaziland depends on South Africa for all of its oil and 85 percent of its consumer goods. There were also more Swazis living in South Africa (many of whom worked in the gold mines) than there were in Swaziland. Sobhuza II was careful with his foreign policy. He condemned apartheid and praised freedom fighters in Rhodesia and Mozambique, but he refused to let these rebel movements use Swazi soil for military staging grounds.

Domestically, Sobhuza II tolerated the Western concept of democracy until 1972, when an opposition party managed to win three seats in the House of Assembly. Although Sobhuza's party still held an overwhelming legislative majority, Sobhuza II had had enough. At a public meeting on April 12, 1973, he announced that he was repealing the constitution. Mincing no words, he declared, "I have assumed supreme power in the Kingdom of Swaziland. All legislative, executive and judicial power is vested in myself." He dissolved all political parties, banned public political meetings and demonstrations, and declared that suspects could be held without trial for sixty days and that such detention could be renewed indefinitely.

In 1977, Sobhuza II abolished the parliamentary system altogether and announced that the nation would be ruled by traditional institutions. However, the following year, bowing to the international mania for democracy, he created a bicameral parliament, although he retained the right to appoint ten of the fifty members of the lower house and half of the members of the upper house. The names of the candidates, four for each seat in the lower house, were not announced until the day of the election. Each voter was asked to line up in front of the candidate of his or her choice. Forty-five percent of the registered voters did not show up at the polls, apparently taking the position that this public display would earn them three enemies and only one friend. Actually, the whole procedure was pointless anyway because King Sobhuza II retained the right to veto permanently any bill that the parliament might pass.

Sobhuza II died on August 21, 1982. He had been king for so long that there was confusion about the protocol regarding his burial because no one involved in his father's burial was still alive. He left behind about sixty-five wives from thirty-two different clans, although estimates of his lifetime total of wives ranged as high as 120. He was survived by 110 children, including 40 sons. The royal family ordered a period of mourning to last three moons, during which all plowing and other work-related activities were prohibited. Because the nation was in the midst of a drought, cattle died and food was scarce for months afterward.

KING MSWATI III—Ntomi Tfwala lived in the queens' quarters as a handmaiden to one of Sobhuza II's youngest and most Westernized queens. Sobhuza II picked her out to be a queen herself and, on April 19, 1968, she gave birth to a son. Conceived when Sobhuza II was sixty-eight years old, he was named Makhosetive (King of All Nations) because he was born in the year that many foreign leaders visited Swaziland to celebrate its independence. He was educated at the local Masundvivini Royal School and then sent off to the Lovedale Mission School in South Africa, just as his father had been more than sixty years earlier. Aged fourteen, he was off hunting when Sobhuza II died. It came as a surprise when the royal council chose him to become Swaziland's next king because he was the second-youngest of Sobhuza II's dozens of sons. Five months after being designated heir to the throne, Makhosetive left Swaziland to study at the Sherbourne School in Dorset, England. In September 1983, he returned home during a school holiday and was displayed publicly to a curious citizenry. His mother, in the meantime, had taken over as regent.

Ordinarily, Makhosetive would not have been crowned king until his twenty-first birthday. However, because of political instability in the country, he was enthroned three years early. On April 25, 1986, at the age of eighteen, he was designated King Mswati III.

IT'S GOOD TO BE KING—Because Mswati III was young, had lived in England, and had been exposed to the modern world, there was hope among the educated class of Swazis that he would lead the nation to more up-to-date and democratic ways. However, the traditional perquisites of being king were too much for him to resist. One tradition that Mswati III found particularly appealing was the annual Reed Dance in which thousands of girls and young women dance topless before the king, after which he is allowed to choose a new wife from among them. In recent years, King Mswati III has taken advantage of modern technology to study videotapes of the dancers to help him make his decisions. In 2002, his choice actually precipitated a governmental crisis. In September of that year, after the Reed Dance, he picked out a seventeen-year-old named Zena Mahlangu. Zena's mother, Lindiwe Dlamini, was a telecommunications executive who was furious that the king had "secured" her daughter. Dlamini filed suit against the king, claiming that he had abducted Zena. The nation's judiciary branch, already annoyed by Mswati III's interference in their regular work, eagerly took on the case. Mswati III sent government officials to speak with the three judges in charge of the case and to order them to dismiss the lawsuit or resign. The conflict was resolved when the king presented Zena publicly and announced that she had agreed to become his tenth wife.

Mswati III's choice of Zena Mahlangu created another problem. A year earlier, the king had responded to the alarming rise in HIV/AIDS (33% among girls aged fifteen to nineteen) by instituting a chastity law that prohibited men from having sex with teenage girls for the next five years. When Mswati III himself defied the ban by marrying Zena, he was forced to pay the price: a fine of one cow. Later, he ended the ban one year early, on August 22, 2005. That year he chose as his twelfth wife, a Miss Teen Swaziland finalist.

IT'S GOOD TO BE KING: LIVING BIG—Mswati III has included Michael Jackson and Eric Clapton among the guests at his birthday parties. For his thirty-sixth birthday in 2004, he threw a party for 10,000 guests that cost $612,000. But that was a minor

expense in comparison to his outlays for cars. That same year, Mswati III purchased a $690,000 Maybach 62 luxury sedan and ten BMWs. Because, at the time, the Swazi unemployment rate stood at 40 percent, he prohibited the photographing of his May-bach.

KING MSWATI III WITH FOUR OF HIS WIVES AND HIS CONTROVERSIAL FIANCÉE, ZENA MAHLANGU (FAR RIGHT)
AP Photo

But even the Maybach was not Mswati III's greatest extravagance. In 2002, while half of Swazis were living in homes without running water, the king announced that he planned to buy a private jet that was worth $44.6 million, an amount that was double the annual health budget for the entire nation. The Swazi parliament cancelled the order, but Mswati II overruled the legislature and purchased the jet anyway. The speaker of the house, Marwick Khumalo, was forced to resign his post because he protested the plane purchase too vigorously.

In February 2002, Mswati III flew to Hollywood to celebrate MTV's "Rock the Vote!" campaign. The fact that his own citizens are not allowed to take part in free elections seemed to have no effect on his conscience.

WOMEN—In the siSwati language, the word for woman means "one who dies without speaking of what she endures." According to tradition a woman in Swaziland cannot own property. She also cannot apply for a passport or enter into a contract without the consent of her husband or, if she is unmarried, a male relative. Wives are legally treated as minors and in case of divorce, the children belong to the father. These last restrictions can be overlooked if the couple prepared a prenuptial agreement, but in a nation where 80 percent of the population are peasant farmers, such agreements are rare.

Women who have been widowed less than two years are not allowed to appear in public. In 1998, Mswati III made an exception to this prohibition so that widows could join in the celebrations honoring the thirtieth anniversary of both independence and his birth. However, that same year he used the prohibition to prevent widows from running for office or even voting. Many Swazi women escaped the restrictions at home by becoming nurses and finding work outside the country. But in July 2004, Mswati III put a halt to this practice by blocking overseas employment agencies form obtaining the foreign currency necessary to continue doing business.

DEMOCRACY NO—In April 2003, the League of Churches in Swaziland hosted a forum on "The Disadvantages of Multi-Party Democracy." With the king in attendance, Rev. Khayeni Khumalo summed up the government position bluntly: "Presidents are power-hungry people who are like rapists: they break in and rule. . . . There is not a single verse in the Bible which says there should be a president ruling a country. When the people are given the right to choose, they always choose evil."

King Mswati III first dissolved parliament and ruled by decree when he was only twenty-four years old. Swaziland has continued to hold legislative elections since then, but because the king has the right to overrule anything the parliament does, these elections are nothing more than elaborate publicity stunts and their results are meaningless. When half of the nation's labor force went on strike in 1997, Mswati III simply made strikes illegal.

FREEDOM NO—In response to the fact that Swaziland had been in operation without a constitution for thirty years, the government announced a new draft constitution in August 2003. Another two years passed before Mswati III signed it into law, and it finally took effect in February 2006. However, the new constitution is no document of civil rights. Among its clauses it:

- allows the death penalty for a wide variety of offenses
- bans political parties

- rejects the concept of habeas corpus and allows the holding of suspects for five to ten years without trial
- prohibits investigations into "any matter relating to the exercise of a royal prerogative"

and for good measure,

- gives King Mswati III the right to overrule any rights that are granted elsewhere in the constitution.

There is no protection of freedom of speech or freedom of the press and no public access to government documents. The government has also been known to refuse to release imprisoned suspects even though they have paid bail.

According to both Amnesty International and the U.S. State Department, Swazi prisoners have died in custody after being tortured and suffocated to death. The Swazi authorities have a preference for two particular forms of interrogation. Tube style interrogation involves suffocating the prisoner by putting a rubber tube around his face and mouth. Victims of Kentucky interrogation have their arms and legs bent and then tied with rope or chain, after which they are beaten.

IN HIS WORDS:

"Democracy is not good for us because God gave us our own way of doing things."
                                                        APRIL 2003

ON HUMAN RIGHTS:

"What rights? God created people, and he gave them their roles in society. You cannot change what God has created."
                                                        MAY 30, 2003

"The Bible says, 'curse be unto a woman who wears pants.'"
                                                        MAY 30, 2003

A SWAZI SAYING:

"A king is a mouth that does not lie."

(AP Photo)

13.

PERVEZ MUSHARRAF—PAKISTAN

THE NATION—Pakistan is the sixth most populous nation in the world, trailing only China, India, the United States, Indonesia, and Brazil. Almost all of Pakistan's 166 million citizens are Muslims. Eighty percent are Sunni and 20 percent are Shi'a. The population is ethnically diverse. The largest group, at about 44 percent, are the Punjabis, who live mostly in the east, on the border with India, and have generally dominated Pakistani politics. The Pashtuns (15%) are centered in the region bordering Afghanistan, the Sindhis (14%) live in the south, near India, and the Seraikis (10%) live primarily in the Pakistani Punjab. There are also significant numbers of Muhajirs, who emigrated from India to Pakistan at the time of independence, and Balochis, who occupy the sparsely populated southwest and who also live in Iran and Afghanistan. Since its independence in 1947, Pakistan has fought three wars with India. It has been under military control for half its history, and no elected Pakistani leader has ever completed his or her term of office. The name Pakistan was created in 1933 by the early nationalist leader Choudhary Rahmat Ali as an acronym for Punjab (P), Afghan (a), Kashmir (k), Sindh (s), and Balochistan (tan). In the Persian language "pakstan" means "land of the pure."

THE SWEEP OF HISTORY—Human life in Pakistan dates back to at least the ancient Soan culture in the Pothohar region of Punjab, 50,000 to 100,000 years ago. Many civilizations in the region rose and fell, including the Indus Valley Civilization and that of the Indo-Aryan tribes who came from Central Asia and mixed to produce the Vedic Civilization around 1500 BC. In the sixth century BC the region was conquered by the Persians and in 326 BC by Alexander the Great. The Gandhara Civilization in the north was a center of Buddhism. A series of conquerors swept through the region until AD 712, when the Umayyed dynasty sent an Arab-Muslim army to conquer the Sindh and Multan people in southern

Punjab. Led by Muhammad bin Qasim, the army introduced Islam to the population. The new faith was spread by Sufis, and Muslim rule was firmly established by Muhammad Ghuri in the twelfth century. Beginning in 1526, most of the Indian subcontinent was ruled by the Mughal Empire, which controlled territory in what is now India, Pakistan, and Afghanistan. The empire began to decline in power in 1707, and in 1739 it was defeated by a Persian army led by Nadir Shah.

TOWARD INDEPENDENCE—By the end of the eighteenth century, the British East India Company had gained almost complete political and economic control of the region. In 1857 the Indian War of Independence (also known as the Indian Mutiny) was launched. The British defeated the rebellion after fourteen months, but it laid the foundation for the formation of the Indian National Congress (INC) in 1885, which was created to give educated Indians a greater share in the British administration. In 1920 the pacifist Mahatma Gandhi gained the leadership of the INC. Fearing that the INC would be dominated by India's Hindu majority, Muslims in India formed the All-India Muslim League (AIML) in 1906. The leader of the AIML, Allama Muhammad Iqbal, a poet and philosopher, first proposed a two-nation theory in 1930, calling for the establishment of a Muslim state in Northwest and Southeast India. Around the same time, activist Choudhary Rahmat Ali wrote about the formation of a Muslim state in the Indian subcontinent in a pamphlet entitled "Now or Never: Are we to live or perish forever?" Rahmat Ali founded the Pakistan National Movement in 1933.

If Iqbal and Rahmat Ali first proposed the two-nation theory, it was Mohammad Ali Jinnah who made it a reality. Known as "Quaid-i-Azam" or Great Leader, Jinnah was the founding father of independent Pakistan. A member of the Muslim League since 1913, Jinnah resigned from the Indian National Congress after clashing with Mahatma Gandhi over the best way to achieve self-rule from British control. He served as president of the Muslim League from 1920 to 1930. In 1929 he proposed a fourteen-point plan for the establishment of a unified Indian constitution that would satisfy both Hindus and Muslims. The proposal was rejected by both sides, and Jinnah went into self-imposed exile in England, retiring from politics to practice law. With the encouragement of Iqbal and Rahmat Ali, Jinnah returned to India to reorganize the Muslim League. He raised the idea of a partition of India at the 1940 Lahore Conference and organized a day of civil disobedience on August 16, 1946. The protests, which began peacefully, degenerated into mob violence, resulting in more than 10,000 deaths, including Muslims, Hindus, Buddhists, and Sikhs. By then the British were desperate to get rid of the tumultuous subcontinent. Lord Louis Mountbatten was named the last Viceroy of India and took quick steps to partition the country.

THE CHAOS OF INDEPENDENCE—On August 14, 1947, Pakistan achieved its independence. The Muslim nation was established in two separate regions divided by a thousand miles of Hindu India. The East Pakistan population was Bengali and, other than being Muslims, had little in common with the people of West Pakistan. Riots erupted throughout India and Pakistan as millions of people began to move across the borders from both sides. More than 5.5 million Muslims and 3 million Hindus fled, and approximately half a million people were killed in the violence that erupted. The new nation found itself in a difficult situation. While India inherited the infrastructure left behind by the British, the Pakistanis had to build a government from scratch. In addition to the arrival of millions of refugees, there were few educated or experienced politicians, no working treasury, and a lack of basic equipment, including office space, office furniture, and even writing materials.

Jinnah took the role of Pakistan's governor general and directed the creation of the country. Although he had pushed for a Muslim state, he had never given up hope of a unified Indian state, and he remained a firm believer in a moderate, secular Pakistan that would protect all its citizens, regardless of religion or race. In his first speech to the Constituent Assembly of Pakistan he told them, "You are free. You are free to go to your temples, you are free to go to your mosques or to any other place of worship in this State of Pakistan. You may belong to any religion or caste or creed. That has nothing to do with the business of the State." Unfortunately, Jinnah died of tuberculosis and lung cancer only four weeks after the declaration of independence.

Following Jinnah's death, the country entered a period of political turmoil. His successor, Liaquat Ali Khan, became Pakistan's first prime minister, but proved an ineffectual leader and was assassinated in October 1951. Ali Khan was succeeded by Khawaja Nazimuddin, who had to cope with increasing political squabbling and infighting, as well as riots in the Punjab region and a growing Bengali independence movement in East Pakistan. The Bengalis wanted Bangla to be recognized as a national language alongside the Urdu of West Pakistan. On February 21, 1952, students and activists started a mass protest in Dhaka, the capital of East Pakistan. The police responded with violence, firing on the crowd and killing several students, and sparking what would become the Bengali Independence Movement. After two years of growing turmoil under Nazimuddin, Governor General Ghulam Mohammed dismissed the prime minister and dissolved his cabinet, in the first of what would become a series of coups. Ghulam Mohammed had the support of the head of the army, General Mohammed Ayub Khan, as well as the defense secretary, Iskandar Mirza. When Ghulam Mohammed's health began to fail, Mirza stepped forward and took over leadership of the country as Pakistan's first president. However, the country continued to destabilize as the parliament splintered into factions vying for political power.

THE FIRST MILITARY DICTATOR—For the first few years after independence, the Pakistani military remained under the control of the British. On January 17, 1951, commanding officer Sir Douglas Gracey ceded control of the Pakistani army to General Muhammad Ayub Khan, the first Pakistani to hold the position. Amid the growing political instability, Khan became increasingly disillusioned with the ability of civilian authorities to govern the country. The final straw came in October 1958, when the Khan of Kalat, the ruler of a barren and distant region in Balochistan that had been independent for seven months after the partition of India, declared himself the sole legitimate ruler of his territories and broke his ties to Pakistan. Ayub responded by sending Pakistani troops to seize the Khan's land and throw him in prison. The army did not stop there, however, and the next day it occupied all radio and telegraph stations throughout Pakistan, as well as the major railway stations, airports, and ports. The National Assembly was closed and newspapers were given orders not to publish anything that had not been approved by the military. Finally, Ayub declared the constitution void and banned all political parties. Ayub named himself the Chief Martial Law Administrator and soon forced President Mirza into exile, taking the position for himself.

After a decade of political turmoil and incompetence, many Pakistanis were happy to see Ayub take control. In fact, Ayub was more benign than oppressive, and although he continued to imprison or humiliate opposing politicians, he did not sanction physical violence or execution. Ayub worked to house the huge numbers of refugees surrounding Karachi and commissioned the construction of a new Pakistani capital, Islamabad, in the northwest region of the country. He also established numerous tribunals and committees to crack down on the widespread corruption and bribery taking place within the government, and within a year he dismissed more than 1,500 corrupt officials. Taking a secular stance, he established the Muslim Family Laws Ordinance to protect the rights of women in marriage. As president, Ayub allied himself with the United States, declaring himself their "most allied of allies."

Ayub also took on a political protégé, the young Zulfikar Ali Bhutto. Only twenty-nine years old, the Berkeley-educated Bhutto was given a position within the cabinet and was soon appointed to the post of Foreign Minister. In 1962, Ayub decided to lift martial law and allow the political process to continue. By then, Ayub had become increasingly unpopular in the country, both for his secular approach and for his alignment with the United States. He won the 1964 presidential election, but with a slim majority. The real turning point in Ayub's leadership came in 1965, when Pakistan attempted to retake the disputed territory of Kashmir, leading to an all-out war between India and Pakistan. Although the war ended in a stalemate, almost 7,000 Pakistani soldiers were killed and public opinion turned increasingly against Ayub.

THE UNINTENDED CONSEQUENCES OF DEMOCRACY—In 1967, Bhutto founded the Pakistan People's Party (PPP). He began to wear a uniform similar to those worn by Chinese Communist Party leaders and to push for the introduction of "Islamic Socialism." Bhutto spoke out against Ayub's regime, beginning a nationwide tour with the catchy slogan "Food, Shelter, and Clothing." Bhutto forced Ayub's resignation in 1969 and gave control of the country back to the military. General Agha Muhammad Yahya Khan reimposed martial law and assumed the role of Chief Martial Law Administrator. Just two years after Yahya Khan took control, the country was on the brink of civil war. Yahya Khan declared national elections to be held in October 1970, but flooding in East Pakistan forced him to postpone the voting until December. Just weeks before the election, a cyclone struck East Pakistan, causing a tidal wave that swept more than a quarter of a million people out to sea, making it one of the deadliest natural disasters of modern times. The population of East Pakistan was then angered by what they perceived as the slow response and apathy of the government.

When the ballots were counted, the Alawi League, led by Mujibur Rahman, won a landslide victory in East Pakistan, and thus a majority of the seats in the National Assembly. Bhutto and his party called for the nullification of the results and for a new election to be held. Yahya Khan tried to postpone a decision on this proposition, but demonstrations continued to spread throughout East Pakistan. Instead of listening to their complaints, the Pakistani government sent General Tikka Kahn, a man with a reputation for brutality, to become governor of East Pakistan. On March 25, 1971, under Tikka Kahn's leadership, the army initiated its program to crush Bengali resistance. It started by deporting all foreign journalists and attacking the Bengali opposition, as well as intellectuals and students. As civil war broke out, India contributed its own troops to help the Bengali independence movement and shut off Pakistan's ability to fly over Indian territory, effectively cutting off the Pakistani troops in East Pakistan. By December, the remaining Pakistani troops had surrendered and East Pakistan, renamed Bangladesh, had achieved independence.

Bhutto took advantage of the climate of uncertainty after the war to ascend to power and quickly established autocratic rule. He created a paramilitary force outside of the Pakistani army called the Federal Security Force (FSF), largely made up of former military officers and criminal elements. The FSF was in charge of Bhutto's security and was charged with identifying and arresting anyone suspected of plotting against the state. The FSF soon became an instrument of state violence, carrying out covert operations and assassinations at Bhutto's whim. Bhutto's increasingly intolerant political machine earned him the nickname "Adolf Bhutto." Bhutto was supported by the PPP, which dominated the parliament and extended his term for six years. It even prepared a book of Bhutto's quotations, styled after Mao

Zedong's *Little Red Book.* Any dissention within the PPP was swiftly dealt with, and many of the party's leaders were forced into exile or murdered by the FSF. Bhutto nationalized major industries and all banks and withdrew Pakistan from the Commonwealth of Nations. He was so unpopular that the left and the right joined forces and gained mass support. When Bhutto announced that his party had won a sweeping victory in the elections of March 1977, it was clear that he had rigged the results. Tens of thousands of people took to the streets, many from the main Islamic parties, who accused Bhutto of undermining Islamic tradition. When the FSF was unable to restore order, Bhutto called out the army. But many soldiers resented Bhutto's creation of the FSF and refused to fight to protect him, joining the protests instead. In a last-ditch effort to retain power, Bhutto tried to appease the Islamists by issuing a decree that outlawed alcohol, gambling, nightclubs, and movie theaters. The fundamentalists were not impressed.

On July 5, General Muhammad Zia-ul-Haq, whom Bhutto had appointed Chief of Army Staff the previous year, seized power in a military coup and declared martial law. Zia-ul-Haq put Bhutto into prison, but then released him. Bhutto immediately set out on a tour of Punjab, the stronghold of his PPP, where he attracted huge crowds. In September the military arrested him on charges of ordering the political murder of an opponent. Bhutto was convicted and sentenced to death. The Supreme Court of Pakistan ruled that the sentence be commuted to life in prison, but Zia-ul-Haq ordered that the death penalty be carried out anyway. On April 4, 1979, Bhutto was hanged.

THE MILITARY DICTATORSHIP RETURNS—WITH A VENGENCE—

Zia-ul-Haq created a new version of the legislature, the Majlis-i-Shura, and announced that he would appoint all 284 members. He tried to legitimize his regime through the increased Islamization of the military. Army promotions went only to practicing Muslims, and civil workers were judged not just by their performance, but according to their adherence to daily prayer and their knowledge of Islam. In 1979, Zia-ul-Haq enacted the Hudood Ordinance, which criminalized all extramarital sex and which is still in force. For unmarried couples, the punishment is 100 lashes; for an adulterer, the punishment is death by stoning. Rape can only be prosecuted if the victim can produce four Muslim male witnesses to testify. The Hudood Ordinance also criminalized drinking alcohol, punishable by eighty lashes, and made the punishment for theft the amputation of the right hand at the wrist. Zia-ul-Haq built up an appalling record of human rights abuses that included torture, arbitrary imprisonment, and public floggings of journalists and political dissidents.

At the end of 1979, the Soviet Union invaded Pakistan's neighbor, Afghanistan, and three million Afghan refugees flooded into Pakistan, which also was thrust onto the front lines of the Cold War. Suddenly, Zia-ul-Haq found himself in the position of being a key ally of the United States, which inundated him with money and weapons. Realizing that the United States needed him so much that they did not care about his human rights abuses, Zia-ul-Haq cracked down even harder on civil society, banning all public gatherings and imposing a curfew in major metropolitan areas. He also instituted a 10 percent military quota for all civil service, government, and corporate positions. Soon, a generation of fundamentalists had jumped up the ranks of the military, the civil service and, especially, the Inter-Services Intelligence (ISI), the Pakistani secret police. The ISI began covert operations in support of the Afghan resistance movement and played a central role in building up the Taliban, one of the most extreme of the religious, anti-Soviet forces in Afghanistan. When the Soviet troops finally left Afghanistan in 1989 the ISI continued to support the Taliban and other militant groups.

In December 1984, Zia staged a referendum, the wording of which seemed to be a vote for or against Islam, but which in fact affirmed his right to remain in power for five more years. Two months later he held elections for the National and Provincial Assemblies, but only on a nonparty basis, and won easily. On August 17, 1988, Zia boarded a Pakistani Air Force plane at Bahawalpur bound for Islamabad. With him were most of the senior military cabinet as well as U.S. ambassador Arnold Raphel. A few minutes after takeoff, the plane crashed, killing everyone onboard. The results of the official inquiry into the crash were never released to the public.

THE DECADE OF CORRUPT CIVILIANS—Because the crash that killed Zia ul-Haq also took out most of the top military brass, it opened the way for a civilian government once again. A former civil servant, Ghulam Ishaq Khan, the presiding officer in the senate, was sworn in as president. Ishaq's first act as president was to declare a state of emergency.

He then turned the government over to Benazir Bhutto, the thirty-six-year-old daughter of the former president, who was the leader of the newly reformed PPP, one of the two dominant parties in the country. The other powerful party was the Islamic Democratic Alliance or IJI (Islami Jamhoori Itihadi), led by Nawaz Sharif. The two political leaders fought bitterly for control of the country. As prime minister, Bhutto used the military frequently to crack down on dissidents or protesters, but like almost all Pakistani rulers

COMPETING TO BE THE MOST CORRUPT:
NAWAZ SHARIF AND BENAZIR BHUTTO
Reuters/Corbis

before her, she was unable to control the extremist elements in the country. Seventeen months into her seven-year term, Bhutto was forced out by Ishaq, with the backing of the military. Ishaq then ordered another election, which Nawaz Sharif won easily. Bhutto became the leader of the opposition. The country slid even deeper into political chaos when Ishaq announced the dissolution of Sharif's government in 1993. Sharif took his case to the Supreme Court, who ruled that both Sharif *and* Ishaq had overstepped their authority and forced them both to resign. In the interim, a caretaker government was formed under Moen Qureshi, former vice president of the World Bank, until another election was held. Benazir Bhutto again took power—and was dismissed a second time in 1996.

NAWAZ SHARIF—In 1997, Nawaz Sharif was elected prime minister in a landslide election. With the support of more than two-thirds of the National Assembly, he had the opportunity to work toward greater political stability and economic reform. Instead, he quickly moved to consolidate his own power. He amended the constitution to eliminate the power of the president to dissolve the government and he removed the chief justice of the Supreme Court. Sharif cracked down on the opposition in parliament and harassed and imprisoned journalists who were critical of his administration. He was also immensely corrupt, using the state coffers as a personal bank account and installing friends and relatives in national positions.

In 1998, army chief General Jehangir Karamat called for military representation on the National Security Council, a move that Sharif took as a threat to his power. Sharif wanted to install his close friend, Lt. General Khawaja Ziauddin, as Chief of Army Staff, but Ziauddin was busy as the head of the Inter-Services Intelligence. Three generals were in line to ascend to the position. Two had strong political backing, so, as a temporary solution until Ziauddin could take charge, Sharif chose the third: Pervez Musharraf.

THE MAN—Pervez Musharraf was born, the second of three sons, on August 11, 1943, in the Daryaganj neighborhood of Delhi, India. His family fled to Pakistan in 1947 during the riots that followed India's partition. His father, Syed Musharraf-ud-Din, was a diplomat, having originally joined Pakistan's Foreign Service as a clerk. At one point Syed Musharraf spent seven years working in the Pakistani embassy in Ankara, Turkey, where Pervez spent part of his childhood, learning to speak fluent Turkish. Pervez's mother, Begum Zohra Musharraf, was an educated and liberal woman who worked for the International Labor Organization (ILO).

A short, pudgy child, Musharraf was nicknamed "Gola," which means "ball." As a child,

Pervez was always overshadowed by his older brother, Javed, who was a year ahead of him at school and much stronger academically. Pervez recalled being scolded by his teachers for not being as smart as his brother. An average student, Pervez admitted to sometimes taking his brother's old school papers and rewriting them to get better grades. Pervez's younger brother, Nareed, was also highly intelligent and went on to become an anesthesiologist in Chicago. Musharraf attended Saint Patrick's High School in Karachi before moving to Lahore to attend university at the Forman Christian College, where he was, as usual, an average student. He was also an enthusiastic, if not outstanding, athlete. His greatest achievement came during his freshman year when he won third place in a bodybuilding competition. Musharraf's participation in sports continued throughout his career. As a top military general he was known for leaving work by 2:00 p.m. to spend the afternoon playing table tennis, tennis, or badminton. Because of his undistinguished grades, Pervez's mother encouraged him to go into the military when he graduated. So in 1961, Musharraf enrolled in the Pakistani Military Academy in Kakul, before moving on to the National Defense College and then the Royal College of Defense Studies in the United Kingdom.

Musharraf fought in the Indo-Pakistani War of 1971 as a company commander for artillery regiments as well as for an armored division. In early 1991 he was promoted to Major General and given command of an infantry division, and by 1995 he had attained the rank of Lieutenant General and was in charge of the prestigious Strike Corps. One of Musharraf's favorite training methods for his troops was to order them to lie as close to a set of railroad tracks as possible and then to make them keep their head up and eyes open as a train passed directly in front of them. In 1998, Musharraf reached the rank of Chief of Army Staff, and the following year he led the army during the Kargil War.

SEIZING POWER—The Kargil conflict erupted between India and Pakistan in May 1999 as a result of Indian anger over the infiltration of Islamic militants into the Indian-controlled territory of Kashmir. As army chief, Musharraf organized a major military operation into the Indian-administered Kargil region of Kashmir. Pakistani troops and Kashmiri militants infiltrated the border and captured the mountains above a vital road used to supply Indian troops, who had been based in the region since 1984. The high altitude and harsh terrain allowed the Pakistani soldiers to hold their position for two months despite larger Indian numbers and bombardment by the Indian air force. International tensions grew to the point that Nawaz Sharif visited Washington, D.C., to try to convince the United States to back the Pakistani position. The Clinton administration instead put so much pressure on Sharif to withdraw that when he returned he announced a pullout. Sharif also provoked the outrage of the military by blaming the army for acting unilaterally. Musharraf, however, emerged from the campaign a military hero.

By this point, relations between Sharif and the army were so strained that the 111 Brigade, a military corps known for overthrowing governments, was placed on fifteen-minute alert to seize civilian buildings in case Musharraf was fired. Sharif tried to smooth things over by agreeing to extend Musharraf's term as Chief of Army Staff for an additional two years. At 3:45 p.m. on October 13, just after Musharraf boarded a plane in Colombo, Sri Lanka, Sharif met with General Ziauddin in his home. A camera crew was there and they taped Sharif installing Ziauddin as army chief. The tape was sent to the national television station, PTV, to be broadcast at 5:00 p.m. and again during the six o'clock news. Policemen were also stationed at the national airport in Karachi, Musharraf's final destination, with orders to prevent his plane from landing. Meanwhile, Ziauddin was to remove the top generals suspected of being loyal to Musharraf.

One month before the attempted removal, Musharraf had replaced two of the country's nine military commanders with men loyal to him. The remaining generals had anticipated the possibility of an attempt to remove Musharraf and immediately put their own plans into place. By 5:30, less than two hours after the removal, soldiers took over the PTV building and cancelled the 6:00 p.m. broadcast of the video. At the same time, three army trucks arrived at Sharif's residence and took control of the building. Soldiers also occupied the airport and the national radio station and placed Ziauddin, Sharif, and several cabinet ministers under house arrest. Meanwhile, Musharraf's plane, which had been circling for hours, was finally allowed to land, with only a few minutes of fuel left. Forty-eight hours after landing, Musharraf appeared on television to announce the removal of Nawaz Sharif and to declare a state of emergency in the country. He appointed himself "Chief Executive" and suspended the constitution, declaring that "the whole of Pakistan will come under the control of the Armed Forces." Throughout the entire coup, not a shot was fired. Sharif was thrown into prison and eventually put on trial by Pakistan's Anti-Terrorism Courts, which sentenced him to several life sentences for corruption, hijacking, tax evasion, embezzlement, and terrorism. The military government agreed to commute his sentence from life in prison to exile in Saudi Arabia.

Like Pakistan's previous military dictators, Musharraf was initially seen as a welcome change by most Pakistanis. By the time Musharraf took power, the previous administrations of both Benazir Bhutto and Nawaz Sharif had practically run the Pakistani economy into the ground. The country was on the verge of defaulting on its $32 billion debt, and the federal reserves were only $1.5 billion. Almost 60 percent of government revenues were going toward paying off the debt. In 1996, Transparency International ranked Pakistan the second most corrupt country in the world.

CONSOLIDATING POWER—In the aftermath of Musharraf's coup, the Pakistani Supreme Court insisted that he hold general elections by October 12, 2002, three years after taking power. But on June 20, 2001, in a surprise move, Musharraf appointed himself president. He was the fourth military ruler of Pakistan to take the position, after Ayub Khan in 1958, Yahya Khan in 1969, and Zia-ul-Haq in 1977. At the same time, Musharraf removed the current president, Rafiq Tarar, when he refused to resign, and dissolved the national and provincial assemblies. Musharraf was now the sole power in the nation. As October 2002 loomed on the horizon, Musharraf was confronted with his promise to hold general elections. He found himself in a difficult position, as the two main parties, Sharif's Pakistan Muslim League (PML) and Bhutto's PPP, together controlled about half of the popular vote. So instead of a normal parliamentary election with candidates that the constitution required, Musharraf announced a referendum for the end of April 2002. The wording of the referendum was: "For the survival of the local government system, establishment of democracy, continuity of reforms, end to sectarianism and extremism, and to fulfill the vision of Quaid-e-Azam [Mohammed Ali Jinnah], would you like to elect President General Pervez Musharraf as president of Pakistan for five years?" Musharraf learned from Zia-ul-Haq's experience, and he took almost every step imaginable to ensure that he would win in a landslide. In the run-up to the election Musharraf allowed only "constructive" criticism from opposition parties and banned all public meetings. On voting day itself, anyone over the age of eighteen was allowed to vote, without having to produce any ID, which allowed for the casting of multiple votes by the same person. The voting booths themselves were overseen by senior military officers. Incredible as it may seem, Musharraf won 97 percent of the vote. The vote was so obviously rigged that Musharraf later felt compelled to apologize for the "enthusiasm" of his followers.

In August of 2002, Musharraf further strengthened his hold on power. He issued a presidential decree instituting twenty-nine constitutional amendments designed to consolidate power within the military and presidency. Among the amendments was one that gave the president the power to make all senior appointments in the provinces, bureaucracy, and judiciary, including the Supreme Court, and another that allowed Musharraf to retain his role as army chief while also serving as president. He explained his dual roles as president and military leader by stating, "If you want to keep the army out, you have to bring it in." He also introduced a Legal Framework Order as a new article in the constitution, validating all acts of his government since the 1999 coup. Although constitutional amendments required a two-thirds majority in parliament, Musharraf explained that he did not need any other approval for the amendment, because he had secured the Supreme Court's approval. To give the constitution a veneer of democracy, Musharraf insisted that the parliament still has the power to undo the amendments by a two-thirds majority, but he has hinted that if that were to happen he would be forced to choose between resigning and dissolving the parliament.

DEMOCRACY, MUSHARRAF STYLE—Musharraf was now ready for the promised parliamentary elections of October 2002—almost. To be on the safe side, he issued a law stating that no previous prime ministers could serve a third term, even if they had not finished the previous two. The law applied only to Benazir Bhutto and Nawaz Sharif. Musharraf also made it known that if either Bhutto or Sharif were to return from exile they would be immediately arrested by the military under charges of corruption. Neither Bhutto nor Sharif attempted to return. Musharraf also passed legislation that made candidates ineligible to run if they did not have a university degree, if they had bank debts, or if they had failed to pay their utility bills. These strict rules eliminated more than half of the previous parliament, but since Musharraf decided to accept degrees from Islamic madrassa schools, almost all religious candidates were still eligible. Musharraf also banned all public rallies.

To avoid any strong opposition within the country Musharraf encouraged divisions within the Muslim League, the political party of Nawaz Sharif. The Muslim League split between those who were content to cooperate with the new regime and those who remained loyal to Sharif. The pro-establishment politicians formed the Muslim League (Q), or Quaid-e-Aram, "King's Party." The oppositionists formed the Muslim League (N). As a backup plan, in case the PML-Q did not do well in the elections, the military backed 100 independent candidates as well.

Not surprisingly, the Muslim League (Q) won the most seats, 118 of the 342 seats contested. The Muslim League (N) won only fourteen. Benazir Bhutto's PPP won eighty-one seats, and a coalition of religious parties, under the name of Muttahida Majlis-e-Amal (MMA), the United Council of Action, gained sixty seats. Composed of six religious political groups, the MMA represented a broad range of religious factions, including Sunnis, Shi'a, and Barlevis, a more moderate sect of Islam. Although the political leaders varied in their outlook, many were vehemently anti-American. Maulana Fazlur Rahman, the leader of the most powerful MMA group, the pro-Taliban Jamiatul Ulema-i-Islam (Islamic Party of Religious Leaders), made a public threat after the attacks on September 11 that if the United States pursued Osama bin Laden, Americans in Pakistan would be the target of further terrorist attacks. Previously, the religious leaders had been unwilling to cooperate with each other, due to sectarian divisions. This time, however, their anti-U.S. sentiment united them. The MMA gained most of its support in the Baloch and Pashtun populations in the Pakistani tribal lands along the Afghan border, a region with close ties to the Taliban and where U.S. intelligence services believe Osama bin Laden might still be hiding. The MMA gained political control of one of Pakistan's four provinces, the wild Northwestern Frontier Province, as well as shared control, with the PML-Q, of Balochistan. On June 2, 2003, the MMA passed a law instituting Shari'a law in the Northwestern Frontier Province. This included mandatory daily prayer, the veiling of women, and the requirement that men grow beards. An MMA-directed "anti-obscenity" movement led to mobs in the provincial capital of Peshawar tearing down advertisements featuring women, destroying satellite dishes and video rental stores, and attacking the offices of foreign multinational corporations. The MMA also prohibited mannequins from being displayed in shop windows and male doctors from treating female patients.

Musharraf had hoped to use the election to consolidate his own power in parliament, but instead he found himself in a weaker state than before the elections. His party, the PML-Q, had to negotiate with either the MMA or the PPP to achieve a majority in parliament. They began with the MMA, who demanded that the PML-Q disband the National Security Council and withdraw measures allowing Musharraf to dissolve the National Assembly. When the MMA also insisted that Musharraf set a specific date for giving up his role as army chief, the PML-Q cut off negotiations. Next, they turned to Benazir Bhutto, who still exerted significant influence on the PPP despite being in exile. Bhutto entered the negotiations asking the PML-Q to release her husband, Asif Ali Zardarin, from prison and to drop the charges of corruption against both of them. When these negotiations failed as well, Musharraf's party was able to convince some PPP politicians to cross over to the PML-Q, but only after a rule forbidding party defections was waived by Musharraf. On November 21, 2002, the National Assembly voted in a new prime minister, Zafarullah Khan Jamali, a fifty-eight-year-old tribal leader from Balochistan and former national field hockey player. The portly, friendly Jamali was loyal to both Musharraf and the army. Jamali barely made it into office, receiving the bare minimum of votes required, 172.

KASHMIR—Since the Partition of India in 1947, Kashmir has been a contentious and fundamental issue within Pakistan. The last British Viceroy of India, Lord Louis Mountbatten, directed the partition of the subcontinent. Mountbatten, who got along well with India's Jawaharlal Nehru and Mahatma Gandhi, had strained relations with Mohammed Ali Jinnah, and soon abandoned the idea of a unified subcontinent. Under the Partition plan, the former princely state of Kashmir was allowed to choose which side it would join. Though a majority of the population was Muslim, the state was ruled by the Hindu Maharaja Hari Singh, who could not decide in which direction to turn. Fearing that the Hindu Mahajara would choose to join India, Pakistani tribesmen from the Northwestern Frontier Province invaded Kashmir along with Pakistani military forces. India soon sent in troops as well, beginning the First

Kashmir War. After months of intense fighting, the two sides agreed to a ceasefire and established a line of control between the Indian-administered and Pakistan-administered sides of Kashmir. Since then, violence has repeatedly flared up in the region, as both sides continue to claim their right to control the territory. The Second Kashmir War erupted in 1965, and in 1999 the two countries skirted war after the Kargil Conflict. Since the Partition, tens of thousands of soldiers and civilians have died in the fighting. The Pakistanis have accused Indian forces of killing as many as 80,000 Muslims in the Indian territory, while Pakistan has encouraged the infiltration of Islamic militants into the region from training camps in Pakistan.

In August 2002, the situation in Kashmir began to heat up again. Almost one million soldiers massed along the Indian-Pakistani border, sparking global fears of a war. The cause of the tension was complaints about Kashmiri militants infiltrating the border from Pakistan into India. India gave an ultimatum that it would invade the Pakistani-controlled portions of Kashmir if Pakistan did not seal the border and stop the crossings. Under pressure from the United States, Musharraf agreed. He ordered the dismantling of militant training camps in Pakistani-controlled Kashmir, although most simply moved into Pakistani territory. Nonetheless, Musharraf gained many enemies among the militant groups, who felt betrayed by a leader who had supported them for many years.

There is still a strong and widespread belief in Pakistan that it should be allowed to govern all of Kashmir, since the majority of the population is Muslim. In the words of Musharraf himself, "Kashmir runs in our blood." Nevertheless, in November 2004, he declared a unilateral ceasefire along the line of control. India responded by lifting a ban on flights into the country by Pakistan's national airline.

SEPTEMBER 11: THE TWO-EDGED SWORD—Before the September 11, 2001, terrorist attacks in the United States, Musharraf had been the single most enthusiastic supporter of Mullah Mohammed Omar and his Taliban regime in Afghanistan. Like Musharraf, most Taliban were ethnic Pashtuns, and the Taliban could not have gained power without the aggressive support of the Pakistani military. Less than twenty-four hours after the attacks had taken place, the Bush administration gave Musharraf an ultimatum: either side with the United States or with the Taliban. As a man with little ideology other than self-preservation, Musharraf, without conferring with his aides or generals, made the decision to cast his lot with the Americans. He went on television to announce that he was abandoning Pakistan's long-standing ties with the Taliban and speaking out against religious extremism, saying "there is no reason why this minority should hold the majority as hostage." Musharraf also cut off oil and power supplies to the Taliban, agreed to let the United States use two

Pakistani air bases, and promised Pakistan's help in providing military intelligence to U.S. troops. Musharraf was immediately rewarded. By the end of September the Bush administration had agreed to waive economic sanctions that had been in place since Pakistan had tested nuclear weapons three years earlier. Bush also lifted a ban on military sales to the regime. The United States pledged more than $50 million in aid, with Japan and the European Union kicking in another $40 million each. U.S. assistance rose from a meager $5 million in 2001 to slightly more than $1 billion in 2002. In 2003, more than $560 million was allocated in aid and another $1 billion in debt was cancelled. On October 2, 2001, while Musharraf was trying to convince

PERVEZ MUSHARRAF WAS THE WORLD'S LEADING SUPPORTER OF THE TALIBAN. BUT AFTER SEPTEMBER 11, 2001, THE U.S. MADE HIM AN OFFER HE COULD NOT REFUSE. ON SEPTEMBER 19, HE TOLD THE PAKISTANI PEOPLE HE WAS CHOOSING "THE LESSER EVIL."
Reuters/Corbis

the international community that his government was not really a supporter of terrorism, a massive explosion outside the fortified Jammu and Kashmir Assembly complex in the Indian city of Srinagar killed forty-two people. The bombing had been carried out by an ISI-linked jihadist group devoted to retaking control of Indian-administered Kashmir. An embarrassed Musharraf condemned the bombing as a terrorist act, a first for a Pakistani leader.

STAYING IN POWER: THE BALANCING ACT—To avoid being overthrown or even killed, Pervez Musharraf has had to balance the demands of various powerful groups, most notably the military, Inter-Services Intelligence, and religious extremists. At the same time he has tried to convince his financial supporters in the U.S. government that he really is fighting terrorists.

Military spending in Pakistan continues to average more than 30 percent of the national budget. It is also unusually nontransparent, appearing in the budget as a single line. The military remains loyal to Musharraf mainly because he makes sure that it enjoys privileges and prestige. The Pakistani military also owns land and property. The Fauji Foundation, which serves as the financial support mechanism for retired soldiers, is the largest corporation in the country and generates about $30 million per year.

Pakistan's nuclear arsenal was built up as a key deterrent against India. India, with seven times the population of Pakistan and more than twice the number of soldiers, had begun its own nuclear program more in response to India's rivalry with China, and its desire to become a world superpower. Trying to keep pace with India's military spending, in a country with only one-eighth the GDP, has steadily bankrupted Pakistan, with little money left over for the nation's infrastructure or economic growth.

The ISI network includes 10,000 soldiers, spies, and intelligence officers, as well as an unknown number of informers and "assets." It has been described as "a kingdom within a state." Prior to the September 11, 2001, attacks, Egyptian intelligence officers tracked down Taliban member Ahmad Khadr, a close associate of Osama bin Laden and the suspected mastermind of the 1995 bombing of the Egyptian embassy in Islamabad that killed nineteen people. Khadr was hiding in a safehouse in the Pakistani frontier city of Peshawar when Egyptian forces surrounded the building. Lacking the authority to arrest Khadr, they notified General Mahmood Ahmad, the chief of the ISI, so that he could send in his men to capture the known terrorist. Instead, that night a car with diplomatic plates arrived at the Peshawar house, and the Egyptian intelligence officers watched while Taliban militants jumped out, grabbed Khadr, brought him back to the car and then drove him across the border into Afghanistan and beyond Egypt's reach. It was widely suspected that Khadr knew too much about the close ties between the ISI and the Taliban, and that they did not want that information getting out. Six days after 9/11, Musharraf sent Mehmood Ahmed to Afghanistan to try to convince the Taliban leader, Mullah Mohammed Omar, to hand over Osama bin Laden to the United States. Unbeknownst to Musharraf, Ahmed, a known fundamentalist sympathizer, instead urged Omar to continue to resist the United States. When Musharraf eventually learned of this disloyalty he removed Ahmed and replaced him with General Ehsan-ul-Haq, a more moderate and loyal general. Ehsan-ul-Haq was given the task of weeding out from the ISI "the beards," the name given to the Islamic extremists.

Beginning in 1989, the ISI was a covert supporter of Islamic militant movements inside Pakistan and Afghanistan. The militants were trained and armed by the ISI and were encouraged to cross the border into Kashmir to clash with Indian troops. Pakistani extremist groups shared training camps with al-Qaeda fighters and provided funding through a complex network of money-laundering operations, as well as a network of safehouses that allowed them to operate freely. For this operation, the ISI worked almost completely independently of parliamentary control. Even after September 11, 2001, the ISI was unwilling to entirely give up its ties with the Taliban and other extremist groups. Many training grounds that were nominally closed in the months after the terrorist attacks were later reopened, and groups that had been banned throughout Pakistan were allowed to return under different names. Sometimes the ISI strategy has backfired. One of the ISI's extremist groups, Sipah-e-Sahaba, wound up launching a war against the Shi'a minority in Pakistan, and went on to kill more than 3,600 people over ten years. In addition, the main suspects in the kidnapping and murder of American journalist Daniel Pearl in January 2002 all had links to the ISI because of their involvement with the Kashmir conflict. Pakistani ties with the Taliban were so strong that as many as 100,000 Pakistanis went to fight in Afghanistan, and many came back much more militant and radical.

Musharraf's delicate dance between the Islamist extremists and the United States has led to strange contradictions in his actions. On January 12, 2002, he gave a speech detailing his new alignment with the United States. He banned the five most extreme Islamic groups, began monitoring mosques, and arrested 1,900 suspected militants. Using ISI intelligence, an estimated 600 al-Qaeda suspects have been captured and handed over to U.S. authorities. Most of them were shipped to the military base in Guantánamo. Among moderate Pakistanis, Musharraf's alignment with the United States earned him the nickname "Busharraf." At the same time, Musharraf faced a huge backlash after his announcement to support the United States, both among the public and inside the military. Riots spread through Quetta, near the Afghan border, leaving several people dead, and mobs burned foreign-owned businesses and clashed with the police in Karachi and Islamabad. Indeed, Musharraf has proved himself unwilling to really go after the militants, especially those in the military and the ISI. In order to appease the Islamist forces, at the end of 2002, Musharraf released from prison 1,500 militants. In the summer of 2003, U.S. soldiers captured a group of suspected Taliban agents in Afghanistan. Three of the men were Pakistani officers. Meanwhile, some of the supposedly banned extremist groups have resurfaced under new names, and many extremist clerics and militant leaders are still free to travel and to preach hate.

THE DEADLIEST GAME—Pakistani scientist Abdul Qadeer Khan is hailed as the "Father of the Islamic Bomb." Khan worked for the Dutch lab URENCO, which had perfected the technology for building gas centrifuges, an important method for enriching uranium for use in nuclear weapons. Khan stole blueprints and returned to Pakistan in 1976, where he began to work at the Kahuta nuclear facility (later renamed the A.Q. Khan Research Lab) for two decades to enrich enough fuel to make dozens of atomic bombs. On May 28, 1998, Khan watched as Pakistan detonated its first nuclear weapon in a desert in Balochistan.

Internationally, Khan was also a part of a widespread underground network trading in nuclear materials and technology, involving shell companies and various middlemen to exchange sensitive parts and materials for nuclear programs. Khan orchestrated a nukes-for-missiles trade with North Korea in which Pakistan gave Kim Jong-il's regime plans to build gas centrifuges in exchange for 600-mile capability Nodong missiles, which were reworked and renamed Ghauri missiles. Khan was also suspected of sharing centrifuge technology with other dictatorships, most notably Iran and Libya, in exchange for raw uranium and military technology. After the story of Khan's network broke, there was an international outcry and

Musharraf placed Khan under house arrest. Musharraf, who claimed, rather dubiously, to have known nothing about Khan's activities, gave Khan a full pardon. The Bush administration responded by praising Pakistan for its "serious efforts to end the activities of a dangerous network."

THE RICH GET RICHER—Musharraf brought in a team to improve the failing Pakistani economy. Led by Finance Minister Shankat Aziz, a former Citigroup executive, and Central Bank chief Ishrat Hussain, a former World Bank economist, the nation's GDP grew 5.1 percent, second in the region only to China. At the same time, the Karachi Stock Exchange grew 125 percent in twelve months, the best performance in the world during that period, and the country drew up plans to prepay its $1 billion in loans to the IMF, the World Bank, and the Asian Development Bank. Foreign direct investment rose to $800 million, almost double the $485 million it had been previously. All this made Musharraf popular with international investors, but back home it was another story.

Despite the economic successes, the number of poor people in Pakistan actually grew 10 percent per year, more than five times as fast as the general population growth. Throughout the country more than 37 percent of Pakistani citizens live on less than $1 a day. In a survey of 1,724 members of Pakistan's middle class conducted by Transparency International in 2002, all but six respondents who had sought help from the government or the police reported having been asked for a bribe of some sort.

ASSASSINATION ATTEMPTS—Musharraf lives with the constant threat of assassination. He is said to carry a silver-plated derringer in his chest pocket and he travels in an armor-plated Mercedes, with two other identical vehicles taking separate routes to act as decoys. The ISI is still in charge of Musharraf's personal security. In April 2002, a militant group with ties to al-Qaeda planted a car bomb on a road taken by Musharraf to Karachi. It failed to explode. In December 2003, there were two unsuccessful attempts on Musharraf's life. In the first, a bomb was placed under a bridge along the president's transportation route, exploding just moments after the convoy had crossed. Eleven days later, on Christmas Day, there was a second attack on Musharraf's convoy, as it returned to his home in Rawalpindi. This time, two suicide bombers drove explosive-packed trucks directly into the path of the first and last cars in the convoy, killing sixteen people and injuring fifty others. Musharraf escaped without injury, although the windshield of his car was destroyed. The attackers had successfully avoided the two other decoy convoys, and it was later discovered that they had been given information from a member of Musharraf's security force about which convoy was the real one. Following the attacks, members of Musharraf's security force were banned from carrying cell phones.

MORE IMPORTANT THAN DEMOCRACY—In November 1999, Musharraf created the National Accountability Bureau for the purpose of exposing and combating the widespread corruption within the Pakistani government. The Bureau was given sweeping powers of arrest and is allowed to hold suspects for up to ninety days on corruption charges without the need for a court appearance. The Bureau soon became a political tool as well, used to detain members of the opposition, and it came under increasing criticism from human rights groups for its arbitrary arrests and abuse of detainees.

Musharraf has shown his willingness to use his executive powers. In June 2004, he removed from office Prime Minister Mir Zafarullah Khan Jamali, who had served in the post for nineteen months. Jamali had become increasingly unwilling to follow Musharraf and had publicly declared that Musharraf should resign as army chief at the end of 2004, as he had originally promised to do. Jamali was replaced by Shankat Aziz, the former finance minister who had no previous experience in politics and who earned the nickname "Short-Cut."

On December 29, 2004, Musharraf announced that he had changed his mind about resigning as head of the military, claiming that the nation needed to unify its political and military elements and that only he could provide this unity. He justified his decision by stating, "I think the country is more important than democracy." The Pakistani legislature then passed a bill enabling him to hold both military and civilian positions until 2007. In 2005, Musharraf declared that Benazir Bhutto and Nawaz Sharif would not be allowed to come back to the country or participate in the next elections, scheduled for 2007. Despite the nominal return to civilian rule, many Pakistanis see the possibility of another coup, in which Musharraf either suspends or dissolves the National Assembly. In addition to his executive powers, his control over the National Security Council, and his position in the military, Musharraf is supported by more than 600 military officers occupying key jobs in various ministries and corporations.

14.

ALEKSANDR LUKASHENKO—BELARUS

THE NATION—Belarus, with a population of ten million, has the dubious distinction of being the last dictatorship in Europe. It is also the ex-Soviet republic with the least distinct national consciousness. For example, it was not until 1910 that anyone bothered to write a history of Belarus as a separate entity.

HISTORY—The area that is now Belarus was originally settled by Baltic tribes, who were overwhelmed by massive migrations of East Slavic tribes in the eighth and ninth centuries. In the thirteenth century, Western Belarus and Eastern Lithuania were consolidated into the Grand Duchy of Lithuania and Russia. In 1569 the Grand Duchy was absorbed into Poland. When the Polish Commonwealth was partitioned in 1795, almost all of Belarus was handed over to the Russian Empire. The nineteenth century saw increasing conflict between the Russian Czarist government and the Belarusan people. The Russians attacked Belarusan culture by prohibiting Belarusan youth from studying abroad (1823), ordering all school instruction to be carried out in the Russian language (1836), and banning the use of the Latin alphabet in Belarusan works (1859). Meanwhile, there were major anti-Russian uprisings in 1794, 1830–1831, and 1863–1864. When Czar Alexander II was assassinated in 1881, one of the assassins was Belarusan.

In 1884, Belarusan students in St. Petersburg made the first formal calls for an independent Belarus. With the 1905 revolution in Russia, the prohibition on printing in the Belarusan language was finally lifted. The chaos engendered by the First World War and by the 1917 Russian Revolution allowed Belarusan nationalists a glimmer of hope. In December 1917, the All-Belarusan Congress held in Minsk proclaimed a republican government. The Bolsheviks disbanded the government, but three months later, on March 25, 1918, the Congress declared Belarus an independent nation. Meanwhile, however, the Germans had occupied Western Belarus since 1915. When Russia and Germany signed an armistice agreement on March 3, 1918, they simply ignored Belarus' demand for rights. Belarus was taken over by the USSR and in January 1919, the Bolsheviks announced the formation of the Belarussian Soviet Socialist Republic (BSSR) within the USSR.

At the end of the Russian-Polish War in 1921, Belarus was divided between Poland and the BSSR. Life did not proceed smoothly for Belarusans on either side of the border. In Poland it began well, as Belarusans contested and won seats in the Polish parliament. By 1924, however, the Polish government had shut down 400 Belarusan schools and at least fifteen Belarusan newspapers. In 1927 the Poles made sweeping arrests of Belarusan leaders and in 1934 they created the Bereya Kartuska concentration camp for the incarceration of Belarusan activists. The following year, the Belarusans lost their last seat in the Polish parliament.

Russian treatment of the Belarusans was mild in the beginning, but in 1929 the Soviet government began to repress Belarusan intellectuals and advocates of Belarusan culture. On February 2, 1931, the president of the Belarusan Academy of Sciences committed suicide as a protest against Soviet persecution. The Communists responded by imprisoning educated Belarusans. In 1937, the Soviets established a death camp in Kurapaty, north of Minsk, and, over the next four years, up to 250,000 civilians were executed there. It is estimated that during the rule of Josef Stalin, more than two million Belarusans died unnatural deaths.

As bad as their situation appeared to be, life for the Belarusans was soon to become even worse. On September 1, 1939, Germany kicked off World War II by invading Poland. Polish resistance collapsed quickly. On September 17, the Soviet army occupied West Belarus (the part that had been controlled by Poland). The Germans gained control of Belarus in 1941. During the next three years, 2.2 million Belarusans were killed, while the German occupation led to the destruction of 209 cities and towns and 9,200 villages, including 628 in which the Germans burned the inhabitants to death.

With the defeat of the Nazis, Belarusans found themselves reincorporated into the Soviet Union. Once again, they were allowed a deceptively hopeful beginning. Belarus, like Ukraine, was invited to join the United Nations as if it was an independent nation. Since this was not really the case, over the next forty-five years Belarus cast the same vote as the USSR on every single issue. As part of Stalin's drive for "Russsification," he began purging Belarusan leaders in the Communist Party in 1946 and replacing them with Russians. The 1950s saw an increasing suppression of the Belarusan language, even after Stalin died in 1953. Speaking in Minsk in January 1959, Soviet premier Nikita Khrushchev put it bluntly when he told Belarusans, "The sooner we all start speaking Russian, the faster we shall build Communism."

Between 1965 and 1980, the BSSR was ruled by Pyotr Masherov, who soon gained a reputation as one of the least corrupt Communist leaders in the Soviet Union. Belarus was transformed into a major industrial region, specializing in the manufacture of machines and precision equipment. Living standards for Belarusans rose well above the Soviet national average. Eventually, Soviet premier Leonid Brezhnev became wary of Masherov's popularity and, in October 1980, Masherov was killed in an automobile accident. To this day, Masherov is well thought of in Belarus and it was nostalgia for the Masherov years that Aleksandr Lukashenko would later exploit in his rise to power.

The Soviet leadership continued to punish manifestations of Belarusan nationalism. On April 20, 1986, the Communist Party encouraged members of a group of veterans of the Afghan War to set upon and beat up young people in Minsk who had been participating in a spring folklore festival. As disturbing as this incident was, it was forgotten because of a traumatic event that happened only six days later.

In the early morning of April 26, 1986, explosions in Reactor Number Four of the Chernobyl Nuclear Power Facility in northern Ukraine released massive amounts of radioactive material into the air. Because of prevailing winds, 70 percent of the toxic fallout landed in Belarus. Eighty percent of the country was contaminated by radioactive iodine, including 20 percent that was severely contaminated. The Soviet response to this disaster was sluggish and secretive. Belarusan discontent grew until July 1989, when a mass rally was held, calling for an investigation of the Soviet government cover-up of the causes and health consequences of the Chernobyl disaster.

During this period, Belarusan public opinion was galvanized by another issue as well: the unearthing of hundreds of mass graves from the Stalinist period. In June 1988, 10,000 people demonstrated, calling for an investigation of Stalinist abuses and their cover-up. Four months later, the Soviet military violently dispersed a demonstration in Minsk commemorating the victims of Stalinism.

As Communist rule in Eastern Europe collapsed and as the USSR itself edged toward disintegration, Belarusans were less than enthusiastic about the prospect of independence. The Supreme Council of the BSSR pushed through reforms declaring Belarusan the republic's official language and, on July 27, 1990, declaring sovereignty and announcing that Belarus would henceforth be an internationally neutral, nuclear-free zone. Yet a poll taken in March 1991 showed that 82.7 percent of Belarusans supported keeping the USSR as a federation of sovereign states. Nonetheless, Belarus declared independence on August 25, 1991. The Soviet flag was taken down and the Supreme Council elected Stanislau Shuskevich, a physicist whose parents were writers who had been persecuted by Stalin, chairman of the new Republic of Belarus. Shuskevich was a leader of the movement to investigate the consequences of the Chernobyl disaster.

The immediate result of the breakup of the Soviet Union was acute economic hardship for all of Belarus. The Supreme Council, which was overwhelmingly controlled by ex-Communists, put off elections until June 23, 1994.

THE STEADY RISE OF LUKASHENKO—Aleksandr Grgoryevich Lukashenko was born August 30, 1954 in a small town in the Vitebsk Region of Belarus. Considering that he would later promote himself as a champion of the common, rural people, he has kept secret his family history and the details of his own childhood. In 1975 he graduated from the Mogiliev Pedagogic Institute with a major in history and social studies. Two decades later his wife Galina was asked why she was reluctant to leave her home village of Ryzhkovichi and join her husband in the presidential palace in Minsk. Galina replied, "I'd better wait for him at home. My Sashka never stays in one place for more than two years anyway."

Indeed, Lukashenko had most definitely established a pattern of two-year hitches. After university graduation, he began with two years as an instructor in the ideology department of a unit of KGB border troops in Brest. Next came two years as secretary of the Komsomol Committee of the Mogiliev City Grocery Retail Department and two years as the secretary of the "Knowledge" Society of the town of Shklov. It was during this stint, in 1979, that Lukashenko joined the Communist Party, although his official biography claims that he was never a member. He moved on to two years as ideology chief of a tank division in Mogiliev, two years as deputy chairman of a collective farm, two years as deputy director of the Shklov Plant of Constructive Materials, and then two years as secretary of the Communist Party of a collective farm. In 1987 he became director of another collective farm. Lukashenko's run of two-year jobs was finally broken in 1989, but not for want of trying. In 1989, he ran for the post of people's deputy, but lost the election by 1 percent to Vyacheslav Kebich, who, one year later, was installed as prime minister.

In 1990, Lukashenko won election to the Supreme Soviet, the parliament of the USSR. Although he was a vocal critic of Stanislau Shushkevich, it was Shushkevich who gave Lukashenko his big break when, in June 1993, he appointed the thirty-eight-year-old Lukashenko to be chairman of the anticorruption committee. Lukashenko's report on corruption, released in December 1993, accused Shushkevich of embezzlement and, although the charges were never proven, Shushkevich was deposed as chairman of the parliament. Lukashenko then launched attacks on Vyacheslav Kebich and other leaders, who terminated the anticorruption committee, thus boosting Lukashenko's popularity.

THE ELECTION OF 1994—There were four major candidates in the election to choose Belarus' first democratically elected president. As the highest-placed member of the transition government, Vyacheslav Kebich fell into the role of the "establishment" favorite. The organized opposition split between Stanislau Shuskevich and Zianon Pazniak, who had played a leading role in the investigation of the Chernobyl disaster and of the Stalinist mass graves. Both men accused Kebich of relying too heavily on Russia to bail out the Belarusan economy. The fourth candidate was Aleksandr Lukashenko. The other candidates did not take Lukashenko seriously, dismissing him as an anti-intellectual buffoon. But it was Lukashenko, with his anticorruption credentials, who best understood the nature of free elections. While Kebich, Shuskevich, and Pazniak debated the issues, Lukashenko fashioned a simpler and more amorphous campaign, reaching out to the elderly, to rural voters, and to members of the military. He ran a modern campaign, shamelessly advocating opposing points of view depending on his audience and on the ebb and flow of public opinion. He supported uniting Belarus and Russia, while at the same time championing Belarusan sovereignty. He criticized market reforms and he supported privatization. He accused top officials of corruption, but he also promised that if elected, he would not purge the leadership. As if this was not enough, Lukashenko's supporters let it be known that his opponents were all fat and flabby, and that Lukashenko was the only candidate who was a "potent man."

On election day, Lukashenko won 44.8 percent of the vote. Kebich picked up 17.3 percent, Pazniak 12.8 percent and Shushkevich 9.9 percent. On July 10, Lukashenko defeated Kebich in a runoff, 80 percent to 20 percent. Four days later, Lukashenko declared, "I promise you that there will be no dictatorship."

IN POWER—Despite his promise, Lukashenko wasted little time before consolidating his power. On May 15, 1995, he sent Belarusans to the polls to vote on four carefully chosen issues, all of which passed with at least 75 percent of the vote. The Soviet-era state flag was restored; the Russian language was put on a par with Belarusan; Belarus joined with Russia as an economic unit and, in the words of Russian president Boris Yeltsin, "The border between Russia and Belarus no longer exists." In addition to these matters, Lukashenko slipped through a referendum that gave the president the authority to dissolve the parliament.

Lukashenko continued to appeal to his base of support by nostalgically invoking the days of benevolent Communism when Pyotr Masherov was in power, while periodically denouncing corruption. At the same time, supporters of true democracy were growing increasingly suspicious of Lukashenko's autocratic ways. On April 4, 1996, 20,000 people in Minsk staged a peaceful protest against a treaty Lukashenko had signed with Russia. Twenty thousand demonstrators in a nation of ten million may not seem significant, but Lukashenko saw the handwriting on the wall—and threatened to expel any foreign journalist who covered the demonstration. (The prospect of the domestic media covering the event was out of the question.) Three weeks later, on the tenth anniversary of the Chernobyl explosions, 50,000 people marched in Minsk to demand Lukashenko's resignation.

To further consolidate his power, Lukashenko staged another referendum in November 1996. This time, the electorate was asked to extend Lukashenko's term of office for two years until 2001; to give him the right to reject decisions by local councils; to give him the right to designate half of the judges of the Constitutional Court; and to dissolve parliament and create a new one. Lukashenko dominated media discussion of the ballot issues. His opponents also objected to the fact that ballot boxes were carried from apartment to apartment by hand. Not surprisingly, the final vote total showed that 70 percent had voted yes. Lukashenko immediately established a new legislature, including an upper house to which he personally appointed all 110 members.

As most of the rest of Eastern Europe began to experience freedom and democracy, Lukashenko shoved Belarus back into the bad old days of Communism. He ordered the arrests of opposition politicians on live television and, in a campaign for "discipline in the workplace," he mandated a return to "mutual surveillance." Workers were encouraged to use "trouble telephones" to inform on one another.

By March of 1997, U.S. president Bill Clinton had had enough of Lukashenko and, citing his abysmal human rights record, Clinton suspended $40 million in aid to Belarus.

PRESIDENT CLINTON SURRENDERS TO A PHOTO OP WITH ALEKSANDR LUKASHENKO.
Dmitri Messinis/AP Photo

This did not stop Lukashenko from physically cornering Clinton at a meeting in Istanbul in 1999 and forcing a photo opportunity that was shown on Belarusan television to demonstrate (falsely) that Lukashenko was respected by world leaders.

In October 1997, Lukashenko, declaring all of his opponents "enemies of the people," signed a law against "injury to the honor and dignity of the Republic *and* the president," thus making it illegal to criticize him. In June 1998, Lukashenko ordered all foreign envoys to abandon their embassies and residences in the Drozdy district of Minsk because they were too close to the presidential compound.

On July 20, 1999, both the European Union and the United States, citing the bogus vote to extend Lukashenko's term of office, declared Lukashenko's legitimacy as president to have expired. Increasingly isolated, Lukashenko turned more violent. On September 16, 1999, opposition leader Viktar Hanchar disappeared and was never seen again. Death squads committed thirty murders. When word of this outrage got out to the public, Lukashenko appointed Viktor Sheiman to be the prosecutor-general in charge of investigating the death squads. This might have been viewed as a move toward justice, but for the fact that Sheiman was one of the leaders in charge of the death squads.

By the time of the next presidential election on September 9, 2001, Lukashenko had lost much of his domestic support. Ever resourceful, he utilized various tactics that compensated for this little problem. For example, he denied the registration of many opposition candidates; he raised monthly salaries and offered free fuel at harvest time; he confiscated the equipment of an independent printing house, seized hundreds of thousands of copies of the election issue of the *Nash Svaboda* newspaper, and had police raid the offices of election-monitoring organizations. Finally, for good measure, he threatened to fire any state employee who did not vote for him. Not surprisingly, Lukashenko won the election with more than 75 percent of the vote. He immediately purged state officials who had chosen not to endorse him and charged them, as usual, with "corruption." Other opponents were branded "allies of NATO."

In November 2002, fourteen of fifteen members of the European Community announced that Lukashenko would not be allowed to enter their countries. Furious at this embarrassing rebuke, Lukashenko threatened to stop policing Belarus' borders and to allow drug traffickers and illegal immigrants to enter the European Union. But Lukashenko had little problem finding allies elsewhere. He once appeared on Iranian television offering to sell Iran "everything it needs." And when Saddam Hussein won reelection as president of Iraq in October 2002, with more than 99 percent of the vote, an envious Lukashenko sent Saddam a message that the election "vividly demonstrated the Iraqi people's striving for independence in making decisions on their own fate." By 2002, Belarus, despite its small population, had moved into the top ten of the world's arms exporters, as Lukashenko brazenly supplied both sides in the Russian-Chechen War.

A poll released in April 2003 showed that only 17 percent of Belarusans would approve constitutional changes that would allow Lukashenko to run for a third term of office. Yet when exactly that issue was put to a vote in October 2004, election officials claimed that, with an 86 percent turnout, 77 percent voted yes. On March 19, 2006, Lukashenko was reelected president with the announced support of 82.6 percent of voters. The result was not surprising considering that the campaign of his opponent, Aleksandr Milinkevich, was so severely restricted by the government that he was reduced to surreptitiously distributing fliers that gave a phone number where he could be reached for an hour.

QUOTES:

> *"To penetrate the soul and the mind of everybody is, of course, a most challenging art form."*
>
> AUGUST 13, 2003

> *"I look at our old people and the middle-aged generation who are nostalgic for the Soviet Union, and they can see that Lukashenko is a good chap."*
>
> MAY 13, 1997

ON THE POSSIBILITY OF DEMONSTRATIONS PROTESTING HIS REELECTION:

> *"We will wring the necks of those who are actually doing it and those who are instigating these acts."*
>
> JANUARY 27, 2006

FROM HIS OFFICIAL BIOGRAPHY:

> *"The activities of A.G. Lukashenko are inseparable from the life of the country."*

> *"He is proud of being called* batka *(dad) by the people."*

> *"He is the only politician in Europe who perceives the truth as, above all else, a category of conscience."*

SIGNIFICA

- Belarus is the only ex-Soviet republic to retain the name KGB for its security services.

• Lukashenko calls himself an "orthodox atheist."

• Lukashenko is married to Galina Rodionovna and the couple has two sons, Viktor and Dmitry. However, the Belarusan first lady does not appear in public and few Belarusans know what she looks like.

• Aleksandr Lukashenko is an obsessive sports fan and is especially fond of ice hockey. In May 1997, he appointed himself president of the National Olympic Committee of Belarus. Although his travel to the Olympic Games has been limited due to the refusal of many countries to grant him a visa, Lukashenko did attend the 1998 Winter Olympics in Nagano, Japan, and managed to insert himself into the proceedings. In the 10-kilometer biathlon race, a sport that combines skiing and shooting, Aleksandr Popov of Belarus was in first place when officials halted the competition because of heavy snow and fog, and ordered it restarted the next day. This time Popov performed poorly and finished in fifty-fifth place. Lukashenko, who was present at the original race, called its cancellation "a mafia-style injustice," and accused the organizers of stopping the race to punish the skiers from Belarus, Russia, and Latvia.

LUKASHENKO WINS A CROSS-COUNTRY
SKI RACE IN BELARUS.
AP Photo

(Jorge Silva/Reuters/Corbis)

15.

FIDEL CASTRO—CUBA

THE NATION—Cuba is an island about the size of Pennsylvania, in the Carribean Sea ninety miles south of Florida. The nation of Cuba, which has a population of more than eleven million, includes several smaller islands. Internationally, it was known as little more than a producer of sugar and as a gambling haven until, in the midst of the Cold War, Cuba's dictator, Fidel Castro, turned his country into the Soviet Union's leading client state in the Americas.

EARLY HISTORY—When Christopher Columbus landed on Cuba on October 27, 1492, the island was inhabited by approximately 200,000 indigenous people. In 1511, Diego Velázquez de Cuéllar led the Spanish invasion of the island and became the first Spanish governor. Before long, the vast majority of the native people had been killed or enslaved.

In 1868 the Dominican general Máximo Gómez led a revolt that turned into a ten-year War of Independence. The first clash took place on the tenth of October, in the town of Yara, and would later be commemorated as the "Grito de Yara," or Cry of Yara. The Count of

Valmaceda, who led the Spanish defense of the island, used ruthless ethnic cleansing techniques against the rebels and put General Valeriano Weyler in charge of the army. Weyler earned the nickname "The Butcher" for rounding up several hundred thousand men, women, and children and incarcerating them in detention camps, where thousands died. Ultimately, General Gómez was unsuccessful in overthrowing the Spanish, but his rebellion continued to spark unrest. These uprisings became known as the "little war," or "guerilla" in Spanish, and ultimately gave rise to the term "guerrilla warfare."

THE NATIONAL HERO—José Martí was born in Havana in 1853 to Spanish parents, but began protesting against Spanish policies at an early age. He published his first political writings at the age of sixteen and founded the newspaper *La Patria Libre,* the Free Fatherland, speaking out against slavery and the injustices of Spanish rule. That same year he was sent to jail and forced to work in the rock pits at Isle of Pines. Martí was sent into exile twice, the first time living in France, Mexico, and Guatemala, and the second time in the United States, where he formed the basis of the Cuban Revolution.

Martí and his forces landed on the Cuban coast on April 11, 1895, at Maisí Cape, hoping to incite a wide-scale rebellion against General Weyler and the Spanish. In a symbolic act, Martí rode a white horse into battle against the full force of the Spanish army. During the battle, which became known as the Battle of Dos Rios, he was shot and killed. Years later, one of his poems would be put to music in the famous song "Guantanamera."

REMEMBER THE MAINE—On Feburary 15, 1898, the USS *Maine* was blown up while at anchor in Havana harbor, killing 266 American seamen. The cause of the explosion was never discovered and may have been accidental, but newspaper publishers William Randolph Hearst and Joseph Pulitzer, seeing a chance to increase the circulation of their papers, egged on the public in the United States with the popular slogan "Remember the Maine! To hell with Spain!" President William McKinley declared war on Spain on April 25 and fighting against the Spanish began in the Philippines. War in Cuba itself was launched in June when U.S. Marines landed at Guantánamo Bay. The battle for Cuba was short, and included the charge up San Juan Hill, led by Lt. Colonel (and future president) Theodore Roosevelt and his Rough Riders. Spanish troops all but surrendered by July 16. When the action was over, the American flag was hoisted over the governor's palace and Cuba became "independent."

The United States lost no time in protecting American business interests. Although the right to self-determination was included in the peace agreement signed by the United States and Cuba, U.S. troops did not pull out until 1902, and only then after forcing the Platt Amendment on the Cuban constitution. The Amendment gave the United States the right to intervene militarily whenever it perceived a threat to its interests; prevented Cuba from entering into any agreements with other countries without U.S. approval; and allowed for the establishment of U.S. bases on Cuban soil, including the military base at Guantánamo, which would rise to notoriety more than 100 years later. In 1902, Tomás Estrada Palma was elected Cuba's first peacetime president. However, after his four-year term, the U.S. military again occupied Cuba, staying until 1909. American troops returned in 1912 and again in 1917.

During the 1920s, as global sugar prices soared, wealth began to pour into the country. During that time, which would become known as the Dance of Millions, vast fortunes were made almost overnight, and country clubs, casinos, and palaces sprang up throughout the capital of Havana. Cuba developed into a major tourist destination and began to earn its reputation for vice and corruption, as organized crime and gangs gained influence. General Gerardo Machado, who had been one of the youngest generals in the Cuban War of Independence, was elected president in 1925 by an overwhelming majority. Once in office, however, he quickly asserted authoritarian control over the press and over civil society. His thugs murdered hundreds of people suspected of disloyalty, and, when it became a hotbed of dissidence, he closed the University of Havana. Machado ultimately rewrote the constitution to stay in power for a second term.

THE PRETTY MULATTO—Fulgencio Batista rose to power in Cuba in 1933 as part of the Sergeant's Revolution that finally succeeded in unseating Machado. The son of a mulatto worker from Banes, Batista earned a reputation for being ruthless and open to bribery. Batista began his military career as a telegraph officer, eventually moving up to become chief of staff from 1934 to 1940, a position that held much more power than the actual presidency. He installed a series of puppet presidents until he was voted into the presidential post himself from 1940 to 1944. Because of his straight hair and dark skin, Batista was known by the derogatory nickname of "El Mulato Lindo," the pretty mulatto. Cuban society was so highly stratified that Batista, despite being president, could not manage to be elected a member of the Havana Biltmore Yacht Club because of his mixed-blood parentage.

In 1944, Ramón Grau San Martín, a populist physician, was elected president, primarily because Batista allowed him to be, and Batista went into semiretirement in Florida. Grau had been instrumental in passing the 1940 Constitution, which was regarded as one of the most progressive in Latin America in terms of human rights. He was succeeded by Carlos Prío Socarrás, who quickly became known for his corruption and violence.

A DICTATOR IS BORN—Fidel Castro was born on August 13, but like much of his life, the year in which he was born is surrounded by controversy. Castro himself claims the year was 1926, but his sisters have said that he was actually born a year later in 1927. He was definitely born in Manacas, a farming community in the municipality of Birán, in the Mayarí region of northern Oriente, which is literally closer to Haiti, Jamaica, and even the Bahamas than it is to Havana.

Castro's father, Ángel Castro y Argiz, was born in Lancara, Galicia, Spain, and emigrated to Cuba in 1898. He spent five years working in a brick factory owned by his uncle before moving to Mayarí, which was then dominated by the United Fruit Company. Ángel began to work on the railroad being built by the company, laying down tracks and performing manual labor, before starting a business selling lemonade to workers in the fields. He used the profits to expand his business, going from town to town selling goods and merchandise. Eventually, Ángel leased land from the United Fruit Company, planting sugarcane and employing small farmers. The lands owned or rented by the Castro family grew to some 26,000 acres, with about 300 families living and working on the property. By the time Fidel was born, the family was quite wealthy. The Castros lived in a two-story country house, built in the Galician style with wooden stilts and a space underneath for farm animals. Ángel's first wife, María Argota, gave birth to two children, Pedro Emilio and Lidia. Although accounts are sketchy, it appears that María died after the birth of her second child, although Juana Castro, Fidel's younger sister, insists that she simply left the family. With María gone, Ángel soon took up with young Lina Ruz González, who had been working in the Castro household as a maid or cook. The pair had three children out of wedlock, Ángela, Ramón, and Fidel. They married shortly after Fidel's birth.

The Castro household was unusual. Although wealthy and powerful for the region, their lifestyle remained extremely rural, with livestock and chickens wandering throughout the house. To bring the family in for meals, Lina would shoot a gun outside the kitchen door. Meals were always eaten from a communal pot while standing. Fidel was named after Fidel Pino Santos, a wealthy Oriente politician and a close friend of Ángel Castro. Fidel also means "faithful," a fact that Castro would later use in speeches. Fidel was not christened until he was five or six years old, and as a result the other children in Birán called him "Jew."

Like his father, Fidel was prone to violent tempers, and he could be a very sore loser. His sisters recall him starting a baseball team in Birán with equipment bought by his father. If the game was going poorly or his team began to lose, Fidel would simply stop the game, gather up the equipment and walk off. Castro's close friend, novelist Gabriel García Márquez, wrote, "I do not think anyone in the world could be a worse loser. His attitude in the face of defeat, even in the slightest events of daily life, seems to obey a private logic: he will not even admit it, and he does not have a moment's peace until he manages to invert the terms and turn it into a victory."

As a child, Fidel was sent to study in Santiago, the second-largest city in Cuba. He spent his first two years in Santiago living with his godparents, during which time he was home-schooled. Eventually, he was enrolled in the Marist school La Salle, along with his older brother Ramón and his younger brother Raúl. Fidel quickly gained a reputation as a trouble-maker and a bully, starting fights with the other boys as well as with the priests.

Ángel received a report that his sons were cheating and that they were "the three biggest bullies" who had ever gone to the school, so he decided not to send them back to La Salle. Fidel, who was in the fourth grade, responded by threatening to burn down the house. Ultimately, Fidel was reenrolled in school, but this time at a more demanding Jesuit institution. When his father threatened to cut off his allowance if his grades slipped, Fidel forged his report cards with the highest marks to take home, while forging his father's signature on his real report card.

Although he was a mediocre student, the young Fidel was known for his almost photographic memory. A fellow classmate, José Ignacio Rasco, recalled Castro impressing the other students by reciting the pages of their textbook from memory. The children would call out a page number and Fidel would repeat the exact contents of the page, including whether or not the last word ended in a hyphen.

In November of 1940, Castro wrote a letter to U.S. president Franklin Delano Roosevelt: "My good friend Roosevelt, I don't know very English, but I know as much as write to you. I like to hear the radio, and I am very happy, because I heard in it, that you will be president of a new era. I am a boy but I think very much but I do not think that I am writting [sic] to the President of the United States. If you like, give me a ten dollars bill green America, in the letter, because never, I have not seen a ten dollars bill green American and I would like to have one of them." Castro received a letter in reply but no money.

Fidel continued his education at the exclusive Jesuit Belén College in Havana. It was here that he learned the skills of public speaking and oration for which he eventually became famous. He attempted to enroll in the Avellaneda Literary Academy, the oratory school at Belén, but was rejected twice after failing to complete a ten-minute speech without notes. Eventually, he earned acceptance and learned to control the stage fright that had paralyzed him.

In another violent episode, Castro got into a fight with a student who called him "crazy." Fidel bit the student and ran out of the room, only to return with a pistol and brandish it until a priest subdued him. Despite rumors to the contrary, he did not graduate at the top of his class. He was remembered, however, for having received the longest and most enthusiastic ovation from his fellow classmates.

UNIVERSITY DAYS—In October of 1945, Castro entered law school at the University of Havana. At the time, the university was an autonomous and self-governing body, and neither the police nor the army was allowed to enter the campus. As a result, the university became a haven for gangsters and political movements. Between 1944 and 1948, more than 120 mob-style murders were attributed to the gangs. It was also while at university that Castro met some of the people who would become closest to him, including Alfredo Guevara (no relation to Ernesto "Che" Guevara). Guevara would later recall Castro as "a boy who will be José Martí or the worst of the gangsters . . ."

Around this time, President Grau approved a rise in bus fares that provided the impetus for Castro's first political action. He organized a demonstration against the fare increase and led a group of students on a march to the presidential palace. The students were beaten by police forces and Castro was slightly injured. Castro was quick to use the incident to his advantage, gaining newspaper coverage. Three days later, Castro was part of a student delegation that went to meet President Grau. As they waited in the president's office for Grau to arrive, Castro joked with the other three students that when Grau entered they should pick him up and throw him from the balcony, then get on the radio and proclaim the victory of the student revolution.

Two main gangster groups were vying for control of the University of Havana, the Socialist Revolutionary Movement (MSR) and the Insurrectional Revolutionary Union (UIR). The MSR was led by Rolando Masferrer, one of Batista's worst henchmen, while the UIR was headed by Emilio Tró. Conflicts between the two groups were frequent and violent. When Castro entered the university he began to maneuver between the two groups. Initially he tried to foster a relationship with the MSR's Manolo Castro, then president of the Students' Federation. In December of 1946, Lionel Gómez, a member of the UIR, was shot in the lung. He named Fidel Castro as his attacker, although there was little evidence actually linking Castro to the crime. Nonetheless, it was widely believed that Fidel had attempted the assassination to ingratiate himself with Manolo Castro and thereby gain entrance into the MSR. Surprisingly, it was Emilio Tró, the head of UIR, who took Fidel under his wing, giving him a pistol, which he took to carrying with him at all times.

Castro's association with the UIR brought him into conflict with the MSR. Rolando Masferrer sent him an ultimatum: leave the gang scene or face the consequences. Instead, Castro volunteered for a planned invasion of the Dominican Republic. The campaign was being led by a group of Dominican exiles, including future president Juan Bosch, and was largely a response to the horrors of the regime of Rafael Trujillo, who had been in power since 1930. During this time, Trujillo's troops had massacred at least 12,000 Haitians along the border, and Trujillo had personally killed people at his opulent home, dumping their bodies in the river.

On July 29, 1947, Castro and his companions sailed to Cayo Confites, the launching point for the invasion. The Cayo Confites forces numbered about 12,000 men, mostly students. Fidel received his first military training, although it lasted only a week. The rest of the time was spent waiting on the mosquito-infested island for the order to launch. Unfortunately for the would-be invaders, Trujillo had long since heard about their plans and had had time to prepare his defense and even to complain to the United States. On September 27, after the invading fleet was already on its way, the leadership called off the attack. With the campaign officially over and the Cuban military rounding up the revolutionary vessels, Castro chose to jump ship and swim for shore. After swimming for eight or nine miles, he reached shore and appeared at his family home.

While Fidel was on Cayo Confites, Emilio Tró was killed in Havana by MSR thugs in a gun battle that lasted hours. Less than six months later, Manolo Castro was killed outside of a Havana movie theater that he owned. Castro, sensing a more promising direction for his future, moved away from the gangsters and became more involved in political actions. He once declared that Al Capone was a stupid man because he had never formed an ideology. If he had, Castro insisted, he would have been world famous, and not remembered only as a gangster.

In 1947, Castro participated in a trip by law students to the Isle of Pines, the location of Cuba's new "model" penitentiary. Returning to Havana, Fidel criticized the prison and the treatment of the inmates. Six years later, Castro would end up a prisoner in the same penitentiary. In 1948 he traveled to Bogotá, Columbia, with three other students from Havana University, including Alfredo Guevara. The trip was part of a Latin American student congress and was financed by Juan Perón, the leader of Argentina. Arriving in Columbia on April 7, Castro and the other students met with Jorge Gaitán, the leader of the Liberal Party and the man expected to win upcoming elections. They were invited to return on April 9 for a meeting at 2:00 p.m. Less than an hour before their scheduled meeting, Gaitán was shot and killed by a mentally deranged man, Juan Roa Sierra. Bogotá erupted in riots, in which Castro was swept up for two days. During the riots, he became involved in the takeover of a police station. By the time the riots subsided, approximately 3,500 people had been killed and a third of the city had gone up in flames.

SERIOUS POLITICS—Back in Cuba, Castro aligned himself with Senator Eduardo "Eddy" Chibás, the voice of the anti-Grau opposition. Despite coming from a wealthy family, he had spoken out against the corruption of Cuba's political elite, running on the slogan "Shame of Money." Disgusted with the state of Cuban politics, Chibás had created the Cuban People's Party, known as the Ortodoxos because they claimed to stand for the orthodoxy of José Martí's principles. Castro joined the Orthodox Party and campaigned hard for

Chibás in his unsuccessful bid for the presidency in 1948. While Fidel presented himself as Chibás' protégé and political heir, in private the two were never close. Chibás resented the young Castro, while Fidel saw Chibás as an obstacle to his own power. In order to be taken seriously as a politician, Castro knew he had to break free of his gangster ties. In late November 1949, he decided to make a clean break, denouncing the actions of the gangsters in front of a large crowd at the university and naming names and pacts. Not surprisingly, the speech put Castro in a dangerous situation and he was forced into hiding, eventually fleeing to New York City for three months.

Castro eventually graduated with a law degree and briefly started a law practice, although he actually practiced little law, concentrating instead on politics. Meanwhile, he led a relatively quiet social life. He was never known to dance, something exceedingly uncommon in Havana in the 1940s, and he was generally awkward and shy around women. Finally, he met Mirta Díaz-Balart and married her in 1948. Mirta was considered an exceptionally beautiful woman, with blonde hair and green eyes. She came from one of the wealthiest families in Cuba, with close ties to Batista. At their wedding, Mirta's father gave the young couple $10,000 for a three-month honeymoon in the United States, with $1,000 in spending money provided by Batista. The couple spent most of their honeymoon in New York City, where Fidel learned English and sat in on courses at Columbia University. Castro later recalled going into a bookstore in Manhattan and being shocked to see Karl Marx's *Das Kapital* available.

Upon their return to Cuba, the newlyweds moved into a hotel located across the street from a military camp. On September 1, 1949, Mirta gave birth to Fidel Castro Díaz-Balart, nicknamed Fidelito. Castro would never be close to his first son, but he was protective of him.

On Sunday, August 5, 1951, Senator Eduardo Chibás went on his weekly radio program and spoke out, as usual, against the corruption of the political system, accusing the education minister, Aureliano Sánchez Arango, of using political funds to buy a large mansion. At the end of his radio show, Chibás urged the Cuban people to wake up to the corruption in government. He then took out a .38 Colt and shot himself in the abdomen. Unfortunately for Chibás, his speech had gone on a little too long. Several minutes before the pistol shot rang out, the radio engineer had cut him off to play a series of radio commercials, including one advertising a brand of coffee that was "good to the last stomachful." Chibás was taken to a hospital, where he lingered for eleven days before dying. During this time, Castro kept close to the politician's bedside. While Chibás lay in state in the University Hall of Honor, Castro stood by as part of the honor guard for more than twenty-four hours and he appeared on the front page of several newspapers.

As the military prepared to move Chibás' body in a large procession, Castro tried to convince Captain Máximo Rávelo, the army captain commanding the escort of the gun carriage transporting the casket, to divert the procession route to the presidential palace. Castro was apparently convinced that he could trigger a mass uprising. Fearing military action and a possible bloodbath, Rávelo refused. President Carlos Prío himself had packed a bag and prepared a plane in the event that a mass uprising did occur.

Castro continued his political pursuits by running for the Chamber of Deputies in 1952. He sent out 100,000 letters to all the members of the Orthodox Party asking for their support. With broad support from the urban and rural poor, Castro was in line to be elected. In fact, he would have been a strong contender for an eventual seat in the senate, and perhaps ultimately might have been elected president through democratic means. However, the planned elections were disrupted on the morning of March 10, 1952, when Batista walked into the army's Camp Columbia in Havana along with his officers. They met no resistance, and by the time dawn broke Batista had taken power and Prío had fled the country. When news of Batista's coup spread, Fidel and his brother Raúl immediately went into hiding. Hours later the secret police arrived at both their houses looking for them.

By this time, Castro had become involved with Natalia Revuelta. "Naty" was known as one of the most beautiful women in Havana, tall, fair, and prosperous. She was well educated, having been raised in France and the United States, and was married to a well-known Cuban heart surgeon, Orlando Fernández-Ferrer. She was also a secret admirer of Castro, and she offered him the use of her apartment as a hiding place. Eventually, Naty became central to Fidel's revolution, providing money and helping print and distribute pamphlets, and even agreeing to let him store firearms and ammunition in her house. The two became lovers, and when Mirta found out, she asked for a divorce in July 1954.

ORGANIZING THE REVOLUTION—Although Castro had been well on his way to being an elected official, Batista's coup gave him the opportunity to play his favorite role: revolutionary leader. He lost no time in gathering a movement for liberation, choosing to create his own organization rather than working with the Communists. Castro saw the Communists as out of touch with the masses and too large for him to control, while the Communists, who enjoyed some support from Batista, had no need of the young revolutionary.

Castro gathered his forces from Eddy Chibás' former Orthodox Party and from within the University of Havana. He and his supporters set up a small revolutionary newspaper, which they printed on a mimeograph machine that they hid inside the trunk of a car. Castro also secured two small two-way radios and began broadcasting regular programs. Within fourteen months, Castro had amassed about 1,200 men. During this time of organizing, he drove more than 30,000 miles, some forty times the length of the island.

From the outset, Castro ran his movement like a military organization, with no democratic processes whatsoever. He passed down orders to his officers and they were expected to obey without question. Castro forbade the drinking of alcohol and imposed strict sexual standards, several times forcing his men to marry their girlfriends. He also ordered that weekly meetings be held to analyze the conduct of the movement's members, and infractions could be punished by expulsion or even death. When another group of student revolutionaries was betrayed by an insider and thrown in prison, Castro became even more security conscious, rarely attending the military training sessions that his group held on university grounds, using the basements of buildings as well as the rooftops of the science building. Many members did not even know that Castro was their leader. Castro developed and employed guerrilla tactics that are still used by underground movements and terrorists today. He based his organization on a cell structure, and nobody within a cell knew people in other cells. Meeting places were kept secret until the last minute.

Soon, Castro faced a critical problem. Although he had the men, he did not have the weapons needed to undertake an armed revolution. Not only that, he did not have enough money to purchase arms for all his men. Castro's solution was to attack a military base and seize its weapons. He chose the military base in Moncada because it was located in the traditionally rebellious province of Oriente and, in those days of limited communications, it was far enough away from Havana that it would take some time for the action to become known to Batista. Castro also fantasized that the attack would spark a larger armed rebellion throughout the province. The arms seized from the military base would be handed out to the population, who would then join in securing the zone from Batista's military. Simultaneous to the Moncada attack, a smaller force would attack the Bayamó Barracks, farther to the west, gaining more munitions and closing off the roads into the province, thus creating a "Liberated Zone" within Cuba.

The Moncada attack was planned for the morning of July 26, 1953, but it ran into problems from the start. The 162 revolutionaries bundled into a 26 car motorcade. One car had a flat tire almost immediately after leaving the farm that served as the staging area. Another car took a wrong turn into the center of town and did not arrive until after the attack had already begun. Finally, a group of four students decided not to participate in the attack at all. Fidel told them to wait until the rest of the cars had left, but they wound up leaving in the middle of the convoy. When they took the turn for Havana, the car behind them mistakenly followed. By the time the would-be revolutionaries in this car realized their error, they had gone well past Santiago and were too far away to participate in the attack. Once the remaining cars arrived at Moncada, their problems continued. The plan had been to attack the morning after Carnival, while most of the government soldiers would be sleeping off the previous night's excesses. As it turned out, however, many of the soldiers were just getting back from their partying, and they had brought back with them to the base even more soldiers to join them in further festivities. The attack was completely unsuccessful. Eight of the revolutionaries were killed and, within a week, the rest had all been captured. Sixty-nine of the rebels were brutally tortured and then killed in prison.

Castro and his co-conspirators were tried before a military tribunal. Castro used the trial as an opportunity for publicity, railing against the Batista regime, denouncing the torture and murder of the prisoners and demanding that the perpetrators be brought to justice. Castro was sentenced to fifteen years in prison. However, his defense statement, "History Will Absolve Me," would become the most famous of his speeches. The text would later be smuggled out of the prison, written in lemon juice between the lines of letters he would write to his friends and family.

Castro ended up in the Isle of Pines prison, which had originally been built by General Machado in 1931 to house the increasing numbers of political prisoners. When Castro and his rebels arrived, they quickly adopted it as a training ground and school. Castro maintained more strict controls on the behavior of his men than did the guards themselves. If the men were ordered by the guards to get up at 6:00 a.m. Castro would make them get up at 5:30. The rebels became noted for their impeccable behavior and were given more freedoms. They eventually began offering classes in Cuban history, grammar, geography, and English. At one point, Castro was put in solitary confinement for fourteen months as punishment for organizing fellow prisoners to sing a revolutionary anthem during a visit by Batista.

In 1954, running unopposed, Batista was elected president. By the following year, enjoying the support of the U.S. government, he felt secure in his control over the country. On May 6, in a bargain with the Orthodox Party and under pressure from the public and Congress, Batista granted Castro and the rest of the rebels amnesty, announcing that it was a Mother's Day present. Less than two years after their failed attack on Moncada, Castro and his men walked out of prison.

THE MEXICAN SOJOURN—Castro continued to publish attacks on the government, but after two dissidents were severely beaten by Batista's thugs and one was killed, he was increasingly worried about his safety and never slept in the same house two nights in a row. Two months after leaving the Isle of Pines, Castro decided to leave Cuba for Mexico. To finance the trip, his sister Lidia sold her refrigerator. Once in Mexico, Castro contacted Alberto Bayo, a former soldier in the Spanish Civil War and an expert on guerrilla warfare who was running a small furniture shop in Mexico. Castro asked Bayo to take charge of training his men. Castro's forces in Mexico began as a small group of sixty or seventy, living in six rented houses. The members of each house were kept under strict control, forbidden to leave without permission or to visit any of the other houses. They could not use the telephone or speak to anyone on the street. Each house included a rebel tribunal that enforced the rules and meted out punishment, which, in at least one instance, included death. Castro next contacted former Cuban president Prío, who was living in Texas. The two met only once, but the elder politician agreed to give Castro $100,000 to finance the revolution. In exchange, Castro agreed to give Prío advance warning before his assault, so that the two could coordinate their efforts. In fact, Castro had no intention of doing so, and instead planned his attack to coincide with a simultaneous uprising on the island, led by Frank País, the head of a separate revolutionary movement.

It was in Mexico that Fidel met a man who would become central to the Cuban revolution. Ernesto "Che" Guevara was born in Rosario, Argentina, into an upper-class family. The son of a doctor and the eldest of five children, Guevara suffered from frequent and debilitating asthma attacks which would plague him his entire life. A doctor by the age of twenty-three, he set out on an odyssey through Latin America, eventually moving to Mexico with his Peruvian wife Hilda. When Castro and Guevara met, Guevara was already a self-described Marxist and was far more of an ideologue than Fidel.

THE REVOLUTION—Castro chose to launch his revolution from the Mexican port of Tuxpan. He found a small, sixty-foot boat called the *Granma* that he bought from an American for $20,000. The boat was designed to carry at most twenty-five people and was powered by two small diesel engines. When the eighty-two rebels finally took off, the boat sat so low in the water that they were in constant danger of capsizing. Like the Moncada attack, the assault on Cuba ran into problems from the start. Traveling at 7.2 knots, the tiny ship was battered by bad weather. Two days into the voyage it became clear that the crossing would take at least seven days, instead of the estimated five, and that the landing would therefore miss the planned uprising in Cuba. On the fifth day, still at sea, the rebels heard news over the radio of País' attempted revolt, and its bloody defeat by Batista.

On December 2, 1956, the rebels landed, or as Che would describe it, shipwrecked, at a muddy place called Purgatory Point. Within an hour, Batista had learned of the force and had sent planes to strafe and bomb the area. According to Castro, only twelve men survived the initial landing and attack. The number was probably chosen more for its religious significance than its accuracy, and other historians have estimated the force to be either eighteen or twenty. The men marched for three days through the forest, covering just twenty-two miles while being continually hounded by bombings and ground troops. On the third day they were surrounded and attacked by a group of soldiers, during which Che was wounded in the shoulder. The rebels hid in a sugarcane field, but with no food or water they were forced to drink their own urine to survive.

Eventually, the rebels reached the Sierra Maestra, where they settled among the rural peasants and began to regroup. The locals, who felt no allegiance to Batista, received them warmly, providing food and supplies. On January 17, 1957, Castro led his men, now numbering thirty-three, on their first attack, against a small garrison in La Plata. The rebels killed two soldiers and wounded five, and carried off a number of guns and munitions. They also behaved according to their strict rules of morality, allowing wounded soldiers to receive medical aid and releasing all prisoners after the initial attack.

A month later Castro felt the time was right for some controlled media coverage, so he sent a rebel to Havana to bring back a foreign journalist. The man chosen was Herbert Matthews of the *New York Times,* who was sent to the Sierra Maestra to confirm that Castro was actually still alive. Although the rebels still numbered less than fifty, Castro ordered columns of men to march past the camp, then change uniforms and march back again, to make it appear that their forces were larger than they really were. At one point Castro even had one of his officers interrupt the interview to say that a separate regiment of troops had just arrived, a regiment that never in fact existed. The ploy worked, and Matthews wrote a three-part story about the massive buildup of rebels in the mountains.

As the movement grew, Castro began to clash with other members of the revolution, especially Frank País. País, who had survived the failed uprising in December, had continued to lead the guerrilla movement in the cities, a much more difficult and dangerous operation. A strong, handsome, and charismatic leader, he was one of the few people who dared to challenge Castro's control, and he often clashed with Fidel on how to organize the rebellion. País came from an upper-class background and was vehemently anti-Communist. He wanted to replace Castro's strict top-down hierarchy with a more democratic and decentralized structure. Unfortunately, País was being tracked ever more closely by Batista and his men. Despite appeals for support to Castro, País was eventually surrounded in one of his hideouts and killed by an assassin.

Popular support for the rebels continued to grow, and more and more Cubans joined their forces. In March 1958, Raúl Castro was given command of the Second Front, based in Oriente, which began to operate semi-independently of the Sierra Maestra group. Although still under his brother's command, Raúl showed his talent as a military tactician, capturing or destroying many of Batista's planes, trains, and military vehicles. In April of the same year, Fidel called on the people of Cuba to participate in a general strike, which he hoped would spark a nationwide uprising. When Batista heard about the strike he gave orders to execute anyone who participated. More than 140 activists, mostly young people, were gunned down. However, Batista's harsh response only served to increase Castro's popularity.

By the end of the summer it was clear that the tide was beginning to turn. In September, Che Guevara and Camilio Cienfuegos led two forces of rebels on what would become known as the "Westward March." Batista's troops put up practically no resistance, either giving up town after town or actually deserting to the rebels. By November the rebels controlled almost all of the transportation lines in Oriente and were moving slowly but surely toward Havana.

VICTORY—On the night of December 31, 1958, Batista resigned and fled the country. Fearing a takeover by a military junta, Castro and his men left at dawn for Santiago, arriving on January 2. That night Castro gave a speech in front of 200,000 people. He was flanked on one side by the new president, Manuel Urrutia, a quiet judge who had joined the rebel army, and on the other by Archbishop Enrique Pérez Serantez, the priest who had baptized him and whose efforts had gotten him freed from prison. That same day Che Guevara and Camilio Cienfuegos entered Havana and took control. In grand style, Castro chose a symbolic march toward Havana at the head of the victorious rebel army. The march took five

FIDEL CASTRO DURING HIS FIRST
WEEK IN POWER.
Lester Cole/Corbis

days, and he used every opportunity to showcase in front of the masses. He started in the back of a jeep, wearing his olive-green uniform with his precious M-2 rifle with its telescopic sight slung across his shoulder and a cigar clenched between his teeth. Before he entered Havana, he was riding on the back of a captured military tank, and nine-year-old Fidelito joined him for the final entrance.

The victorious rebel army, numbering only 7,250 fighters, had defeated Batista's 46,000 U.S.-armed troops. The transfer of power was surprisingly orderly. Castro had warned his soldiers against looting and destruction of property. When several caches of arms were found to have been stolen, Castro, worried about the possibility of a separate seizure of power, used his next speech to ask, "Arms for what purpose?" Afterward, the student Directorate, who had taken the arms, sheepishly returned them.

Castro's base of power lay in his blindly loyal rebel army, most of whom were illiterate peasants. He realized that he would need the help of educated people to actually run the country. He chose José Miró Cardona, one of his former professors, to be prime minister; Roberto Agramonte, chairman of the Orthodox Party, to be foreign minister; and Manuel Urrutia, to be president. Castro himself was content to be supreme commander of the armed forces, while keeping his closest allies in the background.

Behind the scenes, Castro began to lay the foundation of a parallel system of power, in which he held complete control. Under the name "Bureau for Revolutionary Planning and Coordination," Fidel brought together many of his old friends from the movement, including Raúl Castro, Che Guevara, Camilio Cienfuegos, and Alfredo Guevara. The group met regularly at Castro's headquarters, the top three floors of the Havana Libre Hotel (formerly the Havana Hilton). Castro was known as the Máximo Lider (Maximum Leader).

In the weeks after the revolution, some 550 Batista "criminals" were courtmartialed and summarily executed. The worst incident occurred in Santiago de Cuba, where seventy prisoners were killed by rebel soldiers at the command of Raúl Castro and then dumped in a mass grave. Three of Batista's most notorious thugs were put on public trial in the athletic stadium in Havana. The angry crowd chanted "Parédon!", meaning "Up against the wall." By the end of the year there had been about 1,900 executions.

In May 1959, Castro instituted a program of agrarian reform, nationalizing foreign holdings on the island, especially those of the U.S. sugar producers. He also created the National Agrarian Reform Institute (INRA), which gave structure to his hidden government. Soon INRA was responsible for nearly all decisions, including the building of infrastructure. INRA was supported by the reconsolidated military, the Revolutionary Armed Forces, under the control of Raúl Castro.

IF YOU DON'T SUPPORT ME, YOU ARE THE ENEMY—With the INRA, backed by the Revolutionary Army, making the political decisions, there was little need for the puppet government. By July, Castro had decided that he no longer needed President Urrutia. On July 16, Castro announced his resignation, saying that he could no longer work with the president and accusing him of betrayal. Castro then disappeared for several days. As planned, the Cuban population responded with massive protests and calls for Urrutia's removal. Humiliated and fearing for his safety, Urrutia disguised himself as a milkman and took refuge in the Venezuelan embassy before going into exile. Ten days later, Castro was back in power. He cemented his control by placing his most loyal allies in key positions of power. Fidel put Raúl Castro in control of the military and made Che Guevara, despite his complete lack of any relevant economic experience, director of Cuba's Central Bank.

Still, the purges continued. The next to go were former members of Castro's own July 26 Movement. In October, Huber Matos, a former Sierra Madre fighter who was in charge of the economically important Camagüey province, sent Fidel Castro a letter of resignation. In it he expressed his concern with the direction of the government and his wish to return home. He did emphasize that he continued to support Castro and wished him success in the future. To Castro, however, anyone not wholly supportive of his regime was his enemy, and he ordered Matos' arrest, as well as that of forty officers who shared his views. Although Raúl wanted Matos shot, Fidel settled with having him sentenced to twenty years in prison. Soon afterward, Camilio Cienfuegos died under suspicious circumstances. Cienfuegos, who was sympathetic to Matos, was on his way to Havana for a meeting with Castro when his Cessna 310 disappeared. No trace of the aircraft or its passengers was ever discovered.

Having removed all allies even remotely suspected of being disloyal, Fidel and Raúl turned their attention to external security. After taking power, they had incorporated many soldiers and officers from Batista's army into the Revolutionary Armed Forces, which numbered approximately 100,000 by the beginning of 1960. Over the next twelve months, the army tripled in size. Additionally, the army was supported by hundreds of thousands of lightly armed militias, recruited from the general population. These militia members were expected to use guerrilla tactics to combat any attempted invasion.

With Castro's blessing, interior minister Ramiro Valdés created a new secret police organization, the G-2, which was supported by the creation of the Committees for the Defense of the Revolution (CDRs), whose task it was to track down suspected saboteurs and traitors. Like Batista before him, Castro soon began to silence critical media, shutting down newspapers, radio stations, and television stations.

CASTRO VISITS THE LINCOLN MEMORIAL,
APRIL 19, 1959
Bettmann/Corbis

FINDING A PLACE IN THE COLD WAR

—In April of 1959, less than six months after taking control of Cuba, Castro, in his first visit as head of state, traveled to the United States. He was welcomed with open arms, both by the American public and the Cuban exile population, and more than 30,000 people came to see his opening speech in New York's Central Park. The U.S. government, on the other hand, played it cooler. President Dwight Eisenhower went on a golfing vacation, leaving Vice President Richard Nixon to meet with Castro. In fact, the CIA was already making plans for Castro's removal, and the U.S. government applied pressure to block the international sale of arms to Cuba.

Back home, Castro made contact with the Soviet Union, and in February 1960, he signed an agreement to trade Cuban sugar for various Soviet products. In July, Raúl Castro traveled to the Soviet Union and reached an agreement with Nikita Khrushchev for a program of military aid. Nevertheless, the leadership of the USSR was wary of the Castro brothers and not yet convinced that it wanted Cuba as an ally.

Castro ordered the American-owned refineries in Cuba to process oil imports from the Soviets. When the companies refused, Castro nationalized their holdings. In response, Eisenhower cut 700,000 tons from the U.S. annual purchase commitment, in what Castro would describe as the American "Dagger Law," designed to stab the revolution in the back. Castro countered by nationalizing all U.S.-owned agricultural and industrial firms on the island, and then all large commercial businesses still under private control. The American Mafia alone had to write off about $100 million of their holdings in the tourist industry. These nationalizations also created a huge expatriation of the Cuban middle class. Between 1960 and 1962, 200,000 highly educated citizens fled the island, mostly settling in Florida. These included doctors, engineers, technicians, economists, and scientists.

BACK IN THE UNITED STATES—In September 1960, Castro made his second trip to New York. He planned to speak at the United Nations and wanted to attract the world's attention. When the eighty-three-person Cuban delegation arrived in New York, they claimed that their rooms at the Shelburne Hotel on Lexington Avenue were far too expensive, and that the hotel had asked for a deposit of $10,000. In dramatic style, Castro's convoy gathered up their luggage, piled into cars and, followed by dozens of reporters, drove to the United Nations building. There, Castro confronted the secretary-general, Dag Hammarskjøld, and told him that they would either sleep in the UN building or in Central Park. Finally, the entire convoy set off for the seedy Hotel Theresa, in the middle of Harlem, where they settled in. It was here that Castro received the leaders of the nonaligned movement, including Indian premier Jawaharlal Nehru and Egyptian premier Gamal Abdel Nasser, as well as Nikita Khrushchev, whom he welcomed with a big bear hug. In fact, the entire affair had been a publicity ploy. The Cubans had been offered a steeply discounted room rate of only $20 per day at the Shelburne Hotel and wound up paying more for their rooms at the Hotel Theresa. When Castro had stormed out of the Shelburne, he had even been offered free rooms at the Commodore Hotel near the UN building. At the UN General Assembly meeting, Castro spoke for four and a half hours, until even his allies were on the verge of falling asleep.

THE BAY OF PIGS INVASION—By March of 1960, relations between Cuba and the United States had become so strained that President Eisenhower gave the green light for the organization and training of a group of Cuban exiles to invade the island. On January 3, 1961, the United States officially broke diplomatic ties with Cuba. When John F. Kennedy

replaced Dwight Eisenhower as president of the United States less than three weeks later, he inherited the planned invasion. At that point, the plot had already been reported in the *New York Times,* and Castro undoubtedly knew that something was afoot. The CIA and the State Department considered several landing sites for the invading forces and decided on the Bahía de Cochinos, or Bay of Pigs. The bay covered a thirty-mile long stretch of coast, in an isolated and swampy region.

Prior to the invasion, on April 15, the United States made a surprise attack on the Cuban air force in an attempt to disable Castro's planes. Castro had already hidden many of his aircraft, and although he lost five planes in the air strikes, in the end he still had more airplanes than pilots: eight planes and only seven pilots. After the air raids, Castro ordered the mass arrests of anyone suspected of being involved in an invasion force. By the time the invaders landed, between 100,000 and 250,000 people had been thrown in prison, scuttling chances for a larger popular revolt.

On April 17, Invasion Brigade 2506, escorted by American destroyers, reached the southern coast of Cuba. The force, which had left from Nicaragua three days earlier, numbered 1,511 men, all of them Cuban exiles. As they pulled out of the port at Puerto Cabezas, the Nicaraguan dictator Luis Somoza told them, "Bring me a couple of hairs from Castro's beard!" The troops landed at dawn at Girón and Larga beaches, but had great difficulty slogging through the swamp to the shore. Many of their small boats got stuck in the reefs, and when the men waded ashore their walkie-talkies became wet, cutting off communication.

Within minutes, word of the landing had reached Castro. He sent his few remaining planes to attack the American support fleet. The Americans were so confident that they had destroyed the Cuban air force that they did not even put anti-aircraft guns in place for defense. By 6:30 a.m. the Cuban planes had scuttled the largest ship, the *Houston,* and had forced a second ship, the *Barbara,* back out to sea, leaving the invading force completely unsupported. At the same time, there were 25,000 Cuban troops and more than 200,000 armed militia in the area. Within sixty-five hours, after heavy losses on the Cuban side, the battle ended when the invading force ran out of ammunition. A total of 114 exile fighters had been killed, and 1,189 were captured. The rest escaped into the swamp or disappeared into the Cuban population. The captured men included many of Batista's former henchmen. Five were executed, and the rest were eventually traded back to the United States in exchange for medical supplies worth $53 million. The attempted invasion of Cuba had failed spectacularly. Dozens of trials were held in front of revolutionary tribunals, resulting in nine executions.

THE NEXT CRISIS—In 1961, Castro announced the creation of the Integrated Revolutionary Organizations (ORI), which would eventually become the Communist Party of

Cuba (PCC). At the same time, his regime began cracking down on anyone suspected of disloyalty to the revolution. Artists, poets, and intellectuals were the first targets. Catholics, Protestants, and members of the Santería cult were also thrown into labor camps. Male and female prostitutes were jailed, as were homosexuals, who had to wear prison uniforms with a large letter "P" on their back, for "pimpillo" or pretty boy.

On December 1, 1961, on national television and radio, Fidel declared "I am a Marxist-Leninist and I shall be a Marxist-Leninist until the day I die." The Soviet leaders in Moscow, however, were still dubious about taking responsibility for Cuba's national defense. In their traditional New Year's message to their friends and allies, they wished Castro, "success in the creation of a new society," but made no mention of his statement. Almost a month passed before they even acknowledged it. On the American side, however, the response was immediate. The State Department moved to bring charges against Cuba in the Organization of American States and called for a meeting of foreign ministers to discuss Castro's removal. In February 1962, the U.S. government imposed a total economic blockade of Cuba, causing the loss of some $600 million in foreign currency earnings. The following month, Castro was forced to place restrictions on basic products. Rations were imposed, and Cubans were given a small book of coupons which were supposed to guarantee them access to a fair share of food and other products. Castro blamed the shortages on the U.S. embargo and the move pushed Cuba even closer to Moscow.

In May, the Politburo in the USSR decided to offer Castro the stationing of Soviet missiles on the island. The original plan called for forty mobile ballistic missile launching pads, with a range of between 1,100 and 2,200 nautical miles. By mid-July, shipments of equipment and weapons began to arrive in Cuba. In October, the United States was finally alerted to the presence of missile sites on the island, and the Cuban Missile Crisis had begun. The first real evidence that Cuba had received missiles from the Soviets came on October 14, when Major Richard S. Heyser flew a U-2 spy plane over the San Cristóbal area of Western Cuba and recorded photographic evidence of nuclear launch sites. For five days President Kennedy and his advisors struggled over whether to take preemptive military action, to blockade the island until weapons were withdrawn, or to reach a political deal with the Soviets. They reasoned that a military air strike might not guarantee the destruction of all missile sites and nuclear weapons, but it would almost certainly result in a Soviet response. Instead, Kennedy announced a military blockade around the island, which would be lifted only after all nuclear weapons had been withdrawn. He also announced that a military strike by Cuba on any country in the Western Hemisphere would be countered with a nuclear attack on the Soviet Union by the United States.

The crisis escalated, and all U.S. strategic missile units were placed on the highest level of alert, while 250,000 troops were put on standby for a possible military landing on Cuba.

Castro sent a letter to Khrushchev urging the Soviets to launch a nuclear strike against the United States if it attempted to invade the island. Events reached a peak on the morning of October 27, when an American U-2A spy plane was shot down over Cuba by a Soviet ground-to-air missile, killing the pilot, Major Rudolf Anderson, Jr. Kennedy was urged to respond with force, but he resisted and the next morning Khrushchev officially announced that the missiles would be removed from Cuba in exchange for a U.S. agreement not to mount an invasion of Cuba nor support an invasion by a third party.

Castro was left out of the decision-making process. Neither Khrushchev nor Kennedy had consulted him, and in the end he only heard about the agreement through radio and newswire reports. From then on, although the Soviets would continue to offer significant economic aid to Cuba, their relationship would be little more than one of convenience. Khrushchev invited Castro to cover up his humiliation by making a forty-day trip through the Soviet Union. The gesture of reconciliation included assurances of generous amounts of economic aid. The U.S. government also took several steps to improve ties with Cuba. Back-channel communications were restarted between Havana and Washington, and Kennedy hinted at ending the economic embargo if Castro stopped supporting guerrilla groups in Latin America and distanced himself from the Soviets.

This warming of U.S.–Cuban relations was derailed, however, when Kennedy was assassinated in Dallas, Texas, on November 22, 1963. Castro was outraged when he heard about attempts being made to link him to the assassination.

COMPAÑERO CHE GUEVARA—Che Guevara, meanwhile, had grown into the ideological brains of the revolution. By 1963, however, Che's socialist idealism had begun to conflict with Soviet economic plans for Cuba. The nation's agricultural output fell by 23 percent, leaving a foreign trade deficit and lower living standards throughout Cuban society. The sugar harvest was the lowest since the end of World War II. As the regime's industry minister, Che was held responsible and he openly criticized aspects of the regime, including its close ties to the Soviets. The following year, Castro signed a five-year agreement to sell Cuban sugar to the Soviet Union at a price above the world-market rate. In 1964, Castro agreed to remove Che from his ministry post and allow him to deal instead with foreign policy. Although he publicly denied having quarreled with Castro, Che began making long trips abroad to support foreign struggles for independence and armed revolutions, spending less and less time in Cuba. He traveled to Algeria, after which Castro agreed to send a battalion of Cuban soldiers and tanks to help the Algerian government in its armed conflict with Morocco. Previously, he had given Cuban military aid to the Algerian National Liberation Front in its struggle against France. Che visited various areas in Africa where colonial struggles were taking place,

including Angola, Mozambique, Guinea-Bissau, Mali, the Congo, Senegal, Ghana, Tanzania, and Egypt. While in Algiers, Che gave a speech criticizing the Soviet Union's economic practices and calling for an end to Cuba's trade agreements with the Soviets.

When Che returned to Cuba on March 15, 1965, he was brought before Fidel and Raúl, and during their closed-door meeting the friendship among the three finally ended. Che left Cuba on April 2, without saying goodbye to Fidel, and set off for the Congo. There he joined a group of guerrilla fighters around Laurent Kabila, who would eventually become that nation's dictator. Che continued to travel, reaching Bolivia in November 1966. Within a year, he had been tracked down by Bolivian officers and soldiers, and was eventually killed by Bolivian soldiers trained by Green Berets and the CIA.

SUGAR FANTASIES—Meanwhile, back in Cuba, Castro had announced sweeping changes to the agrarian system, embarking on what would be a series of agricultural fiascos. The Cuban trade deficit with the USSR had mushroomed to $4 billion, so Castro tried to increase agricultural production. His first plan revolved around the sugar harvest, and he announced a target of 5.5 million tons for 1965, increasing to 7 million tons and eventually reaching 10 million tons by 1970. Castro called 1970 "the year of the ten million tons," but from the beginning, more realistic observers doubted whether the target could be achieved. Castro poured all of Cuba's energy into the sugarcane harvest, leaving almost all other economic activity at a standstill. Virtually the entire Cuban population was put to work cutting cane, including mothers, children, pensioners, white-collar workers, and the military. Even visiting foreign dignitaries were asked to cut cane, and Castro himself cut for four hours almost every day. Christmas was abolished for 1969, and growing cycles were changed to allow for more production. With so much effort going into cutting cane, the rest of the Cuban economy fell between 20 and 40 percent. Worse yet, it soon became clear that the target was indeed impossible to achieve. In July 1970, Fidel was forced to announce that the ten million tons had been a failure. In his usual style, he made an impassioned plea to the people and announced his resignation. The Cuban population responded with their support and he quickly returned to power.

SUPERCOW—In the early 1960s, Castro became increasingly interested in the techniques and science of farming and animal husbandry. His ideas and schemes to improve Cuban agriculture abounded, and included a campaign to rid the island of all weeds, an idea to plant a circle of coffee plants in a huge ring around the island, and a plan to produce a Cuban Camembert that would rival that of Normandy. In 1964, he invited a noted French agronomist, André Voisin, to make a lecture tour of Cuba. Castro had been impressed by Voisin's book, *Grass Productivity.* When Voisin arrived, Castro arranged an exuberant series of dinners, social events, lectures, and sightseeing tours. Evidently the strain of celebrity was too much for Voison because, on December 21, after three weeks of being feted, Voisin suffered a heart attack and died while visiting a state farm. Undaunted, Castro continued to look for ways to improve the Cuban agricultural industry, this time in dairy production.

Prior to the revolution, Cuba had had a population of cattle in the millions, mostly the indigenous Cebú variety. The cattle were well adapted to the tropical climate, but were notoriously poor producers of milk. American Holsteins, by contrast, languished during the dry season but produced far more milk. Fidel ordered the purchase of several thousand of the most expensive Holsteins from Canada. Within the first few weeks, nearly one-third died in the intense Cuban heat. Castro then ordered the construction of special air-conditioned dairy farms, a move that might have benefited André Voisin had Castro thought of it earlier. Castro next announced a plan to cross-breed the Cebú cattle with the imported Holsteins. The resulting F-1 hybrid, he claimed, would inherit the vigor of the tropical cows with the productive capacity of the purebreds. Ignoring the protests of animal husbandry experts and breeders, Castro poured resources and propaganda into the project. One cow, named Ubra Blanca, or White Udder, became so famous that after her death Castro ordered her stuffed and placed in a museum. Unfortunately, the project was a complete failure. Even fifteen years later, the resulting F-1s were still producing less than half the milk of the average American Holstein.

TRYING TO GAIN INTERNATIONAL RESPECTABILITY—Although he was the ruler of a small country, Fidel Castro had dreams of glory. By the end of the 1970s he was providing aid to thirty-five Third-World countries. Part of this outreach had to do with medical training and health care, a legitimate specialty of Castro's Cuba. Even today, Cuba has a lower infant mortality rate and a higher life expectancy than the United States. However, Castro also wasted a lot of his nation's limited resources in support of dubious military ventures, including the bloody civil war in Angola and a war between Ethiopia and Somalia. In September 1979, Castro's international efforts reached their peak when Havana played host to the Sixth Non-Aligned Conference, which made Castro its official spokesman for the next four years.

FLEEING THE SOCIALIST PARADISE—In 1965 the United States declared its willingness to accept any Cubans who sought asylum. Over the next six years, so many

Cubans chose to flee the country that there were fears that almost one in every five Cubans would emigrate. The loss of income and of skilled labor, the "brain drain," was considerable, and Castro finally forbade the flights. Between 1959 and 1980, a total of 800,000 people are estimated to have left the island. This exodus came to a head on April 1, 1980, when a bus crashed through the front gates of the Peruvian embassy in Havana, killing a guard. The six people inside the vehicle asked for political asylum. Outraged, Castro made a tactical error, removing all protection from the embassy. When the news spread that no one would be prevented from entering or leaving the grounds, Cubans flooded into the compound. Within five days, 10,000 people had descended upon the embassy, occupying nearly every square inch. When the Peruvian government refused to accept the refugees, Costa Rican President Rodrigo Carazo offered to allow the Cubans to go to his country. Castro responded by announcing that anyone in the embassy grounds could go home, pack their bags, and leave for wherever they wanted. The next day hundreds of boats packed with families from all over the country left Cuba. By September, when Castro reintroduced travel restrictions, an estimated 125,000 people had fled the country, many headed for the United States. Photographs and video of the massive exodus were shown around the world, delivering a blow to Castro's image of Cuba as a socialist paradise. It is estimated that between the 1959 revolution and the year 2000, 10 to 15 percent of the Cuban population fled the country, with a majority of them settling in Florida.

SUGAR RUSH—In the early 1980s, sugar prices and harvests were so good that the Cuban economy was growing at a rate of 24 percent, while Latin America as a whole declined by 9 percent. Then a worldwide slump in sugar prices drove Cuba's debt to the West from $2.8 billion in 1983 to $6 billion in 1987. Even worse, the Cuban debt to the Eastern bloc rose to almost $19 billion. The Soviet Union tried to save Castro's Cuba by increasing trade between the two countries. In 1989 the Communist governments in Eastern Europe fell apart and all economic agreements with them became worthless. To make matters worse, in the early 1990s, a series of hurricanes swept across Cuba, decreasing sugar production even more and causing almost $1 billion in damage. The struggling economy meant that military spending had to be scaled back, and restrictions placed on food and household supplies. Milk was available only for children and those with special needs, and soap, detergent, toilet paper, and matches became precious commodities. Cooking oil and flour were distributed only on a limited basis, as were fruit, jam, and butter. Every two years citizens were entitled to buy four pairs of underwear or bras, two pairs of socks, one shirt or blouse, and four meters of material to make trousers or dresses. At the same time, the black market shot up, from $2 billion to $14.5 billion in less than four years. Energy consumption was slashed by 50 percent, and electricity became sporadic throughout the country. Tractors were replaced with oxcarts, and people began to wait two to three hours for infrequent city buses.

Faced with an economy on the verge of collapse, in 1993 Castro gave permission for Cubans to start private businesses, mostly in the service sector. He also allowed them to own and spend U.S. dollars. In September 1994, he reestablished farmers' markets. The following year, he enacted a law that permitted foreign investors to own Cuban businesses in almost every area of the economy, a right that had previously been limited to the tourist industry. Cuba's economic output, which had declined 40 percent between 1989 and 1994, stabilized and began to grow.

In 1995, U.S. president Bill Clinton attemped to counter this trend by signing into law the Helms-Burton Act, a strengthening of the thirty-five-year-old embargo against Cuba that included a ban on any loans or financial assistance to the island; a ban on the import from a third country of any products that contained materials processed in Cuba; and a stipulation that the embargo could only be lifted once a transition government was in power in Cuba that moved toward a market-oriented economic system and that did not include either Fidel or Raúl Castro. The act also required the return of all property seized by the rebels from U.S. citizens.

The biggest beneficiary of Castro's economic reforms has been the military, which is run by his brother Raúl. The Ministry of Armed Forces manages GAESA (Grupo de Adminstración de Empresarial), a huge conglomerate of businesses involved in tourism, mining, consulting, construction, and international trade, and is thought to employ at least 20 percent of Cuban workers.

CATHOLICISM AND COMMUNISM—Since the early days of his revolution, Castro had had difficulty with the Catholic Church. In 1962, Pope Pius XII excommunicated Castro after his announcement that he was a Marxist-Leninist. From that point on, Castro restricted and persecuted the church and its followers. Much of its property was confiscated and many members of the clergy were expelled from the county. Castro officially proclaimed Cuba an atheist county. He finally became more tolerant of religion in 1992, allowing religious Cubans to join the Communist Party. In 1998, Pope John Paul II was invited to tour Cuba and give large public masses. The pope spoke out against the human rights abuses within the country, but encouraged greater cooperation and reconciliation between the church and Cuba. That same year Castro approved nineteen visas for foreign priests to take up residence in the country. He also allowed Cubans to celebrate Christmas as a holiday for the first time since the 1960s.

THE OVER-THE-HILL DICTATOR—The 1990s found Fidel an aging, lonely dictator. He had quit smoking his trademark cigars in 1985, as part of an anti-smoking campaign on the island. Most of his close allies had been either killed or exiled. He kept up his practice of not sleeping in the same place more that two nights in a row, and he now traveled in a column of three bullet-proof Mercedes limousines with a heavily armed guard.

By 1999, the Cuban National Assembly approved a series of measures that increased penalties for crimes, including a death penalty for drug-related crimes and longer prison sentences for robbery with violence. Sentences of up to twenty years were threatened against anyone providing information to the U.S. government or any foreign enemy or collaborating by any means with foreign media for the purpose of destabilizing the socialist state. At the time, an estimated 110,000 people, roughly one percent of the population, was serving time in prison or labor camps. Of these, at least 3,000 were presumed to be political prisoners. According to a 2005 report by Amnesty International, "the Cuban authorities continue to suppress any form of dissent by methods such as harassment, threats, intimidation, detention and long-term imprisonment."

THE REVOLUTION DEVOURS ITS CHILDREN—At the same time that Cuba was rising to power in the international sphere, Castro was imposing more restrictions on domestic liberties. In 1971, in response to the arrest of Cuban poet Heberto Padilla, an open letter was published in the French paper *Le Monde,* criticizing the repressive system in Cuba. The signatories included authors of both the left and the right, including Jean-Paul Sartre, Simone de Beauvoir, Mario Vargas Llosa, Carlos Fuentes, Susan Sontag, and Gabriel García Márquez. In 1989, one of the most celebrated "Heroes of the Revolution" was brought down: Arnaldo Ochoa Sánchez, a general in the Cuban army and a veteran of the Sierra Maestra, the Bay of Pigs, and guerrilla campaigns in Venezuela, the Congo, Ethiopia, Angola, and Nicaragua. The popular Ochoa had become a magnet for disaffected army officers and veterans, who gathered at his house in increasing numbers. Sensing a threat, Castro ordered Ochoa and three other high-ranking officers arrested for drug smuggling. The trial was a sham, and it received worldwide attention when all four were given death sentences, despite the fact that the maximum sentence for drug smuggling was twenty years in jail. Ochoa maintained his innocence, and his allegiance to the regime, until his execution by firing squad. He was buried in an unmarked grave. With Ochoa's execution, Castro sent a strong message to the increasingly disillusioned military that he would tolerate no dissent within the armed forces or society in general.

In March 2003, Castro took advantage of the world's preoccupation with the U.S.

invasion of Iraq to crack down again on political activists and dissidents. Cuban police arrested seventy-eight journalists, political students, and independent librarians and charged them with conspiring to overthrow the government. Most were sentenced, in closed-door trials, to between fifteen and twenty-eight years in prison. Over the next year, fourteen of the dissidents were released, but the majority have remained in prison. In response to the arrests, Cuban activist Oswaldo Paya delivered a petition to the Cuban National Assembly with more than 14,000 signatures, demanding a referendum to change the Cuban political system and protect civil liberties. It was the second year that Paya had delivered the petition. When he did so in 2002, with more than 11,000 signatures, Castro responded by conducting his own referendum, winning an overwhelming majority (98.97 percent of the vote according to the Cuban government) to amend the constitution and declare socialism on the island "irrevocable."

CIA PLOTS—Marita Lorenz, Fidel Castro's former translator and lover, was recruited by the CIA in a plot to kill Castro using a pill made from shellfish toxin. At the last moment, however, she could not bring herself to go through with the plan, and instead flushed the pill down the toilet. Two years later, a barman by the name of Santos de la Caridad was hired to slip a botulism pill into Castro's milkshake during his weekly visit to the bar. The plan was foiled, however, when the pills stuck to the inside of the freezer and shattered as they were being removed. Santos was too nervous to pick up the pieces of the pills and put them into the drink. Other CIA assassination ideas included a plan to give Castro a box of poisoned cigars, a plan to coat the inside of his diving suit with tuberculosis bacteria, and a plan involving a rifle disguised as a television camera. The CIA even devised a plan to slip Castro a substance that would make his beard fall out, thus humiliating him and causing him to lose the respect of the Cuban people.

THE NUMBER 26—Castro remains superstitious about certain dates and numbers. He attaches great importance to the number 26, having been born in 1926, on April 13 (which is half of 26) and having started his conspiracy against Batista in 1952, at the age of twenty-six, The attack on the military base in Moncada, for which Castro chose the date, took place on July 26, 1953, and his revolutionary movement took the name The 26th of July Movement. Castro frequently chooses the twenty-sixth day of the month to deliver key speeches or to make major decisions, such as March 26, 1962, when he spoke out against the so-called Sectarians of the Communist Party, who were challenging his rule. Of course, all this good luck would be ruined if he acknowledged that, as his sisters claim, he was really born in 1927.

(Patrick Durand/Sygma/Corbis)

16.

ISAIAS AFWERKI—ERITREA

THE NATION—A small nation of about 4.5 million people on the Red Sea, Eritrea achieved independence, with widespread international support, in 1991 after a thirty-year liberation war against Ethiopia.

BECOMING A NATION—In 1869, Italy purchased the Red Sea port of Assab from two local sultans and established Eritrea as a colony of Italy with a market-based agricultural economy. At its peak at the beginning of World War II, 70,000 Italians lived in the colony. The Italians treated the Eritreans as little more than cheap labor, but they did develop a reasonable infrastructure that included railway lines, all-weather roads, and two airports. When Italian forces were driven out of Ethiopia and Eritrea in 1941, the Allied Powers gave Eritrea to Great Britain to rule as a protectorate. After the war, the fate of the nation was put in the hands of the United Nations. Although the majority of Eritreans wanted independence, the UN, in December 1950, passed a resolution joining Eritrea with Ethiopia in a federation. The Ethiopians, led by Emperor Haile Selassie, gradually took over all control of Eritrea, reducing it to a mere province of Ethiopia. Pro-independence Eritrean guerrillas began a war against Ethiopia in 1961. The liberation armies split into Christian and Muslim factions, as well as regional forces. By the time the Ethiopian monarchy collapsed in 1974, there were about 20,000 Eritrean soldiers and they were beginning to control some of the more remote areas of the country. In the confusion that followed the change of government in Ethiopia, the Eritrean guerrillas occupied almost all of Eritrea. The new Ethiopian government, the Dergue, gained massive military aid from the Soviet Union and Cuba, but the Eritrean People's Liberation Front (EPLF), led by Isaias Afwerki, grew to a force of 110,000, 30 percent of whom were women, and kept the Ethiopian army at bay. As the Soviet armed forces became increasingly bogged down in their war in Afghanistan, they lost interest in helping the Dergue.

THE MAN—Isaias Afwerki was born February 2, 1945, into an Eritrean family that was respected during the reign of Haile Selassie. He studied engineering in the Ethiopian capital of Addis Ababa, but left to join the Muslim-dominated Eritrean Liberation Front (ELF) in 1966. The ELF sent him to be trained in China. Back in Eritrea, he switched to first one liberation splinter group and then another, finally settling on the Eritrean People's Liberation Front (EPLF), of which he soon became the leader. In 1982, Isaias formed an alliance with Meles Zenawi, the head of another guerrilla group, the Tigrayan People's Liberation Front, which was seeking independence from Ethiopia for the Tigrayan people. Together they defeated the ELF and headed toward Addis Ababa. In 1991, they forced out the hated regime of Mengistu Haile Mariam. In April 1993, with numerous international observer teams in attendance, the Eritreans voted overwhelmingly for independence. Isaias became Eritrea's first, and to date only, president.

At first the prospects for the newly independent nation looked promising. Although Eritrea had been damaged by thirty years of war and it had to deal with the return of a quarter-million Eritrean refugees from Sudan, it was greeted enthusiastically by the international community. Even the government of Ethiopia, which was, after all, ruled by Isaias' old friend Meles Zenawi, offered its support. In addition, Isaias' government was surprisingly tolerant considering it had come to power through force of arms. The EPLF soldiers were required to leave their weapons at police posts before entering the capital of Asmara, and the police themselves did not carry guns. Carrying on a practice it had begun in liberated areas during the war, the government acknowledged the importance of ethnic minorities by offering elementary school education in six languages. It also sent out cultural workers to teach the music, dance, and arts of the different nationalities and initiated a project of recording oral histories from elders of all groups. In November 1991, Isaias announced compulsory "national service" for all citizens between the ages of eighteen and forty. University students were sent to rural areas to teach reading and writing, while soldiers built roads and dams and terraced hillsides for agricultural use.

ANOTHER LIBERATION LEADER GOES BAD—Before long, however, it became clear that Isaias had no intention of sharing real power with anyone. In 1997 a constituent assembly ratified a new constitution that then had to be voted on by the Eritrean citizenry before it could be implemented. The election never happened, nor was a full judicial system ever put in place. No group larger than seven is allowed to gather without government approval. The government-run student summer work program began to look suspiciously like forced labor camps. When a newspaper published a first-person account of the mistreatment of student-workers in September 2001, Isaias shut down all of the private newspapers in Eritrea and they have remained closed ever since.

A USELESS WAR—The 1991 split between Eritrea and Ethiopia was amicable, but it left the exact borders in three remote areas unresolved. After months of minor skirmishes, on May 6, 1998, Eritrean troops moved into one of the disputed zones, the Badme Triangle, and fought with local militia. Almost immediately, the old revolutionary comrades Isaias and Meles ordered their armies to engage in a full-out war. This absurd conflict over three meaningless strips of land was particularly tragic for Eritrea, which depended on Ethiopia for two-thirds of its trade. In addition, Eritrea had less than one-sixteenth the population of Ethiopia. Isaias used the supposedly patriotic national service system to round up young people, take them to police stations, and put them on the front lines. He also used precious government funds to purchase expensive MiG-29 fighter jets, planes so sophisticated that he had to hire Eastern European pilots to fly them.

After two years of fighting, the displacement of more than 600,000 Eritreans and the deaths of tens of thousands of soldiers, Ethiopia reoccupied the disputed territories and the war ended. A 2002 decision by an independent Eritrea–Ethiopia Boundary Commission, backed by the United Nations and the African Union, awarded Badme to Eritrea. Although both sides had agreed to abide by the decision of the Commission, Ethiopia's Meles Zenawi refused to turn over the land. Isaias refused to take any responsibility for the war, blaming it all on Meles. In an interview with National Public Radio's "Talk of the Nation" he said, "How much money have we wasted in this war the last three years? How many lives has this conflict cost Eritrea and Ethiopia? Was it worthwhile to use this money, wasted on weapons, wasted on fighting a senseless war? Couldn't that have been used for some useful purpose? . . .

Yes, we squandered money, we spent money, but that was for self-defense." International observers thought otherwise. On December 21, 2005, a commission of the Permanent Court of Arbitration in The Hague ruled that Eritrea was responsible for causing the war when it attacked Ethiopia.

Ethiopia is not the only country with which Isaias has clashed. Eritrea engaged in a three-day war with Yemen in December 1995 over control of the Hanish Islands, and Isaias and Sudan's dictator, Omar al-Bashir, supported guerrilla groups that opposed each others' governments. No doubt inspired by U.S. president George W. Bush's declaration that Iraq, Iran, and North Korea formed an "Axis of Evil," Isaias accused Ethiopia, Yemen, and Sudan of being an "Axis of Belligerence."

(Reuters/Corbis)

17.
BASHAR AL-ASSAD—SYRIA

THE NATION—Syria is the size of the state of Washington, but with more than triple the population—about nineteen million people. Since 1961, Syria has been ruled by the Ba'ath party, the same party that ruled Iraq until the fall of Saddam Hussein. Almost three-quarters of the Syrian population are Sunni Muslims and another 15 percent or so belong to other Muslim groups, most notably the Alawites, who have held the leading political positions in Syria since 1966. Ten percent of Syrians are Christians and they have traditionally been treated well.

A MAGNET FOR INVADERS—On the crossroads of history, Syria was occupied by Akkadians, Amorites, Hittites, Canaanites, Phoenicians, Arameans, Hebrews, Egyptians, Sumerians, Assyrians, Babylonians, Iranians, Greeks, Romans, Arabs, European Crusaders, Mongols, Mamluks, and Turks. Syria is the site of the oldest preserved Jewish synagogue and the earliest identified Christian church. What is now Syria entered the twentieth century as part of the Turkish Ottoman Empire. After World War I and the dissolution of the Ottoman

Empire, nationalists proclaimed the independent Arab Kingdom of Syria with Emir Faisal of the Hashemite dynasty king. However, in July 1920, French troops defeated Faisal's Arab army at the Battle of Maysalun and imposed military rule. Faisal moved on to Iraq, where he was king until his death in 1933.

In 1922, the League of Nations gave Great Britain control of Transjordan and Palestine; and France was given what would evolve into present-day Syria and Lebanon. Nationalist revolts, protests, and strikes continued throughout the 1920s and 1930s, particularly among the Sunni majority. After the Free French and the British drove out the pro-Nazi Vichy government, Syria proclaimed its independence in 1943. In 1945, the French tried to reestablish control, but pressure from the newly created United Nations forced them to withdraw the last of their troops on April 17, 1946. Syria's first decade of independence was chaotic. It saw a failed invasion of Israel in 1948, a military coup in 1949, twenty cabinets and four constitutions.

The Ba'ath Party was founded in 1945 in Damascus by Michel Aflaq, a Christian, and Salah al-Din al-Bitar, a Sunni Muslim. It was conceived as a secular, pan-Arab nationalist party and it gained its greatest popularity in Syria and Iraq. Democracy was restored in Syria in 1954 and Ba'athists won seats in the next parliamentary elections. In 1959, when Syria joined Egypt to form the United Arab Republic, the Ba'ath Party leadership, as part of the union agreement, agreed to disband the party. This did not sit well with the party rank and file, and the union with Egypt was not popular with Syrians in general. A military coup in Syria put an end to the United Arab Republic in 1961. Ba'athist military officers, with help from other nationalists, seized power on March 8, 1963, a month after Iraqi Ba'athists gained control, albeit briefly, in their country. In Syria the Ba'athists banned all other political parties, but factions developed within the party itself. In June 1967, Syria lost the Golan Heights to Israel during the Six-Day War and in 1970 Syrian forces failed in their attempt to invade Jordan. On November 12, 1970, the minister of defense, Hafiz al-Assad, led a bloodless military coup that removed Syria's civilian leadership. Assad and his son have ruled Syria ever since.

THE FATHER—Hafiz al-Assad would prove to be much less interested in ideology than previous Ba'ath leaders. His main concern was securing personal power. The Alawites, the religious minority to which Assad belonged, follow a syncretic version of Islam that combines elements of Twelver Shi'ism with Christian practices. For example, in addition to observing Muslim holidays, the Alawites also celebrate Christmas and Epiphany. They are considered heretics by orthodox Sunni Muslims, some of whom refer to them as "little Christians." The Alawites are centered in eastern Syria. Because they constitute barely 10 percent of the Syrian population, Hafiz al-Assad, in order to stay in power, had to create a coalition of Syria's non-Sunni minorities. During the final years of his life, five of his seven closest advisors were Christians.

Within a few years of seizing power, Assad was supreme commander of the armed forces, head of the Ba'ath Party, and head of the executive branch of the government. He was responsible for choosing all government ministers and their deputies, all senior civil servants, all military officers, and all judges. Although he had allowed the legalization of friendly political parties and of a basically impotent parliament, Assad retained the right to dissolve that parliament. In 1984, Amnesty International released a list of thirty-eight types of torture used by Assad's regime. In addition to the usual practices, Syrian torture included "The Black Slave," in which the victim is strapped onto a device which, when turned on, inserts a heated metal skewer into his or her anus, and "The Chicken," whereby the victim is strapped to a revolving wooden bar resembling a roasting spit and subjected to beating with sticks.

On October 6, 1973, Syria and Egypt attacked Israel in an attempt to regain lost territory. A negotiated settlement ended the fighting after three weeks, but the Golan Heights remained under Israeli control. In 1975, Assad sent Syrian troops into Lebanon, which was immersed in a complex civil war. They remained there for thirty years. In 1982, 200 members of the Islamist Muslim Brotherhood staged an insurrection in the northern city of Hama. Assad responded with overwhelming force, pounding the city with mortars for three weeks and killing more than 10,000 civilians. Beginning in the 1980s, Assad used terrorism as a foreign policy tool. He supported Abu Nidal's Palestinian terrorist group, the Fatah Revolutionary Council, and Abdullah Ocalan's Kurdish Workers' Party, among others. He was also widely accused of supporting numerous terrorist organizations through intermediaries so that he personally could deny involvement in their acts. The terrorists who blew up the Khobar Towers barracks in Saudi Arabia in 1996, killing nineteen U.S. soldiers, planned their attack in Syria.

Assad intended to pass on control of Syria to the oldest of his four sons, the charismatic Basil, but on January 21, 1994, Basil was killed in a car accident while driving to the airport in the Syrian capital of Damascus. Assad then turned to his second son, Bashar.

THE SON—Bashar al-Assad was born in Damascus on September 11, 1965, and attended the elite Fraternity School. Because Basil was the heir apparent, Bashar was free to pursue a relatively normal life. More bookish and intellectual than his flashy older brother, who went straight into military training, Bashar chose to study medicine. This probably pleased his father, who, as a youth, had hoped to become a doctor, but was prevented from pursuing his goal because his family lacked the necessary financial resources. Bashar earned

HAFIZ AL-ASSAD AND SON BASHAR
Reuters/Corbis

his medical degree from Damascus University in 1988 and then met his military service requirement by working as an army doctor. He moved to England in 1992 to do postgraduate training in ophthalmology at the Western Eye Hospital in London. He would later marry Asma Akhras, a Syrian who was raised in London. When Basil died, Bashar returned to Damascus for the funeral and found that his life was about to be turned upside down. Having decided to groom Bashar to be his successor, Hafiz al-Assad set to work to bolster his credentials with the all-important military. Bashar, after his obligatory two years as an army doctor, had left the service with the rank of captain. Now he was enrolled in a course for tank battalion commanders and then put in charge of a tank unit in November 1994. He was promoted to major in January 1995. The following year he enrolled in the command and general staff course at the Higher Military Academy and he graduated with honors in July 1997. He was immediately promoted to lieutenant colonel and put in charge of the same Republican Guard brigade that Basil had commanded. Early in 1999 he moved up to the rank of staff colonel.

To further strenthen Bashar's status, his father insisted that respected members of the military praise him publicly. Even more important, Hafiz set about eliminating from positions of power, in the military and in the intelligence and security agencies, anyone who might challenge Bashar, including Hafiz's own brother, Rifa't. They were replaced by trustworthy loyalists. Bashar's brother-in-law, Asif Shawkat, the husband of Bashar's older sister, Bushra, was given a position in Syrian Military Intelligence and quickly promoted to second-in-command. Hafiz al-Assad also initiated a public relations campaign to sell Bashar to the Syrian citizenry, blanketing the country with posters of Hafiz, Basil, and Bashar with captions that read, "our leader, our ideal and our hope." Acknowledging the public's cynicism about governmental corruption, Hafiz put Bashar in charge of a highly visible anticorruption campaign (just as he had done earlier with Basil) with offices throughout the country where citizens could go to express their complaints. Of course real anticorruption prosecutions were extremely selective, as possible challengers to Bashar found themselves charged with various offenses, while regime loyalists survived unscathed. Bashar was given the chairmanship of the Syrian Computer Society, a position previously held by Basil. However, unlike his late brother, Bashar, an academic, took the post seriously and is credited with promoting the introduction of the Internet to Syria, a development that is rarely a foregone conclusion in dictatorships. Hafiz also gradually educated Bashar in Syria's relationship with Lebanon, and by late 1998, Bashar was handling the management of Lebanese affairs. He met with a wide range of Lebanese political figures and took a particular liking to Hassan Nasrallah, the secretary-general of Hezbollah. Combining his two portfolios, anticorruption and Lebanon, Bashar targeted the Syrian business associates of Lebanon's billionaire prime minister, Rafiq al-Hariri, a Sunni Muslim whom Hafiz al-Assad wanted removed from power.

DICTATOR BY DEFAULT—When Hafiz al-Assad died on June 10, 2000, the Syrian parliament quickly lowered the minimum age for presidents from forty to thirty-four and Bashar was sworn in. Many Syrians and foreign observers found it hard to believe that Bashar al-Assad could stay in power for long and considered him a transitional president until the real powers-that-be decided who would take his place. But Hafiz had done a good job of eliminating Bashar's most dangerous contenders. In addition, the most powerful players in the military, the intelligence services, the government bureaucracy, and the Ba'ath Party were content to leave Bashar alone—as long as he didn't try to rock the boat. For example, Bashar convinced the parliament to pass a law legalizing private banks, but not one private bank actually opened. More significantly, Bashar released more than 600 political prisoners, and he encouraged the formation of political and cultural forums where citizens could discuss democracy. Syrian intellectuals were so refreshed by this climate of openness that they called it the "Damascus Spring." Soon hundreds of pro-democracy advocates were meeting at these forums and circulating petitions promoting a more open society. Even members of parliament were calling for an end to the emergency laws that had been in place since December 1962. Then the crackdown began. The authorities shut down the discussion forums and arrested almost all of their most vocal members. It is unclear whether the dismantling of the discussion groups was an example of the Syrian old guard overruling Bashar's reformist tendencies or if the creation of the forums in the first place was a trick to identify regime opponents.

Bashar has been uncompromising in his anti-Semitism. When Pope John Paul II visited Damascus in May 2001, Bashar used his welcoming speech to denounce the Jews, saying, "They tried to kill the principles of all religions with the same mentality in which they betrayed Jesus Christ and the same way they tried to betray and kill the Prophet Muhammad." At an Arab summit conference in Beirut in March 2002, he declared that all Israelis were legitimate targets for terrorist attacks.

GREATER SYRIA—Syrian troops invaded Lebanon in 1975 to "stabilize" the country during its civil war. This action was not really that surprising considering that Syrians had, for centuries, considered both Lebanon and Palestine part of "Greater Syria." In the current context, the Syrian occupation created a buffer zone that allowed Syria to support anti-Israeli terrorist groups without having them actually operate out of Syria. It also ensured that Lebanon remained a closed market for Syrian products and a place of employment for more than one million Syrians, most of whom would otherwise be unemployed if they had to return to Syria. Assad maintained control of Lebanon through the use of 30,000 troops, an extensive military intelligence network, and financial support of Shiite political parties, including Hezbollah, Shiites constituting one-third of the Lebanese population.

On August 27, 2004, Bashar ordered Rafiq al-Hariri, the longtime enemy of the Assad family, to have the Lebanese parliament amend its constitution to allow the pro-Syrian president of Lebanon, Emile Lahoud, to remain in office after his six-year term expired in November. Although Hariri was humiliated by the way the young Bashar treated him, he pushed through the amendment anyway—in a ten-minute legislative session. One week later, France and the United States co-sponsored a resolution in the United Nations, which was passed by the Security Council, demanding that Syria withdraw its 20,000 remaining troops from Lebanon and disband the armed wing of Hezbollah. This was a stunning development for Bashar and the Syrian leadership because France had always been Syria's leading Western supporter. On October 20, Rafiq al-Hariri resigned as prime minister and began to make plans for the May 2005 parliamentary elections, which would be monitored by international observer groups. On February 2, 2005, Hariri and the Lebanese opposition publicly called for the complete withdrawal of Syrian troops. Twelve days later, Hariri was assassinated by a massive truck bomb in Beirut that also killed nineteen other people. There followed a series of increasingly large street demonstrations, starting with one for Hariri's funeral. On March 8, Nasrallah and Hezbollah mobilized 500,000 pro-Syrian demonstrators. Six days later, the combined Sunni, Christian, and Druze opposition brought out one million people for the largest demonstration in Lebanese history. Following the release of a United Nations report that implicated the Syrian leadership, including one of Bashar's younger brothers and his sister's husband, in the assassination of Rafiq al-Hariri, or at least in a refusal to seek out the perpetrators, Bashar al-Assad agreed to withdraw his troops. The last of the Syrian troops finally left Lebanon on April 26, 2005. Although this was a blow to Bashar's prestige, Syria maintained major influence in Lebanon through its intelligence presence, its deep involvement in Lebanon's security forces, and its business connections.

DANGEROUS GAMES—It is still possible in Syria to be convicted of "opposing the party's revolutionary goals" or "harming the state's reputation." Torture continues to be commonly used. For example, in a February 2005 trial of eighteen Kurds for "activity against the authority of the state," every one of the defendants claimed that they had been tortured with electricity, and one said he had been sodomized with a piece of wood. The Syrian Human Rights Committee of London believes that there are about 4,000 political prisoners in Syria and that more than 17,000 prisoners have disappeared, their fate unknown.

Bashar, like Pervez Musharraf in Pakistan, is playing a dangerous and delicate game, balancing support for Islamist extremists with cooperation with the U.S. government in its battle against terrorism. On the one hand, he has allowed foreign fighters to cross through Syria on their way to join the insurgency in Iraq. On the other hand, he has allowed the United States to send terror suspects to his prisons to be interrogated and tortured.

(Mike Hutchings/Reuters/Corbis)

18.
MELES ZENAWI—ETHIOPIA

THE NATION—Ethiopia is an old and large country in East Africa with a population of almost 75 million. Rare among African nations, it was never colonized, although Italian troops did occupy the country during World War II. There are eighty different ethnic groups, but two of them, the Amhara and the Oromo, account for almost two-thirds of the population. Most Ethiopians are Christian or Muslim, with the Christians predominating.

HISTORY—Ethiopia is mentioned in the Bible, although it is unclear to which area most of these references apply. According to traditional teachings, the Ethiopian monarchy was created by Menelik I, the son of the Queen of Sheba and King Solomon. The Kingdom of Axum was noted by historians in the first century AD and Christianity was introduced to the region in the fourth century. The Christian Church of Ethiopia, a branch of the Coptic Christian Church, was ruled by the Patriarch of Alexandria in Egypt. The Ethiopian Christians were cut off from the rest of Christianity by the Islamic takeover of North Africa in the mid-tenth century and did not reestablish contact for at least another 400 years. The *negus,* or emperor, of Ethiopia sent a message to the king of Portugal requesting help in fighting against Muslim encroachments, and Portuguese troops fought alongside the Ethiopians in the sixteenth century. However, the missionaries who accompanied the Portuguese turned out to follow a different branch of Christianity than the Ethiopians, Roman Catholicism, and they insisted that the Ethiopians convert. In 1632 a war broke out between the Ethiopian Christians and the Catholics, and the Catholic and Jesuit missionaries were expelled. Ethiopia fragmented into regional princedoms until Kassa Hailu united the empire in 1855 and crowned himself Emperor Tewodros II. His reign is usually recognized as the beginning of the modern era in Ethiopian history. Under pressure from Muslim invaders, Tewodros appealed to the British for help. When Queen Victoria did not reply, he imprisoned some British residents, including the consul, whereupon the British forces teamed with local warlords and stormed Tewodros' fortress in 1868. As soon as they breached the gates, Tewodros committed suicide, whereupon the British looted the country and carted off art treasures that ended up in European museums and collections. The British showed no interest in colonizing Ethiopia, but the Italians did. When Ethiopian troops defeated Italian forces at the Battle of Adowa in 1896, the Europeans accepted Ethiopia as an independent nation.

THE KING OF KINGS—From 1930 until 1974, Ethiopia was ruled by Emperor Haile Selassie. Born Tafari Makonnen in 1892, he was made *ras,* or prince, and given the position of crown prince, the heir apparent, in 1916. In the early 1920s, he abolished slavery, gained Ethiopia entry to the League of Nations, and toured Europe. When his aunt, the empress, died in 1930, he was crowned His Imperial Majesty, Emperor Haile Selassie I, King of Kings and Lord of Lords, Conquering Lion of the Tribe of Judah, Elect of God. In 1935, Benito Mussolini's Italian troops invaded Ethiopia and occupied the country, which Mussolini declared a province of Italy. Haile Selassie himself fought against the Italians, but ultimately he was forced to flee the country. In June 1936, he appeared at the General Assembly of the League of Nations in Geneva and gave a dramatic speech on behalf of the Ethiopian people in which he detailed the atrocities committed by the Italians, including the use of chemical weapons, and appealed to the world community to save his nation, concluding, "What reply shall I take back to my people?" Haile Selassie was instantly transformed into an international celebrity and a symbol of the war against Fascism. After British and Ethiopian troops drove out the Italians, he returned to Ethiopia in 1941 and, after World War II, Ethiopia became a charter member of the United Nations.

THE RELUCTANT GOD—Unbeknownst to Haile Selassie, thousands of miles away on the island of Jamaica, four ministers, inspired by his list of titles, created the Rastafarian movement, a religion that worshipped Haile Selassie as God incarnate. In 1961 a delegation of Rastafarians traveled to Ethiopia for the first time and met with the archbishop of the Ethiopian Orthodox Church, who told them that Haile Selassie considered himself a man just like them and that he would be upset if he learned that they considered him God. Far from being discouraged, the Rastafarians were convinced that this humility on Haile Selassie's part was proof of his divinity. In 1966 he agreed to visit Jamaica. When he landed at the international airport in Kingston on April 21, more than 100,000 Rastafarians swarmed all over the airfield and the official government welcoming ceremony had to be canceled. Haile Selassie had to be convinced that his life was not in danger before he would deplane. He was unable to persuade the Rastas that he was not God, but as a gesture he donated land in Ethiopia for the Rastafarians to establish a community.

In an attempt to free himself from dependence on the British after World War II, Haile Selassie turned to the United States for help. With the advent of the Cold War, the Americans were glad to oblige. In exchange, they took a World War II radio station, the Kagnew Station, in Asmara, Eritrea, which was then controlled by Ethiopia, and converted it into a major spy base for the National Security Agency. Between 1946 and 1975 more than two-thirds of U.S. military assistance to Africa went to Ethiopia, and the United States actively provided Haile Selassie with support in his counterinsurgency campaigns against the Eritreans and others.

THE DERGUE—In 1974, after a major drought, the aging Haile Selassie was overthrown by a military committee known as the Dergue ("Committee"). It is believed that the Dergue had Haile Selassie murdered in his bed the following year. The Dergue declared Ethiopia a Marxist military dictatorship. In the chaos that followed, Eritrean guerrillas gained control of their country and Somalia invaded southeastern Ethiopia, which was populated by ethnic Somalis. Until this point, the United States had been supporting Ethiopia and the Soviet Union had been supporting Somalia. Almost overnight the two superpowers switched sides. In December 1976, the leaders of the Dergue signed a military assistance deal with the Soviet Union and, with the help of Soviet arms and advisors and Cuban troops, the Somalis were defeated and the Eritreans driven into retreat.

In February 1977, Dergue member Lt. Colonel Mengistu Haile Mariam seized power after having the nation's two previous leaders executed. He then launched a reign of terror during which thousands of people were tortured and executed without trial. To eliminate support for insurgents, he ordered the poisoning of wells, the withholding of food aid during droughts, and the forced transfer of 600,000 people into resettlement camps. He also created neighborhood organizations, called *kebeles,* that were empowered to kill anyone suspected of opposing Mengistu. Before long, however, Mengistu was unable to handle the droughts, famines, and multiple liberation movements and he lost control. Guerrilla groups representing the Eritrean, Tigrayan, and other peoples joined forces to create the Ethiopian People's Revolutionary Democratic Front (EPRDF).

THE MAN—Meles Zenawi was born May 8, 1955, in Adwa, Tigray. He was a medical student at Addis Ababa University, but after two years he left in 1974 to join the Tigray People's Liberation Front, a hard-line Communist guerrilla group that saw as its model the Stalinist Albania of Enver Hoxha. In February and March 1990, by now the leader of the EPRDF, Meles visited London and Washington, D.C., and convinced the governments of the United Kingdom and the United States that he had renounced Marxism-Leninism and that if he took control of Ethiopia he would be amenable to Eritrean independence.

In May 1991, EPRDF troops reached the outskirts of the Ethiopian capital of Addis Ababa and waited for the outcome of negotiations that were taking place in London. By this time, Mengistu had fled to Zimbabwe, where he was offered sanctuary by fellow dictator Robert Mugabe. As Addis Ababa descended into chaos, the U.S. assistant secretary of state for African affairs, Herman Cohen, encouraged Meles and the EPRDF to enter the capital "to stabilize the situation," which they proceeded to do without hesitation.

The Ethiopians were glad to be rid of Mengistu, but the "situation" was not so simple. Traditionally, the capital, not to mention the central government itself, had been dominated by the Amhara people. Meles was a Tigrayan, an ethnic group from the far north of Ethiopia that made up only 6 percent of the nation's population. Protesters threw stones at the U.S. embassy and called the change of government "Cohen's coup." Many Ethiopians were also infuriated when Meles gave his blessing to Eritrean independence, which turned Ethiopia into a landlocked nation. Meles, who might have been satisfied to have secured independence for his Tigrayan people, now found himself the leader of the entire nation of Ethiopia (minus Eritrea). Although he pledged to turn Ethiopia into a multiparty democracy, staying in power was too hard to resist. Still, he knew that to keep the financial and military support of Europe and the United States, he needed to create an appearance of a multiethnic democracy. In regional elections in 1992, he outlawed the Oromo Liberation Front, which represented Ethiopia's largest ethnic group, the Oromos. By 1994 he was ready to put on a better show. Meles proudly bragged that thirty-nine different political organizations, representing all the major ethnic groups, took part in the June 5 election. In fact, what he had done was to create for each ethnic group a puppet party that supported his government. All of the real opposition parties boycotted the election. In the Ogaden region, where ethnic Somalis continued to wage a war of secession, the elections were not held at all.

WASTING THE LIVES OF HIS PEOPLE—In 1998 one of the most useless wars in modern history broke out between Ethiopia and Eritrea. When Eritrea gained its independence, there were three small areas where the border was left undefined. On May 6, 1998, a few soldiers from Eritrea crossed into the Badme region, one of the disputed zones, and engaged in a brief firefight with local militia in the Tigray Province of Ethiopia. Considering that the leaders of the two countries were once close allies, the incident should have been resolved peacefully and easily. But both Ethiopia's Meles and Eritrea's Isaias were facing

ON DECEMBER 12, 2000, DICTATORS ISAIAS AFWERKI AND MELES ZENAWI AGREE TO A PEACE AGREEMENT AFTER SUBJECTING THEIR RESPECTIVE PEOPLE TO A USELESS WAR.

AP Photo

major political problems at home, and both could use a war for their own benefit, even it would prove ruinous for their people. Meles, who was still viewed with resentment by many Ethiopians for giving away Eritrea, saw a chance to prove that he was a true Ethiopian patriot. Isaias whipped up similar patriotic sentiment to distract attention from the miserable state of the Eritrean economy. The fighting quickly escalated into a full-scale war, displacing hundreds of thousands of people and leaving tens of thousands of soldiers dead. In May 2000, Ethiopian troops cut one of the Eritrean army's main supply lines and occupied a quarter of Eritrea. The Eritreans retreated from the disputed zones and Ethiopia declared victory, ending the war.

However, although the killing ended, the conflict was not over. On December 12, 2000, the two sides, as part of the Algiers Agreement, agreed to binding arbitration in which an Eritrea–Ethiopia Boundary Commission would study the claims of both sides and decide the final borders. In April 2002, the Boundary Commission gave each country some of the disputed territory, but it awarded the Badme region to Eritrea. Meles, despite his earlier agreement to binding arbitration, refused to accept the decision and refused to return the territory to Eritrea. As of July 2006, it remains in Ethiopian hands.

In April 2001, student demonstrations demanding greater academic freedom and the re-

moval of armed police from campuses ignited simmering discontent in Addis Ababa with rising unemployment and deteriorating economic conditions. Soon there was widespread rioting, and security forces killed 130 people and imprisoned hundreds more.

On May 15, 2005, Ethiopia held parliamentary elections. The day of the voting passed
peacefully, but when the results were announced, trouble started. Meles' EPRDF claimed it
had won more than 300 of the 527 seats contested, while the leading opposition parties announced that they were leading in most constituencies. The next evening, Meles declared a
state of emergency and took control of all security forces. Demonstrations against election
fraud grew until June 8, the day that the official results were originally supposed to be announced. That day, police in Addis Ababa shot to death at least thirty-seven protestors and an
estimated 4,000 people were arrested. When the final results were released on July 8, they
showed the EPRDF with 327 seats. Protests continued until November when police killed
another forty-eight people and again made thousands of arrests. Among the 730 protesters
and opposition leaders still in jail in 2006 was the mayor-elect of Addis Ababa, Berhanu
Nega.

THE MEGA CORPORATION—Meles Zenawi is married to Azeb Mesfin, a member of parliament and the director of the Mega Corporation, which Meles created after assuming power. The corporation is involved in import-export, land development, publishing,
advertising, and other fields.

(Patrick Robert/Sygma/Corbis)

19.
PAUL BIYA—CAMEROON

THE NATION—As a political entity, the West African nation of Cameroon was patched together by European colonial powers. The population of more than sixteen million speaks 279 languages. Slightly more than half of Cameroonians are Christians, a quarter follow traditional belief systems, and about 22 percent are Muslims. There are approximately 260 distinct ethnic groups. Since achieving independence in 1960, Cameroon has been ruled by one party and only two presidents. Cameroon is Africa's largest producer of timber and it is the world's fifth-largest producer of the cocoa that goes into making chocolate. The nation has the reputation of being one of the most corrupt countries in the world and actually earned Transparency International's number-one ranking as corruption champion two years in a row, in 1998 and 1999.

PRE-BIYA—The Germans claimed Cameroon as a colony in 1884. Following World War I, the Treaty of Versailles divided the colony between France and Great Britain. The French granted East Cameroon independence on January 1, 1960. On October 1, 1961, the

British gave up control of West Cameroon and it joined East Cameroon to form a single country. French-educated Ahmadou Ahidjo, a Muslim from the north, took over as president and stayed in power for twenty-two years until he unexpectedly resigned on November 6, 1982, apparently because his French doctors told him that he had a terminal disease. Ahidjo did retain his position as head of Cameroon's lone political party. He was replaced as president by the prime minister, Paul Biya, a Roman Catholic from the Beti ethnic group in the south. Ahidjo did not have a terminal illness, but by the time he realized this, Biya had squeezed him out of the party leadership and forced him to flee the country. Ahidjo eventually died in Senegal in 1989.

THE MAN—Born February 13, 1933, Biya studied in Paris and received a degree in public law. After working for two years in the presidential palace, he became director of the office of the minister of education and then moved up to secretary-general of the Education Ministry. After serving as secretary-general of the presidency, Biya was named prime minister by Ahidjo in June 1975.

At the time that Biya assumed office in 1992, Cameroon enjoyed a booming economy with solid exports of cocoa, timber, and coffee and a growing petroleum industry. Thanks to corruption and ethnic cronyism, Biya destroyed the economy. While Biya and his friends grew rich on oil money, the Cameroonian economy shrank for nine straight years beginning in 1987.

In January 1984, Biya stood for election for president and managed to win 99.98 percent of the vote. It is not known what happened to the two-hundredths of one percent of the voters who managed to vote against him. To be on the safe side, Biya eliminated the position of prime minister so that no rival politician could create his own power base. Three months after the election, he put down a mutiny by the mostly Islamic Republican Guard, which he blamed on Ahidjo, who was condemned to death in absentia. To demonstrate that he was not a dictator, Biya changed the name of the only legal political party from the National Cameroonian Union to the Cameroon People's Democratic Movement (RDPC). In 1988, he was reelected president, although his vote percentage slipped to only 98.75 percent.

CONTROLLING THE OPPOSITION—Under pressure at home and from abroad, Biya legalized opposition parties in 1990, but strikes and pro-democracy protests in 1991 left more than 100 dead. Forty-eight parties took part in March 1992 legislative elections. The RDPC won 88 of the 180 seats and, with the help of sympathetic small parties, cobbled together a working majority. Presidential elections had been scheduled for a year later, but Biya moved them up to October 1992 to give the opposition less time to organize.

The U.S.-based National Democratic Institute for International Affairs arrived in Cameroon to help train election officials, but stayed to observe the election and to watch in dismay as the government ignored normal democratic procedures. "It would not be an exaggeration," the observers would later report, "to suggest that this election system was designed to fail." The government-controlled television gave Biya 142 minutes of time to present his case, while allowing the opposition parties a combined total of 12 minutes. Names of eligible voters were crossed off the registry and there were widespread reports of multiple voting and voting by underage residents. In some areas known to be anti-Biya, polling sites were moved without warning to reduce turnout. The territory of Rey-Bouba in the district of Mayo Rey blocked all political party pollwatchers from entering. Results by polling site were never published.

The election took place on October 11. A week later, George Achu Mofor, the governor of East Province, resigned to protest the way the central government had forced him to use any means necessary to ensure a Biya victory in his province. The election results were announced on October 23. Biya won with 39.9 percent of the vote. John Fru Ndi, the English-speaking head of the Social Democratic Front, was given 35.9 percent, an affront which landed him in house arrest; and a third major candidate, former prime minister Bello Bouba Maigari, won 19.2 percent. Demonstrations in English-speaking Western Cameroon were so large that Biya imposed a state of emergency in the region and ordered mass arrests of opposition supporters. Despite the dubious aspects of the election, the French government congratulated Biya on his victory. At the time, the French oil company Elf Aquitaine monopolized oil exploration off the coast of Cameroon.

In 1996, students at the University of Cameroon's Yaounde 1 campus boycotted classes to protest a hike in fees that was so broad that it included usage charges both for the library and for toilets. When the strike spread to other campuses, the government sent in troops who beat a student to death. By the time of the 1997 parliamentary elections, Biya had learned his lesson. His party manipulated the voting much more efficiently and gained a clear majority of the seats. In the presidential election later that year, Biya claimed to win 92.6 percent of the votes.

By this same time, Biya was cracking down on privately owned newspapers, and arresting and imprisoning journalists. In one particularly notorious case, Pius Njame, the editor of an independent French-language newspaper, reported that Biya had suffered a "malaise" and a possible heart attack while attending the 1997 Cameroon Cup soccer final. Njame was convicted of "spreading false news" and served ten months in prison.

THE PIPELINE—Although Cameroon attracted the attention of the oil industry, its reserves were relatively limited. But the industry had other plans for Cameroon. Northeast of

Cameroon, the landlocked nation of Chad was found to have plenty of oil. A consortium of ExxonMobil, Royal Dutch Shell, and Elf Aquitaine drew up plans for a $3.7 billion project that would sink 300 wells in Chad and run the oil to the Atlantic coast via a 665-mile-long pipeline they would build across Cameroon. Because the regimes of both Biya and Chad's Idriss Déby were notorious abusers of human rights, and because of the high potential for environmental degradation, Shell and Elf pulled out of the project. With billions of dollars of profits on the line, ExxonMobil found two new partners, Chevron and Petronas of Malaysia, and plunged ahead in promoting the plan. Construction of the pipeline, which began in October 2000, threatened the destruction of the livelihoods of 100,000 Bagyeli Pygmies living in the region and in some cases their eviction. The World Bank backed the project, making it the bank's single-largest investment in sub-Saharan Africa, and the pipeline was completed in July 2003.

Meanwhile, human rights groups were reporting systemic torture, the kidnapping and disappearance of political dissidents, and a legal code that permitted forced female genital mutilation and allowed rapists to avoid prosecution if they marry their victims. Biya keeps such tight control over the country that his office approves all public appointments all the way down to village police officers. In the words of lawyer Charles Taku, "To get such a job or a business license . . . you have to show that you support the president actively, that you love him and his party."

HUMAN RIGHTS—THE VANISHING ACT—In 2002, Paul Biya caught a break. Cameroon happened to be serving a two-year term as a member of the United Nations Security Council when U.S. president George W. Bush decided to invade Iraq and needed the support of Security Council members. Biya, a longtime friend of France's president, Jacques Chirac, found himself being wooed by Bush and visited him in the White House the day that the United States began its bombing of Baghdad. U.S. secretary of state Colin Powell praised Cameroon as "a place of stability" and promised that "we will do everything we can to strengthen the government." The criticisms of Biya's human rights record, which had been catalogued in the reports of Powell's own State Department, were swept aside as if they had never happened.

CREATIVE ELECTION RIGGING—In 2004, Biya faced a new presidential election and came up with a new and novel tactic in the world of rigged elections. In previous elections he had perfected the arts of suppressing opposition campaigning and stacking the voter rolls. But he faced criticism from international election-monitoring groups. In July 2004, he signed a $400,000 deal with the Washington, D.C., law and lobbying firm of

PAUL BIYA AND
SECOND WIFE CHANTAL
Jacky Naegelen/Reuters/Corbis

Patton Boggs to improve Cameroonian ties with the United States at a time when the State Department had said that Biya's security forces had "committed numerous unlawful killings and were responsible for torture, beatings and other abuses," and that the government "continued to arrest and detain arbitrarily various opposition politicians." One of the Patton Boggs lobbyists, former U.S. Representative Greg Laughlin, a Texas Democrat, put together a bipartisan observer group called the U.S. Association of Former Members of Congress. With Biya's government covering the bills, the Association flew in six ex-congressmen, who observed the October 11 presidential election in which Biya claimed a 71 percent landslide, declared it a free election, and flew home. One of the former congressmen, Ronnie Shows, a Democrat from Mississippi, enthused, "This is what democracy is about." Another observer group from the Commonwealth nations, led by former Canadian prime minister Joe Clark, saw the election process differently. They said that the registration process, which the U.S. group had arrived too late to observe, had "missed a considerable portion of the voting-age population of Cameroon". "We ran into swarms of people who had been declared ineligible to vote," said Clark. The Catholic Bishop's Conference of Cameroon also accused Biya's government of vote-rigging.

THE ECTOPLASM—Biya's first wife, Jeanne-Irene, died in 1992, leaving behind two sons and a daughter. Two years later the sixty-one-year-old Biya married a twenty-four-year-old named Chantal and began spending an increasing amount of time on vacation. Cameroon's leading novelist, the late Mongo Beti, once described Biya as an "ectoplasm" and another time as a "zombie." Because Beti also had harsh words for John Fru Ndi, Biya let him get away with it, although Beti was roughed up by police at demonstrations.

(AP Photo/David Longstreath)

20.
CHOUMMALY SAYASONE—LAOS

THE NATION—A quiet, landlocked Buddhist nation in Southeast Asia, Laos is a true backwater. Many of the country's political and historical developments have been the result of the ripple effects of events in neighboring countries: Thailand, their "cousins" to the west; China, the monster to the north; and Vietnam, the tumultuous and war-ravaged nation to the east. One of these outside influences, Communism, reached Laos after World War II, took hold in the 1970s, and has yet to leave. Only half of Laos' population of about six million is ethnically Lao. The rest belong to one of about seventy different ethnic groups and tribes. About 60 percent of Laotians follow Theraveda Buddhism. Despite being officially banned by the Communist government, spirit cults are also popular. Laos is the world's third-largest producer of opium, behind Afghanistan and Burma.

OUTSIDE FORCES—Laos' Golden Age occurred during the fifty-seven-year reign of King Surinyavongsā (1637–1694), during which his kingdom of Lan Xang was a center of religion and the arts. Surinyavongsā had only one son, Chao Rachabut, whom he ordered executed when he was found guilty of adultery. This left an unclear succession when Surinyavongsā finally died, and Laos was victimized by factionalism and foreign intervention from all sides. In the late nineteenth century, King Unkham, threatened with takeover by either the Siamese (Thai) or the French, chose the French, who bundled the country into French Indochina. Laos had never been mapped, so, in conjunction with the British, the Chinese, and the Thais, France mapped Laos in 1896 and 1897 and created the basic boundaries that still exist. Although the French did impose the *corvée* system of ten days' forced labor a year, for the most part they ignored Laos, considering it little more than a buffer zone against British influence in Southeast Asia. Laos remained reasonably unaffected by World War II until 1945, when the Japanese forced King Sīsavāngvong to declare independence from the French. The country was descending into the beginnings of a multisided civil war when Japan surrendered, ending World War II.

The French regained their role as the dominant player in Laos, but nationalist forces and even the Chinese army entered the fray. Communism was a hard sell in Laos because, unlike in China and Vietnam, the farmers, who made up 90 percent of the population, owned their own land and there were no landlords to rail against. Still, the Communists gained a foothold in the ethnic minority regions and in 1950 started a Lao Communist organization that came to be known as the Pathēt Lao ("Lao Homeland"). The Pathēt Lao operated as a subsidiary of the Vietnamese Communists. Laos gained full sovereignty in 1953, but by that time the Pathēt Lao already controlled part of the country. Before long, Laos, despite its relative remoteness and lack of economic importance, was swept up in the Cold War and, more specifically in the surrogate war that the United States and the Soviet Union were fighting in Vietnam. The Communist North Vietnamese, who had occupied northeastern Laos during their fight against the French, used Laotian territory to deploy more than 75,000 troops. In addition, the Vietnamese built and maintained the Ho Chi Minh Trail to supply Communist forces in South Vietnam and Cambodia. Almost all of the Trail ran through eastern Laos. The Chinese established their own military zone of influence in the northwest. And then there were the Americans. The United States began training the Royal Lao Army and an army of the Hmong ethnic group in 1959. U.S. involvement in Laos was considered a "Secret War," not publicly acknowledged by the government, and American soldiers and CIA agents who died in Laos were listed as having died in Vietnam. Of course it was no secret to the Laotians. Between 1964 and 1973, the United States dropped two million tons of bombs on Laos, one thousand pounds of explosives for each man, woman, and child in the country. In Xieng Khouang Province, the figure reached two tons per person. The Americans dropped an average of one planeload of bombs on Laos every eight minutes, every day for nine years. To avoid the bombing, many Laotian villagers were forced to live for years in caves and to do their farming at night.

COMMUNISM—When Cambodia and Vietnam fell to the Communists in 1975, it was just a matter of time before Laos followed. The Lao People's Democratic Republic was declared on December 2, 1975. The Pathēt Lao harshly repressed the Hmong and anyone else considered unsympathetic to its regime, including the royal family, and tens of thousands of people were imprisoned in "reeducation" camps. Although the Pathēt Lao government received aid from the Soviet Union, Vietnam, and China, under Communism the Laotian economy collapsed and an estimated 400,000 Laotians, about 12 percent of the population, fled to Thailand.

More than thirty years after the Pathēt Lao takeover, Laos remains a one-party state that did not even bother to promulgate a constitution until 1991. By 2005, of the eleven members of the ruling Politburo, eight were active or former military officers. Eventually, the Politburo adopted the "Chinese Model," liberalizing their economy while centralizing political power and aggressively suppressing dissent. Their efforts have met with only moderate success. In 1999, the government released a report that showed that in the valley around the capital of Vientiane, remittances from relatives abroad was a greater source of income for people than agriculture, wages, or business.

From the time the Communists took power in 1975 until his death in 1992, Kaysone Phomvihane, who had led the Lao People's Revolutionary Party (LPRP) since 1955, was the head of the Laotian government, first as prime minister and then as president. Kaysone was something of a mystery figure who refused interviews and was rarely seen, even by the people he ruled. In the late 1980s, he emerged from isolation, traveled around the country, spoke with foreign journalists, and even visited three countries: China, Japan, and Sweden. When he died, General Khamtay Siphandone was promoted to party chairman.

The details of Khamtay's life are as obscure as those of his predecessor. Born in 1924 in Champasak Province near the border with Cambodia and Thailand, it is thought that he spent the World War II years in India and that after the war he was a postal worker. He joined the Lao Issara (Free Lao) movement in 1946 and went with the Pathēt Lao when it split with the Lao Issara in 1949. Like most Communist leaders, he patiently lumbered his way to the top. In 1954 he was appointed chief of staff of the Lao People's Liberation Army, and in 1957 he was selected for membership in the Central Committee of the Lao People's Party, the precursor of the LPRP. In charge of party propaganda and training, he was promoted to supreme commander of the army in 1961. He gradually moved up in the party hierarchy and when the Pathēt Lao took charge of the country, he became minister of national defense, a post he held until 1991. He was also deputy prime minister until moving up to party chief and president.

THE LATEST LUMP—Khamtay retired at the age of eighty-two and was replaced as the head of the LPRP on March 21, 2006, by Vice President Choummaly Sayasone, a three-star general who acceded to the presidency as well in June. The son of a farmer from the remote province of Attapeu in southern Laos, Choummaly joined the Pathēt Lao guerrillas in 1954 at the age of about eighteen. He received military training in the Soviet Union and in Vietnam, retaining particularly close ties to the Vietnamese Communists. After working his way up through the military and party hierarchies, he joined the ruling Politburo in 1981 and became minister of defense in 1991. He moved up to deputy prime minister in 1998 and vice president in 2001. A lifelong friend of Khamtay, Choummaly is considered a conservative even by Laotian standards.

The LPRP is the only legal party in Laos. All candidates for National Assembly are chosen by a committee appointed by the Assembly itself. Voting is compulsory. In March 2006, the party elected a woman to the Politburo for the first time. The government, dominated by ethnic Lao, operates a widespread surveillance network and monitors cellphone and e-mail communications.

CRIME, LAOTIAN STYLE—Many criminal offenses in Laos are so general that they can cover almost anything. For example, in Laos it is illegal to "propagate information or opinions that weaken the state," "distort party or state policies," "slander the state," import a publication "offensive to the national culture," "disturb the peace and happiness of the community," report "misleading news," and participate in acts that cause "turmoil or social instability" or "create division among the people." In recent years, people have been arrested for attempting to organize a pro-democracy demonstration (ten years in prison) and importing Bibles (detained for a few days). Premarital cohabitation is also illegal, as is marrying a foreigner without governmental permission, which often entails paying bribes. In fact, having sexual relations with a foreigner at all is illegal.

Arrestees are allowed to be held without charge or trial for up to one year. There are only fifty attorneys in the country, and during criminal trials defendants must present oral arguments themselves. There are no juries and it is generally believed that verdicts are decided before the trials are held.

21.
A SPECIAL CASE: GEORGE W. BUSH—UNITED STATES OF AMERICA

"If this were a dictatorship, it'd be a heck of a lot easier, just so long as I'm the dictator."

PRESIDENT-ELECT GEORGE W. BUSH
DECEMBER 18, 2000

"It takes a lot of degeneration before a country falls into dictatorship, but we should avoid these ends by avoiding these beginnings."

SUPREME COURT JUSTICE SANDRA DAY O'CONNOR
MARCH 9, 2006

George Bush is not a dictator. He is not a dictator because the United States holds reasonably fair elections and presidents are limited to two terms. The U.S. system for electing presidents is flawed, but, by international standards, it falls within the range of acceptability. In the

United States it is possible to criticize the president, even on national television, and not be arrested. This is a freedom not available to the citizens of the countries described in the other chapters of this book. If George W. Bush was really a dictator, Harriet Miers would be a Supreme Court justice and six major U.S. ports would be run by the royal family of Dubai. George Bush is not a dictator. However, he does use some of the same tactics that real dictators use.

THE BEACON OF DEMOCRACY—The United States declared its independence in 1776, established a constitution in 1787, and enacted the Bill of Rights in 1791. Among other things, the Bill of Rights ensures freedom of speech, freedom of the press, freedom of religion, freedom of assembly, the right to bear arms, protection from unreasonable searches and seizures, the right to trial by jury and the right to counsel, and protection from cruel or unusual punishment. The rights set forth in the Bill of Rights became a model for aspiring democracies and a goal for oppressed people around the world. The U.S. Congress and the states abolished slavery in 1865, established the direct election of senators in 1913, and gave women the right to vote in 1920. In an attempt to prevent the creation of a dictatorship, Congress and the states in 1951 limited presidents from serving more than two terms. In 1961, citizens of the District of Colombia were given the right to vote in presidential elections, and in 1964 poll taxes were outlawed. In 1971, the voting age was lowered to eighteen.

THE DYNASTY—The United States has a reputation as a nation in which anyone, regardless of their economic background, can rise to the top and become president. In recent times, both Ronald Reagan and Bill Clinton came from humble families. However, the United States also has a tradition of family dynasties in politics. The second and sixth presidents of the United States, John Adams and John Quincy Adams, were father and son. The thirty-second president, Franklin D. Roosevelt, was the cousin of the twenty-sixth president, Theodore Roosevelt. Two of John F. Kennedy's brothers were elected to the Senate and two of their sons were elected to the House of Representatives. In this sense, the Bush family dynasty is nothing new. What makes their dynasty unusual is their ability to put into the White House a father and son only eight years apart, thus allowing members and supporters of the first Bush administration to continue shaping national policy in the second Bush administration.

THE GEORGE W. BUSH AGENDA—George W. Bush has repeated so many times that the 9/11 terrorist attacks shaped his presidency that there is a tendency to forget that before they took place he had already been in office for seven and a half months—more than enough time to have expressed and begun enacting an agenda of his choosing. In his campaign he had stressed that as governor of Texas he had reached out to Democrats. Considering that he had just ascended to the presidency despite receiving fewer votes than his opponent and considering that the Senate was split 50–50 between Republicans and Democrats, it was assumed by most observers that President Bush would work closely with the opposition party. However, it became clear almost immediately that he had no intention of doing so, that he and Vice President Dick Cheney and their executive branch advisors had a well-laid-out agenda, and that they expected the Republican leadership in Congress to promote that agenda. Two aspects of that agenda stand out: his foreign policy was based on unilateralism and his domestic policy was based on helping large corporations.

UNILATERALISM—Call it unilateralism or just old-fashioned isolationism, President Bush quickly launched a campaign to have the United States withdraw from various international treaties and agreements. By the end of July 2001, he had announced his opposition to ratification of the Comprehensive Nuclear Test Ban Treaty, joined Somalia as the only countries to refuse to sign the Convention on the Rights of the Child, backed out of the Kyoto Protocol on global warming, opposed the UN treaty to curb international trafficking in small arms and light weapons, announced his intention to withdraw from the 1972 Anti-Ballistic Missile Treaty, and rejected an international treaty to facilitate enforcement of the 1972 Biological Weapons Convention banning the use of germ warfare and biological weapons. He also announced his opposition to the International Criminal Court, an issue that would develop into an obsession with the Bush administration. Bush ultimately demanded that every country in the world sign a bilateral immunity agreement that protected U.S. citizens, including civilians, from prosecution by the International Criminal Court and threatened the cutoff of military aid to any nation that refused to do so. On August 3, 2001, he signed into law the American Servicemembers Protection Act that authorized the use of military force to liberate any citizen being held by the Court. This came as a shock to the Dutch in particular since the International Criminal Court is located in The Hague. On July 1, 2003, Bush did in fact halt military aid to thirty-five countries who refused to sign immunity agreements, including Brazil, Costa Rica, Peru, Uruguay, South Africa, Bulgaria, and Lithuania. He also issued exemptions for forty countries including Israel, Egypt, Jordan, Albania, Uganda, Nigeria, Japan, South Korea, and the members of NATO. On December 7, 2004, Bush signed into law the Nethercutt Amendment that expanded the punishment for nonsigners to include the withholding of aid from the Economic Support Fund, including money to be used for fighting terrorism and drug trafficking.

HELPING THE RICH—No world leader or politician will ever come out and say that the goal of his policies is to help rich people. Instead they use phrases like "stimulate the economy," "provide jobs," "encourage growth," and "increase energy independence." At the Al Smith Dinner to benefit Catholic charities on October 19, 2000, George W. Bush joked, "This is an impressive crowd: the haves and have-mores. Some people call you the elite. I call you my base." It was a good line, but when Bush was inaugurated as president of the United States three months later, it turned out that he wasn't joking. On the first day of his presidency, Bush issued a moratorium on the enforcement of all health, safety, and environmental regulations issued by Bill Clinton during the final days of his term of office. During the first sixty days of his presidency, Bush suspended the "roadless rule" that protected almost sixty million acres of forests from logging and road-building; signed four anti-union executive orders including the prohibition of labor agreements at federal construction sites; repealed ergonomic regulations designed to protect workers from repetitive-stress injuries; issued an executive order stopping Northwest Airlines mechanics from going on strike; abandoned his campaign pledge to regulate carbon dioxide emissions from coal-fired power plants; and overturned a regulation reducing the allowable level of arsenic in drinking water. Then he pulled out of the Kyoto treaty regulating greenhouse gases, including carbon dioxide. On May 16, 2001, Vice President Cheney released his National Energy Policy Development Group task force's National Energy Policy that called for large increases in subsidies for the oil and gas, coal, and nuclear power industries, as well as further weakening of environmental protections. One week later, Congress passed Bush's $1.3 trillion tax cut program. More than half of the cuts went to the richest 10 percent of the population and more than 15 percent of the cuts benefited the richest one-tenth of one percent of Americans.

While most Americans were still reeling from the shock of the 9/11 attacks, the Bush administration continued its aid to the rich. Before the year 2001 was out, Bush had repealed the "responsible contractor rule" that required officers in charge of awarding federal contracts to take into account a company's record of complying with laws relating to worker safety, civil rights, and environmental protection.

President Bush's aid to the rich did not end after his first year in office. For example, two provisions of his original tax cuts dealing with the lifting of limits on itemized deductions and personal exemptions took effect in January 2006, reducing government revenues by at least $150 billion over the next ten years. According to the Tax Policy Center, a joint venture of the Urban Institute and the Brookings Institution, 97 percent of the savings from these cuts will go to the 3.7 percent of households making more than $200,000 a year and only one-tenth of one percent will go to households with an annual income of less than $100,000. In fact, more than half of the savings will go to households with annual incomes of more than $1 million.

HUMAN RIGHTS IN THE UNITED STATES—Most dictators, when they limit people's rights, claim that they have to do so for reasons of national security. For Kim Jong-il or Than Shwe or any other dictator, there is always an "Other," an enemy that is threatening their country and against whom the citizens of the nation must rally. Often there really is such an enemy. The existence of this enemy, whether real or exaggerated, serves as the dictator's excuse to limit or eliminate democracy in his country and to abuse those people he considers a threat to his power. The best kind of enemies, like "imperialists," or "neocolonialists" or people of another religion, are those who can be counted on to continue being there for all of the foreseeable future, thus justifying the permanent abrogation of human rights.

For George W. Bush, the enemy that will not go away in the foreseeable future is Terrorists. Because Islamist terrorists did kill almost 3,000 people in the United States in 2001, there is a tendency for many Americans to trust the president of the United States to do whatever he wants. Unfortunately, President Bush has used his War on Terrorism as an excuse to commit human rights abuses that his own State Department condemns. Since 1977 the U.S. State Department has issued an annual report on the human rights practices of the various nations of the world. The edition of *Country Reports on Human Rights Practices* that was released in March 2006 covered 196 countries. The State Department's Bureau of Democracy, Human Rights, and Labor evaluates each nation based on standards divided into eighteen sections or subsections. The State Department does not issue a report on the United States. However, it is worth evaluating the United States by the same standards by which it evaluates others. In most of the categories, the United States maintains an exemplary record. But there are also seven categories in which George W. Bush engages in practices that his own State Department criticizes when they occur in Iran or Cuba or any other country.

Section 3—Government Corruption and Transparency

> *"Top ruling party officials and businessmen supporting the ruling party received priority in distribution of the country's resources . . ."*
> 2006 STATE DEPARTMENT COUNTRY REPORT ON ZIMBABWE

The Halliburton Company provides products and services to the petroleum and energy industries. Halliburton's engineering and construction subsidiary, Kellogg Brown & Root (KBR), services the energy industry and works on government infrastructure projects. Dick Cheney served as secretary of defense under the first President Bush, George W. Bush's father. In this position, he awarded contracts worth almost $9 million to the Halliburton Company to study how to turn over support for military operations, such as providing food and janitorial services, to a private company. In August 1992, Halliburton was awarded a contract to actually perform these services. From 1995 until he retired to run for vice president in May 2000, Dick Cheney was the chairman and/or chief executive officer of Halliburton. During Cheney's tenure at Halliburton, the company and its subsidiaries did business with the dictatorships of Iraq, Iran, Libya, and Burma, among others. As Cheney put it in a speech to the CATO Institute on June 23, 1998, "The good Lord didn't see fit to put oil and gas only where there are democratic regimes friendly to the United States." In the spring of 2000, Halliburton gave Cheney permission to serve as the head of George W. Bush's vice-presidential search committee. After investigating several candidates, Cheney chose—himself. After he was elected vice president, Cheney was given a $33.7 million retirement package. He continued to hold 433,000 stock options in Halliburton, but two days before being sworn in he signed a Gift Trust Agreement giving after-tax profits from the future sales of his shares to three charities.

Halliburton has reaped enormous rewards during the presidency of George W. Bush. It received $37 million to build prison camps at Guantánamo Bay and $100 million to build a new U.S. embassy in Kabul. While Congress was debating whether to give President Bush the authority to invade Iraq, the army awarded Halliburton a $7 billion no-bid cost-plus contract to extinguish oil fires that might occur during the invasion. Once the United States began its occupation of Iraq, Halliburton hit the jackpot. It received $13.5 billion to provide logistical support for U.S. troops that included the building of prisoner of war camps and support for the search for nonexistent weapons of mass destruction, $2.4 billion to rebuild Iraq's oil infrastructure, and another $1.2 billion to continue oil industry work in southern Iraq. This last contract demonstrates the advantages of being friendly with the party in power. Parsons Corporation also wanted a piece of the oil infrastructure action. Instead of making Halliburton and Parsons bid against each other, the Bush administration gave southern Iraq to Halliburton and northern Iraq to Parsons. One of the most outrageous Iraq-related no-bid contracts was the $45 million given to WorldCom to create a small, temporary cellphone network in Iraq *after* WorldCom had been exposed in the largest accounting fraud scandal in history. WorldCom had no experience in the cellphone field and companies that really were in the business were not informed that the contract even existed until after it had been awarded.

After Hurricane Katrina devastated the city of New Orleans and other parts of Louisiana and Mississippi in August 2005, more than 700 contracts valued at $500,000 or more were awarded by the Federal Emergency Management Administration (FEMA). More than half of these were awarded without competitive bidding.

"In practice the government occasionally denied access to information, citing reasons of confidentiality or national security."
2006 State Department country report on Cambodia

George W. Bush showed a penchant for governmental secrecy even before he became president of the United States. During his first term as governor of Texas, he created a task force made up of business and environmental leaders to deal with air pollution caused by outdated facilities. But when the Clean Air Responsibility Enterprise Committee began to meet, the members discovered that petrochemical executives and state regulators, at the suggestion of Bush, had already held a series of private meetings and drafted a proposal, which, except for minor modifications, would become state policy. Because these meetings were unofficial, the public was not allowed access to documents that described what was discussed. However, according to Public Research Works, employees, lawyers, lobbyists, and family members of the companies that attended the meetings would contribute $1 million to George W. Bush's presidential campaign.

Given this bit of history, it was not surprising that one of the first actions Bush took as president was to create a fourteen-member National Energy Policy Development Group to be headed by Vice President Cheney and to include eight cabinet members. The executive branch would ultimately fight a four-year court battle to keep secret the names of people who met with this task force and what was discussed at meetings of the group. On May 17, 2001, Cheney's task force issued a report calling for expanded drilling and industry-backed tax breaks. The General Accounting Office (GAO), the investigative arm of Congress in charge of monitoring how the U.S. government spends its money, requested documents relating to the work of the energy task force as part of its inquiry into how the Enron Corporation, the leading contributor to George W. Bush's presidential campaign, influenced the formation of government policy. Cheney refused to comply. David M. Walker, the head of the General Accounting Office, accused the executive branch of making Cheney the head of the National Energy Policy Development Group for the very reason that he could claim executive privilege and thus avoid congressional oversight. In February 2002, the GAO filed suit against Cheney for refusing to turn over his records. It was the first time in its eighty-year history that the GAO had sued a member of the executive branch. It was not alone. The conservative public-interest group Judicial Watch had already requested the documents through the Freedom of Information Act, while the more liberal Natural Resources Defense Council had filed suit over related documents held by the Department of Energy. As court rulings see-sawed between Cheney's side and that of the document seekers, the Bush administration became nervous and acknowledged that Enron executives had met six times with members of the task force, and that one of those meetings was a one-on-one session between Vice President Cheney and Enron chairman Kenneth Lay on April 17. When a federal judge forced the Energy Department to reveal some documents, they showed that Energy Secretary Spencer Abraham had refused a request to meet with a coalition of thirty environmental groups because of his "busy schedule." However, in the days that followed, he did find the time to meet with the executives of a half-dozen oil and gas companies, a half-dozen nuclear power corporations, and a half-dozen utility companies.

Eventually, John D. Bates, a Bush-appointed federal district judge, dismissed the GAO's suit on the basis that only a house of Congress or a congressional committee could file such a claim. The suit brought by Judicial Watch, which was later joined by the Sierra Club, was accepted by the Supreme Court, but not without controversy. It seems that between the time the Supreme Court agreed to hear the case and the time it actually came before the Court, Vice President Cheney went duck hunting with one of the Supreme Court justices, Antonin Scalia. Scalia refused to recuse himself from the case, claiming that he "never hunted in the same blind with the Vice President." Scalia voted with the majority to send the case back to an appeals court, which, in May 2005, ruled unanimously that Cheney's involvement with the task force was part of his role as vice president and so he could keep secret the details of his meetings.

On March 23, 2001, only five weeks after assuming the presidency, President Bush ordered the National Archives not to release to the public 68,000 pages of records from the presidency of Ronald Reagan. Under the Presidential Records Act of 1978, the documents were supposed to have been made available to the public after January 20, 2001, twelve years after Reagan left the White House. Bush also kept sealed the papers of Reagan's vice president, who happened to be Bush's father. On November 1, 2001, George W. Bush signed an executive order that went even further. This time he gave former presidents and former vice presidents, and their families after they die, the right to continue preventing the release of their papers. Not only that, but, according to Bush's executive order, even if an ex-president wants to release his papers to the public, the sitting president has the right to bar their release anyway.

After the 9/11 terrorist attacks, the Bush administration raised its level of secrecy even higher. President Bush announced that because of the threat of leaks, he was limiting the sharing with Congress of information about military operations and law enforcement to eight senior House and Senate leaders, and that they would be forbidden to pass on reports to other members of Congress, including those who belonged to the committees responsible for overseeing the activities of the Pentagon, law enforcement, and the State Department. His administration also convinced the National Archives to sign secret agreements with the CIA and the Air Force to remove tens of thousands of pages of historical documents from access to researchers, including many from the 1950s. The agreements required archives employees to refrain from explaining to researchers why the documents had been removed. Attorney General John Ashcroft also told federal officials that the Justice Department was prepared to help them resist Freedom of Information Act requests. On March 25, 2003, President Bush signed an executive order delaying until the end of 2006 the scheduled release of millions of government documents that were supposed to be declassified because they were twenty-five years old. In March 2004, Bush gave the secretaries of Agriculture and Health and Human Services, for the first time, the power to seal records which had previously been open, including data on auto safety, contamination of drinking water, and the sites of potential chemical hazards in communities.

The Bush administration's obsession with secrecy extended to investigations into the terrorist attacks of September 11, 2001. President Bush opposed the creation of an independent commission to study the background and details of the attacks, but on November 27, 2002, he reluctantly signed into law funding for the National Commission on Terrorist Attacks upon the United States, commonly known as the 9/11 Commission. But in a move that would become familiar, he added in an accompanying signing statement that he would withhold from the Commission "information the disclosure of which could impair foreign relations, the national security, the deliberative processes of the Executive, or the performance of the Executive's constitutional duties," a series of exceptions so broad that they could cover almost anything. The main source of the narrative leading up to the attacks is based on statements made by the man who planned the attacks, Khalid Sheikh Mohammed—sort of. The Bush administration refused to allow members of the 9/11 Commission to interview Mohammed and nine other captured members of al-Qaeda. Instead the Commission members had to submit written questions and were given in return answers that supposedly came from them. The Commission was not even allowed to question the interrogators who questioned Khalid Sheikh Mohammed and the others. Only members of the Bush administration know if the answers really came from the captured detainees.

Section If—Arbitrary Interference with Privacy, Family, Home, or Correspondence

> *"Security forces monitored the social activities of citizens, entered homes and offices, monitored telephone conversations, and opened mail without court authorization."*

2006 STATE DEPARTMENT COUNTRY REPORT ON IRAN

President Bush signed into law the USA PATRIOT Act on October 26, 2001. Passed in haste in the wake of the terrorist attacks of September 11, 2001, the Act greatly broadened the government's right to spy on American citizens and residents with the goals of detecting planned terrorist acts before they could be initiated and of identifying supporters of anti-American terrorism. However, in practice, the Bush administration used the powers it gained from the Act to also spy on people and groups not related to terrorism. Section 213 of the USA PATRIOT Act authorized sneak-and-peek search warrants, also known as covert entry search warrants and surreptitious entry search warrants. These allow law enforcement officers to enter a private premise without the permission or the knowledge of the owner or the occupant. In a July 5, 2005, letter, the Justice Department admitted that only 11.8 percent of approved sneak-and-peek warrants had been used in terrorism-related cases.

Some of the Bush administration's spying borders on being silly. In an FBI PowerPoint presentation to a Law School class at the University of Texas, Austin, on March 8, 2006, the group Food Not Bombs was listed as being on a "Terrorist Watch List." The group serves vegetarian food to homeless and hungry people. It seems that the FBI definition of terrorism includes violence against property. Because Food Not Bombs is affiliated with another group, members of which have destroyed property, they too qualified as a possible terrorist group, and U.S. government funds have been used to track their activities. In another case, ten protestors in Houston passed out peanut butter and jelly sandwiches to Halliburton employees as they left work at company headquarters in June 2004. They were trying to call attention to the fact that Halliburton was being accused of overcharging for food contracts in Iraq. The protest was included in the Pentagon's "terrorism threat warning process." Apparently, the U.S. Army's Counterintelligence Field Activity (CIFA) division, which is in charge of tracking threats and terrorist plots against military installations and personnel inside the United States, includes Halliburton and other private companies in its web of protection because they are military contractors. CIFA has also monitored and, in some cases, infiltrated, groups such as the Quakers, the Catholic Workers, and Greenpeace. In June 2002, the FBI investigated a group of environmental activists in Colorado who protested at the annual meeting of the North American Wholesale Lumber Association. The FBI justified the group as a legitimate target because they held a training camp to teach "nonviolent methods of forest defense . . . street theater and banner making."

One of the most controversial incidents of nonterrorist surveillance occurred when the Bush administration was trying to convince the United Nations Security Council to authorize an invasion of Iraq. A leaked memorandum showed that U.S. intelligence wiretapped telephones and intercepted the e-mail communications of the delegations from Angola, Cameroon, Chile, Mexico, Guinea, and Pakistan, not just at their offices, but in the homes of the members of the delegations.

Section 1d—Arbitrary Arrest or Detention

"In practice there is no legal time limit for incommunicado detention nor any judicial means to determine the legality of detention. In the period immediately following detention or arrest, many detainees were held incommunicado and denied access to lawyers and family members. Security forces often did not inform family members of a prisoner's welfare and location. Authorities often denied visits by family members and legal counsel."

2006 STATE DEPARTMENT COUNTRY REPORT ON IRAN

Section 1b—Disappearance

"There were reports of disappearances perpetrated by government forces during the year, some of which may have been politically motivated. In nearly all cases, security forces abducted persons and detained them in undisclosed locations for varying lengths of time ranging from weeks to months."

2006 STATE DEPARTMENT COUNTRY REPORT ON ETHIOPIA

Rendition is the practice of bypassing due process to seize a suspect in a foreign country and transport him to another country where there is a warrant for his arrest. Extraordinary rendition is the practice of seizing a suspect and transporting him to another country for interrogation, even though he is not wanted for a crime. Extraordinary rendition is associated with the Bush administration, but the Bush team actually inherited an existing rendition program from the Clinton administration. On June 21, 1995, President Clinton signed a Presidential Decision Directive that stated, "When terrorists wanted for violation of U.S. law are at large overseas, their return for prosecution shall be a matter of the highest priority . . . If we do not receive adequate cooperation from a state that harbors a terrorist whose extradition we are seeking, we shall take appropriate measures to induce cooperation. Return of suspects by force may be effected without the cooperation of the host government, consistent with the procedures outlined in [National Security Directive 77], which shall remain in effect." National Security Directive 77 was issued by the first President George Bush in January 1993, only days before he left office, and not only its contents, but its title, remain classified. On September 13, 1995, the CIA's Islamic militant unit went after Talaat Fouad Qassem, who had been sentenced to death in absentia for his role in the 1981 assassination of Egypt's president, Anwar al-Sadat. They found Qassem in Croatia and notified Croatian police, who seized Qassem and turned him over to the CIA. U.S. agents interrogated him on a ship in the Adriatic Sea and brought him to Egypt. He was never seen again.

During the summer of 1998, twelve CIA agents helped Albanian authorities wiretap suspected members of the Egyptian-based Islamic Jihad and then pressured the Egyptian government to issue an arrest warrant for Shawki Salama Attiya. Working with U.S. agents, the Albanians killed one suspect and captured five others, including Attiya. They were flown to Egypt at the beginning of July. Once there, they were tortured in several ways, including being beaten, having electric shocks sent through their genitals, and being forced to stand in dirty water up to their knees for extended periods. Two of the five suspects taken from Albania had already been sentenced to death in absentia and were hanged. On August 5, an Arab-language newspaper in London published a letter from the International Islamic Front for Jihad, threatening revenge against the United States for the Albanian action. Two days later, Islamist terrorists blew up the U.S. embassies in Kenya and Tanzania, killing 224 people and wounding more than 5,000.

On September 3, 1998, FBI director Louis J. Freeh told the U.S. Senate Select Committee on Intelligence, "During the past decade, the United States has successfully returned thirteen suspected international terrorists to stand trial in the United States for acts or planned acts of terrorism against U.S. citizens." Freeh added that the *majority* of these renditions had been accomplished with the cooperation of foreign governments. On February 3, 2000, CIA director George Tenet told the Senate Committee on Armed Services, "Since July 1998, working with foreign governments worldwide, we have helped to render more than two dozen terrorists to justice. More than half were associates of Usama Bin Ladin's Al-Qa'ida organization."

Although most of the Clinton-era actions were ordinary renditions, there were some that spilled over into the definition of extraordinary rendition. Abdul al-Yaf'i, a Yemeni, went to Cairo in October 2000 to take his aunt and his brother for medical treatment. At airport immigration, he mentioned that he had been to Afghanistan ten years earlier. Two days later he was imprisoned and interrogated about his visit to Afghanistan and about terrorist bombings. Egyptian security personnel strangled him and accused him "of everything that ever happened in the world." They also asked him to work for them. When he refused, they told him he would be turned over to the United States. He was flown to Jordan, where he was beaten, hung upside-down, beaten on his feet, and ordered to confess. When the Red Cross visited the prison where he was being held, he and others were taken to underground cells. Al-Yaf'i was returned to Yemen in March 2001 without ever having been charged with a crime.

When George W. Bush took over the U.S. presidency from Bill Clinton, his administration was absorbed in its own agenda, and officials in charge of pursuing Islamist terrorists had trouble attracting the new administration's attention. That changed on September 11, 2001. While formulating their response, President Bush and his team embraced the rendition program. On December 18, 2001, hooded security officials at Stockholm's Bronma Airport detained two Egyptian asylum seekers, Muhammad Zery and Ahmed Agiza, who had been convicted in absentia in Egypt for membership in a banned group. U.S. personnel cut off their clothes, forcibly administered sedative suppositories, blindfolded them, placed them in handcuffs and leg irons, and flew them back to Egypt. There they were tortured by having electrical charges attached to their genitals. Agiza, a doctor who had once been associated with Ayman al-Zawahiri, one of the founders of al-Qaeda, was convicted of terrorism and sentenced to twenty-five years in prison, later reduced to fifteen years. Zery, after spending two years in an Egyptian prison, was released to his village.

The Bush administration expanded the program of extraordinary rendition. A sampling of cases whose details have been made public illustrates the program.

Mahmoud Habib, a dual citizen of Egypt and Australia, was seized in Pakistan in October 2001. He claimed that he was looking for an Islamic school for his children. The Americans suspected that he had trained with al-Qaeda in Afghanistan. He was interrogated in Pakistan for three weeks, including by some agents who spoke with American accents. He was then flown to Egypt, where he was interrogated for another six months and where, according to Habib, he was beaten and hung from the ceiling. From there he was sent to Bagram Air Force Base in Afghanistan and finally to the U.S. detention camp at Guantánamo Bay. After the *Washington Post* ran an article about his case, the Pentagon released Habib to representatives of the Australian government. He had spent forty months in U.S. custody without being charged with a crime.

On September 26, 2002, Maher Arar, a Syrian-born Canadian citizen who worked as a telecommunications engineer, was traveling back to Canada after a family vacation in Tunisia, when, while changing planes at John F. Kennedy Airport in New York City, he was grabbed by U.S. agents. He was questioned for thirteen days, primarily about his relationship with the brother of a man with whom he had worked. Arar was then placed in handcuffs and leg irons, placed on a private jet and flown, via Washington, Maine, and Rome, to Amman, Jordan. He was then driven to Syria, where he was imprisoned and tortured until he confessed to anything he was asked to confess to. A year later, after the intervention of the Canadian government, Arar was released from custody and the Syrian government conceded that he had no links to terrorism.

The case of Khaled El-Masri is another example of the excesses of the extraordinary rendition program. A Kuwaiti-born German citizen from a Lebanese family, El-Masri was arrested while on vacation in Macedonia on December 31, 2003, and handed over to U.S. officials. He was handcuffed, blindfolded, and beaten. After three weeks he was flown to Afghanistan, where he was beaten again and put in solitary confinement. He was repeatedly questioned about the 9/11 hijackers and about terrorist training camps in Afghanistan. After five months of being held incommunicado, it became clear to the Americans that they had confused El-Masri with someone who had a similar name. According to El-Masri, a German-speaking man visited him and told him never to mention what had happened because the Americans wanted to keep it secret. El-Masri was flown to Albania, given back his wallet and driven to an airport, where he purchased a ticket back to Germany.

Abu Omar was an Egyptian cleric who sought asylum in Italy after the organization to which he belonged was banned in Egypt. On February 17, 2003, Abu Omar was walking to a mosque in Milan for noon prayers when he was snatched off the streets by CIA agents who flew him, via Germany, back to Egypt. In April 2004, he was released to house arrest and placed a call to his family saying that he had been tortured. He was then rearrested and held in isolation without being charged. Italian lawmakers were so outraged by the abduction that they issued arrest warrants for twenty-two CIA agents, including the station chief, Robert Seldon Lady.

To supplement its extraordinary rendition program, the Bush administration created a network of secret prisons, known as black sites, to which they sent terrorism suspects. Because they planned to treat these detainees in a manner that is considered illegal in the United States, they chose overseas locations for the black sites. Among the nations that are suspected of hosting these prisons or of hosting victims of extraordinary rendition are Thailand, Afghanistan, Poland, Romania, Uzbekistan, Qatar, Djibouti, Syria, Egypt, Jordan, and Morocco. The only public testimony about black sites has involved the case of three Yemenis, Muhammad Bashmilah and Salah Qaru, who were arrested in Jordan in October 2003, and Muhammad al-Assad, who was arrested in Tanzania in 2003. According to Amnesty International, all three were held in secret detention for eighteen months and then returned to Yemen May 5, 2005. The U.S. embassy instructed Yemeni officials to keep them in custody until their case files could be transferred from Washington, D.C. This never happened, so in February 2006, the three pleaded guilty to falsifying travel documents, and they were sentenced to time served in U.S. custody. In March 2006 they were set free. While in U.S. custody, presumably in Afghanistan, they were permanently shackled to a ring fixed in the floor, and they were allowed outside for only twenty minutes a week.

Section 1e—Denial of Fair Public Trial

"The constitution provides for an independent judiciary; the judiciary was under intense pressure to conform to government policies, and the government repeatedly refused to abide by judicial decisions."

2006 STATE DEPARTMENT COUNTRY REPORT ON ZIMBABWE

The USA PATRIOT Act authorized the attorney general to detain any immigrant for seven days and, if the immigrant was charged with an offense, to renew that detention for periods of up to six months with no limit to the number of renewals. The charge did not have to be related to terrorism. Prior to the 9/11 attacks, the U.S. government had always prosecuted accused terrorists in civilian courts. On November 13, 2001, President Bush signed the Military Tribunal Order to try accused terrorists, not in open court, but before closed, military tribunals, without the right of appeal and, for the first time in American history, without access to the evidence against them. The wording of the order was broad enough to include prisoners of war and non-U.S. citizens who contributed to charities that secretly aided terrorists. On August 24, 2004, the first U.S. military tribunal since World War II was called to order in the case of a Yemeni citizen, Salim Ahmed Hamdan, who was accused of being Osama bin Laden's driver. Hamdan was assigned a military lawyer and the case eventually made its way into the civilian legal system as a challenge to the legality of the Bush administration version of military tribunals. On June 29, 2006, the U.S. Supreme Court ruled that the tribunals were illegal and that the president of the United States does not have the sole authority to try detainees without congressional authorization and without the involvement of the judicial branch of government.

Section 1c—Torture and Other Cruel, Inhuman, or Degrading Treatment or Punishment

"The constitution prohibits torture. . . . Nevertheless, there were numerous credible reports that security forces and prison personnel tortured detainees and prisoners."

2006 STATE DEPARTMENT COUNTRY REPORT ON IRAN

In the wake of the 9/11 attacks, George W. Bush and his administration decided to take a no-holds-barred approach to fighting terrorism. From the beginning they knew that the tactics and techniques they planned to use were illegal according to U.S. law. Rather than reject these tactics and techniques, they prepared a series of convoluted legal rationales that they hoped would protect them from prosecution. The War Crimes Act of 1996 made it a federal crime to commit a "grave breach" of the Geneva Conventions, meaning the deliberate "killing, torture or inhuman treatment" of detainees. Violations of the War Crimes Act that result in the death of a detainee carry the death penalty and they do not have a statute of limitations. In a memo to President Bush dated January 25, 2002, the White House counsel, Alberto Gonzales, suggested that Bush find a way to avoid the rules of the Geneva Conventions as they relate to prisoners of war because that "substantially reduces the likelihood of prosecution under the War Crimes Act." A week later, Attorney General John Ashcroft sent a memo to the president also stressing that opting out of the Geneva treaty "would provide the highest assurance that no court would subsequently entertain charges that American military officers, intelligence officials, or law enforcement officials violated Geneva Convention rules relating to field conduct, detention conduct or interrogation of detainees. The War Crimes Act of 1996 makes violation of parts of the Geneva Convention a crime in the United States."

So the Bush administration announced the creation of a new category of captured prisoners. Instead of being "prisoners of war," suspected al-Qaeda members or sympathizers would be "illegal enemy combatants." Since this designation was not mentioned in the Geneva Conventions, they were not protected by its provisions. As for the soldiers fighting for the Taliban government of Afghanistan, they were also "enemy combatants" because Afghanistan was a "failed state" and the Taliban soldiers did not belong to an army, but a "militia."

U.S. Army Regulation 190-8 provides persons captured on a battlefield the right to a military hearing at which they can demonstrate that they are entitled to be held as prisoners of war or to prove that they are innocent civilians picked up by mistake. After the 1991 Gulf War, for example, almost 1,200 captured Iraqis were given such military hearings and hundreds of them were released as innocent civilians. The first President Bush saw this as normal procedure; his son, George W. Bush, did not. After the 2001 invasion of Afghanistan, he declared that no one picked up on a battlefield was entitled to Prisoner of War status, and he refused to allow the U.S. military to hold a single status hearing. Instead, after holding the captured soldiers and others in camps in Afghanistan, he shipped most of them to Guantánamo. The problem was that these prisoners fell into a mishmash of different categories. Some of them really were al-Qaeda members and terrorists-in-training. Others were Taliban soldiers, many of whom considered themselves to be fighting for a national army. The Taliban operated a forced labor system in which villagers were periodically expected to work for the Taliban for about twenty days at a time. Those Afghanis who had the misfortune to be doing their forced labor at the time of the U.S.-led invasion were considered enemy combatants. Because the United States offered a substantial reward for the capture of members of al-Qaeda or the Taliban, entrepreneurial bounty hunters snatched random locals, collected their rewards, and disappeared. Finally, there were innocent civilians who were just picked up by mistake. Unlike his father, George W. Bush did not give any of these people a chance to present evidence of their innocence.

The fact that these prisoners were sent to Guantánamo rather than to a military prison in the United States was another example of the Bush administration's attempts to avoid prosecution under the War Crimes Act. They declared that because Guantánamo was in Cuba and was not part of the United States, anything that was done there was not subject to U.S. laws. They also faced the problem that Sections 2340-2340A of the US Code, Title 18, outlawed torture. So, to be on the safe side, the Bush administration redefined the word "torture." In an August 2, 2002, memo signed by Jay Bybee, the head of the Justice Department's Office of Legal Counsel, the department lawyers proposed sidestepping the law by narrowing the designation of an act of torture as one that caused suffering "equivalent to the pain accompanying serious physical injury, such as organ failure, impairment of bodily function, or even death." Even then it did not qualify as torture if the torturer was seeking information from the victim. An action only counted as torture if the torture was gratuitous. When George W. Bush nominated Alberto Gonzales to replace John Ashcroft as attorney general, and he had to appear before the Senate for confirmation hearings in January 2005, the Justice Department issued a new, less restrictive definition of torture.

By this time, Americans, and others around the world, had been horrified by photographs, released in April 2004, of U.S. soldiers torturing prisoners at the Abu Ghraib prison in Iraq. When this story broke, the Bush administration portrayed the guilty soldiers as "bad apples" who had acted without the approval of their superior officers. Unfortunately, the true story was not so clear. The first group of prisoners from Afghanistan arrived at Guantánamo on January 11, 2002. In November, Secretary of Defense Donald Rumsfeld assigned Major General Geoffrey Miller to take charge of the prison camp because not enough useful information was being extracted from the detainees and he believed the reason was that previous commanders had been too soft on them. Like the rendition program, the torture program began with the goal of preventing terrorist attacks, but gradually morphed out of control. In the words of Alfred McCoy, author of *A Question of Torture: CIA Interrogation, from the Cold War to the War on Terror,* "General Miller turned Guantánamo into a de facto behavioral research laboratory, a kind of torture research laboratory." Employing military psychologists, Miller refined the methods of mental torture to include the exploitation of cultural sensitivities, in particular, with regard to Arab males, matters of sexual identity and sexual roles. The psychologists also helped identify the phobias and weaknesses of individual prisoners.

The techniques used on the prisoners at Guantánamo, which included threatening them with dogs, exposing them to temperature extremes, and shackling them upright to keep them awake, "migrated" to the Bagram Air Base in Afghanistan, where hundreds of Afghanis were tortured. After the invasion of Iraq, the U.S. forces found themselves faced with a growing insurgency that they did not understand. Desperate for information, Rumsfeld ordered General Miller to go to Iraq and "Gitmo-ize" the prisons there. He brought with him a manual of techniques, which he gave to Lt. General Ricardo Sanchez, the U.S. commander in Iraq. Sanchez was put in a bind. The techniques clearly went beyond those allowed in U.S. Army Field Manual 3452, and if he allowed his troops to use them, they could be prosecuted under the Uniform Code of Military Justice. Yet Miller had been sent to Iraq by the secretary of defense, who, in turn, had the support of the commander-in-chief, George W. Bush. In September 2003, Sanchez gave the go-ahead to torture prisoners. An internal investigation by U.S. Army Major General Antonio Taguba, issued on April 4, 2004, detailed some of the abuses committed by members of the U.S. military at Abu Ghraib. They included using unmuzzled dogs to frighten and bite detainees, sodomizing a detainee with a chemical light, urinating on detainees, forcing naked men to wear women's underwear, photographing and videotaping male and female detainees naked, forcing groups of male detainees to masturbate while being photographed and videotaped, punching and kicking detainees and beating them with a chair, and threatening them with a loaded pistol. Taguba estimated that 60 percent of the prisoners at Abu Ghraib were "not a threat to society" and that many civilians who were completely innocent were being held there indefinitely.

On March 21, 2006, Sergeant Michael J. Smith, an army dog handler, was found guilty of six counts, including frightening detainees into urinating and defecating on themselves. He was sentenced to six months confinement. Colonel Thomas Pappas, the highest-ranking military intelligence officer at Abu Ghraib, testified in Smith's trial under a grant of immunity. He stated that he believed that General Miller had given permission to use these techniques. Miller refused to testify, invoking his right against self-incrimination. More than forty detainees died as a result of interrogation techniques used by U.S. military and intelligence personnel.

Section 4—Governmental Attitude Regarding International and Nongovernmental Investigation of Alleged Violations of Human Rights

> "ICRC [International Committee of the Red Cross] access to prison and other detention facilities was restricted . . ."
>   2006 STATE DEPARTMENT COUNTRY REPORT ON ETHIOPIA

The Bush administration's refusal to notify the Red Cross that it is holding individuals in various secret locations is a violation of international humanitarian law. Secretary of Defense Donald Rumsfeld personally ordered the CIA to hide a prisoner, Hiwa Abdul Rahman Rashul, in Iraq from the Red Cross for several months. Army General Paul Kern testified before the Senate Armed Services Committee that the CIA may have hidden as many as 100 "ghost detainees." In 2006, the Bush administration continued to refuse the Red Cross access to suspects, including Jose Padilla, a U.S. citizen who was arrested in Chicago on May 8, 2002.

THE THREE-LEGGED STOOL—For generations American schoolchildren were taught that the U.S. government was a three-legged stool. One leg is the executive branch; one leg is the legislative branch; and the third leg is the judicial branch. For the government to work properly, all three legs have to be of equal length and equal strength. This has not stopped U.S. presidents from trying to make the executive leg longer and stronger. For example, in 1937, President Franklin D. Roosevelt, frustrated by the Supreme Court's opposition to several of his planned New Deal programs, proposed that he be allowed to appoint an extra judge to the Supreme Court for every judge over the age of seventy who had served for ten years and who refused to retire. This proposal, which came to be known as FDR's "court-packing" scheme, would have given him the right to change the balance of the Supreme Court by appointing six new justices. Facing opposition even from supporters in his own party, Roosevelt was forced to withdraw his court reform bill.

In 1952, during the Korean War, President Harry S. Truman, in response to a threatened nationwide strike, seized the steel mills to keep them running. Even though Truman was a Democrat and all nine Supreme Court justices were appointed by Democratic presidents, including four by Truman himself, the court ruled 6–3 that the seizures were not justified by the inherent powers of the presidency or by the president's role as commander-in-chief of the armed forces.

In December 1982, President Ronald Reagan signed into law the Boland Amendment, which prohibited the Defense Department, the CIA, and other government agencies from providing covert military assistance to the Contras, a guerrilla group fighting against the government of Nicaragua. Reagan and his administration used a presumed loophole in the amendment to continue supplying the Contras anyway, some of the funds coming from secret arms sales to Iran. Eleven people were convicted for their roles in the Iran-Contra Affair and two more, including Secretary of Defense Caspar Weinberger, received pre-trial pardons. Reagan himself avoided prosecution by claiming that he was unaware of the illegal aspects of the scheme.

SAWING THE LEGS OF THE STOOL—Almost immediately after the terrorist attacks of September 11, 2001, George W. Bush used them to begin an assault on the traditional separation of powers. Despite the fact that all previous acts of terrorism had been prosecuted through civilian courts, his Military Tribunal Order of November 13, 2001, made it clear that he considered the judicial branch irrelevant in this matter. He also did not bother to ask for congressional authorization. In addition, he declared that his role as commander-in-chief of the armed forces included the right to ignore the Geneva Convention rules pertaining to prisoners of war and to authorize the indefinite incommunicado detention of U.S. citizens if he declared them "enemy combatants."

In supporting the August 2, 2002, Justice Department memo justifying the use of torture, President Bush again took the position that he, as commander-in-chief, had the sole authority to decide the tactics to be used in fighting terrorism and that the legislative and judicial branches had no right to interfere with his decisions. However, the torture issue did not go away. In 2005, Senator John McCain of Arizona, who had himself been tortured while spending five and a half years as a prisoner of war in Vietnam, proposed an amendment to a defense appropriations bill that banned the use of torture and cruel, inhumane, or degrading treatment of prisoners in U.S. custody. President Bush threatened to veto the bill if Congress passed it. When it became clear that there was bipartisan support for the ban, Vice President Cheney lobbied to have the CIA exempted from its provisions. Congress refused. So the Bush administration came up with a compromise. The president would sign the bill if another amendment was added. Called the Detainee Treatment Act of 2005, it provided that "no court, justice or judge shall have the jurisdiction to hear or consider an application for a writ of habeas corpus filed by or on behalf of an alien detained by the Department of Defense at Guantanamo Bay, Cuba" or "any aspect of the detention" of anyone held at Guantánamo or in military custody. In other words, President Bush agreed to give up torture in exchange for a law that confirmed that prisoners he deemed "enemy combatants" had no rights—or so it seemed. Congress agreed and, sitting at his ranch in Crawford, Texas, on December 30, 2005, Bush signed the bill. But then, at 8:00 p.m. he sent out by e-mail a "signing statement" that he would interpret the antitorture amendment "in a manner consistent with the constitutional authority of the president . . . as commander-in-chief and consistent with the constitutional limitations on judicial power." In other words, Bush declared himself free to ignore the provisions of the amendment. He had used the antitorture amendment to secure passage of the Detainee Treatment Act and then declared himself not bound by the amendment after all.

On May 20, 2006, as part of a bribery investigation, the Bush administration challenged the nation's traditional separation of powers by sending the FBI to raid the congressional office of Rep. William Jefferson of Louisiana. It was the first time in the 219-year history of the

United States that the executive branch had, without consulting representatives of the legislative branch, authorized a raid on the office of a sitting member of Congress.

VETOING CONGRESS INSTEAD OF VETOING BILLS—For more than 200 years, since the days of George Washington, Congress and the president followed a simple procedure for confronting their differences. After Congress passed a bill, it went to the president to be signed into law. If the president did not like the bill, he vetoed it. Congress could then override the veto by securing two-thirds majorities to do so in both houses. George W. Bush is the first U.S. president since Thomas Jefferson to serve for more than four years without issuing a single veto. Most observers attributed this to the fact that both houses of Congress were controlled by the president's party. But it turns out that Bush was using an alternative method for bypassing Congress: the signing statement. Often the courts are called upon to interpret ambiguous clauses in laws. When they do so, they consider the congressional debates that preceded passage of a law. In 1986, President Reagan's attorney general, Edwin Meese, proposed that the president accompany his signing of selected bills with a signing statement that would clarify his position on potentially ambiguous clauses. That way, when the courts considered the interpretation of a law, they would take into account not just the opinions of the members of Congress, but of the president. Presidents George H. W. Bush and Bill Clinton continued this practice. When George W. Bush became president, he expanded the use of signing statements to include his actual application of a law. In the aftermath of the 9/11 terrorist attacks, Bush's actions were largely ignored, but in fact, in his first five years in office, he issued more than 130 signing statements, relating to more than 750 separate laws.

Here is a sampling of President Bush's signing statements other than the one relating to torture:

- When Congress passed the 2002 bill creating the Department of Homeland Security, it included provisions that required that department to share with the appropriate oversight committees information about problems relating to the screening of checked bags at airports and about vulnerabilities at chemical plants. The bill also stated that the department had to provide Congress with unaltered reports that dealt with immigration and visa services. Bush signed the bill, but then released a signing statement that gave him the right to withhold the information and to alter the reports.
- In August 2004 and again in December 2005, Congress passed bills forbidding the military from adding to its files information that was gathered

illegally and that was obtained in violation of the Fourth Amendment's protection against unreasonable searches. Bush signed the bills and then issued signing statements that Congress cannot tell the military which pieces of intelligence can or cannot be used, and that the president alone has that right.

- In October 2004, Congress passed a bill prohibiting Defense Department personnel from interfering with the right of military lawyers to give legal advice to their commanders. After signing the bill, Bush added a statement requiring military lawyers instead to follow the legal conclusions of the administration's lawyers in the Defense and Justice Departments. The same bill required the Pentagon to give guards in military prisons training in the humane treatment of detainees as described in the Geneva Conventions, to perform background checks on civilian contractors operating in Iraq and to prohibit such contractors from performing security and law enforcement functions. In his signing statement, Bush reserved for himself the right to ignore all of these provisions.

- In December 2004, Bush signed an intelligence bill that required the Justice Department to share with Congressional oversight committees copies of administration memos relating to new interpretations of domestic spying laws, as well as details regarding the FBI's use of domestic wiretaps. After signing the bill, Bush released a signing statement claiming that he had the right to withhold this information.

- Article One of the United States Constitution gives Congress the power "to make rules for the government and regulation of the land and naval forces." At least four times Congress passed laws forbidding U.S. troops from engaging in combat in Colombia. Bush signed all of the bills, but each time he attached a signing statement declaring that only the president, not Congress, can restrict the use of U.S. troops.

- In August 2005, Congress passed a bill prohibiting the Department of Energy and the Nuclear Regulatory Commission from firing or punishing employees who inform Congress about wrongdoing. After signing the bill, Bush issued a signing statement saying that only the president or his appointees can decide what an employee tells Congress.

- On the same day, December 30, 2005, that he added a signing statement to the anti-torture amendment, President Bush signed a bill that required that scientific information prepared by government researchers be transmitted to Congress "uncensored and without delay." But in another signing statement, he said that the president can order researchers to withhold information from Congress.

- On March 9, 2006, Bush signed into law a bill that required the Justice Department to provide Congress with reports on how the FBI is using the USA PATRIOT Act to search homes and secretly confiscate papers. Then he added a signing statement stating that the president can order the Justice Department to withhold such information from Congress.

OVERRULING THE JUDICIAL SYSTEM—In 1967, the U.S. Supreme Court

ruled that wiretapping is the equivalent of raiding a home. Applying the Fourth Amendment's ban on unreasonable searches, the justices said that federal agents and police had to obtain a warrant from a magistrate before they could tap a phone. President Richard Nixon argued that in cases involving matters of national security the president could order wiretapping without a warrant. In 1972, in the Keith case, the Supreme Court unanimously rejected this claim, explaining, "These Fourth Amendment freedoms cannot properly be guaranteed if domestic security surveillance may be conducted solely with the discretion of the executive branch." The Court made a point of noting that its ruling did not apply to "the activities of foreign powers and their agents," and suggested that "Congress may wish to consider protective standards" in this regard. With this in mind, and in response to covert action abuses by the Nixon administration, Congress passed, and President Jimmy Carter signed into law, the Foreign Intelligence Surveillance Act of 1978 (FISA), which gave the president and his attorney general the power to conduct electronic surveillance in the United States if they obtained a warrant from a judge on a special court, the Federal Intelligence Surveillance court (FISC), the seven members of which were to be appointed by the chief justice of the Supreme Court. The law made it clear that going through the FISC was the "exclusive means" for authorizing these wiretaps and that to go ahead with such surveillance without a warrant was a crime.

After the terrorist attacks of September 11, 2001, Congress and the Bush administration agreed to modify the law to allow surveillance without a warrant for seventy-two hours, after which the warrant could be obtained retroactively. They also expanded the FISC membership to eleven to ensure that at least four of the justices would be close to Washington, D.C., in case of an emergency.

Between 1978 and 1992, presidents Carter, Reagan, and Bush presented 7,030 applications for warrants and the court approved all of them as submitted. During his eight years in office, President Bill Clinton and his Justice Department presented 6,057 warrant applications. The FISC approved 6,055 of them, modified one, and rejected one. This is not to say that there was no controversy involving the program. Problems developed in 2000, during which the Clinton administration admitted to seventy-five cases of misstatements and factual omissions in FISA applications. There were also cases in which the FBI videotaped a meeting even though videotaping had not been authorized, engaged in unauthorized searches, and continued surveillance after warrants ran out. In one case, the FBI failed to notice that a target had given up his cellphone and that the cellphone number had been reassigned to a new person. The FBI continued this electronic surveillance "for a substantial period of time" even though the new owner of the cellphone number spoke a different language than the target. Despite these problems, the relationship between the executive branch and the FISC appears to have remained harmonious, as indicated by the fact that the court approved without modification 99.97 percent of the Clinton administration requests.

All this changed after George W. Bush became president. The court rejected four Bush administration requests outright and modified 240. Some Bush supporters have tried to characterize the FISC justices as liberal obstructionists. In fact, all eleven members of the Bush-era FISC were selected by conservative Republican Supreme Court Chief Justice William Rehnquist.

The Foreign Intelligence Surveillance Act of 1978 that created the FISC also provided for a three-member Foreign Intelligence Surveillance Court of Review to review applications denied by the FISC. All three current members of this court were appointed by Chief Justice Rehnquist during George W. Bush's presidency. After twenty-four years of idleness, in September 2002 the Court of Review heard its first case because the Bush administration tried to expand the coverage of FISA jurisdiction to allow prosecutors and local law enforcement agencies to be involved in the surveillance program and to have access to information obtained through the surveillance. FISC modified their requests before accepting them and the Bush administration appealed. At the September 9, 2002, hearing before the Court of Review, the Bush administration was represented by ten members of the Department of Justice, led by Solicitor General Theodore B. Olson, who had become famous when he presented the Bush-Cheney case to the Supreme Court during the 2000 presidential election dispute. Other notables included James A. Baker, in his role as counsel for the Office of Intelligence Policy and Review, and John C. Yoo, who has gained notoriety for coauthoring the memos that the Bush administration used to redefine torture and to justify excluding prisoners held in Guantánamo from the protections of the Geneva Conventions. The Justice Department team was joined by Spike Bowman, a lawyer for the FBI, and David S. Addington, a lawyer representing Vice President Cheney's office. Lawyers supporting the FISC decision were not allowed to be present, so the ACLU and others later submitted a written brief to the three justices. The convening of the Court of Review was so novel that the justices had to ask the Justice Department lawyers questions like who submitted the surveillance applications (the attorney general's staff) and how often the FISC met to consider the applications (once a week).

Olson argued that a FISC-approved surveillance could uncover information about a suspect that, although totally unrelated to terrorism, might indicate illegal or illicit activities that could then be used to blackmail or intimidate a terrorism-related suspect into cooperating with the authorities. Such a prosecution or threat of prosecution would be approved by the attorney general who, at the time, was John Ashcroft. It is worth noting that FISA warrants are issued based on a lower-than-usual standard that does not require probable cause, and that if a FISC-approved surveillance leads to a prosecution, even one not related to terrorism, the targets may not be allowed to obtain copies of their intercepted communications.

The administration also wanted to change the phrase "the purpose of the surveillance is to obtain foreign intelligence information" to *"a significant* purpose of the surveillance. . . ." This qualifying word could open the door to all manner of other "purposes" for surveillance. When the Court of Review judges tried to get the Justice Department officials to clarify what other purposes there might be besides suspicion of terrorism or espionage, Olson and Baker were evasive. Exasperated, Judge Lawrence Silberman said, "I'll try one more time and then I'll give up." Olson complained that the judges were asking "very, very difficult questions" and, in the end, Silberman never got his answer.

At one point in the proceedings, Judge Ralph B. Guy, Jr. found "a touch of irony" in the fact that after the PATRIOT Act had expanded the government's power of surveillance and after the FISC had gone twenty-four years without an appeal, suddenly, for the first time, the government was complaining about being restrained by the court. Nonetheless, on November 18, 2002, the Court of Review sided with the Bush administration.

Yet despite this victory, and despite having the expanded powers of the PATRIOT Act, President Bush and Vice President Cheney were not satisfied with the extent of their power and continued to clash with the FISC. In 2003, 2004, and 2005, the court denied four of the Bush administration's applications, forced them to withdraw five, and modified 234. In the twenty-four years prior to 2003, the court had voiced objections to a grand total of eight applications. As it would later turn out, President Bush had already secretly authorized the National Security Agency to intercept international calls without a warrant. In January 2006, Attorney General Alberto Gonzales sent to Congress a legal justification for warrantless wiretapping. He claimed that the president had "inherent constitutional authority to order warrantless foreign intelligence surveillance," that the 1978 Federal Intelligence Surveillance Act was unconstitutional because it interfered with presidential powers and that even if it was constitutional, such surveillance was covered by Congress's post-9/11 granting to the president the power to "use all necessary and appropriate force." Gonzales did not explain why President Bush, if he believed this, had bothered, during his first term of office, to apply to the FISC for warrants 5,645 times. To put it simply, President Bush took the position that he was not bound by laws passed by Congress and that he was not obligated to follow rules established by the federal courts.

WHAT IS THE REAL REASON GEORGE BUSH INVADED IRAQ?—To hear George Bush in 2006, the only reason he invaded Iraq was to introduce democracy to that country, and the reasons U.S. and U.K. troops are still there are to combat the terrorists who entered Iraq after the invasion—and to save face. But in the weeks and months leading up to the invasion it was quite a different story. Back then the Bush administration's pitch to the American people was: "Saddam Hussein has chemical and biological weapons and even nuclear weapons that he plans to give to Osama bin Laden and al-Qaeda who will then smuggle them into the United States and kill tens of thousands of people." Even if you knew nothing about Iraqi history and politics, this argument should have appeared dubious on the face of it. In the terrorist attacks that *have* taken place inside the United States, including the World Trade Center bombing of 1993, Timothy McVeigh's bombing of the Murrah Federal Building in Oklahoma City, and the 9/11 attacks, none of the perpetrators needed to smuggle weapons into the country. Whatever they needed, they found without difficulty inside the United States.

There were three important informal groups within the Bush administration that were anxious to invade Iraq, although certain individuals belonged to more than one group. These groups were (1) war profiteers (2) neoconservative ideologues, and (3) supporters of Israel.

WAR PROFITEERS: It is a simple fact of life that when there is a war, there is money to be made. If the whole world was at peace, weapons makers would go out of business. But if weapons are being used in an actual war, bullets, missiles, and bombs have to be built and sold to replace the ones that have been shot or detonated. Parts for tanks, fighter jets, and all sorts of other equipment also have to be replaced regularly. So there is a certain class of individuals and companies that, for reasons having nothing to do with politics, roots for wars to start and then to go on as long as possible. There are also huge profits to be made in the reconstruction industry, which moves in to rebuild what war has destroyed. War is great for business—if you happen to be Halliburton or Bechtel or Boeing or Lockheed Martin or Northrop Grumman or the Parsons Corporation.

NEOCONSERVATIVES: On January 27, 1998—more than three and a half years before the 9/11 attacks—the Project for the New American Century published an open letter in the

Washington Times urging President Clinton to invade Iraq and overthrow Saddam Hussein. Among the eighteen signatories to this letter were ten people who would later join the Bush administration. They are:

- Donald Rumsfeld: Secretary of Defense
- John Bolton: U.S. Ambassador to the United Nations
- Paul Wolfowitz: President of the World Bank and formerly Deputy Secretary of Defense
- Zalmay Khalilzad: U.S. Ambassador to Iraq
- Robert Zoellick: Former Deputy Secretary of State
- Elliott Abrams: Deputy National Security Advisor
- Peter Rodman: Assistant Secretary of Defense for International Security Affairs
- Paula Dobriansky: Under Secretary of State for Global Affairs
- Richard Armitage: Former Assistant Secretary of Defense
- Richard Perle: Former Chairman of the Pentagon's Defense Policy Board

Among the other founders of the Project for the New American Century were Dick Cheney, Lewis (Scooter) Libby, Jeb Bush, and Dan Quayle.

In 1998, these neoconservatives wanted to overthrow Saddam Hussein because it was "almost certain" that he would "acquire the capability to deliver weapons of mass destruction," thus putting at risk American troops, Israel, moderate Arab states, "and a significant portion of the world's supply of oil." Sure enough, five years later, when the neocons got their invasion and Iraq was descending into chaos and looting, U.S. troops made a beeline to secure its oil facilities. It is not only Republicans who would send American soldiers to war to protect oil fields. In 1979, a Democratic president, Jimmy Carter, declared, "Any assault on the Gulf will be regarded as an assault on the vital interests of the United States."

SUPPORTERS OF ISRAEL: Saddam Hussein was not involved in anti-American terrorism, but he was a supporter of anti-Israeli terrorists. He hated Jews and he wanted Israel destroyed. [Even before the neocon letter to the *Washington Times,* David Wurmser (since 2003 Vice President Cheney's Middle East advisor), coauthored a 1996 report, "A Clean Break: A New Strategy for Securing the Realm," that advised Israeli president Benjamin Netanyahu to overthrow Saddam Hussein.] Saddam Hussein provided tens of millions of dollars to groups that committed terrorist acts in Israel, and Israel is safer with him out of power—particularly as the Israeli government and its army were able to sit back while American troops and money did the job. Some members of the Bush administration, like Wurmser, Perle, and Wolfowitz, at best miscalculated that what is good for Israel is always good for the United States.

Once the various administration supporters of invading Iraq came together, all that was necessary was to convince President Bush. George W. Bush no doubt did take seriously the potpourri of reasons that his advisors presented him, but it is possible that the reason that pushed the president over the top in deciding to invade Iraq was more personal. In 1991, Bush told Queen Elizabeth that he was "the black sheep" in his family. Once he was president, he had the chance to show his father that he could do something his father had failed to do: take out Saddam Hussein.

In his book, *Plan of Attack,* Bob Woodward relates what happened when he asked President Bush if he asked his own father for advice about going to war against Iraq. According to Woodward, Bush replied that he had not asked his father for advice because, "He is the wrong father to appeal to for advice, the wrong father to go to, to appeal to, in terms of strength. There's a higher father that I appeal to." It is common for a president of the United States to appeal to God for advice and strength. However, under normal circumstances, if a president of the United States was considering invading Iraq, and a living ex-president had once done just that, he would ask that ex-president for advice—not spiritual advice, but practical advice, like how to interact with your generals and your Middle East experts, how to deal with the different ethnic and religious factions in Iraq, how to work with traditional allies, and how to win over fence sitters. George W. Bush chose not to consult that experienced ex-president.

It is not hard to guess what George Bush the father would have advised his son had he been asked. In 1998, the first President George Bush coauthored a book with his National Security Advisor, Brent Scowcroft, entitled *A World Transformed.* In chapter nineteen they wrote about the first Gulf War, "Trying to eliminate Saddam, extending the ground war into an occupation of Iraq . . . would have incurred incalculable human and political costs. Apprehending him was probably impossible. . . . We would have been forced to occupy Baghdad and, in effect, rule Iraq. The coalition would instantly have collapsed, the Arabs deserting it in anger and other allies pulling out as well. Under the circumstances, there was no viable 'exit strategy' we could see, violating another of our principles. . . . Had we gone the invasion route, the United States could conceivably still be an occupying power in a bitterly hostile land."

The father had it right, while the son got it wrong. George W. Bush's ill-advised attempt to outdo his father led to the deaths of thousands of Americans and tens of thousands of Iraqis, the loss of U.S. credibility around the world, and the creation in Iraq of a terrorist training ground where none existed before.

TO DICTATE OR NOT TO DICTATE—George W. Bush is not a dictator, and to say that he is is an insult to people who live in countries where they are not free to express their opinions, not free to practice the religion of their own choice, not free to vote, and are not allowed to travel freely inside and outside their country. However, President Bush has used the terrorist attacks of September 11, 2001, as an excuse to try to alter the balance of power among the three branches of the government of the United States and to bypass the traditional respect for the rights of even the "worst of the worst" that has, for more than two centuries, made the United States a model for oppressed people who want to bring freedom and democracy to their own nations.

22.
OVERTHROWING DICTATORS

It would be reassuring to know that there is an existing historical pattern for ousting dictators from power and replacing them with functioning democracies. Unfortunately, it is not so simple. However, examining the overthrow of dictators over the past thirty years, it is clear that the various methods that have been used successfully do vary in terms of their effectiveness in actually improving the human rights and living conditions in the countries the dictators ruled.

FOREIGN INVASION—Many people, when confronted with the atrocities and human rights abuses committed by dictators, respond by urging the United States and other countries to invade the dictator-run nations, overthrow the tyrants, and organize elections. As the administration of U.S. President George W. Bush learned the hard way in Iraq, overthrowing the dictator is usually the easy part. Establishing a safe, functioning democracy afterwards is the hard part. In the case of Iraq, attempts were complicated by the fact that the removal of Saddam Hussein without any involvement by Iraqis unearthed ethnic conflicts that had been in existence long before Saddam Hussein was even born.

When Vietnam invaded Cambodia in 1979, the Vietnamese freed the Cambodian people from the grip of one of the worst regimes in modern history, that of Pol Pot and the Khmer Rouge. The Vietnamese installed in Pol Pot's place a friendly (to the Vietnamese) dictator named Hun Sen. More than twenty-five years later, Hun Sen is still the prime minister of Cambodia.

Sometimes foreign invasions do lead to a democratic government. In 1989, the United States invaded Panama, killed several hundred people, arrested Panama's thuggish dictator, former U.S. ally Manuel Noriega, and installed a government that has stayed democratic, albeit often corrupt and inefficient. By a stretch of definition, one could add the example of Grenada. On October 23, 1983, suicide bombers attacked a U.S. Marine barrack in Beirut, Lebanon, killing 241 people. To deflect attention from this humiliating tragedy, President Ronald Reagan ordered the invasion, two days later, of the small Caribbean island nation of Grenada, overthrowing the military dictatorship of Bernard Coard. Of course Coard had only been in power for twelve days, but Grenada has managed to remain democratic ever since. Perhaps the lesson is that foreign invasions can work if the nation being invaded is small and lacks a meaningful army. If this is the case, there is one dictator in this study who is ripe for overthrow by foreign invasion: Teodoro Obiang of Equatorial Guinea, a nation that is small, has an insignificant army, and whose population would overwhelmingly be thrilled to see Obiang forced into exile. Overthrowing Obiang would be so easy that it could probably be done by the Pittsburgh Steelers.

REBEL AND FOREIGN ARMIES TOGETHER—Dictators have also been overthrown by foreign invaders working in concert with local rebel armies. Idi Amin of Uganda was disturbingly clever as dictators go. He once wore a kilt to a royal funeral in Saudi Arabia and he is alleged to have sent President Richard Nixon a "Get Well Soon" card after the Watergate scandal broke. He was also a horrifyingly brutal tyrant. In October 1978, Amin invaded the neighboring country of Tanzania. The Tanzanian army joined forces with Ugandan rebels and, in April 1979, drove Amin out of Uganda and replaced him with the equally dictatorial Milton Obote. Yoweri Moseveni has ruled the country since 1986. To describe Uganda in the twenty-first century as a "shaky democracy" would be polite.

Joseph-Désiré Mobutu, supported by Belgium and the CIA, seized power in what is now the Democratic Republic of the Congo (DRC) in 1965. Mobutu was a Cold War darling of the Western powers and ultimately received more than $1.5 billion in U.S. military and economic aid. He was a colorful character who changed his name in 1972 to Mobutu Sese Seko Koko Ngbendu Wa Za Benga: "The all-powerful warrior who, because of his endurance and inflexible will to win, will go from conquest to conquest, leaving fire in his wake." Mobutu was also a vicious murderer who stole the profits from the sale of his nation's resources. He lasted in power for thirty-two years until rebel Congolese forces, supported by armies from Rwanda, Uganda, and elsewhere, drove him into exile. Almost ten years after Mobutu's downfall, the DRC is a divided country where civilians are killed by various armies and militia on a regular basis.

In October 2001, U.S.-led forces invaded Afghanistan and aided existing ethnic armies that opposed the Afghan Taliban government, as repressive a regime as any that existed at that time. The Taliban leader, Mullah Mohammed Omar, fled to the mountains on the Pakistani border and the Taliban continues to fight a guerrilla war against the troops of the central government and thousands of soldiers from the United States and NATO. In Kabul and parts of Afghanistan, the people live in significantly more free and democratic conditions than in the days of Taliban rule. But a good 40 percent of the population of the nation continue to live under the control of warlords. Their rule is oppressive and elections held in these areas are elections in name only. According to Human Rights Watch, more than half of the members of the Afghan parliament that was elected in 2005 are connected to regional armed groups or personally have records of past human rights abuses.

REBEL ARMIES ALONE—Sometimes rebel armies depose dictators with only material support from abroad. Anastasio Somoza Debayle was the third member of his family to rule the Central American nation of Nicaragua in a dynasty that lasted more than forty years. Somoza was so corrupt and so violent that he alienated almost every element of Nicaraguan society. He was finally driven from power in 1979 by a Marxist rebel army, known as the Sandinistas, who were armed by Venezuela, Panama, and Cuba. The Sandinistas ruled Nicaragua until 1990, when they were defeated in an election. Nicaragua continues to be democratic.

Master Sergeant Samuel Doe gained power in the West African nation of Liberia in 1980 when he led a group of noncommissioned officers who stormed the Executive Mansion and killed and disemboweled the president, William Tolbert. Doe became a good friend of the U.S. government, opening his country as a staging base for the CIA, while raking in more than $400 million in U.S. aid. By the end of the decade, Liberia was embroiled in a bloody, ethnically based civil war. On September 9, 1990, one of the rebel forces captured Doe as he left the Executive Mansion and tortured, mutilated, and executed him, a process they thoughtfully preserved on videotape. Doe's overthrow was followed by continuous civil war until Nigeria's dictator, Sani Abacha, negotiated a ceasefire and elections were held in 1997.

In Chad, the murderous regime of Hissène Habré was brought down in 1990 by a rebel army led by General Idriss Déby, Chad's current dictator. Habré went into exile in Senegal, from which human rights groups have tried to have him extradited to stand trial for crimes against humanity. In the East African nation of Somalia, the twenty-two-year regime of Siad Barre finally collapsed in 1991 when the country descended into civil war. That same year, Ethiopia's appalling dictator, Lt. Colonel Mengistu Haile Mariam, fled before a rebel army and was given sanctuary by Zimbabwe's dictator, Robert Mugabe. Mengistu was replaced by another dictator, Meles Zenawi, who remains in power today.

COUPS AND ASSASSINATIONS—Dictators are often overthrown by coups or simply assassinated. However, these methods rarely lead to democracy. Jean-Bédel Bokassa of the Central African Republic crowned himself emperor—literally—when he placed a 2,000-diamond crown on his own head in 1977, eleven years after he seized power in a military coup. Increasingly autocratic and despised, he was overthrown by his cousin while he himself was off visiting Muammar al-Qaddafi in Libya in 1979. The Central African Republic is still only bordering on democracy more than twenty-five years later.

The thirty-five-year regime of one of the most notorious old-fashioned South American dictators, Alfredo Stroessner, finally came to an end in 1989 when the commander-in-chief of the Paraguayan military, General André Rodríguez, took advantage of Stroessner's ill health to boot him out of office. Since then, Paraguay has developed into a corrupt, chaotic, and weak democracy.

As for assassinations, Park Chung-hee, South Korea's dictator of eighteen years, was shot to death by the head of the Korean CIA in 1979. South Korea continued to be a dictatorship. Pakistan's unpopular dictator of eleven years, Mohammad Zia-ul-Haq, died in a plane crash in 1988. It is still unclear whether the crash was an accident or an assassination. Either way, Pakistan stumbled through a decade of corrupt civilian rule before returning to its status as a military dictatorship.

NONVIOLENT POPULAR UPRISINGS—There is no question that, when successful, overthrowing a dictator through a nonviolent or primarily nonviolent popular uprising is the most effective method of ensuring that a country makes a successful transition to freedom and democracy. It also helps enormously if foreign countries are prepared to provide both moral and financial support.

For twenty years, Ferdinand Marcos ruled the Philippines with iron fists and well-lined pockets. In February 1986, he claimed victory in an election that was clearly fraudulent. Philippine citizens gathered in the streets in protest and to support the real winner of the election, Corazon Aquino, the widow of a politician assassinated in 1983. Leaders of the Catholic Church and high-ranking members of the military sided with the demonstrators.

U.S president Ronald Reagan, a good friend of Marcos, was convinced that Marcos had really won the election and that Aquino and the protestors were soft on Communism. Finally, Reagan's advisors talked him into changing his mind. Marcos flew to Hawaii, where he died in exile. The Filipino "People Power Revolution" established the Philippines as a democratic nation.

When the Communist system collapsed in Eastern Europe in 1989, nonviolent protests forced the resignation of the Communist leaderships in Poland, Czechoslovakia, Hungary, East Germany, and Bulgaria. These nations all made a successful transformation from authoritarian states to democracies. In Romania, the dictator, Nicolae Ceauşescu, was harder to bring down. Hailed by U.S. president Jimmy Carter as "a great national and international leader," Ceauşescu was in fact a vicious tyrant who insisted on complete control over all aspects of Romanian society. Forced to flee the capital after a mass uprising, he was hunted down and executed by members of the Romanian military. Every one of these countries, including Romania, established multiparty democracies.

In Chile, another longtime strong-arm dictator, General Augusto Pinochet, gradually lost control of his country as popular opposition spread, and in 1990 he was actually voted out of office after twenty-six years. Chile is now a solid democracy. Indonesia's authoritarian dictator, Suharto, was overthrown when widespread demonstrations and rioting forced him to resign in 1998 after thirty years in power. Indonesia now holds multiparty elections, although the military remains an important force in the nation's political life.

Serbia's horrible dictator, Slobodan Milošević, tried to ignore the results of national elections in 2000, but mass demonstrations forced him to give up power. He was arrested for war crimes and crimes against humanity and forced to stand trial in The Hague, where he died in prison. Serbia is now a multiparty democracy.

Charles Taylor of Liberia escaped from a jail in Massachusetts, where he was being held on charges of embezzlement, and returned to Liberia, taking charge after the killing of Samuel Doe. Taylor won a democratic election, but then assumed dictatorial powers. In 2003, a United Nations tribunal charged Taylor with war crimes. Taylor resigned and fled to Nigeria on the condition that he would not be extradited. In November 2005, Ellen Johnson-Sirleaf was elected president of Liberia, becoming the first woman to be elected the leader of an African nation. In March 2006, the Nigerian government agreed to turn over Taylor to a United Nations–backed special court. Taylor tried to flee to Cameroon, but was captured by Nigerian troops on March 28.

All of these happy tales may give the impression that once a nation's populace joins together to demand their dictator's resignation, he will leave and all will be well. Unfortunately, it does not always work that way. The Iranian revolution of 1979 is a cautionary example.

The Shah of Iran was reviled by almost all segments of the population. The demonstrations against him were huge, and when he was overthrown, jubilation in Iran was widespread. However, the Ayatollah Khomeini and the other religious leaders who gained power in Iran created a constitution that ensured that they would retain ultimate control over all aspects of the nation's operation no matter how people voted in elections.

In Burma and in China, massive pro-democracy demonstrations did not lead to the overthrow of those nations' dictatorial governments. In Burma, nationwide protests in 1988 forced the military government to hold an election in 1990, which it lost in dramatic and overwhelming fashion. The military refused to recognize the election results and arrested opposition leaders. What should have been a celebration of democracy in Burma failed. Among the contributing factors in this failure was that none of the members of the ruling junta chose to side with the pro-democracy movement. The opposition movement was almost too diverse. Once it became clear that the military junta would not step down, the students, monks, and ethnic armies that had joined forces for the election fell back on their separate agendas and had trouble coordinating their efforts. In addition, foreign governments, although sympathetic in words, showed little interest in actually supporting the pro-democracy movement.

A similar fate befell the pro-democracy movement that rose in China in 1989. Although it was centered in the Tiananmen Square protests in Beijing, demonstrations actually spread to 132 cities. Unlike the popular uprising in Burma, the one in China rose almost spontaneously. When the Communist government ordered its crackdown, the demonstrators were not sufficiently organized or unified to counter the repression. They also had not had time to articulate a democratic program to replace the existing system. The foreign media happened to be in Beijing to cover a visit by Mikhail Gorbachev, so the images of the demonstrations were displayed around the world. However, although people in other countries might have been uplifted by the sudden promise of the collapse of the Chinese Communist Party, their governments were reluctant to commit themselves to supporting the pro-democracy movement, apparently because they feared that if the movement failed, the Chinese government would carry out economic retribution against its foreign supporters. With no real support from abroad, the demonstrators were no match for the Communist Party.

HOLDING HANDS WITH DICTATORS—In his book *Breaking the Real Axis of Evil: How to Oust the World's Last Dictators by 2025,* Mark Palmer addresses the fact that although some dictators have a tenuous grasp on power and are susceptible to popular movements, others, like North Korea's Kim Jong-il, have such overwhelming control over their countries that it is difficult for their citizens to even find out what is happening outside their

HOW NOT TO OVERTHROW DICTATORS: GEORGE
W. BUSH WITH KING ABDULLAH AND JACQUES
CHIRAC WITH TEODORO OBIANG.

Jason Reed/Reuters/Corbis and Luc Gnago/Reuters/Corbis

borders, much less speak out against their government. In cases such as these, opening the nation to outsiders is more important than isolating or boycotting the country. However, in general, the democratic nations of the world could help by ending their support of dictators. Human rights activists winced when George W. Bush went out of his way to be photographed holding hands with Saudi dictator King Abdullah. Although U.S. politicians all speak in favor of democracy, the fact is that their foreign policy decisions are driven more by geopolitical considerations and by what is best for American business than they are by what is best for the citizens of a dictatorship. American policy relating to democracy and dictatorships has traditionally been schizophrenic. On the one hand, the United States has used military force to liberate many countries from the grips of dictators, most notably during World War II. On the other hand, the United States has supported the overthrow of elected governments, including in Iran in 1953, in Guatemala in 1954, in the Congo in 1960, in Ecuador in 1961, in the Dominican Republic in 1963, in Brazil in 1964, in Chile in 1973, and in Haiti in 2001. As recently as 2006, U.S. secretary of state Condoleeza Rice traveled to the Middle East to urge the dictators of Saudi Arabia and Egypt to join with the United States in opposing the democratically elected government of Palestine.

In an ideal world the United Nations would take the lead in organizing the world's response to dictators and to human rights violations. In the real world the UN is constrained by the fact that it was created to give each nation a vote without taking into account the nature of the regime that rules the nation. By 2005 the UN Commission of Human Rights included so many human rights violators that it had lost all credibility. In May 2006 the UN held an election for a new Human Rights Council that would, presumably, operate as a more serious body. Unfortunately, when the votes were counted, among the 47 nations that earned a place on the new council were several dictatorships, including China, Saudi Arabia, Pakistan, Cuba, and Cameroon. Clearly, the United Nations is not the proper venue for enforcing human rights. As an alternative, it should be possible to create a new Council of Democracies for nations that hold free elections and that respect basic human rights. There are currently about 117 nations that would qualify. If these nations increased trade with each other and tried to boycott the dictatorships, it would make it more difficult for dictators to keep their countries from collapsing. Of course dictators could trade with each other, which they already do, but it is just not the same. As Egypt's Anwar Sadat once expressed it when describing the difference between doing business with a dictatorship and a democracy, "The Russians can give you arms, but only the United States can give you a selection."

FOR MORE INFORMATION ON HOW TO HELP—Readers who want to know more about human rights and how they can help should refer to the following organizations, all of which oppose dictatorships of both the left and the right.

Human Rights Watch
350 Fifth Avenue, 34th floor
New York, NY 10118-3299 USA
Tel: 1-212-290-4700; Fax: 1-212–736-1300
http://www.hrw.org

Amnesty International
5 Penn Plaza - 14th floor
New York, NY 10001
Tel: 1-212-807-8400; Fax: 1-212-463-9193
http://www.amnesty.org/actnow

Freedom House
1301 Connecticut Ave., NW
6th Floor
Washington, D.C. 20036
Tel: 1-202-747-7000; Fax: 1-202-822-3893
http://www.freedomhouse.org

Reporters Without Borders
5, rue Geoffroy-Marie
75009 Paris, France
Tel: 011-331-4483-8484; Fax: 011-331-4523-1151
http://www.rsf.org/rubrique.php3?id_rubrique=20

The author may be reached by writing to viciousgnu©aol.com.

APPENDIX

OVERTHROWN MODERN-DAY DICTATORS AND THEIR FATE					
NATION	DICTATOR	REIGN	OVERTHROW	PERSONAL FATE	FATE OF NATION
Uganda	Idi Amin	1971–1979	Foreign & exile invasion	Died in Saudi Arabia	Dictatorship
Central African Republic	Jean-Bédel Bokassa	1966–1979	Coup (France)	Exile in France/ Returned/ 6 years in prison/died free	Shaky democracy
Equatorial Guinea	Francisco Macías Nguema	1968–1979	Family coup	Executed	Dictatorship
Uganda	Milton Obote	(1962–1971)			
		1980–1985	Military coup	Died in South Africa	Shaky democracy
Chad	Hissène Habré	1982–1990	Rebel army	House arrest in Senegal	Dictatorship
Liberia	Samuel Doe	1980–1990	Rebel army	Executed by rebels	Elected dictatorship
Ethiopia	Mengistu Haile Mariam	1977–1991	Rebel army	Exile in Zimbabwe	Dictatorship

(continued)

NATION	DICTATOR	REIGN	OVERTHROW	PERSONAL FATE	FATE OF NATION
Somalia	Siad Barre	1969–1991	Rebel army	Died in Nigeria	Divided/ Ongoing war
DR Congo	Mobutu Sese Seko	1965–1997	Foreign invasion /Rebel army	Died in Morocco	Divided/ Ongoing war
Liberia	Charles Taylor	1997–2003	Forced to flee	Prison	Democracy
Cambodia	Pol Pot	1975–1979	Foreign invasion (Vietnam)	Guerrilla war/died under control of rival guerrilla	Weak democracy
Iran	Mohammad Reza Pahlavi	1941–1979	Nonviolent revolution	Died in Egypt	Dictatorship
South Korea	Park Chung-hee	1961–1979	Assassinated by KCIA		Dictatorship
Philippines	Ferdinand Marcos	1965–1986	Nonviolent revolution	Died in Hawaii	Democracy
Afghanistan	Mohammad Najibullah	1986–1992	Rebel army	Executed	Dictatorship
Pakistan	Mohammad Zia-ul-Haq	1977–1988	Died in plane crash		Dictatorship
Indonesia	Suharto	1967–1998	Nonviolent uprising	House arrest	Democracy
Afghanistan	Mohammad Omar	1998–2001	Foreign invasion/ rebel army	Hiding	Divided democracy
Iraq	Saddam Hussein	1979–2003	Foreign invasion (U.S.)	Prison	Shaky democracy/ Ongoing war

NATION	DICTATOR	REIGN	OVERTHROW	PERSONAL FATE	FATE OF NATION
Romania	Nicolae Ceauşescu	1965–1989	Revolution	Executed	Democracy
Czechoslovakia	Gustav Husák	1969–1989	Nonviolent uprising/resigned	Died free	Democracy
East Germany	Erich Honecker	1971–1989	Nonviolent uprising/resigned	Died in Chile	Democracy
Bulgaria	Todor Zhivkov	1954–1989	Nonviolent uprising/resigned	Died in house arrest	Democracy
Poland	Wojciech Jaruzelski	1981–1990	Nonviolent uprising/resigned	Free	Democracy
Serbia	Slobodan Milošević	1990–2000	Election/ Nonviolent uprising	Died in prison	Democracy
Nicaragua	Anastasio Somoza Debayle	1967–1979	Rebel army (lost U.S. support)	Assassinated in Paraguay	Democracy
Haiti	Jean-Claude Duvalier	1971–1986	Fled after protests	Exile in France	Shaky pseudo-democracy
Panama	Manuel Noriega	1983–1989	Foreign invasion (U.S.)	Prison	Democracy
Paraguay	Alfredo Stroessner	1954–1989	Military coup	Exile in Brazil	Weak democracy
Chile	Augusto Pinochet	1973–1990	Election	House arrest	Democracy

SUGGESTED READING LIST

General

Amnesty International Report: The State of the World's Human Rights. 2002, 2003, 2004, 2005 editions. London: Amnesty International, 2002, 2003, 2004, 2005.

Blum, William. *Killing Hope: U.S. Military and CIA Interventions Since World War II.* Monroe, ME: Common Courage Press, 1995.

Brooker, Paul. *Defiant Dictatorships: Communist and Middle-Eastern Dictatorships in a Democratic Age.* New York: New York University Press, 1997.

———. *Twentieth-Century Dictatorships: The Ideological One-Party States.* UK: Palgrave Macmillan, 1995.

Clodfelter, Michael. *Warfare and Armed Conflicts: A Statistical Reference to Casualty and Other Figures, 1500-2000.* 2nd ed. Jefferson, NC: McFarland, 2002.

Human Rights Watch World Report. 2003, 2004, 2005, 2006 editions. New York: Seven Stories, 2003, 2004, 2005, 2006.

Piano, Aili and Arch Puddington, eds. *Freedom in the World: The Annual Survey of Political Rights and Civil Liberties.* 2003, 2004, 2005 editions. Lanham, MD: Rowman & Littlefield, 2003, 2004, 2005.

U.S. Department of State. "2005 Country Reports on Human Rights Practices." March 8, 2006. www.state.gov/g/drl/rls/hrrpt/2005/index.htm.

Omar al-Bashir—Sudan

El-Battahani, Atta. "Multi-Party Elections & the Predicament of Northern Hegemony in Sudan." In Michael Cowen and Liisa Laakso, eds., *Multi-party Elections in Africa.* Oxford: James Currey, 2002.

Burr, J. Millard and Robert O. Collins. *Revolutionary Sudan: Hasan al-Turabi and the Islamist State, 1989-2000.* Social, Economic and Political Studies of the Middle East and Asia. Leiden, The Netherlands: Brill, 2003.

Johnson, Douglas H. *The Root Causes of Sudan's Civil Wars.* African Issues. Oxford: International African Institute, 2003.

Jok, Jok Madut. *War and Slavery in Sudan.* Philadelphia: University of Philadelphia Press, 2001.

Lesch, Ann Mosely. *The Sudan: Contested National Identities.* Bloomington: Indiana University Press, 1998.

O'Ballance, Edgar. *Sudan, Civil War and Terrorism, 1956-99* Houndmills, UK: Macmillan, 2000.

Petterson, Don. *Inside Sudan: Political Islam, Conflict, and Catastrophe.* Boulder, CO: Westview, 2003.

Verney, Peter et al. *Sudan: Conflict and Minorities.* London: Minority Rights Group, 1995.

Kim Jong-il—North Korea

Breen, Michael. *Kim Jong-Il: North Korea's Dear Leader.* Singapore: John Wiley & Sons, 2004.

Cumings, Bruce. *North Korea: Another Country.* New York: New Press, 2004.

Goulden, Joseph C. *Korea: The Untold Story of the War.* New York: Times Books, 1982.

Institute for South-North Korea Studies. *The True Story of Kim Jong-II.* Seoul: Institute for South-North Korea Studies, 1993.

Kim Jong-il. *Kim Jong Il: On the Art of Opera.* Honolulu: University Press of the Pacific, 2001.

———. *On the Art of the Cinema.* Honolulu: University Press of the Pacific, 2001.

———. *The Great Teacher of Journalists: Kim Jong Il.* Amsterdam: Fredonia Books, 2002.

Kim, Su Hi. *North Korea at a Crossroads.* Jefferson, NC: McFarland & Company, 2003.

Martin, Bradley K. *Under the Loving Care of the Fatherly Leader: North Korea and the Kim Dynasty.* New York: Thomas Dunne, 2004.

North Korea Foreign Languages Publishing House. *Kim Jong Il: The People's Leader.* Pyongyang: FLPH, 1983.

Oh, Kongdan and Ralph C. Hassig. *North Korea: Through the Looking Glass.* Washington, DC: Brookings Institution Press, 2000.

Suh, Dae-Sook. *Kim Il-Sung: The North Korean Leader.* New York: Columbia University Press, 1988.

Than Shwe—Burma

Fink, Christina. *Living Silence: Burma Under Military Rule.* Bangkok: White Lotus, 2001.

Human Rights Documentation Unit. *Human Rights Yearbook: Burma 2004.* Thailand: HRDU, 2005.

Human Rights Watch. *"My Gun Was as Tall as Me": Child Soldiers in Burma.* New York: Human Rights Watch, 2002.

San Suu Kyi, Aung. *Aung San of Burma.* Edinburgh: Kiscadale, 1991.

———. *Freedom from Fear.* London: Penguin, 1995.

Steinberg, David I. *Burma: The State of Myanmar.* Washington, DC: Georgetown University Press, 2001.

Robert Mugabe—Zimbabwe

Chan, Stephen. *Robert Mugabe: A Life of Power and Violence.* Ann Arbor: University of Michigan Press, 2003.

Hill, Geoff. *The Battle for Zimbabwe: The Final Countdown.* Cape Town: Zebra Press, 2003.

Meredith, Martin. *Our Votes, Our Guns: Robert Mugabe and the Tragedy of Zimbabwe.* New York: Public Affairs, 2003.

Norman, Andrew. *Robert Mugabe and the Betrayal of Zimbabwe.* Jefferson, NC: McFarland & Company, 2004.

Islam Karimov—Uzbekistan

Akbarzadeh, Shahram. *Uzbekistan and the United States: Authoritarianism, Islamism & Washington's Security Agenda.* London: Zed Books, 2005.

Karimov, Islom. *Uzbekistan: Along the Road of Deepening Economic Reform.* Houston: Uzbekistan, 1996.

Levitin, Leonid and Donald S. Carlisle. *Islam Karimov—President of the New Uzbekistan.* Vienna: Agrotec, 1995.

Rashid, Ahmed. *Jihad: The Rise of Militant Islam in Central Asia.* New Haven, CT: Yale University Press, 2002.

Hu Jintao—China

Fairbank, John K. "The Reunification of China." *The People's Republic, Part 1: The Emergence of Revolutionary China 1949-1965.* In Roderick MacFarquhar and John K. Fairbank, eds., *The Cambridge History of China, Vol. 14.* Cambridge: Cambridge University Press, 1987.

Fairbank, John King and Merle Goldman, *China: A New History.* Cambridge, MA: Belknap, 2006.

Gernet, Jacques. *A History of Chinese Civilization.* Cambridge: Cambridge University Press, 1996.

Li, Cheng. *China's Leaders: The New Generation.* Lanham, MD: Rowman & Littlefield, 2001.

MacFarquhar, Roderick. "Epilogue." *The People's Republic, Part 1: The Emergence of Revolutionary China 1949-1965.* In Roderick MacFarquhar and John K. Fairbank, eds, *The Cambridge History of China, Vol. 14.* Cambridge: Cambridge University Press, 1987.

Nathan, Andrew J. and Bruce Gilley. *China's New Rulers: The Secret Files.* New York: New York Review Books, 2003.

Roberts, J.A.G. *The Complete History of China* London: Sutton, 2004.

King Abdullah—Saudi Arabia

AbuKhalil, As'ad. *The Battle for Saudi Arabia: Royalty, Fundamentalism, and Global Power.* New York: Seven Stories Press, 2004.

Aburish, Said K. *The Rise, Corruption and Coming Fall of the House of Saud.* New York: St. Martin's Griffin, 1996.

Al-Rasheed, Madawi. *A History of Saudi Arabia.* Cambridge: Cambridge University Press, 2002.

Chamption, Daryl. *The Paradoxical Kingdom: Saudi Arabia and the Momentum of Reform.* New York: Columbia University Press, 2003.

Fandy, Mamoun. *Saudi Arabia and the Politics of Dissent.* New York: Palgrave, 2001.

Holden, David and Richard Johns. *The House of Saud: The Rise and Rule of the Most Powerful Dynasty in the Arab World.* New York: Holt, Rinehart and Winston, 1982.

Kostiner, Joseph, ed. *Middle East Monarchies: The Challenge of Modernity.* Boulder, CO: Lynne Rienner, 2000.

Lacey, Robert. *The Kingdom.* New York: Harcourt Brace Jovanovich, 1981.

Unger, Craig. *House of Bush, House of Saud: The Secret Relationship Between the World's Two Most Powerful Dynasties.* New York: Scribner, 2004.

Saparmurat Niyazov—Turkmenistan

Niyazov, Saparmurat. *Independence, Democracy, Prosperity.* Alma-Aty, Kazakhstan: Noy Publications, 1994.

———. *Rukhnama: Reflections on the Spiritual Values of the Turkmen.* Ashgabat: State Publishing Service Turkmenistan, 2003.

Rashid, Ahmed. *Jihad: The Rise of Militant Islam in Central Asia.* New Haven, CT: Yale University Press, 2002.

Seyed Ali Khamenei—Iran

Afshari, Reza. *Human Rights in Iran: The Abuse of Cultural Relativism.* Philadelphia: University of Pennsylvania Press, 2001.

Daneshvar, Parviz. *Revolution in Iran.* New York: Palgrave Macmillan, 1996.

Hiro, Dilip. *The Essential Middle East: A Comprehensive Guide.* New York: Carroll & Graf, 2005.

———. *Iran Under the Ayatollahs.* London: Routledge, 1985.

———. *The Iranian Labyrinth: Journeys Through Theocratic Iran and its Furies.* New York: Nation Books, 2005.

Hooglund, Eric, ed. *Twenty Years of Islamic Revolution: Political and Social Transition in Iran Since 1979.* Syracuse, NY: Syracuse University Press, 2002.

Menashri, David. *Iran: A Decade of War and Revolution.* London: Holmes & Meier, 1990.

Mohammadi, Ali, ed. *Iran Encountering Globalization: Problems and Prospects.* London: Routledge Curzon, 2003.

Moslem, Mehdi. *Factional Politics in Post-Khamenei Iran.* Syracuse, NY: Syracuse University Press, 2002.

Stevens, Roger. *The Land of the Great Sophy.* New York: Taplinger, 1979.

Zahedi, Dariush. *The Iranian Revolution Then and Now: Indicators of Regime Instability.* Boulder, CO: Westview, 2000.

Teodoro Obiang Nguema—Equatorial Guinea

Decalo, Samuel. *Psychoses of Power: African Personal Dictatorships.* Boulder, CO: Westview, 1989.

Febley, Randall. *Equatorial Guinea: An African Tragedy.* New York: Peter Lang, 1989.

Liniger-Goumaz. *Historical Dictionary of Equatorial Guinea.* 2nd ed. African Historical Dictionaries 21. Metuchen, NJ: Scarecrow Press, 1988.

Obiang Biko, Adolfo. *Equatorial Guinea: From Spanish Colonialism to the Discovery of Oil.* Libreville, Gabon: MONALIGE, 2000.

Muammar al-Qaddafi—Libya

Bianco, Mirella. *Qadafi Voice from the Desert.* Paris: Longman, 1975.

Blundy, David and Andrew Lycett. *Qaddafi and the Libyan Revolution.* London: Weidenfeld and Nicolson, 1987.

———. *Commentary on the Green Book.* Tripoli: World Center for Researches and Studies of the Green Book, 1984.

El-Kikhia, Mansour O. *Libya's Qaddafi: The Politics of Contradiction.* Gainesville University Press of Florida, 1997.

al-Qaddafi, Muammar. *Escape to Hell and Other Stories.* Montreal: Stanki, 1998.

———. *The Green Book. Tripoli:* Public Establishment for Publishing, n.d.

King Mswati III—Swaziland

Kuper, Hilda. *Sobhuza II: Ngwenyama and King of Swaziland.* London: Duckworth, 1978.

———. *The Swazi: A South African Kingdom.* New York: Holt, Rinehart and Winston, 1986.

Pervez Musharraf—Pakistan

Abbas, Hasan *Pakistan's Drift into Extremism: Allah, the Army, and America's War on Terror.* Armonk, NY: M.E. Sharpe, 2005.

Chanda, Bipan et al. *India's Struggle for Independence.* London: Viking, 1988.

Cloughley, Brian. *A History of the Pakistan Army: Wars and Insurrections.* 2nd ed. Oxford: Oxford University Press, 2000.

Haroon, A. *Muhammad Bin Qasim to General Pervez Musharraf.* Lahore: Sang-e-Meel, 2004.

Mahmood, S. *The Musharraf Regime and the Governance Crisis: A Case Study of the Government of Pakistan.* Huntington, NY: Nova Science, 2000.

Ziring, Lawrence. *Pakistan: At the Crosscurrent of History.* Oxford: One World, 2003.

Aleksandr Lukashenko—Belarus

Balmaceda, Margarita M., James I. Clem, and Lisbeth L. Tarlow, eds. *Independent Belarus: Domestic Determinants, Regional Dynamics, and Implications for the West.* Cambridge, MA: Harvard University Press, 2002.

Garnett, Sherman W. and Robert Legvold. *Belarus at the Crossroads.* Washington, DC: Camegie Endowment for International Peace, 1999.

Zaprudnik, Jan. *Belarus: At a Crossroads in History.* Boulder, CO: Westview, 1993.

———. ed. *Historical Dictionary of Belarus.* European Historical Dictionaries 28. Lanham, MD: Scarecrow, 1998.

Fidel Castro—Cuba

Castro, Fidel. *History Will Absolve Me: Fidel's Courtroom Speech in His Own Defense, October 16, 1953.* New York: Center for Cuban Studies, n.d.

Dorschner, John and Robert Fabricio. *The Winds of December.* New York: Coward, McCann & Geoghegan, 1980.

Geyer, Georgie Anne. *Guerrilla Prince: The Untold Story of Fidel Castro.* Kansas City, MO: Andrews McMeel, 2001.

Gott, Richard. *Cuba: A New History.* New Haven, CT: Yale University Press, 2004.

Kenner, Martin and James Petras, eds. *Fidel Castro Speaks.* New York: Grove, 1969.

Quirk, Robert E. *Fidel Castro.* New York: W.W. Horton & Company, 1993.

Skierka, Volker. *Fidel Castro: A Biography.* Cambridge: Polity, 2004.

Skulc, Tad. *Fidel: A Critical Portrait.* New York: Perennial, 1986.

Bashar al-Assad—Syria

George, Alan. *Syria: Neither Bread nor Freedom.* London: Zed, 2003.

Leverett, Flynt. *Inheriting Syria: Bashar's Trial by Fire.* Washington, DC: Brookings, 2005.

Seale, Patrick. *Asad of Syria: The Struggle for the Middle East.* Berkeley: University of California Press, 1995.

Choummaly Sayasone—Laos

Evans, Grant. *A Short History of Laos: The Land in Between.* Crows Nest, Australia: Allen & Unwin, 2002.

A Special Case: George W. Bush—United States

Amnesty International. "United States of America: Below the Radar: Secret Flights to Torture and 'Disappearance'." *AI website,* April 5, 2006. web.amnesty.org/library/index/ENGAMR510512006.

Denbeaux, Mark and Joshua Denbeaux. "Report on Guantánamo Detainees: A Profile of 517 Detainees Through Analysis of Department of Defense Data." *Seton Hall website.* law.shu.edu/news/guantanamo_report_final_2_08_06.pdf.

Ginger, Ann Fagan. *Challenging US Human Rights Violations Since 9/11.* Meiklejohn Civil Liberties Institute. Amherst, NY: Prometheus, 2005.

Martin, Kate and Joe Onek. " 'Enemy Combatants,' The Constitution and the Administration's 'War on Terror'." *American Constitution Society for Law and Policy.* August 2004. www.acslaw.org/pdf/enemycombatants.pdf.

Mayer, Jane. "Outsourcing Torture: The Secret History of America's 'Extraordinary Rendition' Program." *The New Yorker,* February 14, 2005.

Presidential Signing Statements 2001–2006. www.cohertbabble.com/signingstatements/about.htm

"Sneak and Peek Search Warrants and the USA PATRIOT Act." *Georgia Defender,* September 2002. www.law.uga.edu/academics/profiles/dwilkes_more/37patriot .html.

Special Investigations Division. "Halliburton's Performance Under the Restore Iraqi Oil 2 Contract." U.S. House of Representatives Committee on Government Reform—Minority Staff. Prepared for Rep. Henry A. Waxman. March 28, 2006.

Readers interested in receiving a copy of the full bibliography for this book should send an e-mail request to viciousgnu©aol.com with the heading "Tyrants Bibliography."

ACKNOWLEDGMENTS

First thanks go to my father and my sister for agreeing to let me run my first list of Most Repressive Governments in *The Book of Lists #2* in 1980, and to Lee Kravitz and my friends at *Parade* magazine for publishing, beginning in 2003, my annual list of Worst Dictators Currently in Power. For their help in the research process, I want to thank Jaime Loucky, Maryan Soliman, Dave Shukla, Ben Warner, Theodore Long, and Steve Commins; and for their aid in the preparation of the manuscript, Flora Chavez and Aman Gill. To my agent Ed Victor and to Judith Regan, Cal Morgan, Doug Grad, and others at ReganBooks, thank you for your patience.

INDEX